WASHINGTON, D.C.

PUBLICATIONS OF THE GERMAN HISTORICAL INSTITUTE

Edited by Detlef Junker
with the assistance of Daniel S. Mattern

The German Historical Institute is a center for advanced study and research whose purpose is to provide a permanent basis for scholarly cooperation among historians from the Federal Republic of Germany and the United States. The Institute conducts, promotes, and supports research into both American and German political, social, economic, and cultural history, into transatlantic migration, especially in the nineteenth and twentieth centuries, and into the history of international relations, with special emphasis on the roles played by the United States and Germany.

Recent books in series

Sibylle Quack, editor, *Between Sorrow and Strength: Women Refugees of the Nazi Period*

Mitchell G. Ash and Alfons Söllner, editors, *Forced Migration and Scientific Change: Emigré German-Speaking Scientists and Scholars after 1933*

Manfred Berg and Geoffrey Cocks, editors, *Medicine and Modernity: Public Health and Medical Care in Nineteenth- and Twentieth-Century Germany*

Stig Förster and Jörg Nagler, editors, *On the Road to Total War: The American Civil War and the German Wars of Unification, 1861–1871*

Norbert Finzsch and Robert Jütte, editors, *Institutions of Confinement: Hospitals, Asylums, and Prisons in Western Europe and North America, 1500–1950*

David E. Barclay and Elisabeth Glaser-Schmidt, editors, *Transatlantic Images and Perceptions: Germany and America since 1776*

Norbert Finzsch and Dietmar Schirmer, editors, *Identity and Intolerance: Nationalism, Racism, and Xenophobia in Germany and the United States*

Manfred F. Boemeke, Gerald D. Feldman, and Elisabeth Glaser, editors, *The Treaty of Versailles: A Reassessment After 75 Years*

Susan Strasser, Charles McGovern, and Matthias Judt, editors, *Getting and Spending: European and American Consumer Societies in the Twentieth Century*

Manfred F. Boemeke, Roger Chickering, and Stig Förster, editors, *Anticipating Total War: The German and American Experiences, 1871–1914*

To the Memory of
Jürgen Heideking (1947–2000)

Republicanism and Liberalism in America and the German States, 1750–1850

Republicanism and Liberalism in America and the German States, 1750–1850 represents the cooperative effort of a group of American and German scholars to move the historical debate on republicanism and liberalism to a new stage. Until recently, the relationship between republican and liberal ideas, concepts, and worldviews has almost exclusively been discussed in the context of American revolutionary and late-eighteenth-century history. Although the German states did not experience successful revolutions like those in North America and France, republican and liberal ideas and "language" deeply affected German political thinking and culture, especially in the southern states. The essays published in this book expand the time frame of the debate into the first half of the nineteenth century, applying an innovative and comparative German-American perspective. By systematically studying the similarities and differences in the understanding of republicanism and liberalism in the United States and the German states, the collection stimulates new efforts toward a comprehensive interpretation of political, intellectual, and social developments in the "modernizing" Atlantic world of the eighteenth and nineteenth centuries.

Jürgen Heideking was Professor of Modern History and Director of the Institute of Anglo-American History at the University of Cologne, Germany. He was a senior research fellow and member of the Academic Advisory Council of the German Historical Institute in Washington, D.C.

James A. Henretta is Priscilla Alden Burke Professor of History at the University of Maryland. He has held research fellowships from the Charles Warren Center at Harvard, the National Endowment for the Humanities, the American Council of Learned Societies, and the Woodrow Wilson Center for International Scholars. He has served as a Fulbright Senior Scholar and as the Harmsworth Professor of American History at Oxford University.

Republicanism and Liberalism in America and the German States, 1750–1850

Edited by

JÜRGEN HEIDEKING

University of Cologne

JAMES A. HENRETTA

University of Maryland

with the assistance of

PETER BECKER

European University Institute

GERMAN HISTORICAL INSTITUTE
Washington, D.C.
and

 CAMBRIDGE
UNIVERSITY PRESS

PUBLISHED BY THE PRESS SYNDICATE OF THE UNIVERSITY OF CAMBRIDGE
The Pitt Building, Trumpington Street, Cambridge, United Kingdom

CAMBRIDGE UNIVERSITY PRESS
The Edinburgh Building, Cambridge CB2 2RU, UK
40 West 20th Street, New York, NY 10011-4211, USA
477 Williamstown Road, Port Melbourne, VIC 3207, Australia
Ruiz de Alarcón 13, 28014 Madrid, Spain
Dock House, The Waterfront, Cape Town 8001, South Africa

http://www.cambridge.org

First published 2002

Printed in the United Kingdom at the University Press, Cambridge

Typeface Bembo 11/13 pt.   *System* QuarkXPress [BTS]

A catalog record for this book is available from the British Library.

Library of Congress Cataloging in Publication Data
Heideking, Jürgen, 1947–
Republicanism and liberalism in America and the German states, 1750–1850 / Jürgen
Heideking, James A. Henretta.
p. cm. – (Publications of the German Historical Institute)
Includes bibliographical references and index.
ISBN 0-521-80066-8
1. United States – Politics and government – 1775–1783. 2. United States – Politics and
government – 1783–1865. 3. Germany – Politics and government – 1740–1806.
4. Germany – Politics and government – 1806–1848. 5. Political culture – United
States – History. 6. Political culture – Germany – History. 7. Liberalism –
United States – History. 8. Liberalism – Germany – History. 9. Republicanism –
United States – History. 10. Republicanism – Germany – History. I. Henretta,
James A. II. Title. III. Series.
E302.1 .H45 2001
320.51′0943′09033–dc21

00-065464

ISBN   0 521 80066 8   hardback

Contents

List of Contributors

Willi Paul Adams is a professor of history at the Free University of Berlin.

Hans Erich Bödeker is a senior research fellow at the Max Planck Institute for History, Göttingen.

Otto Dann is a professor of history at the University of Cologne.

Jürgen Heideking was a professor of history at the University of Cologne.

James A. Henretta is a professor of history at the University of Maryland, College Park.

Paul Nolte is an assistant professor of history at the University of Bielefeld.

Vera Nünning is a professor of history at the University of Cologne.

A. G. Roeber is a professor of history at Pennsylvania State University.

Robert E. Shalhope is a professor of history at the University of Oklahoma.

Edmund Spevack is a research fellow at the German Historical Institute.

Amy Dru Stanley is a professor of history at the University of Chicago.

Robert J. Steinfeld is a professor at the State University of New York, Buffalo, School of Law.

Rudolf Vierhaus is a professor emeritus of history at the University of Göttingen and former director of the Max Planck Institute for History, Göttingen.

Rosemarie Zagarri is a professor of history at George Mason University.

Introduction

JÜRGEN HEIDEKING AND JAMES A. HENRETTA

Transatlantic comparisons in the period from 1750 to 1850 are often limited to the American and French revolutions, and recent bicentennial celebrations of the Declaration of Independence and the French Revolution have reinforced this tendency. Indeed, these two epochal events are the focal points of what R. R. Palmer has called the "age of democratic revolution" and therefore deserve the closest historical scrutiny.[1] However, there is much to be gained by broadening the perspective in order to view these revolutionary upheavals as part of a continuous transformation of Western society and culture. Moreover, Palmer's concept of a transatlantic "democratic revolution" is widely acknowledged to be flawed because terms such as *democratic* and *democracy* do not precisely convey the content and meaning of late-eighteenth-century texts. In fact, as other scholars looked closely at the sources they discovered that the revolutionary mind in America and Europe was deeply affected by republican maxims, principles, and values. Beginning in the 1970s the reconstruction and evaluation of this "republican ideology" became a major task of historians on both sides of the Atlantic. American, British, and French scholars took a leading role in this effort, whereas historians in Germany and other central European countries remained on the sidelines. In Germany the debate on the relationship between republicanism and liberalism, and the crucial importance of these ideologies for understanding the birth of the modern world has only recently begun to inspire research and generate controversy.

To push forward this transcontinental dialog, a German-American conference on "Republicanism and Liberalism in America and the German States, 1750–1850" was convened in 1996. Under the auspices of the

---

1 R. R. Palmer, *The Age of Democratic Revolution: A Political History of Europe and America, 1760–1800*, 3d ed., 2 vols. (Princeton, N.J., 1962).

German Historical Institute, Washington, D.C., with additional financial support from the Fritz Thyssen Foundation, this conference took place at the University of Wisconsin at Madison on October 3–6, 1996. The task defined for the conference participants was threefold: to take stock of the present state of the debate over the influence of republicanism and liberalism in the revolutionary era; to extend the discussion into the first half of the nineteenth century in order to profit from fascinating new research on subsequent political, social, and cultural developments; and to explore the possibilities of comparative German-American studies, especially in the field of ideas and *mentalités*, from the late eighteenth to the late nineteenth century. This volume assembles most of the papers delivered at the conference, revised in the light of our discussions.

I

Bernard Bailyn, Gordon S. Wood, and Pauline Maier initially explored the impact of British opposition ideology – both republican and dissenting Whig – on the American Revolution.[2] Their studies drew in part on the work of J. G. A. Pocock and other scholars, who had traced the course of republican thinking from classical times to Renaissance Italy and from there to early modern Britain.[3] Other historians, among them Joyce Appleby, insisted on the significance of Lockean liberalism during the revolutionary era. Subsequently, scholars have tried to evaluate the relative importance of these intellectual outlooks and traditions in the creation of the American nation, and also to relate them to specific social groups and interests.

In essence, three interpretive models have dominated discussions over the past two decades: (1) British opposition ideology reflecting either a "dissenting Whig" outlook (Bailyn) or a "neoclassical republican"[4] tradition (Wood) strongly influenced the early stages of the American

2 Bernard Bailyn, *The Ideological Origins of the American Revolution*, enlarged ed. (Cambridge, Mass., 1967; reprint, 1992); Gordon S. Wood, *The Creation of the American Republic, 1776–1787* (Chapel Hill, N.C., 1969); Pauline Maier, *From Resistance to Revolution: Colonial Radicals and the Development of American Opposition to Great Britain, 1765–1776* (New York, 1972); Robert E. Shalhope, *The Roots of Democracy: American Thought and Culture, 1760–1800* (Boston, 1990).

3 See these works by J. G. A. Pocock: "Machiavelli, Harrington, and English Political Ideologies in the Eighteenth Century," *William and Mary Quarterly* 22 (1965): 549–83; *The Machiavellian Moment: Florentine Republican Thought and the Atlantic Republican Tradition* (Princeton, N.J., 1975); "The Machiavellian Moment Revisited: A Study in History and Ideology," *Journal of Modern History* 53 (1981): 49–72; *Virtue, Commerce, and History: Essays on Political Thought and History, Chiefly in the Eighteenth Century* (Cambridge, 1985); and the collection he edited, *Three British Revolutions: 1641, 1688, 1776* (Princeton, N.J., 1980).

4 This term is often used to distinguish eighteenth-century British republican thought (also variously called Old Whig Country, commonwealth, oppositionist, or neo-Harringtonian) from the republicanism of Aristotle and other Greek and Roman writers. The question of how many classical elements still resided in the "neoclassical" tradition is not easy to answer. See Paul A. Rahe, *Republics Ancient and Modern: Classical Republicanism and the American Revolution* (Chapel Hill, N.C., 1992).

Revolution, but in the aftermath of independence it was replaced by a more modern, individualistic, "liberal" ideology. In politics, this transition to a liberal outlook meant that republican government did not rest on the traditional foundations of "civic virtue" and communal morality but rather on institutional mechanisms, such as a functional division of power, checks and balances, and federalism. In particular, the adoption of the U.S. Constitution in 1787–8 signaled the triumph of the modern concept of an "extended republic" with a complex system of representative government over the traditional idea of a small, harmonious republican commonwealth. In economic matters, this ideological transition symbolized a shift from agrarian austerity and self-reliance to competitive individualism and commercialism.[5] (2) Although there were dissenting Whigs and neoclassical republicans in colonial America, the ascendant intellectual tradition was that of Lockean liberalism, especially with respect to property rights (Appleby). The struggle for American "rights" during the revolution further enhanced the significance of Lockean liberalism even as independence resulted in the creation of state governments organized in accord with many traditional republican values. Thus, it happened that republican principles were important with respect to certain issues and in certain settings, whereas liberal ideas were more influential in other respects. The debate over the Constitution in 1787–8 produced a clash between these intellectual currents as Federalists and Anti-Federalists undertook a fundamental re-examination of the nature of American government.[6] (3) Liberalism and republicanism are philosophical constructs or "ideal types"; as such, they do not exactly reflect or correspond to the political and social realities of late-eighteenth-century America. Consequently, although these sets of ideas can be analytically distinguished and described by scholars, the historical actors did not perceive them as separate and competing choices. Instead, the

---

5 In essence, this was Gordon S. Wood's thesis in *The Creation of the American Republic*, which caused intense discussion and stimulated many new studies. Important early responses include J. R. Pole, "The Creation of the American Republic," *Historical Journal* 13 (1970): 799–803; Robert E. Shalhope, "Towards a Republican Synthesis," *William and Mary Quarterly* 29 (1972): 49–80. Ten years later, Shalhope reviewed the course of the debate in "Republicanism and Early American Historiography," *William and Mary Quarterly* 39 (1982): 334–56. For another ten-year assessment, see Robert E. Shalhope, "Republicanism, Liberalism, and Democracy: Political Culture in the Early Republic," in Milton M. Klein et al., eds., *The Republican Synthesis Revisited: Essays in Honor of George Athan Billias* (Worcester, Mass., 1992), 37–90. In 1985 the *American Quarterly* devoted a special issue (vol. 37) to this scholarly debate.

6 See, esp., these works by Joyce Appleby: "Liberalism and the American Revolution," *New England Quarterly* 49 (1976): 3–26; "The Social Origins of American Revolutionary Ideology," *Journal of American History* 64 (1978): 935–58; *Capitalism and a New Social Order: The Republican Vision of the 1790s* (New York, 1984); and "Republicanism in Old and New Contexts," *William and Mary Quarterly* 43 (1986): 20–34.

revolutionary era was characterized by a fusion of republican and liberal ideas.[7] These concepts "were linked and blended" in the minds of early modern individuals whose thinking changed as they attempted to assimilate and manage new phenomena and new events, but who were neither truly classical nor fully modern in their thinking.[8]

With respect to this ongoing debate, the papers and discussions at the conference in Madison tended to support the growing consensus that republicanism and liberalism are best conceived of as "complex webs of ideas" or "languages" and that neither clearly dominated the revolutionary and constitutional discourse.[9] As the scholarly discussion continues, the task will be to assess the proportional share or the specific "mixture" of ideas, concepts, and values from republican and liberal sources.

Moreover, over the past decade the main focus of research has shifted to the early nineteenth century. In *The Radicalism of the American Revolution* Gordon Wood argued that around 1810 the United States was "a giant, almost continent-wide republic of nearly 10 million egalitarian-minded bustling citizens. . . . Americans had become, almost overnight, the most liberal, the most democratic, the most commercially minded, and the most modern people in the world."[10] These claims elicited considerable controversy. Some historians doubted that the social order of colonial British

7 This position was advanced initially by Lance Banning who elaborated it in a number of articles on the American founding period. See, esp., "Republican Ideology and the Triumph of the Constitution, 1789 to 1793," *William and Mary Quarterly* 31 (1974): 167–88; "Jeffersonian Ideology Revisited: Liberal and Classical Ideas in the New American Republic," *William and Mary Quarterly* 43 (1986): 3–19; "Some Second Thoughts on Virtue and the Course of Revolutionary Thinking," in Terence Ball and J. G. A. Pocock, eds., *Conceptual Change and the Constitution* (Lawrence, Kans., 1988), 194–212; "The Republican Interpretation: Retrospect and Prospect," in Klein et al., eds., *Republican Synthesis*, 91–117. It has now been adopted, in slightly different versions, by many of those working in the field. See Drew R. McCoy, *The Elusive Republic: Political Economy in Jeffersonian America* (Chapel Hill, N.C., 1980); Isaac Kramnick, "Republican Revisionism Revisited," *American Historical Review* 87 (1982): 629–64; Isaac Kramnick, "'The Great National Discussion': The Discourse of Politics in 1787," *William and Mary Quarterly* 45 (1988): 3–32; Isaac Kramnick, *Republicanism and Bourgeois Radicalism: Political Ideology in Late Eighteenth-Century England and America* (Ithaca, N.Y., 1990); John Murrin, "Can Liberals Be Patriots? Natural Rights, Virtue, and Moral Sense in the America of George Mason and Thomas Jefferson," in Robert P. Davidow, ed., *Natural Rights and Natural Law: The Legacy of George Mason* (Fairfax, Va., 1986); James T. Kloppenberg, "The Virtues of Liberalism: Christianity, Republicanism, and Ethics in Early American Political Discourse," *Journal of American History* 74 (1987): 9–33; Jürgen Heideking, *Die Verfassung vor dem Richterstuhl: Vorgeschichte und Ratifizierung der amerikanischen Verfassung 1787–1791* (Berlin, 1988); Daniel T. Rogers, "Republicanism: The Career of a Concept," *Journal of American History* 79 (1992): 11–38; Horst Dippel, "The Changing Idea of Popular Sovereignty in Early American Constitutionalism: Breaking away from European Patterns," *Journal of the Early Republic* 16 (1996): 21–45.
8 Lance Banning, *The Sacred Fire of Liberty: James Madison and the Founding of the Federal Republic* (Ithaca, N.Y., 1995), 215.
9 Ibid., 472n75.
10 Gordon S. Wood, *The Radicalism of the American Revolution* (New York, 1992), 6–7.

North America had been as hierarchical, patriarchal, and deferential as Wood suggested. Many scholars also took exception to the sweeping character of his depiction of the United States in 1810, especially because it largely ignored the South – where nearly 1.5 million African-American slaves enjoyed neither liberal rights nor commercial opportunities – and any other "dark side" of the American experiment in republican government.[11]

However, Wood's proposition that liberal ideas came to dominate the lives of many whites in the new nation was widely accepted.[12] A number of scholars had already pointed out that the era of the early Republic witnessed many important changes and innovations: the commercialization of agriculture and the first stages of industrialization; the expansion of regional market economies and, thanks to improvements in transportation, the beginnings of a national market; a shift in the aspirations of producers and consumers, many of whom became full-fledged members of a capitalist "market society";[13] the radical individualism of evangelical reform; the democratization of state constitutions and state politics; the growth of activist political parties on the state and national levels; rapid settlement of the Northwest and Southwest; and the first wave of mass immigration from Ireland and Germany. Yet, many historians pointed out that although these "liberal" changes occurred and society became more individualistic, materialistic, and competitive, the ideology of traditional republicanism continued to permeate public life. For example, republican principles informed the "Commonwealth Idea," providing an intellectual rationale for state governments to foster economic development by chartering banks and subsidizing canals and other projects. Moreover, many ordinary Americans continued to view themselves as members of a cohesive republican community. In particular, various disadvantaged groups – journeymen and wage laborers, women, immigrants, and free blacks – invoked republican ideals

---

11 See, e.g., the discussion of Wood's thesis in *William and Mary Quarterly* 51 (1994): 684–716.
12 John Diggins, *The Lost Soul of American Politics: Virtue, Self-Interest, and the Foundations of Liberalism* (New York, 1984). An important German contribution to this discussion came from Hans Vorländer, *Hegemonialer Liberalismus: Politisches Denken und politische Kultur in den USA 1776–1920* (Frankfurt am Main, 1997), where the author re-evaluates Louis Hartz's thesis of an American "mass Lockeanism" or "natural liberalism," that is, a pragmatic worldview centered on liberty, constitutionalism, limited government, and the protection of private property. See Louis Hartz, *The Liberal Tradition in America* (New York, 1955), 12.
13 Charles Sellers, *The Market Revolution: Jacksonian America, 1815–1846* (New York, 1991). Critical reviews of the new literature in this field are Sean Wilentz, "Society, Politics, and the Market Revolution, 1815–1848," in Eric Foner, ed., *The New American History*, 2d ed. (Philadelphia, 1997), 61–84; Paul Nolte, "Der Markt und seine Kultur – ein neues Paradigma der amerikanischen Geschichte?" *Historisches Zeitschrift* 264 (1997): 329–60; James A. Henretta, "The 'Market' in the Early Republic," *Journal of the Early Republic* 18 (1998): 289–304.

to legitimize their political and social demands.[14] Some of the following essays reinforce the conclusion that republican values remained important well into the nineteenth century. They also suggest that the interplay between republican and liberal principles can be studied most effectively at the local and state levels.[15]

At first glance it seems problematic or even impossible to compare the American experience with developments in the German states from the Seven Years' War to the revolutions of 1848–9. Instead of behaving as actors, the German-speaking peoples during most of this period appeared to be passive observers of the fast-moving events taking place across the Atlantic or in neighboring France. In fact, to win ratification of the U.S. Constitution of 1787 the authors of *The Federalist Papers* used the Holy Roman Empire (the "Germanic empire") as a particularly instructive illustration of the dangers of a loose confederation:

The history of Germany is a history of wars between the Emperor and the Princes and States; of wars among the Princes and States themselves; of the licentiousness of the strong, and the oppression of the weak; of foreign intrusions, and foreign intrigues; of requisitions of men and money, disregarded, or partially complied with; of attempts to enforce them, altogether abortive, or attended with slaughter and desolation, involving the innocent with the guilty; of general imbecility, confusions and misery.[16]

Although this bleak picture does not correspond exactly to the historical facts as reconstructed by modern scholarship, it represented the contemporary American view of the state of affairs in central Europe.[17] During

---

14 See the chapters in James A. Henretta et al., eds., *The Transformation of Early American History: Society, Authority, and Ideology* (New York, 1991); Alfred F. Young, ed., *Beyond the American Revolution: Explorations in the History of American Radicalism* (DeKalb, Ill., 1993). The relationship between politics and race was the topic of a roundtable discussion on James Brewer Stewart's article, "The Emergence of Racial Modernity and the Rise of the White North, 1790–1840," *Journal of the Early Republic* 18 (1998): 181–236.

15 See, e.g., James A. Henretta, "The Slow Triumph of Liberal Individualism: Law and Politics in New York, 1780–1860," in Richard O. Curry and Lawrence B. Goodheart, eds., *American Chameleon: Individualism in Trans-National Context* (Kent, Ohio, 1991), 87–106; Janet A. Reisman, "Republican Revisions: Political Economy in New York After the Panic of 1819," in William Pencak and Conrad Edick Wright, eds., *New York and the Rise of American Capitalism* (New York, 1989), 1–44; see also Robert E. Shalhope's essay in this book (Chapter 8).

16 Federalist paper no. 19, written by James Madison, with the assistance of Alexander Hamilton, Dec. 8, 1787, quoted in Jacob E. Cooke, ed., *The Federalist Papers* (Middletown, Conn., 1979), 119–20.

17 For an overview of recent literature, see Volker Press, "The Holy Roman Empire in German History," in E. I. Kouri and Tom Scott, eds., *Politics and Society in Reformation Europe: Essays for Sir Geoffrey Elton on his Sixty-Fifth Birthday* (London, 1987), 51–77; Volker Press, *Altes Reich und Deutscher Bund: Kontinuität in der Diskontinuität* (Munich, 1995); Jost Dülffer, Bernd Martin, and Günter Wollstein, eds., *Deutschland in Europa: Kontinuität und Bruch; Gedenkschrift für Andreas Hillgruber* (Berlin, 1990); Hans Erich Bödeker and Ernst Hinrichs, eds., *Alteuropa – Ancien Régime – Frühe Neuzeit: Problem und Methoden der Forschung* (Stuttgart, 1991); Rudolf Vierhaus, ed., *Frühe*

the early nineteenth century this negative impression received apparent confirmation as a result of the dissolution of the Holy Roman Empire in 1806, the devastation of the Napoleonic Wars, the establishment of a powerless and dependent German Confederation (Deutscher Bund) at the Vienna peace conference of 1815, the restoration of feudal rule under Metternich, and finally the failure of the democratic revolutions and a national convention in 1849.[18]

Certainly the United States and Germany followed very different paths to modernity, but notions of American "exceptionalism" and a German *Sonderweg* do not preclude a comparative perspective – indeed, they make it all the more instructive. Despite many setbacks and failures, the German states took part in the fundamental transformation from premodern, hierarchical, feudal, and corporate societies to modern nations. Except in the French-occupied Rhineland, Germans did not experience a revolution before the mid-nineteenth century. However, they followed closely the events in America and were deeply influenced by the French Revolution. German philosophers and intellectuals tried to make sense of the great changes they were witnessing and suggested the implications for their own society. Moreover, a rising class of bourgeois activists began to demand constitutionally guaranteed economic and political rights, thereby creating a public opinion or "public sphere" (*Öffentlichkeit*) that was often critical of established authorities. Some radical individuals and groups even strove for popular sovereignty and republican government on the American model.[19]

Neuzeit – Frühe Moderne? Forschungen zur Vielschichtigkeit von Übergangsprozessen (Göttingen, 1992); Helmut Neuhaus, "The Federal Principle and the Holy Roman Empire," in Hermann Wellenreuther, ed., *German and American Constitutional Thought: Contexts, Interaction, and Historical Realities* (New York, 1990); Helmut Neuhaus, *Das Reich in der Frühen Neuzeit* (Munich, 1997); Winfried Schulze, "'Von den grossen Anfängen des neuen Welttheaters': Entwicklungen, neuere Ansätze und Aufgaben der Frühneuzeitforschung," *Geschichte in Wissenschaft und Unterricht* 44 (1993): 3–18.

18 For a comprehensive study of the period, see James J. Sheehan, *Der Ausklang des Alten Reiches: Deutschland seit dem Ende des Siebenjährigen Krieges bis zur gescheiterten Revolution 1763–1850* (Frankfurt am Main, 1994); cf. Horst Möller, *Fürstenstaat oder Bürgernation: Deutschland 1763–1815* (Berlin, 1989); Otto Dann, *Nation und Nationalismus in Deutschland 1770–1990*, 3d ed. (Munich, 1996); Otto Dann, ed., *Die deutsche Nation: Geschichte – Probleme – Perspektiven* (Vierow, 1994); Dieter Langewiesche, "Reich, Nation und Staat in der jüngeren deutschen Geschichte," *Historische Zeitschrift* 254 (1992): 341–81; Dieter Langewiesche, *Republik und Republikaner: Von der historischen Entwertung eines politischen Begriffs* (Essen, 1993); Lothar Gall, "Liberalismus und 'bürgerliche Gesellschaft': Zu Charakter und Entwicklung der liberalen Bewegung in Deutschland," *Historische Zeitschrift* 220 (1977): 324–56; Paul Nolte, "Bürgerideal, Gemeinde und Republik: 'Klassischer Republikanismus' im frühen deutschen Liberalismus," *Historische Zeitschrift* 254 (1992): 609–56.

19 Horst Dippel, *Germany and the American Revolution: A Socio-Historical Investigation of Late Eighteenth-Century Political Thinking* (Wiesbaden, 1978); Horst Dippel, *Die amerikanische Verfassung in Deutschland im 19. Jahrhundert: Das Dilemma von Politik und Staatsrecht* (Goldbach, 1994); Erich Angermann, "Der deutsche Frühkonstitutionalismus und das amerikanische Vorbild," *Historische Zeitschrift* 219 (1974): 1–32; Hermann Wellenreuther, "Die USA: Ein politisches Vorbild der bürgerlich-liberalen

(By contrast, the disastrous history of the First French Republic fueled anti-revolutionary conservatism in Germany, assisting monarchical rulers to survive the Napoleonic onslaught.)

This intellectual and political agitation induced many princely governments – beginning with the South German states – to promulgate constitutions. Simultaneously, a process of party formation began on the local and regional levels, especially in the German Southwest. In the economic sphere, state particularism slowed progress and kept Germany as a whole dependent on foreign imports; nevertheless, the founding of the German Customs Union (Deutscher Zollverein) by several states in the 1830s was an important step in creating a common market and greater national unity. When the revolution broke out in 1848 German society was still premodern in many ways, but the German people were within reach of a constitutional monarchy and stood on the threshold of a liberal and democratic nation.[20]

Consequently, our agenda at the conference included the role played in these German developments by republican and liberal ideas. In this regard as in others, present knowledge allowed only tentative answers, and full agreement was neither expected nor achieved. Some disagreements reflected the great diversity among German localities, states, and regions. The forty-one members of the German Bund included self-governing "free cities" and tiny principalities as well as extended territorial states, such as

Kräfte des Vormärz?" in Jürgen Elvert and Michael Salewski, eds., *Deutschland und der Westen im 19. und 20. Jahrhundert*, pt. 1: *Transatlantische Beziehungen* (Stuttgart, 1993), 23–41; Peter Wende, *Radikalismus im Vormärz: Untersuchungen zur politischen Theorie der frühen deutschen Demokratie* (Wiesbaden, 1975).

20 The best surveys of the revolutionary period are Wolfram Siemann, *Die deutsche Revolution von 1848/49* (Frankfurt am Main, 1985), and Günter Wollstein, *Deutsche Geschichte 1848/49: Gescheiterte Revolution in Mitteleuropa* (Stuttgart, 1986); cf. Dieter Langewiesche, "Republik, konstitutionelle Monarchie und 'soziale Frage': Grundprobleme der deutschen Revolution von 1848/49," *Historische Zeitschrift* 230 (1980): 529–48; Dieter Langewiesche, "Die deutsche Revolution von 1848/49 und die vorrevolutionäre Gesellschaft: Forschungsstand und Forschungsperspektive," *Archiv für Sozialgeschichte* 31 (1991): 331–443; Dieter Langewiesche, "Germany and the National Question in 1848," in John Breuilly, ed., *The State of Germany: The National Idea in the Making, Unmaking, and Remaking of a Modern National State* (London, 1992), 60–79. For the impact of the American example, see Eckhart G. Franz, *Das Amerikabild der deutschen Revolution von 1848/49: Zum Problem der Übertragung gewachsener Verfassungsformen* (Heidelberg, 1958); Günter Moltmann, "Amerikanische Beiträge zur deutschen Verfassungsdiskussion 1848," *Jahrbuch für Amerikastudien* 12 (1967): 206–26, 252–65; Hans Boldt, "Der Föderalismus in den Reichsverfassungen von 1849 und 1871," in Hermann Wellenreuther and Claudia Schnurmann, eds., *Amerikanische Verfassung und deutsch-amerikanisches Verfassungsdenken: Ein Rückblick über 200 Jahre* (New York, 1991), 297–333; Jörg-Detlef Kühne, "Die Bundesverfassung der Vereinigten Staaten in der Frankfurter Verfassungsdiskussion 1848/49," in Wilhelm Brauneder, ed., *Grundlagen transatlantischer Rechtsbeziehungen im 18. und 19. Jahrhundert* (Frankfurt am Main, 1991), 165–88; Jörg-Detlef Kühne, "Bürgerrechte und deutsches Verfassungsdenken 1848–1871," in Wellenreuther and Schnurmann, eds., *Amerikanische Verfassung*, 230–66.

Prussia and Bavaria. Communal republicanism and liberal rights existed in many South German states and distinguished them from their northern neighbors; in addition, the Elbe River formed an East-West divide, separating the modernizing western parts of Germany from a solidly agricultural and conservative East.[21] Given this diverse landscape and the absence of national parties with a clear ideological profile, it was difficult to establish the meaning of "German" republicanism and liberalism. However, as recent studies in American colonial history have confirmed, a "regional" perspective often yields the most accurate interpretations. As conveners of the conference, we hoped that historians working on early modern German history would benefit from this regional approach as well as from the sophisticated arguments developed in the course of the American debate over republicanism and liberalism.

II

In his overview of German political discussions Rudolf Vierhaus (Chapter 1), the former director of the Max Planck Institute for History in Göttingen, traces various "lines of thought" in Germany from the late eighteenth century to the revolution of 1848–9. In the preabsolutist tradition of self-government by localities and estates, Vierhaus suggests, republicanism was often understood and translated as *Gemeinsinn*, the concept of a political and moral "public spirit" binding rulers and ruled together in a quest for the "common good" (*Gemeinwohl*). This political mentality was supposedly found in existing European republics such as the imperial city-states, the Swiss cantons, and the Netherlands, although many critics argued that these governments had declined into oligarchic aristocracies. Vierhaus explains that a new outlook developed in Germany during and after the French Revolution: "Constitutional liberals" envisaged a constitutional monarchy with a representative legislature and a separation of powers. Under such governments the people, aided by enlightened education, would develop patriotism and a "republican attitude." Many members of the growing middle class endorsed this outlook, trusting in peaceful reforms, enlightened government, and public education to turn dependent subjects into patriotic citizens. However, the resulting constitutional monarchies remained "paternal administrative states," as Vierhaus labels them, characterized by a low degree of political participation and the predominance

---

21 Hans Fenske, *Der liberale Südwesten: Freiheitliche und demokratische Traditionen in Baden und Württemberg 1790–1933* (Stuttgart, 1981); Paul Nolte, *Gemeindebürgertum und Liberalismus in Baden 1800–1850* (Göttingen, 1994).

of a public discourse focusing on legal rules. Indeed, Prussia developed a "bureaucratic absolutism," an "obsession for governing everything" that prevented the growth of a genuine "public spirit." Beginning in the 1830s a radical "left" wing among the constitutional liberals demanded a German nation-state in the form of a parliamentary democratic republic. In 1848–9 the advocates of a democratic republic proved stronger than the majority of the liberal revolutionaries had expected, Vierhaus notes, accentuating fears of social upheaval and undermining the solidarity of the reformers. In conclusion Vierhaus emphasizes the continuity of the German traditions of local self-government, private charitable societies and associations, and particularly the ideas of a "state of laws" and the law-abiding citizen. Containing at least a "republican potential," these traditions became part of Germany's political and legal culture in the twentieth century.

The exact nature of this "republican potential" in the late eighteenth century is the subject of the initial five chapters, those by Hans Erich Bödeker (Chapter 2) and Otto Dann (Chapter 3) on Germany, a comparative study of the Prussian county of Weingerode and Pennsylvania by A. G. Roeber (Chapter 4), and essays on women and republicanism in England and the United States by Vera Nünning (Chapter 5) and Rosemarie Zagarri (Chapter 6).

As Bödeker points out in "The Concept of the Republic in Eighteenth-Century German Thought," political writers of that era usually thought of republics as "free" states, small territories or city-states governed by citizens elected to office because of their wealth or renown. Such states, as Vierhaus noted, were believed to have the greatest potential to inspire patriotism or "civic virtue" among their citizens and provide them with "civil" and "political" freedom. However, this claim was contested by those who defended rule by princes and enlightened monarchs and those who pointed out that these governments provided "just laws" that safeguarded the "civil freedom" of individuals – their persons, their property, and their standing before the law. Bödeker demonstrates that many German political writers of the late eighteenth century sought a compromise between these positions by drawing on the writings of Montesquieu and praising the "English model" of a "monarchic republic." In their view, this mixed form of government preserved both the monarchical principle and civil freedom while also providing the people with a modicum of political power – "participation of the citizen in rulership," as the journalist August Ludwig Schlözer asserted in 1793.

The subsequent centrality of monarchical republicanism in German political discourse testified both to the actual power of the princes and to intellectual concerns about "free states" among the middle classes. In their eyes traditional city-state republics – with the notable exception of Hamburg – seemed little more than wealthy oligarchies. (Thus, according to Bödeker, there is little evidence that "classical republicanism" played a major role during the German Enlightenment – a position that is at odds with Paul Nolte's influential study of Baden, which found classical republican values and practices in the towns of Southwest Germany in the early nineteenth century.[22]) To the middle classes, "modern" republics on the model of the First French Republic were even more dangerous, for they threatened rule by the unenlightened, propertyless masses. Consequently, Bödeker concludes, only a committed minority of democratically minded political thinkers celebrated the republican doctrine of popular sovereignty enshrined in the new American states.

Otto Dann's essay on "Kant's Republicanism and Its Echoes" elaborates on and extends the arguments propounded by Bödeker. Dann likewise disputes Nolte's argument that classical republicanism was crucial to the shaping of German liberalism; but, differing from Bödeker, he credits Nolte for having established the presence of this tradition in the political culture of southwestern Germany. As Dann remarks, only further research will determine the significance of Nolte's findings and the importance of traditional republicanism on the local level. Whatever the results of that scholarly effort, Dann is adamant that "modern" republicanism took root in Germany not in 1848 (as Nolte argues) but in 1795, with Immanuel Kant and his students. Through a close reading of Kant's *Zum Ewigen Frieden* Dann explores the ways in which the philosopher modernized the understanding of republicanism by identifying it with representative government and the separation of powers. Kant also defined republicanism as a form of government (and not a type of state) and therefore argued that it could be realized within a traditional monarchical framework: a representative legislature within a constitutional monarchy. It was this synthesis of monarchical and republican principles, Dann argues, that Kant established as the primary discourse of political debate in Germany during the first decades of the nineteenth century.

In his comparative German-American analysis of "Constitutions, Charity, and Liberalism," A. G. Roeber likewise notes the importance of princely power in shaping the course of German ideology and state building. He recounts the efforts of the Pietist counts of the tiny Prussian county of Wernigerode to maintain local control over education and poor relief,

---

22 See note 75 of Bödeker's essay (Chapter 2), which specifically disputes Nolte's argument.

a struggle that was doomed to failure because of the aggrandizing policies of the electors of Brandenburg and the central Prussian state. This
story had an American dimension because some of the Lutheran pastors
who were sent to America to care for the German community in Pennsylvania were subsequently subsidized by Pietist church administrators in
Wernigerode and Halle. Influenced by the Wernigerode practice of "reform Pietism from above," these pastors tried to create a state-supported,
religiously directed system of charity and education in postrevolutionary
Pennsylvania. According to Roeber, they failed primarily because "mutual
mistrust" among the diverse religious societies there made it impossible to
secure funding from the state government, despite its commitment to
"republican" community. Thus, Roeber argues, popular religious concerns
shaped the character of social policies in America, not the aggrandizing
policies of the central state (as in Prussia) or the secular ideologies of
tax-shy liberalism.

The essays by Vera Nünning and Rosemarie Zagarri suggest some additional insights afforded by the comparative analysis of republican ideology.
To a greater extent than women in central Europe, English and American women contributed to the discussion of political and social issues. As
Nünning points out, Elizabeth Macaulay was well known in Europe and
America as a "female Patriot" and republican author. Initially, she espoused
the harsh "manly" values of classical republicanism, but by the mid-1770s,
influenced by the Scottish Enlightenment and the emerging "culture of
sentiment," she insisted on the importance of "polite" values such as ten-
derness, sympathy, and liberal benevolence. Moreover, in her writings on
education Macaulay used Locke's epistemology and republican notions
of social equality as arguments against the subordination of women in the
private and public spheres, thus contributing to the beginnings of feminist
discourse.[23]

Like Macaulay, Mercy Otis Warren blended the language of republican
virtue with the discourse of natural rights. According to Zagarri, Warren
used the concept of "manners," derived from Montesquieu, to resolve the
tension between the republican commitment to the public good and the
liberal pursuit of self-interest. Again like her English counterpart, Warren
found ways to enhance the position of women, arguing that their superior refinement made them uniquely qualified to inculcate republican

---

23 These points are developed in detail in Vera Nünning, *"A Revolution in Sentiments, Manners, and Moral Opinions": Catharine Macaulay und die politische Kultur des englischen Radikalismus 1760–1790* (Heidelberg, 1998).

manners.[24] Just as Kant expanded the "potential" of German republicanism by establishing the necessity of a representative system, so Macaulay and Warren broadened the reach of Anglo-American republicanism to include women and the new "feminine" cultures of manners and sentiment. By the end of the eighteenth century, traditional conceptions of republicanism had been significantly altered.

The next six essays carry the story of republicanism and liberalism to the mid-nineteenth century and explore both the intellectual evolution of these concepts and the ways in which they were embodied in constitutions, political life, and social values. Four of the chapters – by Willi Paul Adams (Chapter 7), Robert E. Shalhope (Chapter 8), James A. Henretta (Chapter 9), and Edmund Spevack (Chapter 12) – are focused case studies, whereas those by Paul Nolte (Chapter 10) and Jürgen Heideking (Chapter 11) are comparative essays.

Adams's analysis of the "First American State Constitutions, 1776–1780" advances three central points about the outlook and values of the revolutionary generation:[25] First, unlike Kant and other German political writers, Americans defined a republic as a form of state that was incompatible with monarchy or a legally privileged aristocracy. Second, Adams argues that some American patriots used the terms *republican* and *democrat* as synonyms, so that even an elitist such as Alexander Hamilton could praise New York's conservative constitution of 1777 as "a representative democracy." Only gradually would conservative-minded Americans recognize that the republican concept of popular sovereignty could be distinguished from the democratic doctrine of universal suffrage. Third, Americans endorsed Lockean principles of a social contract and natural rights, and safeguarded the rights of citizens through written constitutions that provided for representative government, the separation of powers, and the protection of inalienable individual rights. According to Adams, patriot constitutionalists embraced Hume's pessimistic view of a self-interested human nature (an interpretation that is at odds with Zagarri's understanding of the outlook of Warren). And, he suggests, to attain the common good they relied on the mechanisms of representative government rather than the classical republican ideal of "public virtue" or the influence of republican "manners."

---

24 For an elaboration of this argument, see Rosemarie Zagarri, *A Woman's Dilemma: Mercy Otis Warren and the American Revolution* (Wheeling, Ill., 1995).

25 For an earlier treatment of these themes, see Willi Paul Adams, *The First American Constitutions: Republican Ideology and the Making of the State Constitutions in the Revolutionary Era*, trans. Rita Kimber and Robert Kimber (Chapel Hill, N.C., 1980).

The case studies by Shalhope and Henretta show how the ideological trinity of classical republicanism, representative democracy, and liberal constitutionalism were embedded in nineteenth-century American politics and society. In Bennington, Vermont, Shalhope tells us, there initially were three definitions of republicanism: the egalitarian communalism of the Strict Congregationalists, the democratic individualism of the Green Mountain Boys, and the hierarchical elitism of Federalist gentlemen. Over the following decades the interaction of these groups yielded an unexpected result: a liberal, capitalist democracy. This process began when Jeffersonian-Republican leaders elided the classical republican ideal of the virtuous yeoman with Adam Smith's concept of the self-interested individual, thereby justifying the market-oriented activities of commercial farmers and urban entrepreneurs. This ideological synthesis allowed these Jeffersonian lawyers to join with manufacturers and ex-Federalists to create a "village aristocracy" that extolled the liberal social ideals of equality of opportunity, individualism, and free enterprise. Even when the members of this elite split into Democrat and Whig factions, they remained faithful to these capitalist-oriented principles. However, in their political activities they continued to employ the rhetoric of traditional republicanism, labeling their opponents as defenders of "privilege" and "aristocracy." In Shalhope's view, this political rhetoric had taken on a life of its own, obscuring the growing inequality of Bennington society and producing "a society of capitalists oblivious to the spirit of their own enterprise."

This transition from Jeffersonian republicanism to liberal democracy is also the motif of Henretta's study of New York politics. He shows how Martin Van Buren attacked the system of gentry rule and created a new political order based on party discipline, state-subsidized patronage, and a democratic ideology. Under the influence of Van Buren's "Bucktail" faction, the New York constitutional convention of 1821 abolished "republican" property qualifications for voting and instituted a "liberal" concept of citizenship based on the legal autonomy of (white, male) individuals. Subsequently, the rural-based, petty producer "Barnburner" faction of Van Burenites pushed forward this democratic, populist program in the constitutional convention of 1846. They devised a Jacksonian constitution that undermined the quasi-feudal leasehold practices of the great "manor lords" of the Hudson River Valley and, adopting the liberal economic ideology of Adam Smith, prohibited state assistance to entrepreneurs, business corporations, and other "special interests." In the social sphere, the Barnburners joined with men of wealth to introduce new welfare policies that replaced traditional charity with a work regime for the urban poor.

However, at midcentury, this liberal, Jacksonian, small-government blue-print for New York (and the American Republic) was challenged by the influx of millions of immigrants and the specter of a permanent proletariat as well as class and ethnic warfare.

Similar themes of economic and ideological change inform Nolte's wide-ranging comparison of "Republicanism, Liberalism, and Market Society" in Jacksonian America and *Vormärz* Germany. Like Shalhope and Henretta, Nolte suggests that political ideas penetrated deeply into society only when they were harnessed to the interests of social groups and polit-ical parties. His analysis reveals many similarities between the United States and Germany during these years: Both societies utilized the "language of republican liberty"; both experienced the economic and cultural dis-ruptions of the "market revolution"; and both developed strongly partisan political cultures. Indeed, the similarities extended to specific policies. Both in Germany and the United States (until 1840) most politicians backed state financial support for canals, railroads, and other transportation ven-tures. However, among German liberals and Jacksonian Democrats (includ-ing those in Shalhope's Bennington and Henretta's New York) there was fear that capitalist development would create a "monied aristocracy," destroy the *Mittelstand* (petit bourgeoisie) of independent citizens, and increase social inequality. Consequently, just as rural and small town Barnburner Jacksonians in New York campaigned to prevent the state from subsidizing corporations, so small town liberals in Baden lodged a petition against gov-ernmental assistance to three factories. Yet, as Nolte points out, German liberals did not divide into rival parties (as did the American Whigs and Democrats): Whatever their differences over economic policy, German lib-erals remained united in order to contest the power of princes and bureau-crats. The different structures of political institutions and power in the United States and Germany meant that the two societies would embrace republican and liberal ideas in markedly different ways.

Thus, as Heideking demonstrates, the public celebrations and political rituals of the two societies followed very different trajectories. In the United States, he tells us, the rituals and symbols of the festive culture of the Amer-ican Revolution were derived from the English radical "plebeian" oppo-sition; however, beginning with the Grand Federal Processions of 1788, these antiauthoritarian tendencies were replaced by disciplined displays of civic republicanism – with thousands of self-governing people marching in ordered groups and carrying festive banners. These harmonious American civic celebrations survived the partisanship of the first party system but gradually vanished in the decades after 1830, victims of growing social and

political divisions, ethnic conflicts, and "particularistic" celebrations by temperance reformers, abolitionists, nativists, and other groups.

Whereas American festive culture fragmented, Germans created nationalist symbols and festivals to unite their politically and religiously divided
society. In October 1814 a great outpouring of national sentiment marked
the first anniversary of the Battle of Leipzig, expressed with processions,
bonfires, patriotic speeches, and church services in hundreds of German
towns. Four years later, when these festivities at the Wartburg promoted the
controversial political issues of constitutionalism and national unity, government repression checked their growth. Subsequently, festivals such as the
Oktoberfest in Munich created a sense of regional identity. Then, in 1832,
the Hambacher Fest honoring the Bavarian constitution turned into a
major demonstration for democratic rights and national unity, sentiments
that were reiterated over the following decades by local festivals and the
meetings of *Vereine* (middle-class choral, gymnast, and rifle associations). As
Heideking concludes, the German bourgeoisie used festivals symbolically
to "construct" a German nation, even as the divisions in the American
polity were reflected in (and pushed forward by) the fragmentation of its
celebratory culture.

The adventurous life of Charles Follen, as narrated in Spevack's chapter,
mirrored both the quest for German nationality and the threats to the
American central state. Before emigrating to the United States in 1824
Follen was a radical German nationalist and left-wing republican who
advocated revolutionary violence to create a united German Reich with
a single Christian state church. Forced to flee to America, he married a
wealthy Boston woman and took up an academic position at Harvard.
There he disseminated the ideas of Kant and the German Enlightenment
among New England intellectuals. After becoming a radical Unitarian,
Follen developed a religious philosophy based on free will, ethical self-
perfection, and social reform. By the mid-1830s he had become a devoted
Garrison abolitionist, now as passionately dedicated to the struggle against
American slavery as previously to the battle against German despotism.
Because Follen was a "dogmatic republican" committed to human self-
perfection and fundamental social change, Spevak concludes, he was a
radical outsider in both societies.[26] In this regard Follen anticipated the
experience of many of the radical German Forty-Eighters who emigrated
to the United States after the failure of the liberal revolution of 1848–9.

26 For a full-length study, see Edmund Spevack, *Charles Follen's Search for Nationality and Freedom:
   Germany and America, 1796–1840* (Cambridge, Mass., 1997).

By this time liberalism was the ascendant ideology in the United States, and the final two chapters, by Amy Dru Stanley (Chapter 13) and Robert J. Steinfeld (Chapter 14), explore its ambiguities and implications. As Stanley shows in "Possessive Individualism, Slave Women, and Abolitionist Thought," abolitionists maintained that the defining sin of slavery was its denial of property in the self. But in using the suffering female slave as the most powerful symbol of the dispossessed self, antislavery advocates challenged a pivotal premise of established social relations and liberal theory. In classical liberal thought the "inviolable right of self-ownership" was accorded to men and denied married women, who were considered dependents. Seizing on the liberal doctrine of self-ownership, many women abolitionists – both white and black – claimed freedom for themselves, property rights for their children, and equality within marriage and in society. To acknowledge the emancipatory potential of abolitionism for all women (as well as for enslaved men), Stanley suggests, is to acknowledge the authority achieved by the theory of possessive individualism and liberal ideology by the middle of the nineteenth century.

In his chapter analyzing the evolution of modern "free labor" in the United States, Steinfeld, too, emphasizes the importance of the struggle against slavery and peonage. However, he differs from Stanley in downplaying the causal significance of liberal ideology. He reminds us that laws in Prussia (until 1869) and in Britain (until 1875) made workers who failed to perform labor contracts subject to criminal penalties and imprisonment; in the United States (until 1913) somewhat similar "false pretenses" statutes in the southern states subjected black workers to comparable penalties. These legal rules, he suggests, were compatible with the liberal doctrine of "liberty of contract" because these labor agreements were made by choice; however, they were not in accord with the liberal doctrine of "liberty of person," which allowed labor contracts to be terminated at will (subject only to monetary penalties). This "fundamental conflict within liberalism itself," Steinfeld concludes, meant that the outcome depended not on ideology but on "contingent political events." Thus, he credits agitation by labor unions with freeing Britain's workers from penal sanctions and "changing moral standards" for the legal decisions that liberated blacks in the American South from debt peonage.

Ultimately, Steinfeld's argument reflects the point made by Rudolf Vierhaus in his keynote address before the conference attendees: Whatever the "potential" of republican or liberal ideology, its realization depended on a wide array of social, political, and institutional factors. We hope that the chapters in this book suggest both the complexity of that process in

America and the German states and the value of a comparative perspective for unraveling its logic and meaning.[27] Beyond that, we trust that these
essays clarify the causes of particular events and developments in the two
societies and will inspire further research on the character of our common
intellectual and cultural heritage.

27 For important methodological reflections on this topic, see Erich Angermann, *Challenges of
Ambiguity: Doing Comparative History*, German Historical Institute's Annual Lecture series, no. 4
(Washington, D.C., 1991).

Overview

1

"Wir nennen's Gemeinsinn" (We Call It Public Spirit): Republic and Republicanism in the German Political Discussion of the Nineteenth Century

RUDOLF VIERHAUS

I

Karl August Varnhagen von Ense recounts a conversation that took place between Baron Karl vom Stein and the Silesian Count Gustav von Schlabrendorf in 1814 or 1815 in Paris. When Schlabrendorf asked whether Stein was traveling to Vienna on matters of public service, Stein replied that this was impossible because he served no man. "Because you serve everyone," countered Schlabrendorf. He added, "that is a republican attitude that you may have a lot of use for in Germany." Stein replied: "But we don't want a republic in Germany." However, when Schlabrendorf dropped the term *republic* but insisted that no state could survive without a "republican attitude," Stein agreed with the proviso: "But we have another name for it; we call it public spirit" (*Gemeinsinn*).[1]

Just a few words in a casual conversation give us the specific dimensions of one of the dominant lines of political thought in Germany in the first half of the nineteenth century.[2] The republic as a form of government was

Translated from the German by Sally E. Robertson of Arlington, Virginia.

1 Karl August Varnhagen von Ense, *Denkwürdigkeiten und vermischte Schriften*, 2d ed., 9 vols. (Leipzig, 1843), 3, pt. 3:322.

2 For additional reading on this subject, see Wolfgang Mager, "Republik," in Otto Brunner, Werner Conze, and Reinhart Koselleck, eds., *Geschichtliche Grundbegriffe: Historisches Lexikon zur politisch-sozialen Sprache in Deutschland*, 9 vols. (Stuttgart, 1972–97), 5:549–651; Hartwig Brandt, "Republikanismus im Vormärz: Eine Skizze," in Klaus Malettke, ed., *175 Jahre Wartburgfest: Studien zur politischen Bedeutung und zum Zeithintergrund der Wartburgfeier*, Darstellungen und Quellen zur Geschichte der deutschen Einheitsbewegung im 19. und 20. Jahrhundert, vol. 14 (Heidelberg, 1992), 138, passim.

rejected, but there was demand for a political attitude that Stein did not want to call "republican" but to which he ascribed an analogous meaning. To be sure, Stein, an opponent of both monarchical absolutism and democratic republicanism, was aware of the differences between Schlabrendorf's understanding of "republicanism" and his own of "public spirit," but he assumed a basic identity of intention and mentality that is manifest in the readiness of people to contribute to the common weal of the society (*res publica*) in which they live. Stein was convinced that this "public spirit" could also exist outside a republic. The reforms he introduced in Prussia were intended to lay the foundation for the public spirit, partially by the reactivation of preabsolutist traditions of "local self-government," partially by breaking outdated personal and economic ties, and partially through patriotic education.[3]

Rejection of the republic as a form of government and the concept of a political and moral public spirit had a history extending back well into the eighteenth century. It had long been a shared European opinion that a republic could function only in a small state or city-state, but not in a large territorial state, particularly if it consisted of provinces with differing institutions and legal traditions. Therefore, the unprecedented establishment of the "United States" in North America – in other words, the formation of a large federation with a republican (that is, nonmonarchical) constitution that guaranteed general rights of freedom, equality, and political participation – was observed in Germany with fascination and skepticism. Even among those who had welcomed the Declaration of Independence as a revolutionary step into an age of freedom, not a few harbored doubts regarding the stability of the new state, which could fail as a result of internal conflicts and the emergence of rival factions.[4]

This skepticism was bolstered by the increasing criticism of existing European republics, no longer aimed at Venice, Genoa, and the Polish aristocratic republic but at German imperial cities, the Netherlands, and even at Swiss cantons. Until well past the mid-eighteenth century Switzerland had been celebrated by German writers as the land of freedom. The poet, musician, and antiabsolutist journalist Ludwig Schubart wrote: "Go to Switzerland, young man, and then to Hamburg, if you want to know what freedom does for people. Then go to the royal courts to see how slavery chips away at a man until he is so small he can only crawl."[5] In the 1770s,

3 Gerhard Ritter, *Stein: Eine politische Biographie*, 3d ed., 2 vols. (Stuttgart, 1958).
4 Christian Wilhelm Dohm in *Teutscher Merkur*, 17 (1977): 77.
5 Ludwig Schubart, *Schubarts Leben und Gesinnung, von ihm selbst, im Kerker aufgesetzt*, 2d ed., 2 vols. (Stuttgart, 1791–3), 1:78–9.

however, a series of cases of intolerance in the judicial system and death sentences for religious and political crimes prompted enlightened writers to emphatically attack the "despotism" of the decrepit, oligarchic "aristocracies" of nobility or the professions that ruled the cantons. "Is the hereditary aristocracy not the most wretched, hateful, and tyrannical of all forms of government?" asked August Ludwig von Schlözer, "and does not the elective aristocracy of any nation infected by extravagance and wealth degenerate into actual hereditary aristocracy or family conspiracy?" He added: "Democracy is good for people who merely graze together. I assume it is understood that no other freedom, no higher human good is possible in such a society."[6] Like Schlözer, a liberal and anglophile defender of limited monarchy, many German political writers not only criticized absolutism but sometimes leveled even stronger criticisms at the aristocracy. Rule by oligarchies, whether hereditary or elective, whether their members came from the hereditary nobility or from the service nobility, patrician class, or the professions, seemed worse than the absolutist rule of enlightened monarchs. Whereas the former defended their privileges against any kind of social change, modern reforms could be expected from the latter. Schlözer therefore welcomed Prussian intervention in 1788 on behalf of the House of Orange in the Netherlands.

The French Revolution fueled the idea of a republic in Germany, particularly in the French-occupied and annexed territories on the left bank of the Rhine, although the idea was never championed by more than an intellectual minority. The revolution generated a plethora of republican writings, demands, declarations of allegiance, and draft constitutions. German democrats proclaimed a republic in Mainz and its incorporation into the "Franconian" republic. Republic for them meant human rights, freedom, legal equality and unity, self-government by the people, constitution and representation, safety and peace, and civil rights and civic responsibilities. Even the deterioration of the republic in France as a result of the Jacobin terror did not destroy the ideal image of the republic in the eyes of the small group of convinced German democrats. "Grundlinien einer allgemeinen deutschen Republik" (Outline for a General German Republic) appeared in Altona in 1797,[7] and the draft of a republican constitution "such as might be fitting for Germany" appeared in Basle in 1799, the "seventh year of the mother republic."[8] Both were published anonymously;

6 See August Ludwig Schlözer in *Staatsanzeiger* 4 (1784): 149.
7 See Horst Dippel, ed., *Die Anfänge des Konstitutionalismus in Deutschland: Texte deutscher Verfassungsentwürfe am Ende des 18. Jahrhunderts* (Frankfurt am Main, 1991), 114.
8 Ibid., 177.

neither was simply a copy of the French constitution of the Year III.
Both bore a more liberal-republican stamp, were oriented toward
German circumstances, and were guided by the conviction that a shift
to a republican constitution was possible without a political revolution
but with a change of public opinion resulting from unrestricted freedom
of speech and the press. The beginnings of a German constitutional
discussion in the 1790s, triggered by the revolution in France, were
overtaken by increased press censorship and the frightened aversion even
of those who had welcomed the beginning of the revolution, then by
Napoleonic intervention in German affairs, the formation of the Rheinbund (Rhenish Confederation) and the dissolution of the Reich. The discussion resumed under different conditions in the states of the Rheinbund,
in the reformed Prussia, and later in the Deutscher Bund (German
Confederation).

The nonmonarchical "free state," the republic, no longer was a topic of
discussion anywhere in Europe. In Germany it was increasingly rejected as
a form of state and government foreign to German historical experience
and the national mentality. The discussion concentrated on a constitutional
monarchy, with representation and separation of powers. Those working
toward this goal, the constitutional liberals, were convinced that a "republican" attitude, a patriotic public spirit, could develop under this form of
government as well, indeed, that a constitutional monarchy would
inevitably depend on such an attitude in order to function properly and
keep up with the times. It was not until 1830 that the radical left wing of
the liberals began to insist that this development must lead to parliamen-
tarism and a democratic republic. This call was made most spectacularly at
the National Festival of the Germans at Hambach in 1832, where the
"united free states of Germany in a confederated republican Europe" was
raised as a goal.[9] Achieving this goal first required a new consciousness or
political enlightenment that asserted the freedoms of speech, press, and
assembly as the most important demands. The German Federal Diet or
Bundestag sitting in Frankfurt am Main responded with immediate restrictions. This indicates a second line of continuity in German political culture
since the eighteenth century, which we shall now address: the enlightened
liberal line of thought, which united with a national patriotic line of
thought.

9 Johann Georg August Wirth, *Das Nationalfest der Deutschen zu Hambach* (1832; reprint, Vaduz, 1977),
   1:48.

II

In 1759 the Swiss writer Johann Georg Zimmermann called into question the "national pride" of the Germans, which he described as a political virtue characteristic of republics only.[10] He was challenged in 1761 by Thomas Abbt in his book *Vom Tod fürs Vaterland* (On Dying for the Fatherland)[11] and in 1765 by Friedrich Carl von Moser in the pamphlet *Von dem deutschen Nationalgeist* (On the German National Spirit),[12] both of which triggered a journalistic debate significant in the development of German political consciousness. The traditional attribution of certain public virtues to certain forms of government and their qualification had come back into vogue as a result of Baron Montesquieu's *Esprit des Lois* (Spirit of Law).[13] The question of the "spirit" of the German constitution, which Samuel von Pufendorf called "monstrous" because it did not fit into the classical categories, was answered by referring back to the peculiarities of German history.[14] Moser argued that the imperial and corporate constitution of the Reich, in its ideal form, was the expression of the national spirit of all Germans. Abbt asserted that love for and pride in the homeland were also possible in an unlimited monarchy, assuming it had a great and just ruler and "wholesome" laws, for which Friedrich II and the Prussian state were giving evidence. The key concept in this literary, pedagogical, and political discussion was patriotism. To be a patriot, to act patriotically, to sacrifice oneself for the homeland was not only a rhetorical demand but a self-confident claim that was made, in particular, by members of the ascendant educated middle class, which expressed their refusal to be seen as mere subjects of the state. Patriotism as a moral and political attitude meant an interest in the trials and tribulations of one's fellow man, a practical commitment to the homeland, meaning the commonwealth in which the individual lived – city, province, even Reich and nation. "Participation" was a word often applied to this commitment, or, more accurately, to the readiness for such public commitment, not just in the context of the institutions provided for this purpose but in service of one's own choosing and – for the

---

10 Johann Georg Zimmermann, *Vom National-Stolz (1775)*, 4th ed. (Zurich, 1768).
11 Thomas Abbt, *Vom Tod fürs Vaterland (1761)*, *Vermischte Werke* II, (Berlin, 1770), 3–102.
12 Friedrich Carl von Moser, *Von dem Deutschen National-Geist* (1765).
13 Rudolf Vierhaus, "Montesquieu in Deutschland: Zur Geschichte seines Wirkens als politischer Schriftsteller in Deutschland," in Ernst-Wolfgang Böckenförde et al., *Collegium Philosophicum: Studien Joachim Ritter zum 60. Geburtstag* (Basel, 1965), 403–37.
14 Samuel von Pufendorf (pseudonym: Severinus von Monzambano), *Über die Verfassung des deutschen Reiches*, Klassiker der Politik, vol. 3 (Berlin, 1922), 394.

enlightened "educated class" – in contributions to the discussion that was molding public opinion. This discussion, they were convinced, would eventually produce an irresistible drive for social, economic, and political improvements.[15]

This conviction was often upheld and often disappointed. It placed its trust in the power of the press, in increased criticism, in the reasonableness of the rulers, especially of their ministers and counselors, and in enlightened governments and continuing education of the governed. However, it was understood that this patriotism in Germany lacked a decisive prerequisite for political effectiveness, for patriotism does not bring about a free state; rather, the state must be free, and every citizen must feel a part of the state if patriotism is to be possible. This assertion by Johann Georg Schlosser around 1780 addresses a configuration of political power and political thought in Germany that remained in effect under modified circumstances even as late as the nineteenth century.[16]

More an ideal than a reality, more the product of enlightenment and education than a secure civic self-confidence, patriotism was understood as that quality that turns subjects into citizens. The shared patriotic attitude of the governors and the governed should turn the state that the patriotism serves into a commonwealth with laws to which everyone can freely and thoughtfully agree. Such patriotism may have been oriented more toward the conservation of a modified structure of corporate society or toward enlightened liberalism: Both tendencies were fundamentally different from democratic republicanism. The former aligned itself in the nineteenth century primarily with the political system of constitutional monarchy that, in practice, remained a paternal and patronizing administrative state despite all legal checks and balances. Radical tendencies that continued to push for an egalitarian, democratic republic remained unsuccessful in Germany until 1918.

III

With the dissolution of the Old Reich the constitutional question became critical both in the sovereign states of the Rheinbund under Napoleon's protection and in Prussia after the catastrophe of 1807. No discussion was

---

15 Rudolf Vierhaus, "'Patriotimus': Begriff und Realität einer politisch-moralischen Haltung," in Rudolf Vierhaus, ed., *Deutsche patriotische und gemeinnützige Gesellschaften*, Wolfenbütteler Forschungen, vol. 8 (Munich, 1980), 9–29.

16 Johann Georg Schlosser, "Politische Fragmente," in Johann Georg Schlosser, *Kleine Schriften*, 6 vols. (Basel, 1780), 2:237.

heard anywhere about abolition of the monarchy and transition to a republic. The democratic-republican endeavors of the 1790s had been crushed under the weight of the Napoleonic system, and the Rheinbund states had become consolidated in the form of monarchical administrative states. For these, the introduction of a constitution that provided its subjects with non-democratic representation and the right to participate in legislation and tax collection but that did not abolish monarchical prerogatives had the practical aim of integrating the territories annexed through secularization and mediatization and of stabilizing the states' credit.[17] After the collapse of Napoleon's hegemonic system, however, the constitutional question moved to the center of German politics as a problem of reorganization and modernization of the political life, both nationally and in individual states. The political and ideological fronts that established the terms of debate up to the revolution of 1848–9 developed at this time: old-corporate restorers, new-corporate conservatives, and constitutional liberals. Whereas the former soon became insignificant, the new-corporate conservatives increasingly occupied influential positions in governments and administrations, and endorsed a constitution in which the "monarchical principle"[18] remained in full force and progress toward a parliamentary form of government was blocked. Constitutional liberalism, however, underwent an increasing separation between a moderate wing, which also rejected a parliamentary system based on universal suffrage, and a radical wing that called for a united democratic German republic and parliamentary government. The failure of the revolution of 1848–9 split the liberal movement and forever weakened it.

The debate among representatives of the political currents in Germany remained literary and theoretical; it was carried out in newspapers, pamphlets, sometimes in the provincial diets, and at congresses. This was not merely the consequence of the relatively low degree of politicization and the administrative control of public life. It was also the result of the prevailing conviction among educated people, both conservative and liberal, that not revolution but the free and public battle of opinions would bring about a change in public consciousness. This altered political attitude would foster development toward greater civic freedom, more political equality

---

17 Rudolf Vierhaus, "Das allgemeine Landrecht für die Preussischen Staaten als Verfassungsgesetz?" in Barbara Dölemeyer and Heinz Mohnhaupt, eds., *200 Jahre allgemeines Landrecht für die preussischen Staaten: Wirkungsgeschichte im internationalen Kontext*, Jus Commune, Sonderhefte: Studien zur Europäischen Rechtsgeschichte, vol. 75 (Frankfurt am Main, 1995), 1–21.
18 Friedrich Julius Stahl, *Das Monarchische Princip: Eine staatsrechtlich-politische Abhandlung* (Heidelberg, 1845).

and participation, and a transformation of the paternal administrative state into a citizens' and people's state. This is why even the liberal opposition valued the freedoms of press, speech, assembly, and association more highly than the right to vote. When Arnold Ruge, a radical liberal, in his "Selbst-kritik des Liberalismus" (Self-Criticism of Liberalism) in 1843 pleaded for the "transformation of liberalism into democratism," he considered a "new consciousness" to be the most urgent, indispensable step in German political progress. Only a reform of consciousness, not a reform of political institutions, would create the democratic drive for freedom, for which the time was ripe.[19]

IV

An important element in the political development of Germany from the eighteenth to the nineteenth century was the conviction of the enlightened intelligentsia that the illumination of consciousness and the expansion of knowledge, and rational thought and action would necessarily lead to the improvement (or reform) of society and state: to better laws, better administration, greater freedom and self-determination, but also to a better understanding of the historical basis of the existing conditions and the beneficent results of reform. This was the widespread conviction among educated persons, many of whom held or strove for offices in this world of numerous territories, courts, municipal authorities, and manors, of administration, church, and education, that their service would promote the common weal – which it often did. This lent the political discourse in Germany a specific scholarly, juridical, and pedagogical, but also practical, note. The reforms in the early constitutional states during the first half of the nineteenth century were essentially the work of governments and administrations – that is, of officials who cooperated with men of the same educational level and similar political ideas in the state administrations and in the early constitutional representative bodies. These men – not the monarchs – were the targets of criticism from democratic liberals who strove for a parliamentary order and attacked the system of constitutional monarchy for being without separation of legislative and executive functions and without accountability of government and administration to any parliament, a "patronizing" system that was basically still a more or less benevolent "police state."

Between 1815 and the revolution of 1848 Prussia represented the most extreme example of this system: a military state, a patriarchal state, and a state

---

19 Arnold Ruge, "Eine Selbstkritik des Liberalismus" (1843), reprinted in Hans Fenske, ed., *Vormärz und Revolution 1840–1849*, Quellen zum politischen Denken der Deutschen im 18. Jahrhundert, vol. 4 (Darmstadt, 1976), 80.

of laws, but above all a monarchical state without a written constitution. The
continuity between the so-called enlightened absolutism and the succeed-
ing bureaucratic absolutism was evident here. The 1842 edition of the *Staatslexikon* (Encyclopedia of Political Terms), compiled by Rotteck and Welcker,
was correct in noting that even after the introduction of provincial estates,
one could not speak of a constitution in Prussia unless one considered administrative norms as constitutional laws. Here the protection of civic freedom
rested solely on the "lawful organization of the administration." The "obsession to govern everything" might well be tolerated because of the good will
and the beneficent nature of the government and bureaucracy, yet it aug-
mented the "political immaturity" of the governed[20] and – one might add –
rendered impossible the public spirit that Stein had equated with republicanism, a virtue that had been largely stifled by the absolutist state and could
be revived only through reform of the state, the practice of self-government,
and education. Or, as Harscher von Almendingen stressed in 1814, through
the free election of representatives who were materially independent and
who, without being "tools of the government" – that is, officials – could gain
political influence in the "school of public life."[21]

The complaint about a lack of public spirit was often repeated; the suggestions on how to overcome this deficit always cited the prerequisites for
its development: civic and political freedom, the rule of law, the welfare of
all. Which constitution, which form of government would fulfill and secure
these preconditions was vociferously debated. Even the majority of moderate and national-minded liberal theorists and politicians was convinced
that public spirit could flourish in a constitutional monarchy and did
not require a democratic republic, especially not in nineteenth-century
Germany with its peculiar political traditions and its retarded constitutional
development.

V

After the dissolution of the Old Reich and the collapse of the Napoleonic
hegemonial system, German statehood was reconstructed as a confederation of sovereign monarchical states and city-states with discrete

20 W. Lüders, "Preussen (Staatsrecht)," in Carl von Rotteck and Carl Welcker, eds., *Staatslexikon, oder
Encyklopädie der Staatswissenschaften*, 13 vols. (Altona, 1842), 13:81–3; Rudolf Vierhaus, "The Pruss-
ian Bureaucracy Reconsidered," in John Brewer and Eckhard Hellmuth, eds., *Rethinking Leviathan:
The Eighteenth-Century State in Britain and Germany* (Oxford, 1999), 11–19.
21 Ludwig Harscher von Almendingen, "Politische Ansichten über Deutschlands Vergangenheit,
Gegenwart und Zukunft" (1814), in Hartwig Brandt, ed., *Restauration und Frühliberalismus
1814–1840*, Quellen zum politischen Denken der Deutschen im 19. und 20. Jahrhundert, vol. 3
(Darmstadt, 1979), 149.

constitutional structures. The dominant and competing members of the German Confederation, Austria and Prussia, both multinational states without written constitutions, blocked further constitutional development and national unification by which democratic tendencies inevitably would be strengthened. Although the Bundestag in Frankfurt, the permanent representation of the state governments, tried to suppress these tendencies and aspirations, the politicization of German public opinion made headway and culminated in the revolution of 1848–9. There was strong support for the demand for incontestable civil rights, for representation of the people, and for control of the executive on the state and federal levels. The resistance of the majority of the Frankfurt National Assembly to increasing democratic and republican demands, and of Austria and Prussia to national unification, resulted in a wave of reactionary politics and the restoration of the German Confederation.

The failure of the revolution produced a deep change in the German political mentality and led to the formation of a new political constellation. The resolution of the "German Question" in 1870–1, which meant national unification without Austria, was not enforced by the united will of the German people but by the Prussian politics of Otto von Bismarck. The new federal constitution of the second "Reich" was not based on the will of the nation but on a convention of the German monarchs and magistrates of the city-states. The imperial parliament or Reichstag was based on general election, yet the government was not accountable to the parliament. Until the end of World War I the constitutional system of the Reich and its particular status was that of a constitutional monarchy, characterized by the predominance of the executive. The discrepancy between a nonparliamentary, nondemocratic form of government and a growing politicization of public life under the impact of rapid industrialization, class conflict, and partisanship remained the crucial and unresolved problem of domestic politics in the Kaiserreich.

There were, however, a few "republican" traditions that were revived during the nineteenth century, namely, those of corporate society, power sharing among the estates, and, more important, local self-government[22] – exercised in the imperial cities, in large commercial towns, seaports, and regional centers by the representation of citizens and by elected municipal magistrates. Although increasingly controlled by "absolutist" governments, they often retained the right of self-administration.

---

22 Heinrich Heffter, *Die deutsche Selbstverwaltung im 19. Jahrhundert: Geschichte der Ideen und Institutionen*, 2d ed. (Stuttgart, 1969).

Stein, the Prussian minister and imperial knight, drew on these traditions early in the century for the Prussian Municipal Ordinance of November 19, 1808, the essential aim of which was the revival, as he put it, of
"the participation of citizens in the common weal, to which nearly all of
the larger, good institutions that are still present in the cities owe their existence as works of the public spirit. . . . The city as an independent common
weal shall manage its own affairs through elected bodies, as an active community endowed with a life of its own, as a community inherent in the
unified body of citizens as a whole."[23] Otto von Gierke, who described the
goal of the Municipal Ordinance in these terms, saw in it the starting point
for the "revitalization of corporate self-government."[24] Indeed, self-
government (*Selbstverwaltung*) not only was a strongly supported demand
in the German political discussion in the nineteenth century but was a
reality on the intermediate local and provincial levels. Its importance within
the German political discussion and its function as compensation for a non-
democratic government demand further investigation of the structure of
German political culture.

A second tradition that I must mention in this context is that of the
activities of private associations for the common weal. Beginning in the
eighteenth century, the number of patriotic and charitable societies or local
associations (*Vereine*) for the promotion of public education, the modernization of agrarian production, the development of cultural life, and for
other good causes, increased rapidly. Professional and trade associations,
chambers of commerce, provincial insurance and savings institutions, and
regional commissions for the regulation of traffic, water, and economic
activity resumed public responsibilities. All these institutions, some of them
acknowledged as corporations under public law (*Körperschaften des
öffentlichen Rechts*), produced and maintained a mentality of civic responsibility and a "moral economy" of civic honor.

A third tradition is the Natural Law doctrine of the Enlightenment in
its specifically German, state-oriented version: Society is based on a social
and political contract of individuals endowed with unalienable rights, delegating government to a sovereign bound by law. Corporate rights are
understood as privileges granted by government. The relation between
persons as well as between government and the governed are considered
to be legal relations. In the general common law of the Prussian states of

---

23 "Mediatbericht der Minister Schroetter und Stein," Königsberg, Nov. 9, 1808, reprinted in
   Freiherr vom Stein, *Briefe und amtliche Schriften*, vol. 2, pt. 2: *Das Reformministerium 1807–1808*
   (Stuttgart, 1969), 930.
24 Otto von Gierke, *Die Steinsche Städteordnung* (1907), Libelli, vol. 38 (Darmstadt, 1968), 191.

1794, freedom is an individual right, its protection exclusively the responsibility of the government, which enacts laws to this end and binds itself
to them. Under a government of law the governed are "citizens by law"
whose fundamental rights are protected by the government and who are
entitled to claim this legal right even against government and administration. Immanuel Kant asserted that a state ruled by laws corresponding to
the common weal of the governed has a "republican constitution."[25]

In the process of political reorganization after the dissolution of the Old
Reich, the restoration or modernization of the constitutional system of the
particular states as well as of the German Confederation remained the
central and most heavily debated political problem. Whereas a written
formal constitution granting civil rights, separation of powers, and representation of the people was considered by the liberals to be the indispensable precondition for the further development of a public spirit, the
conservatives feared and resisted the inherent democratic (and national)
tendencies, especially the introduction of a parliamentary government.
What was called "constitutional monarchy," which was characterized by the
predominance of executive power and which existed in Germany at the
state and national levels until the collapse of the Kaiserreich in 1918, did
not suffocate the public spirit in the liberal sense, but it did retard its development into democratic republicanism. The instability of the "improvised
democracy" of the Weimar Republic was a consequence of the fundamental
weakness of republican elements in German political culture.[26]

25 Immanuel Kant, *Zum ewigen Frieden: Ein philosophischer Entwurf* (1796), reprinted in Immanuel Kant,
   Werke in zehn Bänden, ed. Wilhelm Weischedal (Darmstadt, 1968), 9:191, 204.
26 Theodor Eschenburg, *Die improvisierte Demokratie der Weimarer Republik* (Laupheim, 1954).

The Republican World

2

The Concept of the Republic in Eighteenth-Century German Thought

HANS ERICH BÖDEKER

I

The European states that were constitutionally designated as "free" were of special interest for the politicized public that began to develop in the 1760s and that so intensively examined the nature of the different forms of state and government and the degree of freedom they afforded.[1] This public sought to clarify its relationship to the existing governmental orders, critically comparing the monarchic absolutism dominant in Germany with contemporary and ancient republics. A new trend of thought began to emerge that, in a nutshell, accorded only the "republics" the attribute of "freedom," investing this term with the meaning of "free state."[2] Opponents did not want to restrict the label of freedom to institutional participation of citizens in political decision making. Instead, they attempted to

---

Most of this chapter was translated from the German by Sally E. Robertson of Arlington, Virginia.

1 This chapter does not cover recent discussions in Germany of early modern republicanism. On this, see Heinz Schilling, "Gab es im späten Mittelalter und zu Beginn der Neuzeit in Deutschland einen städtischen 'Republikanismus,'" in Helmut Koenigsberger, ed., *Republiken und Republikanismus im Europa der Frühen Neuzeit* (Munich, 1987), 101–43, and Heinz Schilling, "Stadt und Frühmoderner Territorialstaat: Stadtrepublikanismus versus Fürstensouveränität: Die politische Kultur des deutschen Stadtbürgertums in der Konfrontation mit dem frühmodernen Staatsprinzip," in Michael Stolleis, ed., *Recht, Verfassung und Verwaltung in der Frühneuzeitlichen Stadt* (Cologne, 1991), 19–39. Such reconstructions of "urban republicanism" make far-reaching claims in their analysis of the political practices of town oligarchies without referring to clearly established theoretical considerations. Renate Dopheide, in "Republikanismus in Deutschland: Studien zur Theorie der Republik in der Publizistik des späten 18. Jahrhunderts," Ph.D. diss., Ruhr University Bochum, 1990, has reviewed important material. See also Joist Grolle, "Republikanische Wanderungen: Die Fussreisen des Jonas Ludwig von Hess aus Hamburg durch die 'Freien deutschen Reichsstädte' 1789–1800," *Zeitschrift des Vereins für Hamburgische Geschichte* 83, no. 1 (1997): 299–321. I am planning a systematic survey of the research. The present chapter also excludes an interpretation of Kant's concept of republic, although this is vital, because a separate essay in this book is devoted to this topic (Chapter 3).

2 See Rudolf Vierhaus, "Politisches Bewusstsein in Deutschland vor 1789," *Der Staat* 6 (1967): 175–96; for the European contexts, see Franco Venturi, *Utopia and Reform in the Enlightenment* (Cambridge, 1971).

establish a positive relationship with the absolutist states and disputed the claim of the existing republics to the label of "free state."

To better understand the term *republic*, it is illuminating to read the relevant article in Zedler's *Universallexikon*, the leading encyclopedia of the time. In addition to the broad definition of "common entity," Zedler also considered a narrower "republic in specific terms, meaning a free people, country, city, or town knowing no leader, or only one of a certain limited thought." He distinguished three varieties:

1. Those which elect a leader for life or for an established short period, such as Venice, Genoa, etc.; 2. those which elect several of the wealthiest or most renowned citizens of their city or state to govern alternately or for life, such as most imperial cities; 3. several provinces, estates or cities which confederate to form a republic with each maintaining its own form of government, such as Switzerland and the Netherlands.[3]

The scope of this definition was undoubtedly influenced by the fact that the concept of republic was being fed from a wide variety of wellsprings of history and political philosophy. In reconstructing the sometimes contradictory and overlapping definitions of republic, the first step is to examine the theory of political participation[4] from the profession-based "mechanistic state" of enlightened absolutism to the liberal society featuring individual ownership of private property, and the transition from there to democratic republicanism (see II below). Since enlightened republicanism is not limited to certain models of political rule, the second step is to draw a distinction that shapes the entire discussion, the distinct between forms of state and forms of government (see III below). Finally, we trace the link between enlightened republicanism and enlightened patriotism (see IV below).

II

The division of the concept of freedom into the civil and the political,[5] as occurred from the late eighteenth century on, was the linguistic expres-

3 "Republik," in *Grosses vollständiges Universallexikon aller Wissenschaften und Künste*, 46 vols. (Leipzig, 1742), 31:665. For the concept of "republic" in the late eighteenth century, see Inge Stephan and Johann Gottfried Seume, *Ein politischer Schriftsteller der deutschen Spätaufklärung* (Stuttgart, 1973), 69–76. Indispensable is Wolfgang Mager, "Republik," in Otto Brunner, Werner Conze, and Reinhart Koselleck, eds., *Geschichtliche Grundbegriffe: Historisches Lexikon zur politisch-sozialen Sprache in Deutschland*, 9 vols. (Stuttgart, 1972–97), 5:549–651.
4 See Jörn Garber, "Politisch-soziale Partizipationstheorien im Übergang vom Ancien régime zur bürgerlichen Gesellschaft (1750–1800)," in Peter Steinbach, ed., *Probleme der politischen Partizipation im Modernisierungsprozess* (Stuttgart, 1982), 23–65.
5 See Jürgen Schlumbohm," *Freiheit – Die Anfänge der bürgerlichen Emanzipationsbewegung in Deutschland im Spiegel ihres Leitwortes (ca. 1760–1800)* (Düsseldorf, 1975), 133–57, and Diethelm Klippel, *Politische Freiheit und Freiheitsrechte im deutschen Naturrecht des 18. Jahrhunderts* (Paderborn, 1976).

sion of the fact that, above and beyond the call for constitutionality
and equality under the law, there were also the concept and demand that
governmental authority be subject to control of the governed. The conclusion was that only both parts together could be described as complete
freedom.

Johann Michael Afsprung used this argument in 1787. He quite consciously differentiated "political freedom" as the right of the citizen "to a
voice in determining legislation" from "civil freedom" as the opportunity
of the citizen to exercise his power within the necessary legal constraints.
In doing so, he expressly turned away from the amateur and professional
"sycophants" who advocated the absolutist "state of law." Whereas the latter
considered that state to be most free which "is ruled by laws," Afsprung
justified his additional demands by avowing that the citizen is "more assured
of civil freedom" and "makes better use of it . . . when he enjoys political
freedom as well." In an absolute monarchy, laws may be "born of ignorance
or passion" and, moreover, rulers cannot be forced to adhere to the laws at
all times.[6]

More than a few of those who expressly distanced themselves from
republican tendencies and from the French revolutionaries, and who
declared themselves loyal subjects of their princes and fundamental adherents of a monarchic form of state may have viewed political freedom, that
is, overcoming of absolutism, as a long-term goal. For example, the high-
level Prussian official Ernst Ferdinand Klein emphasized that, for him, civil
freedom was the "main thing," that "political freedom has value only inas-
much as it supports civil freedom"; that is, that a monarchy with civil
freedom makes any kind of republicanism superfluous. Nevertheless, he did
not hide his "concerns" that abuses might be "unavoidable" in the long run
in an unchecked government.[7]

This distinction between civil and political freedom ran largely parallel
with that between "civil society" and "state," "private" and "public."
Johann August Eberhard, the popular philosopher from Halle, claimed in
1784 to be the first to differentiate precisely between civil and political
freedom by saying that "political freedom" consisted of "participation in
sovereignty" whereas "civil freedom" signified the "right . . . to do and not

6 Johann Michael Afsprung, *Über die Vereinigten Niederlande in Briefen an Fräulein von . . .* (Ulm, 1787), 32–4. See Julius Endriss, *Die Ulmer Aufklärung* (Ulm, 1942), 34–40.
7 Ernst Ferdinand Klein, *Freiheit und Eigentum, abgehandelt in acht Gesprächen über die Beschlüsse der Französischen Nationalversammlung* (Berlin, 1790), 164, 171, 173, 182; see Eckart Hellmuth, "Ernst Ferdinand Klein: Politische Reflexionen im Preussen der Spätaufklärung," in Hans Erich Bödeker and Ulrich Herrmann, eds., *Aufklärung als Politisierung – Politisierung der Aufklärung* (Hamburg, 1987), 222–36.

to do as I please with regard to actions not specified by the laws of the state."[8] Civil freedom, therefore, consisted of the free discretion of one's property and person, the private sphere of human life, sheltered from arbitrary acts of intervention by the state. That same year, an essay in the journal *Das graue Ungeheuer* offered a similar definition of civil freedom. The concept of political freedom explicitly concerned a limited monarchy – more or less in the spirit of Montesquieu – defined as the "most perfect equilibrium between the free powers of the state: the ruler, the government and the people."[9]

More and more, however, enlightened thinkers such as August Ludwig Schlözer called for the "citizen to share in rulership" as they distinguished between a special political freedom and civil freedom. In 1793 he expressed the twin needs for control and for limits on the scope of state power.[10] The then counterrevolutionary Friedrich Gentz recognized this as well, which is why, in 1795, he took on the "misunderstandings" brought about by the term *political freedom* and proposed that the subdivision of the concept of freedom be abandoned, that "the title of freedom in the political sense be devoted exclusively to civil freedom, that is, the condition of the individual ruled only by just laws . . . and that civil and political freedom be made completely synonymous."[11]

On the other hand, those who subscribed to the idea that the purpose of political freedom was distribution of power could, against the backdrop of the increasingly radical French Revolution, use this principle which mainly targeted monarchic despotism to fight radical French democrats as well.[12] Even an absolutist state like Prussia could in this way be described as free if the principle of distribution of power was interpreted so abstractly as to require only a division of power among various government departments and not that the people possess part of the power.[13] Prussian offi-

---

8 Johann August Eberhard, "Über die Freiheit des Bürgers und die Prinzipien der Regierungsform," in Johann August Eberhard, *Vermischte Schriften*, 2 vols. (Halle, 1784), 1:6–8.

9 Wilhelm Ludwig Wekherlin, ed., *Das Graue Ungeheuer*, 6 vols. (1784), 2:74–5.

10 August Ludwig Schlözer, *Allgemeines Staatsrecht und Staatsverfassungslehre* (Göttingen, 1793), 37; see Bernd Warlich, "August Ludwig von Schlözer 1735–1809 zwischen Reform und Revolution: Ein Beitrag zur Pathogenese frühliberalen Staatsdenkens im späten 18. Jahrhundert," Ph.D. diss., University of Erlangen-Nuremberg, 1972.

11 Friedrich Gentz, ed., *Neue Deutsche Monatsschrift* 2 (1795): 296. See Günther Kronenbitter, *Wort und Macht: Friedrich Gentz als politischer Schriftsteller* (Berlin, 1994), 59–64.

12 See Schlumbohm, *Freiheit – Die Anfänge*, 147–57, and Klippel, *Politische Freiheit*, 157–75.

13 See Christian Wilhelm Dohm, "Mémoire sur la constitution politique des anciennes nations," in *Mémoires de la société des antiquités de Cassel* (Kassel, 1780), 209–22; see also Ewald Friedrich von Hertzberg, *Abhandlungen über das dritte Jahr der Regierung Königs Friedrich Wilhelm II. und zu beweisen, dass die Preussische Regierung nicht despotisch ist, welche den 1. 10. 1789 in einer öffentlichen Versammlung der Akademie der Wissenschaften zu Berlin vorgelesen wurde* (n.p., 1789).

cials pointed, in particular, to the separation of jurisprudence from general administrative functions as proof that their state was free.[14]

When the civil servants of absolute monarchs addressed the problem of political freedom in this way, the determined corporative disciples of Montesquieu objected.[15] They were unable to acknowledge judicial and administrative organs as *pouvoirs intermédiairs* (intermediate powers) ultimately responsible to the prince. Instead, they perceived a need for territorial estates composed, for example, of nobility and municipalities, which – unlike the Prussian system – would have real "legislative rights."[16]

To be sure, there were not many defenders of the old estate systems in the political public of Germany at the end of the eighteenth century. In general, the practical effectiveness of these bodies was ill-suited to eliciting political interest. The middle class viewed the old estates largely as part of the embattled system of privilege, not as a jumping-off point for their own participation. However, a number of prominent authors – including some from the middle class – either defended the existing estates as the locus of political freedom against absolutism, or, increasingly, contemplated less thorough reforms as a means of turning the estates into the watchdog of freedom for the "third estate" as well.[17] Some of the most important spokesmen for this philosophy were connected to the estates by either personal or official relationships. One advocate for this philosophy, the Hannover bureaucrat Ernst Brandes, referred explicitly to England and declared it to be the "freest state," not based on Montesquieu's theories but on a knowledge of the English constitutional reality. The existing constitution and the responsibilities it assigned seemed to him to be entirely satisfactory. He also saw a bit of constitutional, that is political, freedom in the power which remained in the German territorial estates.[18] For, although he admitted that most of the German territorial estates had a "theoretically poor

14 See Ernst Ferdinand Klein, ed., *Annalen der Preussischen Gesetzgebung*, 14 vols. (Berlin, 1789), 4:331–62.

15 On the impact of Montesquieu on German enlightened political theories, see Rudolf Vierhaus, "Montesquieu in Deutschland: Zur Geschichte seiner Wirkung als politischer Schriftsteller im 18. Jahrhundert," in Ernst-Wolfgang Böckenförde et al., *Collegium Philosophicum: Studien, Joachim Ritter zum 60. Geburtstag* (Basel, 1965), 403–37.

16 See Johann Georg Schlosser, *Fünfter Brief über den Entwurf des Preussischen Gesetzbuches, insbesondere über dessen Apologie in den Annalen der Preussischen Gesetzgebung* (Frankfurt am Main, 1790), 123, 126–8; and Johan van der Zande, *Bürger und Beamter: Johann Georg Schlosser 1739–1799* (Stuttgart, 1986).

17 See Klaus Epstein, *The Genesis of German Conservatism* (Princeton, N.J., 1966), 260–86; Vierhaus, "Politisches Bewusstsein," passim; and Geraint Parry, "Enlightened Government and Its Critics in 18th-Century Germany," *Historical Journal* 6 (1963): 178–92.

18 Ernst Brandes, *Politische Betrachtungen über die Französische Revolution* (Jena, 1790), 87.

constitution," he did not see that as sufficient reason "to wish for a change in the way they were constituted."[19]

From the plethora of political statements made by August Ludwig Schlözer, Germany's leading publicist of the late eighteenth century, it is difficult to get a clear picture of his concept of political freedom. He directed his pen against "abuses" wherever he found them, one moment against royal "despotism," the next against "ochlocratic" or "oligarchic" republics.[20] In his "Staatsrecht," however, in 1793 he gave the fundamental definition of political freedom as "participation of the citizen in rulership"[21] and recommended "a mixed form of government" based on the English model: a hereditary monarchy with one hereditary and one elected chamber, as well as free expression of public opinion.[22] He recognized the freedom of a nation as the "restriction of its . . . sovereign by estates,"[23] but this was not unconditional for him. If estates wish to be worshipped as the "guardian angels of freedom," he said, then they must above all guarantee "publicity" as a mechanism for public control over the effectiveness of the estates. This was not the rule in Germany.[24]

Thus, this constitutional concept of freedom also resonated in journalistic circles. Although there was little middle ground between the estates, absolutism, and democracy for the fundamentally reform-oriented adherents of the Enlightenment, they were all the more hopeful that they could, by force of reason, convince the princes and privileged classes that only far-reaching reforms from above, and not reactionary repressive measures, could effectively counter the threat of revolution. The journal *Genius der Zeit* eloquently expressed this philosophy. Much as one would like to believe the apologist for the old powers, the journal wrote, "that freedom is entirely independent of the republican form of government . . . what good is possibility in the face of reality? What good is . . . schoolbook proof without example and action?" And the reality of the monarchies taught only too well that, even when a monarch pursued enlightened policies, everything was still vested in his person. The most striking example for the German Enlightenment was Prussia, where the vaunted "press freedom and religious tolerance" of Friedrich II were succeeded by the counterreaction of Friedrich Wilhelm II. Thus, the policies of monarchies had themselves

19 Ernst Brandes, *Über einige bisherigen Folgen der Französischen Revolution in Rücksicht auf Deutschland* (Hannover, 1792), 134–6.
20 See Warlich, "August Ludwig von Schlözer," passim.
21 August Ludwig Schlözer, *Allgemeines Staatsrecht und Staatsverfassungslehre* (Göttingen, 1793), 37.
22 See Warlich, "August Ludwig von Schlözer," 272–420.
23 August Ludwig Schlözer, editor of *Staatsanzeigen* 14 (1790): 362.
24 Ibid., 18 (1793): 311.

brought about a situation where "freedom and republic . . . were considered synonyms." The very "continuation of the current system paved the way for revolution." The only remedy was "peaceful movement toward legal freedom and equality," a "radical restructuring of monarchic government and transition to a republican system," in particular "abolition of privileged classes, dismantling of the feudal system, establishment of the representative body from all classes chosen by free election by the people," who must be granted a "share in the sovereignty."[25]

This concept of freedom, which found its way into daily newspapers as well, pointed unambiguously beyond the bounds of absolutism and the old estate system, and envisioned a "modern" representative constitution. It did not necessarily imply, however, full equality of citizenship rights or universal suffrage. It was precisely worries regarding excessive influence of the "unenlightened" and propertyless masses that drove the landed, educated segments of the middle class into repeated compromises with absolutism, even as they pushed in principle for political rights.[26] This was also one of the central aspects of August Ludwig Schlözer's commentary on the popular revolutionary movements of his time. Anyone who equated freedom and democracy assumed that "all or most members of the democracy are enlightened and patriotic beings." However, he wrote, "to conceive of an entire population, that is, millions of people, as an aggregate of practical philosophers, runs counter to all we know of psychology and world history."[27]

In addition to authors striving more or less cautiously toward participation and political power, a radical wing emerged in Germany in the late eighteenth century as democratic citizen movements and revolutions were shaking and transforming North America and Western Europe.[28] In the literary and journalistic arenas, and to a lesser degree in political and practical areas – as in the Republic of Mainz[29] – this wing advocated full

25 August Hennigs, editor of *Der Genius der Zeit* 17 (1799): 334–5, 338, 351, 354; see also Rolf Schempershofe, "August Hennings und sein Journal *Der Genius der Zeit*: Frühliberale Publizistik zur Zeit der Französischen Revolution," *Jahrbuch des Instituts für Deutsche Geschichte* 10 (1981): 137–67.
26 See Schlumbohm, *Freiheit – Die Anfänge*, passim.
27 August Ludwig Schlözer, ed., *Briefwechsel*, 4 vols. (Göttingen, 1778), 2:202–4. See also *Staatsanzeigen* 14 (1790): 140, 153; *Staatsanzeigen* 14 (1790): 497–9; *Staatsanzeigen* 1 (1782): 488; and *Staatsanzeigen* 4 (1784): 141–3.
28 See R. R. Palmer, *The Age of Democratic Revolution: A Political History of Europe and America, 1760–1800*, 2 vols. (Princeton, N.J., 1959–64), and Horst Dippel, *Germany and the American Revolution, 1770–1800: A Socio-Historical Investigation of Late Eighteenth-Century Political Thinking* (Wiesbaden, 1978).
29 See Franz Dumont, *Die Mainzer Republik von 1792/93: Studien zur Revolutionierung in Rheinhessen und der Pfalz* (Alzey, 1982).

assumption of state power by the people. For these radicals, the battle cry of political freedom had a democratic and republican tone. It was not, however, simply a continuation of the theoretical tradition of the old republic. To this extent, conservative critics were not wrong in seeing something qualitatively new in the freedom of the French Revolution that was not present, for example, in the old Swiss freedom. Under the banner of civil revolution, the concept political freedom dealt not with preserving the old rights to self-governance of sharply defined corporative entities, but implied instead a tendency toward broadening and equalizing political rights. The goal was to eliminate the differences between full citizens and less privileged groups.

This new democratic spirit was felt as early as 1784 when Johann Michael Afsprung refused to bestow the label of freedom on Switzerland as a whole. On the contrary, he explicitly disputed the applicability of the term to the canton of Zurich, where the urban middle class kept the rural population in a state of political and economic dependency. In contrast, he highlighted democratic Appenzell as a land with "the highest political . . . freedom" where "every man in the land . . . between the ages of 16 and 65" is entitled and obligated to appear on the "territorial council" and where this territorial council holds "the highest power and actual sovereignty" regarding legislation, matters of war and peace, and annual elections of "territorial leaders."[30] If an old example served once again to illustrate new ideas, however, it was to France a few years later that all eyes were turned. Johann Heinrich Campe traveled through the land of the revolution in the summer of 1789 and expected, in the "young French freedom, that there would be not just the appearance, as in other lands, but the reality of representation in the legislative assembly for everyone, even the poorest farmer, that everyone, even the poorest farmer, would be a co-ruler and co-legislator of his country."[31] The French constitution of 1791, however, became the target of severe criticism. The "barrier between active and passive citizens" must be torn down, the critics wrote. "Only vagabonds, criminals and those found guilty of corruption should be excluded from electoral assemblies! All other citizens having reached a certain age must exercise the full scope of their rights, if freedom and equality are to be more than empty words."[32] In England, from the democratic

30 Johann Michael Afsprung, *Reise durch einige Kantone der Eidgenossenschaft* (Leipzig, 1784), 82–3, 98, 288–90.
31 Johann Heinrich Campe, *Briefe aus Paris, während der Französischen Revolution geschrieben*, ed. Helmut König (Paris, 1961), 274, 277.
32 Georg Forster, *Ansichten vom Niederrhein, von Brabant, Flandern, Holland, England und Frankreich im April, Mai und Junius 1790*, ed. Gerhard Steiner (Berlin, 1958), 119.

point of view, it was considered a severe "crime against political freedom" that its laws did not ensure complete representation for the people.[33]

The new, radical democratic concept of freedom also found a footing in the arena of political philosophy. Whereas Kant[34] remained stuck at a level of political rights limited to economic "independence," the young Friedrich Schlegel separated social status from political responsibility and thought the principles of equality and freedom through to their logical conclusion – a call for a "democratic republic." "Poverty and suspected corruptibility, femininity and suspected weakness are not legitimate reasons for complete exclusion from suffrage."[35]

III

By the 1780s at the latest, the differentiation between civil and political liberty had become commonplace. This raised the question of which form of government best allowed freedom to be realized, and whether a hierarchy existed among civil and political freedoms. The question of the best constitution was no longer a purely theoretical one, even in the German Enlightenment. It had been linked to the problem of freedom (most effectively by Montesquieu) and promoted to a central theme of criticism and countercriticism. By the mid-eighteenth century, the constitutional question had begun to be a matter of conflict between the old and new political orders.[36] The new ideal civil constitution was no longer based on "constitutive compacts" but instead on the sovereignty of the people which emanated from equality among citizens; not on the sovereignty of a ruler but instead on a sovereign power of the state organized on the principle of separation of powers; not on just protection of the conventional *iura et libertates* but also on protection of human and civil rights; no longer on the social structure of the estate society but on a society recognizing equality among citizens. This change in constitutional views, and other shifts in political concepts, were accompanied by a general politicization of the public.

---

33 August Hennings, ed., *Schleswigsches Journal* 1 (1793): 390–2.
34 See Gareth Stedman Jones, "Kant, the French Revolution, and the Definition of the Republic," in Biancamania Fontana, ed., *The Invention of the Modern Republic* (Cambridge, 1994), 154–72.
35 Friedrich Schlegel, "Versuch über den Begriff des Republikanismus veranlasst durch die Kantische Schrift 'Zum ewigen Frieden'" (1796), in Friedrich Schlegel, *Studien zur Geschichte und Politik*, ed. Erich Behler (Munich, 1966), 15, 17.
36 See Thomas Würtenberger, "An der Schwelle zum Verfassungsstaat," *Aufklärung* 3 (1988): 53–88; Thomas Würtenberger, "Verfassungsentwicklung in Frankreich und Deutschland in der zweiten Hälfte des 18. Jahrhunderts," *Aufklärung* 9 (1996): 75–100; and Thomas Würtenberger, "Staatsverfassung an der Wende vom 18. zum 19. Jahrhundert," in Reinhard Hussgnug, *Wendemarken in der deutschen Verfassungsgeschichte* (Berlin, 1993), 85–121.

In the early 1760s the contrast between free states or republics on the one hand and monarchies on the other was already attracting interest. When asking whether republics were better suited for promoting human happiness and eliminating despotism, the German enlightened thinkers criticized the German imperial cities that were considered republics.[37] They represented the republican exception to monarchic German rule or, more accurately, the corporative exception to sovereign rule. The enlightened thinkers recognized in these city republics – forms of imperial city governments ranging from pure corporative rule to pure aristocratic rule – something no less troublesome than the despotism of a single ruler: the despotism of a small group. August Ludwig Schlözer made this the central target of his criticism. He found a telling example of the "evil matter of hereditary oligarchies" in the imperial cities ruled by aristocracy. "Have they not all visibly declined? And would they not have crumbled completely had they not been rescued by Wetzlar and Vienna?" The fundamental evil, he wrote, is a form of government that allows rulership by a group of people related by blood and marriage and permits them to exempt themselves almost entirely from taxation and avoid any accountability for administrative or financial affairs.[38]

It is telling that most enlightened thinkers had little respect for the corporative entity as a means of ensuring civil and political freedom. Enlightened writers saw as highly corrupt the small oligarchically ruled city republics, where freedom was a continuous topic of discussion but, in actuality, a small clique maintained its dominance. They claimed that aristocratic republics based on the principle of corporative freedom belonged to an older, outdated stage of the development of the state.

Hamburg was repeatedly singled out as the exception among the imperial cities.[39] "I declare," stated Johann Wilhelm Archenholz paradigmatically in 1787 "that . . . with the exception of the British Isles, there is no republic in our part of the world . . . in short, no space on earth that can be found where the people enjoy such freedom as in Hamburg."[40] In his so-called politico-philosophical commentary on the city, he painted a picture of Hamburg as a sort of miniature England. According to Archenholz, since

37 See Rudolf Vierhaus, *Das politische Bewusstsein*.
38 August Ludwig Schlözer, ed., *Staatsanzeigen* 4 (1784): 3–4.
39 See Joist Grolle, "Eine Republik wird besichtigt: Das Hamburg-Bild des Aufklärers Jonas Ludwig von Hess," *Zeitschrift des Vereins für Hamburgische Geschichte* 79 (1993): 1–36.
40 Johann Wilhelm Archenholz, "Etwas über bürgerliche Freyheit und Freystaaten," *Neue Litteratur- und Völkerkunde* 1 (1787): 266–7; see also Ute Rieger, *Johann Wilhelm von Archenholz als "Zeitbürger": Eine historisch-analytische Untersuchung zur Aufklärung in Deutschland* (Berlin, 1994).

the authority of the Hamburg magistrate was "balanced" by the citizens, "who formed a sort of parliament," the people of Hamburg were assured, even without an actual English writ of habeas corpus, "that they will not lose their freedom except by due process of law."[41] The Hamburg constitution, a mixture of aristocracy and democracy crafted with political wisdom, showed strong affinities to the English constitution, Archenholz continued. In both places, he argued, legislative power rested with the people, whereas the Hamburg Senate – similar to the English king – held the executive authority. Moreover, the government could not control any kind of armed citizenry.[42] Archenholz defined a special "characteristic of political freedom" as the privilege of Hamburg citizens to make decisions about the use of government funds, which he equated with the administration of state revenues in England by the House of Commons, the representatives of the people. His commentary concluded by emphasizing Hamburg's role as a trade center, which in combination with the "freedom described above" justified giving Hamburg "a place among the free states of Europe."[43] Adolph von Knigge in 1791 also recommended Hamburg's constitution as a model for republican freedom that should gradually be introduced in all German states.[44]

Constitutional discussions during the Enlightenment made it increasingly clear that it was not the structure of the constitution but its content, not the legal definition of a form of government but its character, the spirit of its actions, which determined the degree not of theoretical freedom, but of legal security. Therefore, the focus of debate in Germany shifted from the comparison between free state and monarchy, with which the discussion had begun at the end of the Seven Years' War, to the demand for a constitutional state that could be realized under any form of government. Thus, the "spirit of the government" and not the form of the constitution was the essential factor. It was the constitutional state unfettered by any particular form of government that took central stage in this discussion.[45] This was what enlightened thinkers meant when they spoke of moderate, legal, limited rulership, regardless of the institution through which the moderation and limitation were achieved. In this way, any state could be a free state, whether monarchy or republic, as long as "its members are ruled as

41 Ibid., 268.   42 Ibid., 268–9.
43 Ibid., 273.
44 Adolph von Knigge, *Joseph von Wurmbrang, Kaiserlich abyssinischen Ex-Ministers, jetzigen Notarii caesari in der Reichstadt Bopfingen, politisches Glaubensbekenntnis, mit Hinsicht auf die französische Revolution und deren Folgen*, ed. Gerhard Steiner (1792; reprint, Frankfurt am Main, 1968), 54–5.
45 See Vierhaus, *Das politische Bewusstsein*; Schlumbohm, *Freiheit – Die Anfänge*; Klippel, *Politische Freiheit*; and Würtenberger, "An der Schwelle zum Verfassungsstaat."

free people – as citizens – and not as slaves."[46] In the context of this discussion, "republic" was not a discrete form of government but a form of
rulership. Consequently, the terms *republicanism* and *despotism* lost center
stage in the discussion and were used only as qualifiers to one of the various
forms of rulership.[47]

At the same time, the German Enlightenment was developing a theoretical foundation for a constitutional monarchy. Precursors of constitutional theory were cautiously uttered with increasing frequency in the last
decades of the eighteenth century.[48] In addition to Johann Heinrich
Gottlob von Justi[49] and others, Johann Jakob Reinhard as early as the 1760s
described a constitution in his commentaries as a model "composed of
monarchy and democracy, where the king and the people share the legislative power, but the former alone holds the executive power. The people
are represented by their delegates."[50] Johann Jakob Reinhard viewed the
English constitution as a model, and had particular praise for the balance
of powers. In 1785, a determined call for constitutional reform was issued
in the *Berlinische Monatsschrift*: "If a prince wishes to give his laws a lengthy,
though not eternal, life span, then he must give the state a constitution.
. . . He must ensure that, from that time on, no law is passed without the
assent of the state as a whole; in a word, he must transform the state into
a republic of which the head of the ruling family is merely the president."[51]
Such statements must not be interpreted in an overly democratic light.
Based on the compact – related concept of the state – they point the way
through a constitutional monarchy to a constitutional state. In practice,
however, the defenders of such views held fast to a monarchy in which
power was limited by law and freedom ensured through legislation. Enlightened thinkers, whose political awareness was illumined by ideas from
natural law, believed that agreement between the governing powers and the
governed regarding political convictions was the safest foundation for the
development of a constitutional state in which a monarchy was transformed
into a republic, and subjects into citizens.

46 See Vierhaus, *Politisches Bewusstsein*.   47 *Staatsanzeigen* 2 (1778): 175.
48 See Würtenberger, "An der Schwelle zum Verfassungsstaat," 58–70.
49 See Horst Dreitzel, "Justis Beitrag zur Politisierung der deutschen Aufklärung," in Bödeker and
   Hermann, eds., *Aufklärung als Politisierung*, 158–77; see also Uwe Wilhelm, "Das Staats- und
   Gesellschaftsverständnis von J. H. G. von Justi: Ein Beitrag zur Entwicklung des Frühliberalismus in
   Deutschland," *Der Staat* 30 (1991): 415–41.
50 Johann Jakob Reinhard, *Vermischte Schriften*, 2 vols. (Frankfurt am Main, 1760–9), 1:963; see Klaus
   Gerteis, *Bürgerliche Absolutismuskritik im Südwesten des Alten Reiches vor der Französischen Revolution*
   (Trier, 1983).
51 Anon., "Über die neue Unsterblichkeit der Fürsten," *Berlinische Monatsschrift* 5 (1785): 247.

The strict distinction between forms of state and forms of government, propagated by Kant[52] among others, was by no means accepted by all German thinkers of the Enlightenment. Considering the ancient republics and Rousseau's teachings of the nontransferability of the people's sovereignty, the illegitimacy of existing ruler-subject relationships, and the necessity of anchoring the natural equality of humans in constitutional law, some enlightened thinkers considered the republic a concept for opposing arbitrary and illegitimate rulership by individuals. Republic was understood as any form involving multiple rulers as opposed to a single ruler. Most enlightened thinkers were largely unanimous in their rejection of a pure democracy because they mistrusted the "rabble."

England, which extensively limited the rights of the monarch and laid the foundation for parliamentarianism in its Bill of Rights (1698), could be held up as an example of the republican form of state. In a manner typical for the Anglophilic German Enlightenment, England was characterized as a free state or republic in spite of its monarchy.[53] The German Enlightenment interpreted a "constitutional monarchy" as a "monarchic republic" of the British type.[54] From this perspective, the English constitution was a fitting and timely model of a republic for a large state. However, in the process of politicization, particularly in the light of the American battle for independence, the renowned "British freedom" was revealed as spurious. The radical democratic philosophy excluded England from the circle of republican states and governments.

The American War of Independence was a decisive factor in the longterm trend to defining republic in the sense of free states. It caused England to be viewed by republicans as one of the despotic colonial powers, and the new representative republic became a new model.[55] One notable example of a positive judgment regarding such a republican system of political freedom and equality prior to the French Revolution was a 1786 essay titled "Über Frieden und das freie Amerika."[56] The anonymous author took everything that middle-class writers considered enlightened and progressive severely to task. Swiss freedom was for him a "free state without civil rights," ruled by "aristocratic coalitions" and "overblown Landvogts." He

52 See Stedman Jones, "Kant, the French Revolution."
53 See Sisko Haikala, *"Britische Freiheit" und das Englandbild in der öffentlichen deutschen Diskussion im ausgehenden 18. Jahrhundert* (Jyväskyla, 1985).
54 See even Le Comte de Hertzberg, *Huit Dissertations tenue pour l'anniversaire du Roi Frédéric II* (Berlin, 1787), 144–6.
55 See Dippel, *Germany and the American Revolution*; see also Haikala, *Britische Freiheit*.
56 *Über Frieden und das freie Amerika, ein Wissenschaftliches Magazin für die Aufklärung* 2 (1786): 276–306.

sharply criticized the English constitution, which many writers considered the ideal of a moderate monarchy. "The English nation," he wrote, "has civil freedom, in other words, the property, honor and person of a British citizen are protected by a law against any kind of arbitrary power. But his political freedom is restricted on all sides by the power of the king, the privileges of the House of Lords, the system of a dominant religion and the unequally distributed rights of representation." The very sort of personal, civil, and private freedom praised by most writers was described by the anonymous author as insufficient unless accompanied by full political freedom. A limited monarchy, he declared, forged the chains of freedom. He saw equality as a necessary supplement to freedom. The characteristic feature of American freedom, he said, was absolute political equality for all citizens regarding all civil rights, "as a result of which there is no ruling class in the country." Every one enjoyed "the innate sovereign rights of all humans, and the right to participate in legislative and administrative functions." The author did not predict, as most enlightened writers did, that human freedom would come from internal transformation or the spread of rational principles, but would come instead from political institutions: "When a free state no longer has a permanent ruler, when no class has privileges greater than any other, when all privileges are distributed by the hand of the nation, when they apply only to individuals and only for a limited period, only then will the freedom of the people be secured against internal enemies as much as it is within human power to do so."[57]

In the course of the French Revolution, the term *republic* came to be associated with democratic and liberal ideas, as formulated in 1776 and 1789 in the declarations of human rights and in the constitution of the French Republic of June 24, 1793.

Even formerly enthusiastic proponents of the revolution soon turned away in disgust at the atrocities in France. This was due not merely to abhorrence of revolutionary terror, but must also be seen in the context of the different interpretation of *republic* by the German Enlightenment. The majority of German republicans still associated the term *republic* with quite aristocratic or monarchic views, which were irreconcilable with the democratic practice emerging in France. In Germany the republican pathos of the 1780s cooled decisively in proportion to the growth of the democratic element during the French Revolution.[58]

The front lines between the monarchists and the republicans, which had relaxed during the discussions of the 1780s, now solidified. A pronounced

57 Ibid., 276.   58 See Rudolf Vierhaus, *Politisches Bewusstsein*.

polarization came about between the two camps and was reinforced by the fact that, under the protection of French occupation forces, the Upper Rhineland was transformed in October 1792 into the first modern republic on German soil. Faced with emerging modern republics, the opinions of German republicans were divided once and for all. From this point on, the *republic* was unthinkable without the revolutionary democratic ideas of freedom, equality, and brotherhood. Consequently, supporters of the French constitution of 1793 represented a minority in the political world of the late German Enlightenment. Constitutional ideas of a "democratic republic" were espoused only by Johann Adam Bergk, Wilhelm Joseph Behr, the young Friedrich Schlegel, Georg Wedekind, and Georg Forster.[59]

IV

"Political virtue" (Thomas Abbt) was a central element of this multifaceted republican discourse on constitutional theory in the German Enlightenment. The intellectually independent, honor- and dignity-conscious, legally free citizens of moral integrity had the obligation to promote the common good and the right to collaborate on common matters, for the true citizen was at once an active, well-meaning, enlightened patriot. This concept described an attitude in which moral and political motives were interwoven indistinguishably.[60] For Thomas Abbt, the citizen and patriot were identical. "To help his fellow citizen toward the civil freedom is man's natural state." It is a meritorious deed, valuable in itself and serving the common good.[61] By such deeds, he continued, a man revealed himself as a citizen with the noblest of all attitudes, that of "goodwill." There was only one political virtue that eliminated all class differences: Everyone was a "citizen."[62] Being a patriot, thinking and acting patriotically, was synonymous in those decades with the title of an enlightened thinker. The enlightened man, the true citizen and the true patriot, acted according to reason

59 See Jörn Garber, "Literatur und demokratischer Republikanismus: Kants Metaphysik der Sitten und ihre radikaldemokratische Kritik durch J. A. Bergk," in Otto Büsch and Walter Grab, eds., *Die demokratische Bewegung in Europa im ausgehenden 18. und frühen 19. Jahrhundert: Ein Tagungsbericht* (Berlin, 1980), 251–89.
60 See Rudolf Vierhaus, "'Patriotismus' – Begriff und Realität einer moralisch-politischen Haltung," in Rudolf Vierhaus, ed., *Deutsche patriotische und gemeinnützige Gesellschaften*, Wolfenbütteler Forschungen, vol. 8 (Munich, 1980), 9–30; see also Günter Birtsch, ed., *Patriotismus* (Hamburg, 1991).
61 Thomas Abbt, *Vom Verdienste*, 2d ed. (Berlin, 1766), 214; see also Hans Erich Bödeker, "Thomas Abbt: Patriot, Bürger und bürgerliches Bewusstsein," in Rudolf Vierhaus, ed., *Bürger und Bürgerlichkeit im Zeitalter der Aufklärung* (Heidelberg, 1981), 221–54.
62 Thomas Abbt, *Vom Tod fürs Vaterland* (Berlin, 1766), 15.

and public spirit, convinced that the individual interest, properly understood, was identical to the common interest. This patriotism meant the conscious appropriation of, and service to, the political community, often
reminiscent of practice in the ancient republics, as well as a constant willingness to actively participate in the state. Patriotism was a significant document of political self-determination in the German Enlightenment.

Patriotism expressed the transition in the citizen's self-image from
"subject" to "citizen of the state." Citizens were no longer satisfied to play
a passive part in the development of the state. Instead, they wanted to participate on their own initiative in public responsibilities, reform, and social
and governmental progress. Patriotism had helped, without doubt, to bring
harmony to the relationship between subjects and rulers in the monarchy,
and promoted the emotional willingness of the citizens to accommodate
themselves to the royal families. The concept of patriotism was associated
primarily, however, with the demand for civil and political freedom. Thomas
Abbt tied it to the condition that the state to which it applied should have
"beneficial laws" that took no more freedom away from the individual than
was necessary for the best interests of the state as a whole. A citizen could
love such a state, Abbt declared, seized by a sense of honor and willing to
make sacrifices for the state.[63] The Badian bureaucrat Johann Georg
Schlosser demanded, for example: "The state must be free, each citizen must
be himself a part of the state, patriotism is to be possible."[64] The idea of a
connection between the individual and the state made patriotism seem possible only were the citizen able to perceive himself as an active participant
in the state: "Indisputably, the patriot as a human being must thoroughly
fulfill his obligation to care for himself. At the same time, however, as a
social component of the state as a whole, he must view the interest of his
homeland as his own."[65]

Beginning in the mid-eighteenth century, constitutional consciousness
and patriotism were linked.[66] This led some writers to predict consequences
related to constitutional reform: "Freedom is excellent food for such a
happy outgrowth of patriotism. This daughter of sweet reason and love for
mankind will have been given her due if we attribute primarily to her both

63 Ibid., 11.
64 Johann Georg Schlosser, "Politische Fragmente," in Johann Georg Schlosser, *Kleine Schriften*, 6 vols.
     (Basel, 1780), 2:237.
65 August Gottlieb Preuschen, "Der Patriotismus," *Oberrheinische Mannnigfaltigkeiten: Eine gemeinnützige
     Wochenschrift* 1 (1781): 290.
66 See Würtenberger, "An der Schwelle zum Verfassungsstaat," 81–4, for discussion of the term
     Verfassungspatriotismus.

the origin and preservation of true patriotism."[67] "For this reason, in all ages, the greatest and bravest patriots have been found in republics and republican constitutions," including the Greeks, Romans, Genoese, Dutch, and Swiss.[68]

Freedom, republicanism, or a constitutional monarchy allowing a certain measure of equality were at this time viewed as prerequisites for patriotism. The connection between patriotism and republicanism was made as early as the 1760s. Thomas Abbt in his short treatise "Vom Tode fürs Vaterland" (1761) merely reflected the dominant opinion when he wrote that "only a republican could be proud of his homeland, and that, in a monarchy, [patriotism] was nothing but a name, an empty fantasy." From the republican tone of the term "patriotic" to the conflating of republican with patriotic, a powerful trend can be seen. In his "Versuch über den Patriotismus" (1793), H. Christoph Albrecht of Hamburg postulated that "patriotism can become a passion only in a republic."

The enlightened thinker called on poets to become political by becoming active members in the republic and to awaken in citizens an enthusiasm for freedom. Kotzebue accurately assessed the situation at the time when he wrote of French poetry: "The poetic art is valued only to the extent that it fires the enthusiasm of the people."[69] The Jacobin H. N. Deyer of Mainz wanted to use the theater to bring "republican virtues" and the "common good" to the people. He condemned the aesthetic practices of the ancièn regime for dulling the minds of people, saying they "had been turned into sweet poppy juice for too long by canning despotism . . . rocking our souls into idle slumber, when otherwise they would certainly not have been unreceptive to great ideas." The task now at hand was "to stand upon the stage and fan that spark of freedom and republicanism from a glowing ember in few souls into a bright flame in everyone."[70]

Thus there gradually developed the beginnings of a constitutional consciousness and a constitutional patriotism with the idea of the modern constitutional state as a reference point.[71] "A nation's conviction," according to John Adam Bergk, determined the "life span of a constitution."[72] A constitutional consciousness or consensus was thus the standard of measure of

67 Preuschen, "Der Patriotismus," 306.   68 Ibid., 305–7.

69 August von Kotzebue, *Unpartheyische Untersuchung über die Folgen der französischen Revolution auf das übrige Europa* (Thorn, 1794), 101.

70 H. N. Deyer, "Aufruf an meine Mitbürgerinnen, gesprochen in der Gesellschaft der Volksfreunde am 19. Jänner im zweiten Jahr der Frankenrepublik," in Claus Träger, ed., *Mainz zwischen Rot und Schwarz: Die Mainzer Revolution 1792–1793 in Schriften, Reden und Briefen* (Berlin, 1963), 365.

71 See Würtenberger, "An der Schwelle zum Verfassungsstaat," 81–4.

72 Johann Adam Bergk, *Untersuchungen aus dem Natur-, Staats- und Völkerrechte* (Leipzig, 1796), 51.

a constitutional judicial system. Constitutional patriotism saw in a constitution the foundation of a democratic political order and the hope of political freedom: "Patriots are free people who obey laws they have chosen for
themselves – free citizens who participate in the legislative and administrative processes of the common body. Patriots enjoy the full forms of
human rights, for their laws are based on these rights – the rights of
freedom, equality, and security of property."[73] The patriot enjoyed civil
freedom, equality, and security of property, and in return was willing to
defend his homeland. For Johann Adam Bergk, patriotism was "an internal
love and unalterable attachment to the external law, which is organized by
means of a constitution. We respectfully obey a constitution which protects
our human rights and considers our freedom to be its responsibility."[74] In
general, the enlightened thinkers found a political and intellectual home
only in a constitutional order based on natural and rational law.

This constitutional patriotism that developed at the end of the eighteenth century provided the theory and consciousness that formed the
foundation of liberalism at the beginning of the nineteenth century. The
conviction that power can be limited by law, and freedom ensured through
intellect, was the most significant legacy of the philosophy of legal protection and development of the state which took place under the banner of
the Enlightenment. It remained the "last belief" of nineteenth-century
liberalism.[75]

---

73 *Über Deutschlands verlorene Freyheit, seine politische Verfassung, den Despotismus der Fürsten* (n.p., 1798),
   42.
74 Bergk, *Untersuchungen aus dem Natur-, Staats- und Völkerrechte*, 212.
75 Theodor Schieder, "Die Krise des bürgerlichen Liberalismus," in Theodor Schieder, *Staat und
   Gesellschaft im Wandel unserer Zeit* (Cologne, 1958), 59. The problem of the continuity or disconti-
   nuity between the German Enlightenment and Liberalism has been addressed repeatedly. Fritz Val-
   javee, *Die Entstehung der politischen Strömungen in Deutschland 1770–1815* (Munich, 1951), remains
   valuable notwithstanding theoretical confines. The issue is extended in an essay by Rudolf
   Vierhaus, "Aufklärung und Reformzeit: Kontinuitäten und Nauansätze in der deutschen Politik des
   späten 18. und beginnenden 19. Jahrhundert," in Eberhard Weis, ed., *Reformen rheinbündischen
   Deutschland* (Munich, 1984), 287–308, and an article by Dieter Langewiesche, "Spätaufklärung und
   Frühliberalismus in Deutschland," in Eberhard Müller, ed., *". . . aus der anmuthigen Gelehrsamkeit!"
   Tübinger Studien zum 18. Jahrhundert. Dietrich Geyer zum 60. Geburtstag* (Tübingen, 1988), 67–80.
   Paul Nolte has dealt with this problem in his *Gemeindebürgertum und Liberalismus in Baden
   1800–1850: Tradition, Radikalismus, Republik* (Göttingen, 1994), as well as in a number of articles.
   Nolte insists on the influence of "classical republicanism" on the development of early nineteenth-
   century liberal theory and political culture. He has not, however, shown any proof of the existence
   of classical republicanism in the German Enlightenment. Moreover, key principles of liberal
   theory quite reasonably can also be interpreted in terms for natural law. Indeed, on the basis of the
   current research, much is to be said for natural law as the dominant political language of the early
   nineteenth century.

3

Kant's Republicanism and Its Echoes

OTTO DANN

Today *republicanism* is purely an academic concept. It is used to refer to a tradition of political thought that arose in antiquity and disappeared in the nineteenth century. For the past twenty years, particularly in the United States, this tradition of "classical republicanism" has been the focus of an academic discourse that continues to the present day.[1]

The term itself played a role at a turning point in the republican tradition, although this has hardly been noticed and rarely discussed. The earliest evidence comes from the decade of the French Revolution, when the first modern republics were being established in Europe. In Germany, it was the philosopher Immanuel Kant who first threw the concept of republicanism into the political debate. In doing so, he opened up a discourse on republics and republicanism that can be traced in a broad sweep through to the revolution of 1848.

In the thematic and chronological framework of this chapter, I focus first on the new meaning of republicanism, its origin and spread in Germany, and its meaning from the perspective of *Begriffsgeschichte* (history of concepts). I then investigate Kant's writings more closely to explain his conception of republic and republicanism. Finally, I examine the context and

This chapter was translated from the German by Sally E. Robertson of Arlington, Virginia.

1 See the overview by Paul Nolte, "Ideen und Interessen in der amerikanischen Revolution," *Geschichte und Gesellschaft* 17 (1991): 114–40. The discussion was triggered by and remains centered on J. G. A. Pocock, *The Machiavellian Moment: Florentine Political Thought and the Atlantic Republican Tradition* (Princeton, N.J., 1975). However, we must not forget the initial impetus for this discourse, which came from Hans Baron; see Wilfried Nippel, "Bürgerideal und Oligarchie: Klassischer Republikanismus aus althistorischer Sicht," in Helmut Koenigsberger, ed., *Republiken und Republikanismus im Europa der frühen Neuzeit* (Munich, 1988). It is he who deserves the credit for stimulating the discourse in Europe in 1985 (see his "Schlussbetrachtung," ibid., 185–302). This line was pursued by Paul Nolte, "Bürgerideal, Gemeinde und Republik: Klassischer Republikanismus im frühen deutschen Liberalismus," *Historische Zeitschrift* 154 (1992): 609–56. However, the *Begriffsgeschichte* (conceptual history) of republicanism has yet to be discussed.

traditions within which Kant's republicanism stood. Proceeding from these explorations into the genesis of the concept, I inquire in three stages into the further development of republican thought in Germany: in the years around 1800, in the era following the antirepublican backlash in European constitutional history initiated by Napoleon in 1804, and, finally, in the *Vormärz* republicanism that began in 1830 and reached its climax in the first months of 1848, the year of revolution.

This investigation of the history of republicanism in Germany, presented here only in skeleton form, uses the term itself as a guide, while focusing on the philosophical and constitutional literature. It should be remembered, however, that "republic" and "republicanism" have always been more than simple constitutional concepts. They stand for a political and civic culture that presents the historian with great difficulties regarding research and interpretation. Therefore, I shall return in the conclusion to the academic discourse mentioned at the outset, the most recent developments touching directly on our theme.

I

In the decade of the French Revolution, beginning in 1793, Kant joined the political discussion through his writings. It was not until 1795, however, in his treatise *Zum Ewigen Frieden* (On Eternal Peace), that the concept of the republic appears, immediately taking center stage. Kant declares that a republican constitution is the first prerequisite (definitive article) for a condition of lasting political peace. In this context, he casually introduces the new term *republicanism*, but not without immediately defining it:"Republicanism is the governmental principle of separating the executive power (of the government) from the legislative power." Kant then states that the opposite is *despotism*, already well established in Germany, which he distinguishes from republicanism as follows: "Despotism is the (governmental principle) by which the state autonomously executes laws that it has made itself, where the public will is treated by the ruler as his private will."[2] Republicanism and despotism are described here as "governmental principles" and elsewhere as "constitutional principles"; Kant sees them as forms of government.

However, Kant associates with republicanism not only the principle of separation of powers, as explained above, but also "the representative system,

---

2 Immanuel Kant, *Werke in 6 Bände*, ed.Wilhelm Weischedel, 6 vols. (Frankfurt am Main, 1964), 6:206 (B 25). Hereafter, the Kant citations include volume number, page(s) in the Weischedel edition, followed in most cases by the original pagination in parentheses.

which is the only one in which a republican mode of government is pos-sible."[3] It must also be noted that Kant characterizes republicanism as a "possibility," a possible form of government that can "finally [be reached] through gradual reforms."

Republicanism, therefore, describes a process of political reform, the goal of which is a republican constitution. This process is associated, not least of all, with the peacekeeping function of republicanism. When Kant returned to the question of a secured peace in his *Rechtslehre* (Theory of Law) of 1797, he described "the republicanism of all states together" as the global constitution "which seems most suitable to us" for guaranteeing a perma-nent peace.[4]

This is the extent of the statements that Kant made regarding "republi-canism," a term he had introduced more offhandedly than deliberately. The individual statements are difficult to integrate into a system. Kant's departure from the central concept of republic in the modern tradition – republic as a nonmonarchical constitutional form – is noteworthy and can probably only be explained in the context of his political theory.[5]

Here I focus on the remarkable coinage of the term *republicanism*. What motivated the 70-year-old Kant to add the "-ism" suffix to a central concept of old European state typology, the self-characterization of states of his time, thereby moving it into another, modern context of political opinion? It was apparently the contemporary political context itself. Revolutionary France, the largest and most modern state in Europe, had declared itself a republic in 1792, thus rekindling the discourse on the republic as a constitutional form.

Reinhart Koselleck has already pointed out this general practice of neol-ogism. In the context of *Zur Semantik moderner Bewegungsbegriffe* (On the Semantics of Modern Terms for Political Movements), he specifically refers to the dynamization and temporalization of political concepts in the age of the French Revolution:

"Time" has worked its way into all parts of the language and colored the entire political and social vocabulary since the French Revolution. Since then, there has hardly been a central concept of political theory that did not contain a temporal coefficient of change. . . . Notable in this regard is the long series of "-ism" con-structions which extrapolate historic movements into the future, in league with which they justify their actions.[6]

3 Kant, *Werke*, 6:208 (B 29).   4 Kant, *Werke*, 4:478 (B 264).
5 Immanuel Kant, *Metaphysische Anfangsgründe der Rechtslehre* (Königsberg, 1797), chap. 3.
6 Reinhart Koselleck, "Neuzeit: Zur Semantik moderner Bewegungsbegriffe," in Reinhart Koselleck, *Vergangene Zukunft: Zur Semantik geschichtlicher Zeiten* (Frankfurt am Main, 1989), 339.

Koselleck mentions the "concept of republicanism as a political movement" as his first example and defines such semantic neologisms as "concepts of political movements – enriched by the philosophy of history – that call for action in everyday political life.""The accompanying opposite concepts," he added,"fundamentally relinquish to the past the associated behaviors or constitutional elements and their representatives on the intended time axis."[7] In the case of Kant's republicanism, of which Koselleck was also aware, we think of the opposite concept of despotism, and we understand, thanks to Koselleck's illuminating interpretation, the contemporary context in which Kant's neologism is to be classified and explained.

Did Kant have predecessors in the use of the term republicanism, perhaps some with whom he was himself familiar? This question must remain largely unanswered. The -ism concept had yet to arise in the context of the great French debate over the republic as a form of state that had been going on since Varennes in 1791–2. We can refer only to Thomas Paine's *The Rights of Man*, the second part of which, appearing in February 1792, contains a discussion of the forms of a republic and mentions the term republicanism in passing, in exaggerated form in the context of an argument with Edmund Burke, who apparently used the term pejoratively.[8]

No usage of the term republicanism is known in Germany prior to Kant. All the more surprising, then, is the spontaneous response to Kant's "republicanism." The best known, even today, is the response of a young Romantic from Jena. Friedrich Schlegel entitled his discussion of Kant's peace treatise *Versuch über den Begriff des Republikanismus* (Essay on the Concept of Republicanism). He places the focus on Kant's casual mention of the term and systematically expands it to a "deduction of republicanism."[9]

---

7 Ibid., 340–1. In addition, see Otto Brunner, Werner Conze, and Reinhart Koselleck, eds., *Geschichtliche Grundbegriffe: Historisches Lexikon zur politisch-sozialen Sprache in Deutschland*, 9 vols. (Stuttgart, 1972–97), 1:850ff. The concept of "despotism" was already in use prior to the French Revolution, however. See Horst Dreitzel, *Monarchiebegriffe in der Fürstengesellschaft: Semantik und Theorie der Einherrschaft in Deutschland von der Reformation bis zum Vormärz*, 2 vols. (Cologne, 1991), 1: chap. 3.
      Going beyond Koselleck's thesis and perhaps refining it, we must therefore ask when and where those "ism" constructions first appeared in the political language of Europe. In this context, we should remember the central concept of patriotism, widespread since the beginning of the eighteenth century and evidently coined in England; see Viscount Henry St. John Bollingbroke, *Letters, on the Spirit of Patriotism, on the Idea of a Patriot King, and on the State of Parties, at the Accession of King George the First* (London, 1736).
8 Thomas Paine, *The Rights of Man* (1791–2; London, 1963), 174ff., esp. 178. A German translation had been on the market since 1793. Was Kant familiar with it?
9 Friedrich Schlegel, *Versuch über den Begriff des Republikanismus, veranlasst durch die Kantische Schrift "Zum Ewigen Frieden"*, first published in the Berlin journal *Deutschland* 3 (1976). See Anita and Walter Dietze, eds., *Ewiger Friede? Dokumente einer deutschen Diskussion um 1800* (Leipzig, 1989), 161–76, esp. 164ff.

In addition to this prominent response, Fichte's critique,[10] and particularly the usage in the literature of the German Jacobins,[11] shows that the term *republicanism* remained in use in Germany at the time, became more widespread in the last years of the century, then probably receded, and may have reappeared in phases of political tension, for example, in the *Vormärz* period.[12] There does not yet exist a satisfactory analysis of the conceptual history of the term in German or any other language.[13] It is therefore necessary to go beyond the use of the term *republicanism* to examine the entire range of concepts of the republic, first in Kant's own writings and then in the contemporary context.

II

Republics did not have a good reputation in eighteenth-century Europe. They were marginal entities within a political world characterized by *Stände* (estates) and monarchies. Even an enlightened scholar like Kant believed an enlightened monarchy capable of more cultural freedom than a "free state."[14] It was not until late in Kant's writings that the concept of "republic" and its derivative terms appeared. As late as 1793, he used the term *patriotic* as the opposite of despotism in describing the basic principles of a good civil constitution.[15] In 1795, however, when repeating these principles in the first definitive article of *Zum Ewigen Frieden*, Kant subsumed them under the term *republican*. He writes there that the republican

---

10 Dietze and Dietze, *Ewiger Friede?*, 217, first published in Friedrich I. Niethammer, ed., *Philosophisches Journal einer Gesellschaft teutscher Gelehrten* 4 (Jena, 1796).

11 Numerous references in Axel Kuhn, *Linksrheinische deutsche Jakobiner: Aufrufe, Reden, Protokolle; Briefe und Schriften 1794–1801* (Stuttgart, 1978), 247, 260. This volume also documents the inflationary usage of "ism" constructions in political writings of the late eighteenth century; see 238–9 and 262–3.

12 See the article on "Radikalismus und Republikanismus" in *Brockhaus-Konversationslexikon*, 8th ed. (Jena, 1840), vol. 4. Citation in Wolfgang Mager's article on the concept of "Republik," in Brunner, Conze, and Koselleck, eds., *Geschichtliche Grundbegriffe*, 5:628. Reference could be made throughout this chapter to Mager's comprehensive conceptual analysis of history; I thank him for many findings and clarifications.

13 Even Mager does not address the semantic dimension of the term *republicanism* in any detail, describing its origin only briefly; see Mager, "Republik," 602–3. Koselleck published his analysis of Kant's concept in the context of the conceptual history of "democracy" in Brunner, Conze, and Koselleck, eds., *Geschichtliche Grundbegriffe*, 1:850ff. Even Wolfgang Kersting, who has gone the furthest to date toward an interpretation of Kant's republicanism, achieves only a metaphorical circumlocution: "Republicanism means republic in a foreign form, in other words, incorporating the spirit of the original contract into that which is fundamentally in conflict with it, into rulership which had a natural and violent origin" ("Die bürgerliche Verfassung in jedem Staat soll republikanisch sein," in Otfried Höffe, ed., *Immanuel Kant: Zum Ewigen Frieden* [Berlin, 1995], 104).

14 See "Was ist Aufklärung?" (What is Enlightenment?), 1784, in Kant, *Werke*, 6:61 (A 493).

15 See "Über den Gemeinspruch," in Kant, *Werke*, 6:146 (A 236).

constitution is "the only one which is derived from the idea of the original contract on which all the rightful legislation of a people must be
based."[16] This is a surprise: The republican constitution is differentiated from
other forms and declared to be the ideal, normative constitution.

The republican constitution according to Kant is characterized by three
basic principles, which are named and explained in the first definitive article
of *Zum Ewigen Frieden*: human freedom, civil equality, and democratic legislation.[17] Under such a constitution, the individual is no longer a subject
but a citizen.[18] Kant refers expressly to two institutional prerequisites for
implementing such a constitution. For him, the principle of separation of
powers is fundamental, that is, that the legislative power represents a separate institution from the government. Since the governmental power of
states in the eighteenth century rested almost entirely in the hands of the
princes and the aristocracy, Kant called for an institution through which
the civil society – Kant speaks of the *Volk* – could gain political influence.
"The legislative power must fall exclusively to the united will of the
people," he states tersely in the *Rechtslehre* of 1797.[19] To attain such a
legislative body, a new procedure for representation would be necessary.
Therefore, Kant insists on a "representative system, in which alone a republican form of government is possible, without which it is despotic and
violent (regardless of what constitution it has)."[20] Differentiating this from
the old European republic, Kant adds the comment: "None of the old, so-
called republics knew this."

It is again evident that Kant saw the republican constitution not as one
possibility among many but as the best possible constitution, assuring
freedom and equality in a system of natural rights, the only alternative being
a despotic constitution, just as despotism was the alternative to republicanism. These statements also show the tradition of political thought to
which Kant's concept of republic belongs: Montesquieu's principle of separation of powers, more particularly Rousseau's theory of a social contract
and the general will, and with respect to the new, anti-estate theory of
representation probably also Thomas Paine, whose *Rights of Man* had been
available in German translation since 1793.[21]

Kant's republicanism, his statements regarding the republican constitution, must have been interpreted in 1795 as an argument in favor of the
young, modern republics that existed on both sides of the Atlantic at that
time and whose numbers were increasing with each passing year due to

16 Kant, *Werke*, 6:204.   17 Ibid., 6:204 (B 20).
18 Ibid., 6:206 (B 24).   19 Ibid., 4:432 (B 195).
20 Ibid., 6:208 (B 29).   21 See note 8 to this chapter.

the armed victories of France to the west. Kant did not protest this interpretation, but he had other intentions for his republicanism. Whereas the
modern republics saw themselves as an alternative to monarchy, Kant
sought a way to combine enlightened monarchy with a republican, representative constitution. He therefore did not place his concept of republic
in the context of the tradition of modern state typology, which Machiavelli
first summarized at the beginning of his *Il Principe*: "All states, all powers
that rule over humans are either republics or principalities."

Only once did Kant draw a distinction between his and the "old
republics" and added a "so-called"[22] to indicate that he had a very different concept of republic, the concept of a "true republic," as formulated
most clearly in the *Rechtslehre* of 1797: "Every true republic is and can only
be constituted by a representative system of the people. Such a representative system is instituted in the name of the people, and is constituted by all
the citizens being united together, in order, by means of their deputies, to
protect and secure their rights."[23] Kant describes this republic as the "only
rightful constitution." In his treatise *Der Streit der Fakultäten* (The Conflict
of the Faculties), which appeared in 1798, he calls it a *respublica noumenon*,
a "Platonic ideal."[24] However, it is by no means an "empty fantasy," he continued, but rather "the eternal standard for any civil constitution anywhere."
It becomes clear that Kant's concept of republic is not an empirical concept
but a normative one in a qualified sense. Since it applies to all forms of
state, it is closer to the classical, medieval *res publica* than to the republic of
modern state typology.

In order to distinguish his concept from the latter even more clearly,
Kant introduced a distinction between forms of state (*forma imperii*) and
forms of government (*forma regiminis*) and expressly described the republican constitution as a form of government.[25] It takes its shape solely in its
distinction from despotic forms of government, which are characterized by
the assertion of various kinds of private interests.[26] Any ruler, Kant points
out repeatedly, can use the republican form of government as the guide for
his actions. Thus, even "monarchs, though they rule autocratically, [can] rule
in a republican fashion, in other words treat the people according to principles consistent with the spirit of the laws of freedom (such as a people
operating by mature reason would set for themselves)."[27]

In his arguments for a republican constitution, Kant was not talking
about introducing a new form of state. The reader is here referred to his

22 See Kant, *Werke*, 6:208 (B 29).
24 Ibid., 6:364 (A 155).
26 Ibid., 6:207.
27 Ibid., 6:364 (A 156); 6:360 (A 148); and 6:207 (B 27).

23 Ibid., 4:464 (B 242).
25 Ibid., 6:206.

strict rejection of the legality of revolution.[28] However, he consistently supported political reforms, and the implementation of a republican constitution was unthinkable without a change in political and legal conditions.
The peace policy argument that he combines with the argument for republicanism also points in this direction.[29] When Kant argues for republican
constitutional reform,[30] he uses a new verb – *republicanize* – in addition to
the new term *republicanism*.[31] This is yet another political neologism. Where
such constitutional reform has taken place in the form of a revolution, it
may not be rescinded. This is how Kant justified the French Revolution in
retrospect, even in its second stage – the transition to a republic – which
was scorned by most Germans. In his *Streit der Fakultäten*, he describes the
participation of the public in that revolution as the most important "historical sign" of the time, yielding hope for realization of a true republic, of
the "idea of a constitution consistent with the natural rights of man."[32] The
objective of Kant's republic theory, which goes beyond the limits it set for
itself, was representative democracy, which he – and only a few others in
his time – considered possible even within the framework of a monarchy.

III

Kant's theory of republicanism can be compared not only to the French
Revolution but also to a more far-reaching European tradition. Kant's
concept of the "true republic" (*respublica noumenon*) takes its place unmistakably in the old European tradition of the republic as an umbrella concept
for any political community since the medieval interpretation of Aristotle
that combined the Greek *politeia* with the Roman *res publica*. Wolfgang
Mager, in particular, has pointed out the long heritage of this broad concept
of republic in the German-speaking world.[33]

Hardly noticed in this context was the concept of the *res publica literaria*
(republic of letters), which had developed out of this tradition since the
sixteenth century: the imaginary but also real and effective community of
a European intelligentsia educated in literature, by means of which even a
philosopher in distant Königsberg was integrated into a European society
republican in character. This was based on the freedom and equality of the
members and on the political facilitation of religious freedom and pub-

---

28 See writings as early as ibid., 6:154 (A 251–2), and 6:230–4 (B 73ff.).
29 Ibid., 6:205 (B 23), and 6:358 (A 145).   30 See, e.g., ibid., 4:464 (B 243).
31 See, e.g., ibid., 6:358 (A 145).   32 Ibid., 6:364; see also 6:357–8.
33 Mager, "Republik," 588. Mager's discussion of the conceptual history of the term *republic* was used
as a resource throughout this chapter.

lishing activity that Kant adopted as constitutive elements of his political theory.[34]

In addition to the general concept of the republic as a community, which was increasingly replaced with the modern concept of state, the narrower political constitutional concept already addressed by Machiavelli had established itself since the Renaissance: the republic as a nonmonarchical form of state for which the term *Freistaat* (free state) became established in the German-speaking world.[35] After the North American "free states" were established, this constitutional concept became more and more dominant in modern Europe. Kant, however, as we have already seen, distanced himself from this; he also did not use the term "republican" to describe the proponents of these systems.

Rousseau combined the tradition of the city republics of old Europe with a constitutionalism grounded in natural law to establish the modern republican democratic tradition. Kant was obviously influenced by him, although he rejected Rousseau's principle of representation that was based on the city republic.[36] The modern principle of representation as an element of a republican constitution was first brought into the European discussion in earnest by the United States. It was powerfully communicated by Thomas Paine, beginning in 1792.[37]

That year, revolutionary France was in the dramatic phase of its transition to a republic. The monarchy had been suspended since Varennes and a discussion began in the summer of 1791 regarding the character of the constitution for the French state. Robespierre argued for a broad concept of republic in an attempt to achieve a combination of monarchy and republic. Sieyès made a similar argument. In 1792 he published an article in German translation titled "Über den wahren Begriff der Monarchie" (On the True Concept of Monarchy) in a Göttingen journal. In this article he described the republic as a "representative government" that could have any number of different forms of state. The connection to Kant's later arguments is obvious.[38]

34 See Kant, *Werke*, 6:244–5 (B 98ff.).
35 Ibid., 580ff.; also Wolfgang Mager's article on "Republik" in Joachim Ritter and Karlfried Gründer, ed., *Historisches Wörterbuch der Philosophie*, 10 vols. (Basel, 1971–98), 8:858–78.
36 Rousseau, *Contract Social* 3.15; see also 2.6–7, as well as the classical presentation by Irin Fetscher, *Rousseaus politische Philosophie* (Neuwied, 1960), 90ff.
37 Paine, *Rights of Man*, 174, 177ff. See his formula of "representation ingrafted upon Democracy"; also Mager, "Republik," 627.
38 Emmanuel J. Sieyès, "Über den wahren Begriff der Monarchie," *Neues Göttinger historisches Magazin* 1 (1792): 341ff. See Mager, "Republik," 608, who claims that Kant was familiar with this article but does not prove it. For the French discussion, see Mager, "Republik," 596–7.

With the establishment of the French Republic in September 1792, revolutionary France took on a clearly republican identity. The turning point in political self-image associated with this step was manifested, for example, in the establishment of a new calendar, in new national symbols, and in the proclamation of the unity and indivisibility of the national territory. "L'essence de la République ou de la démocratie est l'égalité," declared Robespierre.[39]

The challenge associated with the republicanization of Europe's leading country cannot be overstated. It was considerably greater than that of the revolutionary transformation of 1789 and was escalated in Germany by the fact that the German governments were in a state of war with France. In this war, shortly after the birth of the republic, French troops were able to cross the borders of the German empire and conquer the central Rhine region all the way to Mainz. Societies of supporters of the revolution were soon established in the region, especially in Mainz, the members of which described themselves as "republicans," sought to convince their countrymen of the advantages of a republican constitution, and pushed for annexation by the French Republic. It is in this context that the terms "German free state" and "German republic" first appear in the source material. One republican declared, for example: "To be a republican means to be an upstanding man, honest and just. Republic and realm of justice are one and the same."[40] These are the first republican declarations in the German-speaking world in which the idea of a republic was used in regard to the modern nation. They triggered no particular response at first, but were significant in the building of the regional tradition and have become noteworthy since their historical discovery in recent decades.

There was ample occasion in the German states after 1792 to ask what the attitude toward the republic on the other side of the Rhine should be. Wieland, who was widely read, probably expressed the opinion of the majority of educated people in his journal *Teutscher Merkur* in 1794. He declared, on the one hand, his abhorrence of the "democratic insanity" of this "arrogant republic," the establishment of which was associated with the September 1792 murders in Paris and the execution of the king. He argued, on the other hand, that this republic should be given political recognition as a neighbor state and that war should no longer be waged against it.[41]

---

39 Speech on Feb. 5, 1794, cited in Mager, "Republik," 598.
40 Reprinted in Claus Träger, ed., *Die Französische Revolution im Spiegel der deutschen Literatur* (Leipzig, 1979), 587. See also evidence provided by Mager, "Republik," 599ff.
41 Christoph Martin Wieland, "Über Krieg und Frieden," reprinted in Dietze and Dietze, eds., *Ewiger Friede?*, 59–68.

Another example of this first encounter with the French republican challenge is an essay by Johann Erich Biester – *Einige Nachrichten von den Ideen der Griechen über Staatsverfassungen* (Some Information Regarding Greek Ideas of the Constitution of Governments) – in his *Berlinische Monatsschrift*, which Kant read regularly. In response to the "champions of a very general republican constitution," who liked to associate themselves with ancient Greece, he attempted to show "that the concepts of pure democracy, unity of the republic, destruction of the aristocracy, hatred of monarchs, equality of citizens – in short, all the concepts which are so firmly attached to the current crusade to improve the world – are not in the least confirmed by Greek examples."[42]

This was the climate in which Kant began to speak about politics in the 1790s. Pronounced self-consciousness and an essentially negative attitude toward the republican challenge from France were widespread in educated German society. Kant's political statements began after the republicanization of France. In an essay in the *Berlinische Monatsschrift* in 1793, Kant established the level of argument that he considered appropriate for political discussion. In 1795, he made his first direct statement regarding the French Revolution and its constitutional concept in *Zum Ewigen Frieden*. Compared to the aforementioned authors, who were leading representatives of the Enlightenment in Germany, it is impressive even today how autonomously Kant handled the controversial subject, how positively he took up the republican challenge, and how independently he addressed it.

Immanuel Kant can be regarded as the founder of modern republicanism in Germany. He demonstrated with philosophical stringency that only a republican constitution can guarantee the political achievement of modern human rights and a system of legal security and international peace, and thus provide a future for a civil society in the process of emancipating itself. Kant's republicanism is based on the principles of freedom, equality, and a constitutional state. Its most important institutional elements are separation of powers, the principle of national representation, legislation by the people, freedom of public opinion, and a legally constituted international association of all nations. Kant conceived republicanism as an evolutionary political development program and emphasized that it could be achieved even within monarchies.

---

42 *Berlinische Monatsschrift (1783–1796): Auswahl* (Leipzig, 1986), 279. Biester also points out that the ancient Greeks "were unfamiliar with a representational system" (281) and that the idea of human rights had no validity with them.

IV

The response to Kant's *Zum Ewigen Frieden* was surprisingly strong. The essay, self-published as a treatise, appeared in a new edition in 1796, followed shortly thereafter by translations in France, England, Denmark, and Poland and by literary reactions. In addition to the peace theme, it was primarily Kant's "republicanism" that aroused interest. Goethe and Schiller saw it as cause for an epigram: "Kant and his interpreters: See how a single rich man can feed so many beggars! When the kings build, the carters have work."[43]

The literary fallout of this interest shows that Kant succeeded in triggering a qualified constitutional debate and raising the political discussion of republican France to a new level. Many productive responses to Kant furthered the development of the theme of republicanism.

Friedrich Schlegel, the nimble writer from the Romantic circle of Jena, emphatically adopted the new term *republicanism*. His remarks show the possibilities but also the dangers of a "concept of a political movement." Schlegel recognized republicanism as the political development principle of his age. He perceptively uncovered the democratic tendency contained in Kant's republicanism: "Republicanism is necessarily democratic."[44] Similarly, Schlegel trumped the logical ideal of the true republic with the concept of global republicanism as the goal of historic development: "Only universal and complete republicanism would be a valid and only adequate definitive article for eternal peace." Just a few years later, Schlegel retracted his Jena "democracy"; in his philosophy lectures in Cologne in 1804, he considered "the republican constitution [to be] a necessary source of eternal civil war which [must] be given a more persistent and permanent foundation by means of a monarchical principle."[45]

The circle of those who based their argumentation directly on Kant included not only the Romantics but also the lawyer and democratic popular writer Johann Adam Bergk. His writings after 1795 focus on both Kant and republican France. He amplified Kant's republican ideas to a model for a "democratic republic." The republic for him is a form of state imbued with the democratic principle, characterized by the separation of powers, representation, election of all officials, and equal rights for all citizens, including women.[46] He distinguishes this republican–democratic

---

43 Reprinted in Dietze and Dietze, eds., *Ewiger Friede?*, 229.
44 Reprinted in ibid., 166; regarding Schlegel, see also note 9 to this chapter.
45 Friedrich von Schlegel, *Sämtliche Werke*, 15 vols. (Vienna, 1846), 13:125.
46 Johann Adam Bergk, *Untersuchungen aus dem Natur-, Staats- und Völkerrechte, mit einer Kritik der neuesten Konstitution der französischen Republik* (1796; reprinted, Kronberg im Taunus, 1975), 88ff.; regarding the following points, see 240ff.

model of state from other forms of state in a forceful and populist manner. He lists the characteristic differences between the modern republic and the old European one. The convincing nature of his argumentation rests largely on the French Republic as a concrete example.

Georg Friedrich Rebmann of the Rhineland-Palatinate was among those who became ardent republicans as citizens of the French Republic in the region to the west of the Rhine. By 1797 his personal experience with the French authorities led him to the following, somewhat resigned conclusion: "In France, the republic formed republicans instead of republicans forming a republic! A true republic must be established only after the republican form is established. . . . We must first revolutionize and republicanize the governments in order to be able to republicanize the people!"[47] These statements show how advanced, reflective, and discriminating these discussions about a republic were at the time in the Rhineland.

Others clung longer to their republican convictions, such as the southern German author who in 1799 published the *Entwurf einer republikanischen Verfassungs-Urkunde, wie sie in Deutschland taugen möchte* (Draft of a Republican Constitutional Document as Suited to Germany), modeled largely on the French constitution of 1795.[48] Not least among them is the writer Johann Gottfried Seume, who inserted a republican critique of Napoleon's policy into his *Spaziergang nach Syracus* in 1803:

I have nothing against the First Consulate. But its power was too exorbitant, and the duration was not republican. . . . Minor appointments may and must be for life in a republic, but if it is the major ones, the road leads to despotism. History teaches us this. . . . Throughout the Revolution, the French showed many republican outbursts, frequent republican enthusiasm and occasional republican rage, but rarely republican intent and spirit, and never republican reason. . . . Since Bonaparte again seriously threatens to carry freedom with him to his grave, I have the feeling of having just become a republican for the first time. I believe that a well-ordered republic provides the best possibility for human dignity, human value, general justice, and general happiness. If the boy born tonight in the furthest straw hut in the land cannot one day legitimately run the highest government body of his homeland, then it is nonsense to speak of a serious republic. Privilege of any kind is the grave of freedom and justice.[49]

I have quoted in some detail this "republican of reason," whose position outlasted the French Republic, because he is representative of the

---

47 Georg Friedrich Rebmann, *Holland und Frankreich, in Briefen geschrieben auf einer Reise . . . im Jahre 1796 und dem 5. der Französischen Republik* (Paris, 1797), reprinted in Claus Träger, ed., *Die Französische Revolution*, 828–9.
48 Reprinted in Theo Stammen and Friedrich Eberle, eds., *Deutschland und die Französische Revolution: 1789 bis 1806* (Darmstadt, 1988), 427ff.
49 Ibid., 490–1.

intellectual and political independence associated among his German contemporaries with a republican position stemming from Kant.

This demonstrates that, in the years of political transition around 1800,
when the Holy Roman Empire collapsed and the rule of the German
princes became unstable and questionable, a modern republican way of
thinking became established in German society against the backdrop of the
American and French revolutions, although the political conditions for the
establishment of a German free state would not exist for some time yet.
Using the guiding principle of the republic, the essential characteristics of
a democratic system were developed conceptually in those years, as if in
anticipation of the political constitutional reforms that did not become feasible until our century.

V

After Napoleon was crowned emperor, the nineteenth century soon
witnessed a major contraction of the young republican traditions. In 1808,
the name of the republic was deleted from French coins. Memories of the
republic became associated more and more with the stigma of the Jacobin
dictatorship. The Bonaparte family sought connections to the German
princes, who profited from the stimulus toward modernization provided
by Napoleonic rule. The princes in Germany no longer represented a
"despotic" system; the old absolutism had been crushed. This new climate
required a change in the understanding and categorization of the concept
of republic.

The constitutional law specialist Karl Salomon Zachariä, who had been
publishing academic and other writings since the beginning of the century,
reflected the shifting trends. In his 1802 treatise *Janus*, which addressed Kant
and the peace problem, he recommended "representative democracy, when
simultaneously organized as a republic," as the optimal form of state because
"the peaceful voice of the people must be the most decisive voice in a constitution in which public officials owe their power to a vote of the people
and cannot exercise this power against public opinion without risking the
loss of power."[50] Here, again, as shown above with Johann Adam Bergk,
the Kantian concept of republicanism, when thought through, led to a
concept of representative democracy. In the 1820s, it was monarchy that
Zachariä placed at the center of his system, using the term *Einherrschaft* –
the most constant form of state in Europe, except for Switzerland, which

---

50 Cited in Dietze and Dietze, eds., *Ewiger Friede?*, 454.

was transforming itself into a nation-state. He combined it, however, with the principle of representation of the people and used the term *republic* to describe it. He described as republics those constitutions in which "the people are called upon to exercise or share in the exercise of legislative power," that is, both the representative democracy and the "republican monarchy or *Einherrschaft.*"[51]

The states of the German confederation now resorted in many cases to the combination of monarchy and republican constitutional principle that Kant had proposed as a reform policy for principalities. It was a rejuvenation of the old European concept of republic as the well-constituted community of citizens, a bit of "classical republicanism" in modern garb. The entry on "republic" in the Brockhaus encyclopedia of 1820 refers to the "republic in the ancient sense of *res publica*, a community of citizens" and saw it as being realized at least in a "republican administration." "Therefore, if all monarchs and ministers were republicans, one would fear neither democratic excesses nor aristocratic abuses, and the restless demand of the people for republican freedom would automatically dissolve."[52] This wish intended more than administrative reform, however. This is evident in the *Staatsrecht der konstitutionellen Monarchie: Ein Handbuch für Geschäftsmänner, studierende Jünglinge und gebildete Bürger* (Law of Constitutional Monarchy: A Handbook for Merchants, Students, and Educated Citizens), first published in 1824 by Johann Christoph von Aretin, and very widely read in the German *Vormärz* period. The principle of sovereignty of the people is placed unmistakably at the beginning of this publication, and it is emphasized that "all governmental rights originally belong to the body of the people as a whole and that the government exists only by and for the people." He sees constitutional monarchy as "democracy applied over a larger area and a longer period" and considers it the best manifestation of this principle in his time. The constitutional monarchy, he says, can therefore "produce that civic virtue which would otherwise be considered the principle of the republic. It can therefore rightfully be called a republican monarchy."[53]

Also notable in this historic line is Karl von Rotteck, who received a professorship in Freiburg in the eighteenth century, stayed faithful his entire life to the natural law of the Enlightenment and the basic views of Kant, and became a guiding figure of southwestern German liberalism by virtue

51 Karl Salomo Zachariä, *Vierzig Bücher vom Staate*, 7 vols. (Stuttgart, 1820–32), cited in Mager, "Republik," 624.
52 Ibid., 626.   53 Ibid., 622–3.

of three widespread works and his position as a delegate to the Baden Landtag. In his *Lehrbuch des Vernunftrechts* (Textbook of the Law of Reason), under the heading "On the True Republic," he stated precisely in the spirit of Kant: "The essence of the republic is rulership by the true common will. To the extent that a constitution appears suitable for accomplishing this basic idea, it is a republican constitution and the state a true free state." Despotism and anarchy, as for Kant, were the negative opposites of republicanism.[54] Similarly, Rotteck endorsed the modern representational system in the spirit of Kant by strictly distinguishing between the old European system of "feudal estates" and territorial estates "in the spirit of the representative system." The latter were "a committee representing the entirety of the people united as the society of a state" and he described them as forms of "national representation."[55] In the entry on "democratic principle" in his *Staatslexikon* of 1837, however, Rotteck went a step further and described as republics only forms of state that were distinguished from monarchy. What he had earlier called "republican," he now described as a "democratic principle" and explained: "The democratic principle should therefore never be confused with the republican principle." Legal inequalities and slavery are also to be found in republics, he claimed, pointing to both the classical civilizations and the United States. He concluded that "the republican principle needs to be ennobled by the democratic principle."[56]

VI

Rotteck thus took into account the political transformation that had taken place since 1830 and which led, in Germany, to a breakthrough for the democratic movement. This movement laid demonstrative claim to the republic as the form of state for its program of replacing the rulership of the princes with rulership by the people. A direct link was again forged in Germany to the revolutionary republic of 1792. This was apparent as early as 1832 at the Hambacher Fest, where August Wirth proclaimed "Three cheers for the united free states of Germany! Three cheers for confeder-

54 Carl von Rotteck, *Lehrbuch des Vernunftrechts und der Staatswissenschaften*, 4 vols. (Stuttgart, 1840), 2:208. See also the entry on "state constitution" in Carl von Rotteck and Carl Welcker, eds., *Staatslexikon: Encyklopädie der sämmtlichen Staatswissenschaften für alle Stände*, 12 vols. (Altona, 1845–8), 12:3.
55 Rotteck, *Lehrbuch des Vernunftrechts*, 235–6.
56 See entry on "democratic principle," in Rotteck and Welcker, eds., *Staatslexikon*, 4:260–1.

ated republican Europe!" and Heinrich Brüggemann of Cologne expressed the hope that Germany, as a "powerful, popular free state, [would] watch over the rebirth of the rest of Europe with a sheltering and protective love."[57] The democrats resurrected the label "republicans" to define their new identity. "I am a republican from the bottom of my soul," declared Siebenpfeiffer before the court of assizes in Landau, "for I consider a representative republic to be the only form of state suitable for a large population which feels its dignity, the only form possible today."[58] In this movement, democracy was conceivable only in a republic, and a solution to social problems was also causally associated with this form of state. "Community property is the first and most necessary condition of a free democratic republic," wrote Karl Schapper in 1838.[59] It is therefore not surprising that the Brockhaus of 1840 combined "republicanism and radicalism" into one entry as synonymous concepts.[60]

Spurred on by the proclamation of the Second Republic in Paris in February 1848, a "social democratic republic" was, for members of the nascent democratic movement in the German revolution, the central program point for solving the national question. They assembled in June 1848 in Frankfurt as the "First Congress of the German Democratic Republicans."[61] On April 12 in Constance, Friedrich Hecker had opened the April revolution of Baden with the proclamation of a German republic.

The question of a republic became the central constitutional issue in the first months of the German revolution. It was directly connected to the question of continuing the revolution against the rule of the princes. The overwhelming majority of Germans recoiled from this. The German public identified republic with a wholesale overthrow of the status quo, a sentiment expressed by David Friedrich Strauss in Württemberg: "The question of constitutional monarchy versus republic means asking ourselves whether we want reform or overthrow."[62]

Despite the moving republic poems of Ferdinand Freiligrath, which accompanied the movement behind the revolution of March 1848 (*Die Republik, die Republik! Wohlan denn, Rhein und Elbe!* [The Republic, the Republic! Hail, Rhine and Elbe!]), the call for a republic in the German

---

57 Mager, "Republik," 68.
58 Cited in Hartwig Brandt, ed., *Restauration und Frühliberalismus: 1814–1840* (Darmstadt, 1979), 423–4.
59 Cited in Mager, "Republik," 631. 60 Ibid., 628.
61 Ibid., 633. 62 Ibid., 636.

revolution all too quickly became a partisan issue, an issue of the radicals, particularly the political emigrants who were streaming back into Germany. Among them were Karl Marx and the Communist alliance with a revolutionary program that began with the slogan: "Germany is hereby declared to be a single, indivisible republic." By the summer of 1848 the democratic movement had split over the republic issue, and in the fall of 1848 the left wing Donnersberg faction in the Paulskirche no longer dared to include the call for a republic in its program.

This was the end of modern republicanism in Germany's long nineteenth century. It was a democratic reform program, stimulated largely by Kant, and, beginning in 1832, developed into a revolutionary, antimonarchical project. Like the majority of Europeans, however, Germans in midcentury still saw no acute reason to deny a political role to the princes.[63]

VII

The tradition of democratic republicanism in Germany traced here must be distinguished from the "classical" republicanism that has been at the center of a scholarly discussion for the past two decades. When one considers the historical turning points in classical republicanism that have been identified by that discourse, one arrives at the following thesis: European discussions of republicanism began in the same period in which classical republicanism in the United States was experiencing its last hurrah.

In the current scholarly historical discourse, two different concepts of republicanism are being used: republicanism as the political culture in premodern and early modern republics (so-called classical republicanism) and republicanism as a political program oriented toward the modern constitution of representative democracy. These two concepts refer to very different political contexts. It is important to be clear about this in order to progress in this important matter.

The main question to be asked regarding the United States in the long nineteenth century has to do with the echoes of classical republicanism – not an unimportant question in light of the fact that "classical" refers not only to ancient civilizations but also expresses a permanent commitment.

How are the developments in Germany to be classified in this scholarly discourse? Paul Nolte deserves credit for making the first proposal in this

---

63 In keeping with Kant, the imperial constitution of 1849 can therefore be seen as a solution to the German constitutional problem. However, there were good reasons to refer to Kant in 1919 as well. The final page has yet to be written in the story of Kant's effect on German constitutional history.

regard.[64] Nolte revealed a culture of classical republicanism among the middle classes of southwestern German towns in the first half of the nineteenth century. He made a connection to Peter Blickle's references to the traditions of municipalism and republicanism in early modern Germany.[65] Nolte distinguished between this republicanism, which Blickle also called "experiential republicanism," and a so-called dogmatic republicanism, which he said had limited social staying power.[66] Not until the revolution of 1848, Nolte claimed, had modern republicanism really succeeded in German society. Nolte's argument is therefore based on a model largely patterned on the American one: Middle-class revolution serves as the transition from classical to modern republicanism.

The German tradition of republicanism demonstrated in this chapter is hard to reconcile with Nolte's thesis. It was not in 1848 but rather in 1795, in Kant's wake and with the so-called Jacobins, that the concept of modern republicanism first caught on in Germany. We can trace its origins to intellectual reactions to the reality of the first French Republic. This republicanism did not constitute a rejection of the institution of monarchy but was associated with a program of representative democracy. This concept was enthusiastically adopted by the democratic movement in Germany beginning around 1830 and became part of the national constitutional program in the revolution of 1848.

Modern republicanism with its various options in state forms was undoubtedly a part of the tradition of German liberalism, which always focused on constitutional questions. However, the thesis that early German liberalism was "classical republicanism" is not tenable in the form in which Nolte expressed it.[67] Nolte's argument ignores the 1790s, the Hambacher Fest, and the subsequent democratic movement centered in southwest Germany, along with other important dates. Although considered the great theoretician of classical republicanism, Karl von Rotteck, I argue, was influenced by the Enlightenment, not least of all by Kant, and contributed to the development of modern republicanism in Germany. Should one not rather argue that the traditions of modern and classical republicanism were combined in the person of Rotteck?

Nolte should be lauded for demonstrating classical republicanism, still based largely on a privileged version of civil rights, in the political culture

---

64 See Nolte, "Bürgerideal, Gemeinde und Republik."

65 Ibid., 626ff.; cf. Nolte's other works cited there. Peter Blickle, "Kommunalismus und Republikanismus in Oberdeutschland," in Koenigsberger, ed., *Republiken und Republikanismus*, 57ff.; Peter Blickle, "Kommunalismus, Parlamentarismus, Republikanismus," *Historische Zeitschrift* 242 (1986): 546ff.

66 Nolte, "Bürgerideal, Gemeinde und Republik," 615–16.   67 Ibid., 614.

of Germany prior to March 1848. It therefore seems natural to speak of a co-existence of modern and classical republicanism in the *Länder* and towns up to the mid-nineteenth century. Further research is required to define this co-existence more precisely. That research should focus on the following questions: When and how did modern republicanism replace classical republicanism? Should the two forms of republicanism be viewed as alternatives to one another? What forms of co-existence of classical and modern republicanism can be observed? Was classical republicanism perhaps more widespread on the municipal level and modern republicanism on the national level? These questions make it clear that we must comprehend, research, and discuss the era of democratic revolution – the epoch from 1770 to 1850 – as a whole, in Germany and elsewhere.

4

Constitutions, Charity, and Liberalism by Default: Germany and the Anglo-American Tradition

A. G. ROEBER

For English-speakers, "Germany" signals many impressions of political and constitutional history, primarily of a "statist" tradition, easily contrasted with the "liberal" heritage of Britain, France, and North America. Eighteenth-century attempts by Prussia to consolidate central state power at first seem the logical first step in tracing the later, more troublesome German *Sonderweg* in political and constitutional thought.[1] Yet resistance to centralized remedies intended to alleviate poverty and promote order in state and society – even if not recognizably "liberal" – continued during the eighteenth century in territories of the Holy Roman Empire, even against Prussian overlords. A distinct American tradition of state formation that began with the written state constitutions crystallized in the 1790s. North Americans diverged from European definitions of the state's "police power," as they contemplated how republics might be called upon to relieve poverty and encourage charity in a virtuous social order.

The author wishes to acknowledge the support of the Historical Commission of Berlin for a fellowship in 1994; additional research was conducted under the auspices of Collaborative Research Grant RO-22406-92 of the National Endowment for the Humanities and the Trans-Coop Program of the Alexander von Humboldt Foundation.
1 For a useful summary of the problems surrounding German national identity and historical writing, see Stefan Berger, *The Search for Normality: National Identity and Historical Consciousness in Germany Since 1800* (Providence, R.I., 1997), 21–55. For the issue of charity and the state tradition, see Hermann Beck, *The Origins of the Authoritarian Welfare State in Prussia: Conservatives, Bureaucracy, and the Social Question, 1815–70* (Ann Arbor, Mich., 1995). 9–11; Michael Doesge, *Armut in Preussen und Bayern (1770–1840)* (Munich, 1991); and Frank Rexroth, "Recent British and West German Research on Poverty in the Early Modern Period," *Bulletin of the German Historical Institute London* 12 (summer 1990): 3–11. See also Richard Gawthrop, *Pietism and the Making of Eighteenth-Century Prussia* (Cambridge, 1993), who argues convincingly for the position that Pietism, even with the rise of Friedrich II ("the Great"), remained a powerful arm of "modern" state policy aiming at the actual change in behavior through coercion (280–4). For a summary of the "liberal" and "republican" positions that reflect the Anglophone literature, see Timothy H. Breen, "Revisions Once More in Need of Revising: Political Ideology and Nationalism in Anglo-American Context, 1740–1790," paper delivered at the Krefeld Symposium in 1996. Breen argues for the need to fix interpretations of the American Revolution "in the recent historiography of eighteenth-century England."

Before the 1790s, despite obvious differences that marked highly developed European from relatively young North American societies and
populations, theologians and politicians on both sides of the Atlantic
had concurred that the "police" role of the state applied to charity
when authorities had to contemplate good order threatened by "outsiders."
Otherwise, local secular and church authorities and institutions were
deemed competent to manage the Christian obligation to care for the poor.
This belief revealed itself in legal and constitutional mechanisms in Great
Britain and in the Holy Roman Empire's varying territories. In North
America a strong localist tradition rooted in English precedents shaped this
conviction as well, despite regional variations that incorporated the expe-
riences of continental immigrants.

Travelers in the eighteenth century would have recognized parallels
between Hamburg's charity practices and those of London. Both urban
centers by mid-century had shifted support away from almsgiving and hospitals toward workhouses and openly expressed worries over the social
unrest among the "working poor."[2] That shift occurred only slightly later
in North American cities. American charity law and practice encouraged
local voluntary and nongovernmental solutions for poverty, drifting away
from an earlier belief shared with Europeans that the state shared responsibility for social justice with what Americans would eventually label "privately supported" relief.

This divergence sprang from no developed "liberal" or "republican"
theory. Rather, antinomian-free church suspicions hostile to state direction
of conscience, particularly south of New England, revived by the 1790s
as North Americans contemplated putting coercive power behind the
lofty visions that some public figures had of constructing "Christian"
republics. "Private" and purely voluntary charity and philanthropy tri-
umphed over a brief temptation to link religious instruction to benevolence and training for good citizenship. Almost simultaneously Prussian
fiscal policy trumped local religious leaders' waning arguments in that
state that they should manage charity schemes and promote social welfare
for the working poor. At first, after the American Revolution, German
speakers in North America assumed that pastoral schemes that looked
to replicate some of the Prussian state's shared responsibility for charity

---

2 The vast literature on charity and philanthropy in British and German contexts defies easy summary;
   for some key essays, see Robert Jütte, *Obrigkeitliche Armenfürsorge in deutschen Reichsstädten der frühen
   Neuzeit* (Cologne, 1984), 1–45; Reinhold August Dorwart, *The Prussian Welfare State Before 1740*
   (Cambridge, Mass., 1971); Donna Andrew, *London Philanthropy in the Eighteenth Century* (Princeton,
   N.J., 1990); and Mary Lindemann, *Patriots and Paupers: Hamburg, 1712–1830* (New York, 1990).

with the churches would work in the American context. Instead, absence of state coercion confirmed a process of Americanization among these former continentals that had begun long before the emergence of the American republics.

I

In his impressive *Religion, Law, and the Growth of Constitutional Thought, 1150–1650* Brian Tierney argued that we will make little real progress toward understanding political thought or state formation in the early modern era until someone undertakes "a systematic study on the ecclesiastical theories of a mixed constitution."[3] Tierney's observation provides a springboard for meditation on how continentals and Anglo-Americans attempted to reconcile the interests of the state and its concern with "police" or good order with the inherited Christian obligation to care for the poor. As Marc Raeff has argued, the concern for "police" in Europe focused on beggary and vagrancy when they were threats from the "outside" but left local details of poor relief to the church and local, that is, "private" law. This was the case in colonial North America.[4]

In the early eighteenth century, Prussia's struggle to construct a well-ordered state operated under a dwindling set of constitutional restraints imposed by the Holy Roman Empire. In 1714, as the Hannoverian dynasty began in Britain, Prussia "mediatized" one of its medieval vassal territories, Wernigerode. The Stolberg-Wernigerode family's appeal to the empire for its support of local independence over "police" matters touching on charity anticipated debates over social virtue and "good order" in the American context, as this remote Prussian story touched eighteenth-century North America as well. Wernigerode's count was an avid Pietist, closely connected to the Francke Foundations in Prussian Halle, who eagerly followed stories of the Great Awakening in Northampton, Massachusetts, and donated monies to the Halle missions via Denmark to Greenland. Lutheran pastors in Pennsylvania, trained at the Francke Foundations, were ordained in Wernigerode, and even after the American Revolution they cherished the illusion that the new commonwealth would perpetuate an alliance with the churches to promote useful charity to benefit the social order and public weal of America.

---

3 Brian Tierney, *Religion, Law, and the Growth of Constitutional Thought, 1150–1650* (Cambridge, 1982), 102.

4 Marc Raeff, *The Well-Ordered Police State: Social and Institutional Change Through Law in the Germanies and Russia, 1600–1800* (New Haven, Conn., 1983), 70–83.

Prussian control over local charity found its final expression in the Prussian law code of 1794, the *Allgemeines Landrecht für die Preussischen Staaten*. This general code evolved from Elector Friedrich Wilhelm I's time when the law faculty at Halle in 1714 began to work on a systematic revision of old Brandenburg law and the relationships between the Elector and his far-flung territories. The former professor and legal scholar Samuel Freiherr von Cocceji directed the project. By the 1740s the results were tested in the newly acquired territory of Silesia and the county of Wernigerode. Since the sixteenth century controversy in Wernigerode had pitted the local town council against the count and the count against the Elector of Brandenburg over respective rights and privileges.

The mediatization of Wernigerode provoked bitter resistance and an appeal to the Holy Roman Emperor on behalf of the young Count Christian Ernst by his mother, Christine von Mecklenburg-Güstrow. The quarrels dragged on for two generations, with each successive skirmish settled more decisively in Prussia's favor. Within the constitutional arrangements of the Holy Roman Empire, appeals of ordinary subjects to the immediate lord or against him to the feudal overlord, or ultimately to the emperor, kept such debates over rights and privileges a matter of constant tension. What began as a quarrel over who was the head of the evangelical church in Wernigerode escalated into practical, fiscal threats to Prussia's need for funds to sustain its military expansion. Local rights and privileges raised the question of who was responsible for the religious and economic dimensions of public order. In the eighteenth-century debates, the four "hospitals" in Wernigerode, relief houses for the elderly, infirm, and widowed, resisted increasing demands to provide a financial account of how they were run and how they administered their funds.[5]

Christian Ernst's mother, deeply influenced by the Halle Pietism of her chaplain, Superintendent Georg Neuss, saw clearly that Prussia's ability to claim sovereignty over religious matters in Wernigerode threatened the reform program she and her son intended for their territory in the Harz Mountains. A reform aimed at abolishing old Lutheran holidays, especially those of the saints and those reflecting local piety, at rewriting the liturgy and the hymnal, at tightening academic performance standards in the

---

5 No scholarly investigation of the hospitals has been done; on the 1740s protest, I have drawn from the Staatsarchiv Wernigerode (hereafter StAWern), X 3368: Die neue Armenordnung 1749–1828, Fach #7; VIII/II 2777: Acta in Sachen der Hospitäler . . . 1752; VIII/II 2776: Akten wegen der veranstalteten Kommission 1740–1750, vol. 1, #2, VIIa/4. For the original 1714 recess and the subsequent protests, see Geheimes Preussisches Staatsarchiv (hereafter GPrStA), Hauptarchiv (hereafter HA), VII Allg. Urkundens #189; Rep 8 188aa 1689–1736, 46–160.

schools, and at ending marksmanship contests and other traditional festivals deemed unsuitably frivolous marked this "reform Pietism from above." But part of these reforms also targeted the poor laws and the administration of the hospitals and the *Armenhöfe* – the areas within the town walls where lands were leased to generate income for local poor relief. Wernigerode's ruling family believed, given its historic role as religious head of Wernigerode, that such matters fell under its "police" competence.[6]

Christian Ernst lost the first confrontation with Friedrich Wilhelm in the 1720s when the Prussians insisted that only the king be prayed for as the head of the church. The somewhat odd religious opinions of Friedrich Wilhelm should not blind us to his genuine if brutal attempt to stamp out vagrancy. He also founded a military orphanage for boys and an orphanage for girls in Potsdam between 1713 and 1724. Local inefficiency or indifference toward the implementation of the laws confounded most of these efforts. To avoid opposition in Wernigerode the Prussians planned to pursue vigorously the collection of excise taxes that had been imposed there in 1698 but had so far not been regularly collected. Reports on cooperative or obstreperous local officials began in the 1720s to come to Berlin from the local excise officer.[7]

In 1729 Christian Ernst tried to promote Christian behavior in Wernigerode by ordering that regular prayers be conducted by the city catechist in the Wernigerode hospitals of St. Nicholas, St. Salvator, St. Johannes, and St. George. He also discovered that the inhabitants of St. Nicholas were not able to survive on the stipends paid them. His church consistory reported that if the lands tied to the hospital could be rented out, it would generate income to promote more successful educational and poor relief efforts.

An unsubtle reminder of how church-related matters dealing with charity now fell under Prussian "police" interests surfaced almost immediately. Johann Heinrich Gutjahr, a fervent, Halle-trained Pietist who had succeeded Neuss as superintendent, attempted to exempt his son from Prussian military service. Friedrich Wilhelm immediately ordered the confiscation of Gutjahr's house in Wernigerode as Prussian property, forcing Count Christian Ernst to find a place for the uncooperative cleric. Gutjahr quickly capitulated. Undeterred by the confrontation, Christian Ernst

---

6 The previous note summarizes archival details discussed in A. G. Roeber and Georg Fertig, *Troublesome Riches: Catholic and Protestant Responses to a Capitalist World, 1698–1806* (forthcoming), chap. 2.

7 For details, see GPrStA, Rep 8: Nr. 188aa (von Stolberg), 117–48. On the Prussian attempts, see Dorwart, *Prussian Welfare State*, 105–11, 189–93.

founded a house for widows and revised the manner in which monies were collected and distributed for poor relief. By 1737 a new and greatly expanded orphanage opened near the castle gardens just outside the city walls. Although influenced by Halle's example, Christian Ernst knew he would never be favored with the magnanimous sponsorship Friedrich Wilhelm and his predecessor had lavished on the Francke Foundations. Halle's privileges included freedom from Prussian excise taxes and the liberty to found its own printing house, apothecary, and orphanage. For Wernigerode, even before the accession of Friedrich II, charity interests had begun to be subordinated to Prussia's new fiscal policies and state interests.[8]

Whereas England's constitutional development by the seventeenth century had ended the appeal to medieval procedures as the basis for establishing legal rights, within the Holy Roman Empire the appeal of people to immediate lord or overlord, the appeal of prince to the emperor, such as that attempted in Wernigerode, continued. Even after the Treaty of Westphalia (1648) local princes worked against the growing tendencies toward centralization. These struggles legitimized speculation on the part of territorial princes and leaders as to whether social concerns such as poor relief were better handled under central state control or under an older, more traditional set of "private" arrangements involving town, local noble, church interests, and ancient rights of the local prince.[9]

The Holy Roman Empire had been reduced in constitutional power to such an extent that its mechanisms failed to prevent successive outbreaks of warfare among constituent members from the 1740s to 1763. Still, Wernigerode, like the imperial knights of the German southwest, employed the constitutional structure of the empire as best it could to defend ancient rights and privileges. Wernigerode's count also drew on older English con-

---

8 On the Gutjahr controversy, see Otto Krauske, ed., *Die Briefe König Friedrich Wilhelms I. an den Fürsten Leopold zu Anhalt-Dessau 1704–1710*, Acta borussica . . . Ergänzungsband (Berlin, 1905), 463, 468, 470–2; on the hospitals, see StAWern, B48.1, Rep H Stolberg-Wernigerode, Nr. 7, Nr. 12; see also Adolf Friedrich, *Geschichte der Wohltätigkeits-Anstalten Wernigerodes* (Wernigerode, 1863), 28–40; and Sylvia Maier, "Studien zur Geschichte des Waisenhauses in Wernigerode im 18. Jahrhundert," M.A. thesis, University of Leipzig, 1992. On the general pattern of Prussia's pursuit of central oversight for financing the state administrative bodies, see Reinhard Mussgnug, "Die Finanzierung der Verwaltung an der Wende vom Ständesstaat des 18. zum Verfassungsstaat des 19. Jahrhunderts," in Gerhard Dilcher, ed., *Die Verwaltung und ihre Ressourcen: Untersuchungen zu ihrer Wechselwirkung* (supplement no. 9 of *Der Staat*) (Berlin, 1991), 79–110.
9 On the fate of the Stolberg-Wernigerode library, see Hildegard Herricht, *Die ehemalige Stolberg-Wernigerödische Handschriftenabteilung: Die Geschichte einer kleinen feudalen Privatsammlung* (Halle an der Saale, 1970), 5–25.

stitutional history and American Pietist experiments to assist in this defense.[10]

Among the handwritten translations Christian Ernst owned, a collection of letters written by the Scottish Presbyterian Samuel Rutherford is particularly instructive. The letters, written in 1636–7, translated into German at Königsberg in 1682, and then hand copied for Christian Ernst, reveal his deep awareness of the constitutional theory that had crossed the Baltic and the North seas in both directions in the seventeenth and eighteenth centuries. Rutherford, best known during England's constitutional crisis for his essay *Lex, Rex,* inspired George Lawson's later essay, the *Politica Sacra.* Rutherford's insistence that God commanded humankind to have government but specified no particular structure or tradition appealed greatly to Lawson, whose concerns focused on a proper balance among monarchy, aristocracy, and democracy in the governance of the Christian church. Later, John Locke began writing with little concern for these ecclesiastical questions but finding Rutherford and Lawson useful in arguing for a more secular, liberal constitutionalism.[11]

The opening of Wernigerode's orphanage in 1737 coincided with the count's support for the Danish missions in Greenland. Two years later Wernigerode noticed Halle's support for the Salzburger colony in Georgia and by the 1740s both the count and his Pietist clergy welcomed the news of the Great Awakening in New England and made small donations to Heinrich Melchior Mühlenberg's efforts to organize Lutherans in Pennsylvania.[12] These initial, promising attempts at linking local control over charity collections to broader, international Pietist reforms that seemed to flourish in the context of British constitutional liberty foundered in the face of the political and fiscal reality dictated by Prussia.

10 For the literature on the constitution of the empire, see, e.g., Heinz Schilling, *Das Reich und die Deutschen: Höfe und Allianzen, Deutschland 1648–1763* (Berlin, 1989); Michael Stolleis, *Geschichte des öffentlichen Rechts in Deutschland: Reichspublizistik und Policeywissenschaft 1600–1800* (Munich, 1988), 334–404, treats the practical implementation of state theory in "police"; on the quasi-federal nature of the empire, Helmut Neuhaus, "Das föderalistische Prinzip und das Heilige Römische Reich Deutscher Nation," in Hermann Wellenreuther and Claudia Schnurmann, eds., *Verfassung und Deutsch-Amerikansches Verfassungsdenken: Ein Rückblick über 200 Jahre* (New York, 1991), 31–53.

11 For the Rutherford letters, see StAWern, Rep H Stolberg-Wernigerode A, Fach 2 A, #37; on Rutherford, Lawson, and the influence on Locke, see Conal Condren, *George Lawson's Politica and the English Revolution* (Cambridge, 1989), 58–9, 89–9; on Lawson's *Politica Sacra et Civilis* (1657) and its ties to Althusius, Christopher Besoldus, and later theory, see Tierney, *Religion, Law,* 71–98; and for a work that surprisingly ignores Lawson and this background in general, see John Marshall, *John Locke: Resistance, Religion and Responsibility* (Cambridge, 1994), 92–5.

12 Halle, AFrSt 5E6 for Ebenezer, Ga.; for Pennsylvania, 4 G 1–4; 4 F4–10; on the New England Awakening, C704 letters of Count Christian Ernst von Stolberg, Mar. 4, 1738, 47; Drees, *Geschichte,* 56–7.

The attempt to put serious money behind schooling, orphan relief, and a home for widows in Wernigerode produced a flurry of edicts from the count. A special commission, under Prussian oversight, produced a systematic review of the hospitals and *Armenhöfe* with an eye toward increasing their efficiency and productivity. Forestry, mining, and general economic administration were drawn together in 1746 in a new cabinet, the *Kammer-Kollegium*. A revised poor law emerged by 1750, and for the first time an *Armenkasse* or formal poor relief fund functioned under the oversight and administration of the count's church consistory. Wernigerode's poor law underwent successive revisions between the 1740s and 1755. Wernigerode's chancellor Julius Leopold von Caprivi became the Prussian minister Cocceji's instrument for introducing the Prussian law code into Wernigerode. The code dictated clearly how charitable donations were to be used for poor relief. Wernigerode officials especially resented Prussian insistence that collections for charitable purposes could no longer remain under the supervision of the count's church consistory but had to be reviewed in Berlin as a fiscal matter. A super-consistory for all Lutheran churches in the Prussian lands came into being by 1750, further negating the local consistory's decision-making powers. Prussian edicts declared that all donations *ad pias causas* be carefully reviewed; all parishes, hospitals, and foundations were to provide a financial account of any gifts, and all mortgages and investments were to be financed through Berlin banks.[13]

Christian Ernst's conscientious Pietist convictions ironically advanced the centralizing state interests of his feudal overlord. Moreover, his admiration for British philanthropy in Georgia did not extend to a liberal view of religious truth as mere opinion to be freely debated in his own territory. The count received a report from one of his subjects, Johann Ludwig Voigt, on a visit to the British capital in 1762. A view of "English freedom of Religion" shocked Voigt. He remarked that if Luther could witness British tolerance and the resulting religious chaos, "he would utter God help us not once but ten times."[14] In the mind of the Lutheran Pietist count, local "police" privileges implied the princely duty to guard against religious error and to promote charitable projects that advanced true reli-

---

13 An exhaustive historical review on the issue of collections, taxation policy, and the police rights was finished Aug. 31, 1743 (see GPrStA, Rep 8 1881, 157–58); for the 1750 rescript establishing the Lutheran Ober-Consistorium (Oct. 4, 1750), see GPrStA, Rep 9, NN, lit. e. On the new poor laws, StArWern, Rep H Stolberg-Wernigerode HA, B 48, Fach 1 #7; B 51, Fach 2, #1; B 48, Fach 3, #6 (1753); Fach 4, #1 (1763); for the Prussian oversight of mortgages and holdings, see B 34, Fach 2, #9 (1769).
14 StArWern, Rep H Stolberg-Wernigerode, K. Privat-Korrespondenz, #865, Voigt to Christian Ernst London, Jan. 20, 1762.

gion. The count was ill-prepared to argue when local merchants and crafts-men wanted to specify where their charitable donations should be applied, pointing to broad-based philanthropic efforts in Britain or even in Berlin where no one Protestant tradition was favored over another. The local boys' school in Wernigerode had for generations enjoyed the privilege of orga-nizing a choir that, on a quarterly basis, sang through the streets asking for alms to supplement their normal support. The count encouraged these col-lections as intended to support a school supposed to train loyal Pietist pastors and teachers. Unfortunately, voluntary contributions in 1750 scarcely increased from their 1740 level. Local tradesmen and artisans in Wernigerode, still annoyed with the Pietist reforms that intruded on folk festivals and other local customs, stopped their donations. Their passive resis-tance further delegitimized the count's arguments with Berlin that he alone should exercise police powers over charity that would produce thrifty, pro-ductive subjects for Prussia. The legitimacy of these collections and local control over them grew even more controversial as the effects of the Seven Years' War threw Wernigerode's economic and social conditions into chaos.[15]

The poor law, reviewed in 1760, was altered again in 1766 as children were sent out by parents to increase household incomes by begging. Beadles now oversaw poor relief distribution more systematically. The most serious burden on charitable funds fell on Wernigerode as hordes of ill soldiers and deserters flooded the territory. The local poor fund stood at the edge of bankruptcy, and no amount of warning off vagrant soldiers or control of military passes stemmed the tide. In desperation, Christian Ernst claimed as a local prince's right the seizure of the property of deserters to provide relief to his poor subjects. Prussia disagreed. After a long exchange of letters with Wernigerode, Friedrich II in exasperation wrote: "Enough! there are not two fiscal officers in Wernigerode; my fiscal rights are not confined solely to the inheritances of deserters!"[16]

Even had arguments by local authorities against absolutist tendencies not foundered on the constitutional inability of the empire to check the rise of states like Prussia, lack of tangible, practical results in dealing with issues of poverty and dependency also weakened their arguments. For example,

---

15 Wernigerode Stadtarchiv, X 3-6689: Verzeichnis des von den Kurrentknaben (the collections aver-aged about 120 reichstaler in 1740, about 160 two decades later. From communicants' lists and other estimates, a more or less stable population is assumed of between 2,000 to 3,000 persons in the town).

16 GPrStA, Rep 8, Nr. 188aa, 1749–76, Mar. 15, 1767, to Nov. 10, 1768; Friedrich's handwritten out-burst is in the Oct. 13, 1767, summary of the dispute.

by the 1780s Wernigerode's local authorities expanded the orphanage to include a spinning house, where unemployed persons were ordered to report to learn the wool-spinning trade. Such workhouse experiments had been in existence in other parts of Europe for decades. Five years later outraged cottage spinners petitioned against the innovation, arguing that state-supported spinning in the orphanage undercut the fair access of individual subjects to market prices based on demand. Admitting that there was little work to support the unemployed and fearful of social unrest and the possibility of renewed appeals to a notoriously anti-Pietist monarch, Wernigerode officials faced a gloomy conclusion. Nearing the century's end, their local police powers had been curtailed or circumvented, and charity schemes had failed to prevent subjects from sliding into the ranks of the dependent. In near desperation the Stolberg-Wernigerode family turned to the thirst for news among their literate subjects as a source for revenue, only to meet with renewed threats from Prussia. By founding a local newspaper, the *Wernigerodischer Intelligenzblatt*, authorities planned to siphon subscription money into poor relief coffers. Perhaps inadvertently, or perhaps already knowing the risk involved, they had violated the monopoly rights of the Potsdam military orphanage, which held exclusive rights to monies generated by subscription to public prints. Prussian officials demanded that the newspaper close, and only the Napoleonic wars prevented Prussian intervention.[17]

The Prussian concessions to the Pietist center at Halle, the Francke Foundation, may have allowed its alumni in Pennsylvania to believe that state and church could work harmoniously to oversee charity efforts. Wernigerode's experiences with Berlin should have given them pause. In North America they quickly found that resistance to state taxation power, coupled with religious pluralism, doomed to irrelevance their Prussian model and European experience in such matters.

II

Before the 1760s few effective legal structures and institutions reflected transplanted traditions of public charity in North America. Charity law

---

17 GPrStA I, Rep. 8, Nr. 188a, 1788–98, 1797–1811: Acta wegen des zu Wernigerode herauskommenden Intelligenz Blattes . . . ; on the Potsdam orphanage, see Bernhard R. Kroener, "Bellona und Caritas: Das Königlich-Potsdamsche Grosse Militär-Waisenhaus: Lebensbedingungen der Militär-bevölkerung in Preussen im 18. Jahrhundert," in Bernhard R. Kroner and Heiger Ostertag, eds., *Potsdam: Staat, Armee, Residenz in der preussisch-deutschen Militärgeschichte* (Frankfurt am Main, 1993), 231–52.

inherited from England prescribed solutions that presumed that both the root cause of and solution to poverty were local. From the 1730s to about 1745, however, it seemed as if German-speaking immigrants in Georgia would construct an American experiment in charitable institutions linking European benefactors to official government approval of institutional poor-relief efforts. The founding of an orphanage in 1737 by the Salzburger immigrant community at Ebenezer, Georgia, at first promised a well-regulated program. By 1744, however, the orphanage housing twenty-four adults and children closed because widows and children found work, room, and board on the farmsteads of the settlement. Despite the attractive feature of enjoying European financial support that enabled the distribution of medical services, educational literature and lessons, and clothes and farming tools free of charge, the orphanage, patterned on Halle's Francke Foundation model, could not compete with the wages that the surrounding farms offered. The experiment in Georgia collapsed not because of undue pressure from other religious groups or because of the Georgia Trustees. Rather, internal economic opportunities and needs, coupled with renewed migration, undercut the attractiveness of the orphanage experiment. Neither did a sufficiently grave number of orphans or widows threaten the Salzburger community's financial or social stability, making it unnecessary to continue a somewhat artificial experiment in benevolent paternalism.[18]

Pennsylvania, the colony that eventually emerged as the preferred new home to a majority of German-speaking immigrants, passed laws between 1712 and 1731 encouraging religious societies to acquire property as gifts and to promote the relief of poverty-stricken members in their denominations. By 1731 Philadelphia's almshouse was in operation, and by 1749 local overseers controlled both food distribution and access to relief, much of which came from voluntary sources. By the time Philadelphia's Bettering House (1767) came into being, it included both the old almshouse and the new house of employment.[19]

Pennsylvania's German-speaking Lutherans exhibited a striking lack of concern over providing charity even to their own. Nowhere does pre-Revolutionary testamentary evidence suggest a major concern for charitable gifts, in part because the patterns of German-speaking arrivals

---

18 See Renate Wilson, "Public Works and Piety in Ebenezer: The Missing Salzburger Diaries of 1744–45," *Georgia Historical Quarterly* 77 (summer 1993): 336–66; and A. G. Roeber, *Palatines, Liberty, and Property: German Lutherans in Colonial British America* (Baltimore, 1993), 160–74.

19 I trace the evolution of charity law in Pennsylvania in greater detail in "The Long Road to Vidal: Charity Law and State Formation in Early America," in Christopher L. Tomlins and Bruce Mann, eds., *The Many Legalities of North America* (Chapel Hill, N.C., 2001), 414–41.

in North America, peaking by 1752, did not produce wealthy testators. Analyses of specific arrivals in Lancaster or Reading, for instance, reveal gifts that ranged from conditional bequests to a church or school to the donation of a collection bag or copy of the liturgy, but no endowments of charity schools or relief funds per se. Unable to comprehend the English law of trusts – which was only dimly understood by English speakers in North America – German-speaking arrivals made no such elaborate provisions for educational improvement or poor relief before the Revolution.[20]

In 1768, two of the last Lutheran pastors sent by Halle for work in the New World, Justus Heinrich Christian Helmuth and Johann Friedrich Schmidt, had been ordained and feted in Wernigerode before their departure. Both men briefly attempted after the Revolution to promote a kind of loose church-state cooperation in charity for the purpose of social betterment. They had reason to think Pennsylvania would prove amenable to such notions.

In 1779, Helmuth succeeded the most eminent Lutheran pastor in North America, Henry Melchior Mühlenberg as one of St. Michael's and Zion parish's pastors in Philadelphia. Encouraged by Pennsylvania's post-revolutionary legislative enactments that put western land grants at the disposal of Anglican, Quaker, Lutheran, and Reformed parish poor schools, in 1785, he and the parish pioneered a parish peer relief society that collected $20 per week for parish members. Pastor Helmuth had worked to secure a new charter for the old German Society in 1781, to alleviate the sufferings of the indigenous poor not previously eligible for the Society's relief. Contributions were invested and the interest was disbursed for food, winter fuel, and clothing for the "worthy poor," and for the congregation's distressed widows, orphans, and mentally ill. A congregational poor house was planned but never erected; should the society disband, its articles of incorporation dictated that capital acquired be

---

20 For Lancaster's Baden arrivals, see Mark Häberlein, *Vom Oberrhein zum Susquehanna: Studien zur badischen Auswanderung nach Pennsylvania im 18. Jahrhundert* (Stuttgart, 1993); records, minute books, and miscellaneous records, Trinity Lutheran Church, Lancaster, Pa., V, 103 A 1758–1825, Lancaster Historical Society – Bequests, pp. 6–8; Lancaster County Courthouse, wills and deeds, inventories, Lancaster County Historical Society; I extracted German names from the Berks County Registry of Wills and compared them with those in Werner Hacker, *Kurpfälzische Auswanderer vom Unteren Neckar: Rechtsrheinische Gebiete der Kurpfalz* (Stuttgart, 1983); Annette Kunselman Burgert, *Eighteenth-Century Emigrants from German-Speaking Lands to North America: The Northern Kraichgau* (Breinigsville, Pa., 1983); Don Yoder, ed., *Pennsylvania German Immigrants, 1709–1786 ("Emigrants from Wuerttemberg: The Adolf Gerber Lists")* (Baltimore, 1980), 1–137. For further details on the complexities of charitable trust law and incorporation, see Roeber, "Long Road to Vidal."

re-invested in the poor school to provide at least a rudimentary form of social improvement.[21]

Helmuth, Pastor Christopher Kunze, and Pastor Johann Friedrich Schmidt also devised plans for funneling the talented among the poor from the charity schools to a *Gymnasium*-like higher school to provide future schoolteachers, pastors, and elite leaders for German speakers. The best and the brightest were then sent to a German college nested in the University of Pennsylvania.[22] Helmuth believed, on the basis of the recent legislative record, that Pennsylvania was prepared to promote Protestant Christianity, even as he opposed an official establishment of, or any form of direct assessment in support of, religion.[23] Successful opposition led by German Reformed, Lutheran, and Episcopal leaders to a proposed public school bill in 1796 also seemed to confirm the preference of Pennsylvania's citizens for using incorporated Protestant churches and schools to provide free education for the children of the poor and local relief as well. Helmuth as late as 1810 could point with pride to Lutheran activity in supporting charity schools – six in Philadelphia to the one or two among Episcopalians, Catholics, Presbyterians, and Reformed, though considerably fewer than those run by the wealthier Quakers.[24]

In 1799, however, the Philadelphia Society for the Establishment and Support of Charity Schools was founded – on nonsectarian lines. The move signaled the beginning of a long retreat in Pennsylvania from the indirect support of sectarian charity schools that had seemed to be the established policy of the Commonwealth. By 1800 an even worse disaster befell Pastor Helmuth's vision of an alliance between Commonwealth and churches that would advance the cause of education and charitable relief: Thomas

---

21 See "Kurze Geschichte der Männlichen Wohltäthigkeits Gesellschaft," Lutheran Archives Center, H10/P5/M6/L5; for the published rules, see *Die Gesellschaft für Unterstützung der redlichen Hülfsbedürftigen Haus-Armen* (Philadelphia, 1790); the above also summarizes the financial records of the society and the parish council records, 1790–1810. For further details, see A. G. Roeber, "J. H. C. Helmuth, Evangelical Charity, and the Public Sphere in Pennsylvania, 1793–1800," *Pennsylvania Magazine of History and Biography* 121 (1997): 77–100.

22 For details, see A. G. Roeber, "Citizens or Subjects? German-Lutherans and the Federal Constitution in Pennsylvania, 1789–1800," *Amerikastudien/American Studies* 34 (1989): 49–68; and A. G. Roeber, "The von Mosheim Society and the Preservation of German Education and Culture in the New Republic, 1789–1813," in Henry Geitz, Jürgen Heideking, and Jurgen Herbst, eds., *German Influences on Education in the United States to 1917* (New York, 1995), 157–76.

23 On the growing misperceptions of competing definitions of "liberty" in a transatlantic context for this period, see A. G. Roeber, "'Through a Glass, Darkly': Changing German Ideas of American Freedom, 1776–1806," in David E. Barclay and Elisabeth Glaser-Schmidt, eds., *Transatlantic Images and Perceptions: Germany and America Since 1776* (New York, 1997), 19–40.

24 Roeber, "Von Mosheim Society," 172.

Jefferson was elected president. Helmuth incurred the wrath of
Democratic-Republicans among the German speaking by refusing to have
prayers said for a man he regarded as a deist. In fact, the election of 1800
in Pennsylvania turned on ethnic-religious fears that Presbyterians in particular would dominate the political future of the Commonwealth and
enforce already extant laws against gaming, blasphemy, and profanation of
the Sabbath. The more abstract national principles of Federalist versus
Democratic-Republican theories of government paled by comparison to
these highly specific examples of behavior and the potential for repression
by adherents of a religious society other than one's own.[25]

Pennsylvania's Quaker past made it more than simply "permissive" of
charity undertaken by the colony's diverse religious groups. Protestant
charity was overtly encouraged but without a state fiscal policy that
would have taxed property and controlled distribution of the resulting funds
in province-wide charity.[26] North American Protestants eventually
endorsed a "voluntary" theory of property that elevated individual rights
to property. For the new states south of New England moral arguments
grounded in a Christian communal sense of obligation failed to emerge.[27]
Locke and classic liberal theorists in general rejected limitations on the
freedom to dispose of private property; Locke's own somewhat infamous
dismissal of the need for institutionalized charity was tempered by his
personal expressions of concern and largesse.[28] But Lockean theory
only marginally touched the history of charity law expressed in North
America through denominational and local institutions. Reasons for the
collapse of a brief experiment among German speakers that might have
linked state interest in charity to the goal of a well-ordered, Protestant
society lay elsewhere than in a conscious adoption of explicitly "Lockean"
theory.[29]

25 See variously Kenneth W. Keller, *Rural Politics and the Collapse of Pennsylvania Federalism* (Philadelphia, 1982) [Transactions of the American Philosophical Society 72, part 6], 32–57; Owen S. Ireland,
Religion, Ethnicity, and Politics: Ratifying the Constitution in Pennsylvania (University Park, Pa., 1995);
and Roeber, "Citizens or Subjects," 58–68.
26 Carl Zollmann, *American Civil Church Law* (New York, 1917), 25, 69; Carl Zollmann, "The Enforcement of Charitable Trusts in America: A History of Evolving Social Attitudes," *Virginia Law Review*
54 (1968): 436–9.
27 Elizabeth Mensch, "The Colonial Origins of Liberal Property Rights," *Buffalo Law Review* 31 (1983):
655–8.
28 See Marshall, *Locke, Religion, and Responsibility*, 318–26. For a confirmation of the judgment that it
is nearly impossible to demonstrate a prior claim for charitable obligation within Locke's defense
of private property, see Jerome Huyler, *Locke in America: The Moral Philosophy of the Founding Era*
(Lawrence, Kans., 1995).
29 Thomas A. Horne, *Property Rights and Poverty: Political Argument in Britain, 1605–1834* (Chapel Hill,
N.C., 1990), 201–51.

The Madisonian state undoubtedly enshrined private property rights along lines that look somewhat Lockean. Yet, commentators on American constitutional thought and the participants in the debates over America's "liberal" or "republican" roots have largely ignored the question of charitable activity that touched evangelical, ordinary people. In theory, that issue might have occasioned a debate over the nature of society and government's role in it. Because the Federalists' most enduring achievement consisted in separating the structure of the national republic's politics from the debate over the need for a "moral" social order, that debate never happened.[30]

No ecclesiastical solution had been found in colonial America for resolving where, in a "mixed" constitutional order, responsibility for the socially weak should be located. Whereas the American constitutional framework after 1789 provided an uneasy but flawed balance to the problem of sovereignty, the police powers of the various states, largely unimpaired, could not be linked to a specific religious, moral, or social agenda for long. Minor scolding for intemperance, blasphemy, or breaking the Sabbath not only survived but even enjoyed a brief renaissance in the early republic. No one, however, dared link the concern for public order explicitly to the state's power to tax in support of charitable efforts aimed at creating a religious, "well-ordered" state and society.[31]

J. H. C. Helmuth's 1792 sermons, published in the hope that sales would help the charity society he founded, accurately discerned why the European linkage could not occur in North America. In a series of reflections on the civic rights and responsibilities of Christians, Helmuth skewered those who confidently proclaimed, "'Our days are enlightened days.' . . . In our days one glorifies general brotherly love; one praises the fact that one is no longer divided by the differences in religious systems . . . one regards everyone as a brother, let him believe what he will." Helmuth conceded that in an "external" way such religious tolerance fulfilled a main tenet of the teaching of Christ. But to his core the Halle-trained pastor, who had witnessed Wernigerode firsthand, doubted that genuine love of others motivated such superficial expressions of charity. Rather, indifference to the

---

30 Jennifer Nadelsky, *Private Property and the Limits of American Constitutionalism: The Madisonian Framework and Its Legacy* (Chicago, 1990), 246–54.

31 See Jack N. Rakove, *Original Meanings: Politics and Ideas in the Making of the Constitution* (New York, 1996), 302–15; Rakove rightly notes that "denying government any authority to legislate" in matters of religion "could never apply to economic regulation and public finance" (315). Although aptly summarizing the federal debate over rights and obligations, Rakove is silent on the point that a state establishment of religion and consequent public order was possible in the nineteenth century but did not evolve.

truth of Christianity lay behind such benevolent expressions. The long-term effect of such indifference, Helmuth thought, produced indifference not only toward belief but toward what happened to one's neighbor as well. Worst of all were those pretend Christians who might even "mingle with the masses of Christians on Sundays; they pray, preach, and 'listen' to the singing . . . from church they go straight to the drinking-houses and the card-tables . . . people who live by ambition, stinginess, whoring . . . whose prayers are swearing and whose singing is cursing; people who cheat widows and orphans; people who, in trade and commerce, even committed perjury and who lied and cheated wherever possible."[32]

Yet Helmuth failed to convince the wealthy among his own parishioners of the necessity of constructing a comprehensive system of education for poor children coupled with relief for the elderly, the infirm, and the destitute that would draw upon public funds. He justified such a scheme by pointing to pre-Revolutionary precedents and even to Prussian examples that had sought to make charity available on a more nonsectarian basis. Whereas the emerging American charity law provided guidelines and careful structures on how trusts and incorporated societies were to be founded and governed, fiscal policy remained firmly divorced from social-relief programs in Pennsylvania and elsewhere in the new republic. In large part, mutual mistrust on the part of the various religious societies and a long tradition of hostility to state coercion of conscience and pocketbook drove Americans in a different direction from that of their European contemporaries.

Much of this history of early debates over charity law in North America has been overlooked in the effort to understand "liberal" and "republican" norms. Equally true, the memory of Wernigerode's earlier history of struggle for its own "police" rights and moral responsibility for charity has been forgotten because of the later association of the ruling house of Stolberg-Wernigerode with the Bismarckian empire.[33] In North America the brief flirtation of states with an explicitly denominational control of education and poor relief persisted into the nineteenth century. Eventually, this too evolved into a preference for "private" incorporation, "liberal" in its defense of a private property ethic, "republican" insofar as the states retained what little moral obligation for minimal charitable activity was deemed essential. Beneath both "theories" mutually fearful religious and ethnic groups

---

32 J. H. C. Helmuth, *Betrachtungen der evangelischen Lehre* . . . (Reflections on the Evangelical Doctrine of the Holy Scripture and Baptism) (Germantown, Pa., 1793), 316–17, 324–5.

33 See, e.g., Konrad Breitenborn, *Im Dienste Bismarcks: die politische Karriere des Grafen Otto zu Stolberg-Wernigerode* (Berlin, 1984).

pursued various chimeras of a "Christian" republic in the era of "benevolence." Never persuaded by the high theory of Lockean Federalists, Americans seemed primarily anxious about what harm the police power of the individual states might wreak if harnessed to religious belief. That anxiety did not prevent some of the more numerically dominant from arguing for a closer bond. The outbreak of the Sabbatarian controversy in Pennsylvania in 1809, driven by the confident convictions of a Congregational-Presbyterian alliance, was but the most visible of the short-lived attempts to revive such a debate and carry it on even at the federal level.[34]

The trajectory of debate on the "well-ordered state" increasingly distanced the United States from nineteenth-century German concerns. Differing understandings of what terms like "freedom" meant reflected the profoundly different histories of constitutional and sociocultural experience in profoundly disparate societies.[35] Still, for populations overwhelmingly dominated by Protestant and Catholic forms of western Christianity, the proximate histories of these societies in the eighteenth century had not originally been as disparate as later events suggest. The recognition of mutual social obligation for the less fortunate, coupled with struggles over how and whether the well-ordered state should be involved in the construction of a compassionate society, reveals a deeper level of shared history that has largely been forgotten. Paris or even London may already have looked closer than Frankfurt to American legal and constitutional theorists.[36] To penetrate the values and attitudes of ordinary citizens and subjects on both sides of the Atlantic in this era, however, we must find new avenues such as the one suggested here to transcend what have become increasingly sterile debates over liberalism, republicanism, and their consequences.

---

34 See Richard John, "Taking Sabbatarianism Seriously: The Postal System, the Sabbath, and the Transformation of American Political Culture," *Journal of the Early Republic* 10 (1990): 517–67.

35 For this argument, see Roeber, " 'Through a Glass, Darkly.' "

36 I lift the phrase from another debate on the uniqueness of American legal constitutionalism; see the discussion of Jürgen Habermas's *Faktizität und Geltung: Beträge zur Diskurstheorie des Rechts und des demokratischen Rechtsstaats* (Frankfurt am Main, 1992), in Kenneth Casebeer, "Paris Is Closer than Frankfurt: The Nth American Exceptionalism" (review essay), *Law and Society Review* 29 (1994): 897–961.

5

Politics and Sentiment: Catharine Macaulay's Republicanism

VERA NÜNNING

The identification of a woman's name with republicanism is rather unusual. After all, the traditional values of civic humanism were "manly";[1] martial valor and participation in national politics, for instance, were obviously not something for a woman in the eighteenth century. Moreover, political philosophy at that time was almost exclusively written by male authors. Nonetheless, Catharine Macaulay left her mark on the eighteenth century as a political thinker and pamphleteer, and even managed to become famous as a "female patriot" in both England and America. In the late eighteenth century, American political thought was steeped in British republicanism, and Macaulay herself knew quite a number of American politicians who thought highly of her work and were grateful for her support of the American cause during the War of Independence. Her eight-volume *History of England*, which was available in many libraries in Great Britain and in the colonies, was praised by politicians like William Pitt and John Adams; George Washington made special preparations when the "celebrated historian" Macaulay paid him a two-week visit at Mount Vernon, and Thomas Jefferson recommended her work as an antidote to that "poison" David Hume's history had injected into the minds of the British people.[2] In addition, Macaulay's political pamphlets were taken seriously by her opponents. Edmund Burke thought her the best author of the radical camp, and only

---

1 See, e.g., Ruth H. Bloch, "The Gendered Meanings of Virtue in Revolutionary America," *Signs* 13, no. 1 (1987): 37–58.
2 For the reception of Macaulay's history, see Bridget Hill, *The Republican Virago: The Life and Times of Catharine Macaulay, Historian* (Oxford, 1992), 135–48. Macaulay's contemporary fame is illustrated by Mildred C. Beckwith, "Catharine Macaulay, Eighteenth Century Rebel: A Sketch of Her Life and Some Reflections on Her Place Among the Historians and Political Reformers of Her Time," Ph.D. diss., Ohio State University, 1953, 123–33. For Jefferson's opinion on Hume, see Andrew A. Lipscomb and Albert E. Bergh, eds., *The Writings of Thomas Jefferson*, 20 vols. (Washington, D.C., 1904), 16:125–6.

half-jokingly admitted that he had been "afraid to answer" her vilification of his pamphlet *Thoughts on the Present Discontents*.[3] Macaulay's modifications of republican thought, which amounted to a cultural updating of the republican tradition and utilized republican tenets in an attempt to improve the position of women in society, were thus put forward by a person respected on both sides of the Atlantic.

The mere fact that Macaulay's writings were regarded as important contributions to the political debate from the 1760s onward is enough to establish her importance as a woman who had proved that at least some members of the female sex were able to hold their own in a traditionally male field of activity. Thus Linda Kerber recognizes Macaulay's impact, arguing that she was one of the few women who could serve as an example to American females aspiring to more than their designated role in the nineteenth century.[4] But more important than her function as a potential role model were two features of Macaulay's work: First, she modified the republican tradition in a way that made it more palatable to polite Britons, who in the last third of the eighteenth century had come to esteem refined and humane virtues that were incompatible with important republican values. Second, she put forward views that emphasized the equality of the sexes in intellect and character, and used republican values as arguments against the subordination of women.

Macaulay was not the most likely person to become celebrated as a radical historian and political pamphleteer. Neither her religious upbringing as a member of the Church of England nor her education, which mainly consisted of the free use of her father's library, nor her status as a married woman of the upper middle class can be regarded as obvious bases for her achievement as a radical thinker. But even in her youth Macaulay loved to read books about Roman patriots sacrificing their lives for the liberty of their nation. At the beginning of her career as a radical historian and pamphleteer Macaulay firmly embraced the values of republicanism, which became more accessible to her after her success as a writer had brought her into close contact with people like Benjamin Rush, Richard Baron, and especially Thomas Hollis, who provided her with many valuable political tracts.[5]

3 Edmund Burke, Aug. 14, 1770, in Thomas W. Copeland, ed., *The Correspondence of Edmund Burke*, 10 vols. (Cambridge, 1958–78), 2:50.
4 Cf. Linda Kerber, *Women of the Republic: Intellect and Ideology in Revolutionary America* (Chapel Hill, N.C., 1980), 196.
5 Macaulay's youth, education, and reading are described in Hill, *Republican Virago*, 1–24, 165–71, and in Bridget Hill and Christopher Hill, "Catharine Macaulay's History and Her Catalogue of Tracts," *Seventeenth Century* 8, no. 2 (1993): 269–85. For a more extensive treatment of Macaulay's

That a woman should advance republican ideals is at first sight rather surprising because the harsh virtues of martial valor, self-restraint, rational command of one's passions, and self-sacrifice for the common good were characteristics that in the seventeenth and early eighteenth centuries were seen as qualities in men of the middle and upper classes. Moreover, the basic prerequisite for political autonomy, economic independence, excluded both the lower classes and (married) women from the political arena. Thus, the disdain for republicanism shown by some bluestockings seems understandable. Elizabeth Montague, for instance, wrote that she was sick of all that patriot din of liberty and averred that she was not sure whether Cato had not kicked his wife.[6] Macaulay's reputation as a female patriot indicates, however, that republicanism did offer some opportunities for women in the late eighteenth century. Although women were not allowed to vote in national elections or sit in parliament, they could wield considerable influence as writers of pamphlets for humanitarian or political reform. Even conservative writers like James Fordyce acknowledged women's social and ultimately political importance as educators of England's future citizens.[7]

The fact that women could fulfill some important functions in late eighteenth-century society was the result of a number of cultural tendencies that served to enhance their status: a fundamental change in the conception of human nature, the growing popularity of the so-called culture of sentiment or sensibility, the upgrading of the private and social circle, the downgrading of classical knowledge, and the implications of John Locke's epistemological theories for the education of young citizens were the most important developments favorable to women. Some of these, of course, also contributed to the decline of republicanism in Britain during the 1780s because they served to popularize values contradictory to that political tradition.

First of all, the prevalent attitudes toward the nature of man changed in a way that made some of the tenets of civic humanism appear superfluous. More and more Englishmen – and Englishwomen – came to accept the view first put forth by Latitudinarian divines and the Earl of Shaftesbury that human nature was basically good. David Hume was one of those who argued that the passions were not something negative and in need of restraint

---

innovative modifications of British radical thought, see Vera Nünning, *"A Revolution in Sentiments, Manners, and Moral Opinions": Catharine Macaulay und die politische Kultur des englischen Radikalismus 1760–1790* (Heidelberg, 1998).

6 See Sylvia H. Myers, *The Bluestocking Circle: Women, Friendship, and the Life of the Mind in Eighteenth-Century England* (Oxford, 1990), 93.

7 Cf. James Fordyce, *Sermons to Young Women* (Philadelphia, 1787), 29.

by superior reason; he even claimed that "reason is, and ought only to be the slave of the passions."[8] Although not everyone agreed that reason should have such a subordinate role, prevalent collocations like the "social passions" indicated that feelings came to be valued as such. The republican view that only superior citizens were able to restrain their passions and sacrifice their private interests for the public good lost ground as people came to believe that feelings were basically supportive of virtuous behavior; or, in Shaftesbury's words, that "*Love of one's Country . . . must also be Self-Love.*"[9]

Many of those changes incompatible with traditional republicanism were in some way related to the culture of sentiment, something that among literary historians is regarded as so important that one of the terms commonly used to designate the second half of the eighteenth century is the "age of sentiment."[10] This culture is much more than just a "literary" phenomenon, manifesting itself in sentimental plays, poetry, and novels in which delicate maids try to preserve their virtue and "men of feeling" demonstrate their refined emotions. Rather, the literature that embodies values of sentiment is just one of several forms in which a new way of looking at man and the world came to be expressed. The new values were modified and popularized in philosophy, medicine, history, education, art criticism, and the sermon, and were practiced in the daily behavior of the middling ranks.[11]

The foundation of the paradigmatic shift in the conception of man that lay behind the values of sentiment and ultimately contributed to undermining the tenets of republicanism was, as George S. Rousseau argued, John Locke's epistemology. Locke had claimed that all human knowledge derived from ideas based on impressions that reached the brain via the nerves.[12] This view, which attributed great importance to the nerves as the mediators of knowledge and virtue, was complemented in the second half of the century by the stress placed on the delicacy of the nerves and fibers. Handbooks for domestic medicine brought home to their readers the idea that sensitive nerves led to a sharp intellect and refined

---

8 David Hume, *A Treatise of Human Nature* (1739–40), ed. Lewis A. Selby-Brigge (Oxford, 1896), 415.

9 Anthony Ashley Cooper, Third Earl of Shaftesbury, *Characteristics* (1711), 3 vols. (London, 1727), 1:119. For Shaftesbury's view of human nature, see Norman S. Fiering, "Irresistible Compassion: An Aspect of Eighteenth-Century Sympathy and Humanitarianism," *Journal of the History of Ideas* 37 (1976): 202.

10 Few historians have so far concerned themselves with this culture. The only book on English culture is G. J. Barker-Benfield, *The Culture of Sensibility: Sex and Society in Eighteenth-Century Britain* (Chicago, Ill., 1992).

11 See Vera Nünning "Die Kultur der Empfindsamkeit: Eine mentalitätsgeschichtliche Skizze," in Ansgar Nünning, ed., *Eine andere Geschichte der englischen Literatur: Epochen, Gattungen und Teilgebiete im Überblick* (Trier, 1996), 107–26.

12 Cf. George S. Rousseau, "Nerves, Spirits, and Fibres: Towards Defining the Origins of Sensibility," in R. F. Brissenden and J. C. Eade, eds., *Studies in the Eighteenth Century III* (Canberra, 1976), 141–5.

feelings.[13] Delicate emotions thus came to be regarded as the most important feature of man. Even the commonwealth man Lord Kames was convinced that "[m]an is distinguished from the brute creation . . . by the
greater delicacy of his perceptions and feelings."[14]

This new conception of man, which was fundamentally opposed to the
republican conviction that feelings had to be restrained by reason, had
ethical and ultimately political implications. Sensibility was cherished
because it gave rise to sympathy and thus to virtue. In its broadest meaning,
sympathy meant the ability of an observer to put himself in another's shoes.
Educators, moralists, and preachers advised their readers to cultivate their
capacity for sympathy because it was thought to lead to compassion, which
in turn called forth benevolence, the highest ideal in mid-eighteenth-
century Britain.[15] Thus, benevolence and morality could be inculcated by
cultivating sympathy.

As a consequence, demonstrating one's sympathy became a way of
proving one's moral worth. According to the prevalent belief in the close
relationship between body and soul, emotions manifested themselves first
in the "natural," allegedly "universal" language of the body – most of all,
in the tears that flowed so abundantly in sentimental literature. Exquisite
emotions also found expression in "true politeness," which, in contrast to
the superficial and hypocritical manners attributed to aristocrats, was held
to be based on sincere emotions. A less obvious embodiment of delicate
feelings was shown by those suffering from so-called nervous disorders,
something only highly sensitive and intelligent people had to endure. Even
sturdy Englishmen like James Boswell were rather proud of suffering from
this sort of disease, also labeled "hypochondria," because it proved one's
superior capacity to feel and thus one's morality.[16]

This new ideal was a far cry from the independent, hardy, and valorous
individual who was considered to be the ideal citizen in the republican tradition. The refined and delicate emotions now held to be characteristic of
virtuous people were incompatible with the rather strict and, in Thomas
Sheridan's words, "painful" values of republicanism.[17] To see the difference
one need only contrast the newly fashionable English indulgence toward

13 Cf. John Mullan, *Sentiment and Sociability: The Language of Feeling in the Eighteenth Century* (Oxford,
   1988), 205–13.
14 Henry Home, Lord Kames, *Elements of Criticism* (1762), 3 vols. (New York, 1967), 2:3.
15 Cf., e.g., John Dwyer, *Virtuous Discourse: Sensibility and Community in Late Eighteenth-Century
   Scotland* (Edinburgh, 1987), 60–3, and Fiering, "Irresistible Compassion," 200–5.
16 Mullan, *Sentiment and Sociability*, 201–40, provides a very good overview of the relation between
   sentiment and "nervous disorders." For the "natural" and universal language of the body, see Kames,
   Elements of Criticism, 2:116–32.
17 Thomas Sheridan, *British Education: or, the Source of the Disorders of Great Britain* (Dublin, 1756), 54.

children and the new market for toys and children's books, on the one hand, and Benjamin Rush's recommendations for plain diet and strict daily discipline for his "republican machines," on the other. To refined Englishmen and women, republican virtues grew increasingly out of touch with their daily lives and new values. For Adam Smith, this was only natural: "Among civilized nations, the virtues which are founded upon humanity, are more cultivated than those which are founded upon self-denial and the command of the passions."[18] Although they often still held center stage in political discourse, self-sacrifice for the common good and protestations of being willing "to seal" reforms "with my Blood" became increasingly unfashionable.[19]

Moreover, even writers interested in the fate of the nation and convinced that Britain was pervaded by such luxury and corruption that national ruin was imminent increasingly looked to sentimental values to find a remedy for the nation's ills. Because many commonwealth men were convinced that public virtue was not to be expected from compatriots of their degenerate age, one means of improving public morals was looking to the moral value of sympathy. Especially Scottish writers hit on the moral value of improving private conversation and recommended cultivating virtue by strengthening sensibility and sympathy as an antidote to the luxury allegedly omnipresent in the public sector.[20]

Interestingly enough, during the first ten years of her writing career Macaulay certainly was not one of those writers in favor of the culture of sentiment. In her numerous letters to republicans on both sides of the Atlantic she presented herself as a patriot and stressed that "the administration of that patriotic virtue which so eminently flourished in the glorious states of Greece and for a short period of time in this Country . . . always subsisted in my character."[21]

In the first five volumes of her *History of England* and in the political pamphlets she wrote in the 1760s and early 1770s she was true to her word. In these writings Macaulay was preeminently a mouthpiece for republican values. As recent scholarship has stressed, this, however, was perfectly compatible with recommending Locke's political works and insisting on the importance of natural rights.[22] In her writings Macaulay, like John

---

18 Adam Smith, *The Theory of Moral Sentiments* (1759), ed. David D. Raphael and Alec L. Mafie (Oxford, 1976), 204–5.

19 Cf. Earl of Abingdon, *Thoughts on the Letters of Edmund Burke* (Oxford, 1777), 68. For the distance between republican ideals and daily life, see Dwyer, *Virtuous Discourse*, 101.

20 Cf. Dwyer, *Virtuous Discourse*, 187. For continuing fears of luxury, see James Raven, *Judging New Wealth: Popular Publishing and Responses to Commerce in England, 1750–1800* (Oxford, 1992), 157–72.

21 Catharine Macaulay to John Wilkes, 1768 or 1769, British Library Add. MSS. 30.870, f. 242.

22 For an early view of this opinion, held by writers such as Lance Banning, Mark E. Kann, and Alan Houston, see Jeffrey C. Isaac, "Republicanism vs. Liberalism? A Reconsideration," *History of Political Thought* 9 (1988): 349–77.

Cartwright, used elements from both traditional republicanism and Locke's writings that served to strengthen her argument. She sometimes referred to the Bible, natural law, the ancient constitution of England, and republican values in the same text. Thus she affirmed that the "doctrine of Christ asserted the equal rights of men"[23] and used Locke's conception of the original compact to refute Thomas Hobbes's absolutist notions in her early pamphlet *Loose Remarks on Certain Positions to be Found in Mr. Hobbes' Philosophical Rudiments of Government.*[24] She also quotes Locke's *Two Treatises* extensively in her *History of England* to justify the conviction and execution of Charles I because of his "breach of trust and nonperformance of obligations."[25] For her it was the inherent right of the people to oppose tyrants to the utmost: "Exclude this position, and all governments are equal tyrannies; the destroyers, not the preservers of the rights of nature."[26]

In her early writings, however, Macaulay based her argument less on natural law than on republican values; J. G. A. Pocock even called her a "simon-pure representative of the old quasi-republican tradition."[27] Although she accepted the "mixed constitution" of king, lords, and an independent House of Commons as an adequate form of government for the rather unenlightened citizens in eighteenth-century Britain, like James Burgh she preferred the republican form of government in theory.[28] In her plan for a constitution for Corsica in 1767 she used elements from James Harrington's *Oceana* and divided the legislative branch into a senate and a house of representatives. Because of her belief that most rulers had a "rage for absolute power,"[29] the executive was under normal circumstances to reside in the house of representatives.[30]

Quite a number of Macaulay's political principles stem from her pessimistic view of human nature. She shared the belief that the drive for

23 Catharine Macaulay, *The History of England from the Accession of James I to that of the Brunswick Line,* 8 vols. (London, 1763–83), 3:329n; for Cartwright's use of three traditions in one sentence, see John Cartwright, "American Independence, the Interest and Glory of Great Britain" (1774), in Paul H. Smith, ed., *English Defenders of American Freedom* (Washington, D.C., 1972), 140.
24 The title continues: *and Society with a Short Sketch of a Democratical Form of Government in a Letter to Signior Paoli;* both tracts were first published by W. Johnston as one volume in 1767 in London.
25 Macaulay, *History,* 4:406; see also 4:404, 407–8.
26 Ibid., 4:408.
27 J. G. A. Pocock, *Virtue, Commerce, and History: Essays on Political Thought and History, Chiefly in the Eighteenth Century* (Cambridge, 1985), 290. For Macaulay's republicanism, see Hill, *Republican Virago,* 164–83.
28 This was the position of nearly all the English republicans; for Burgh, see James Burgh, *Political Disquisitions* (1774–75), 3 vols. (New York, 1971), 3:18.
29 See Macaulay, *History,* 8:64.
30 Macaulay believed that only under extraordinary circumstances should a single man be entrusted with executive power, and the period of his rule should be limited to twelve months at the most. See Macaulay, *Loose Remarks,* 22–3, 27.

power was insatiable and that the passions of man had to be governed by superior reason. Governors should not be trusted; "every degree of confidence in government" was liable to be abused.[31] In her opinion one of the ways of preventing this abuse of power was the rotation of members of parliament. She agreed with Harrington that rotation would put a stop to corruption.[32] Moreover, citizens had to watch their rulers carefully and assert their own rights if necessary. A prerequisite for autonomy and responsible political participation was economic independence. In her early writings Macaulay shared the prevalent view that yeomen and gentlemen with large landed estates were truly independent and had a special interest in the common good.[33] She also set great store by the equality of citizens. Like Locke or Richard Price, however, she only defended *political* equality while emphasizing that there was a "natural subordination established by God himself,"[34] based on personal merit or riches that should not be meddled with. In her opinion the lower sorts not only lacked the intellectual education necessary for a sound understanding of politics, but they were also unable to restrain their passions and recognize the common interest; they were far too irrational to govern themselves, let alone others: "The common herd of men are incapable of judging of argument, and must be led to action by their passions."[35] To Macaulay, their only virtue lay in obedience to the right rulers. When she claimed that the consent of the governed was a necessary prerequisite for a legitimate government, she was referring only to the middle and upper classes of society.[36]

Like other commonwealth men Macaulay modified some of the tenets of republicanism.[37] She was among the first radicals of the eighteenth century to claim extensive rights for the people. As early as 1767 she argued in her proposal for a constitution for Corsica that the wishes of citizens were more important than the opinions of their representatives. The senate should first discuss important questions and then make its conclusions

31 Macaulay, *History*, 1:221n.
32 Macaulay, *Loose Remarks*, 34; see also Catharine Macaulay, *Observations on a Pamphlet, entitled, "Thoughts on the Cause of the Present Discontents"*(London, 1770), 17.
33 Macaulay, *History*, 1:xvi; see also ibid., 1:317, 3:239.
34 Macaulay, *History*, 4: 332n; see also Richard Price, *Additional Observations on the Nature and Value of Civil Liberty* (Dublin, 1777), 34.
35 Macaulay, *History*, 3:152; see also ibid., 7:260. Most radicals at the time held this opinion. See, e.g., Joseph Priestley, *Lectures on History, and General Policy* (1788), 2 vols. (London, 1793), 2:57.
36 See, e.g., Macaulay, *History*, 4:383: "the people under God, are the origin of all just power." See also her *Loose Remarks*, 5–6.
37 I do not want to maintain that there is such a thing as a "pure" republicanism; however, a few of Macaulay's opinions modify republican values in a way slightly different from those of her contemporaries.

known to the people; but the electors should first decide what was to be done: "Let these proposals be promulgated one month before the meeting of the representatives toward the passing them; that the people may have time to deliberate on them, and give what directions they shall judge proper to their representatives."[38] In 1775 Macaulay affirmed the right of English citizens to give their representatives binding instructions.[39] Although she conceded that the wishes of the electorate might not always result in the best policy, she considered it "as a far lesser evil than to submit to an indefinite obligation of obedience."[40] Macaulay thus preferred a bad policy that corresponded to the will of the people over good measures dictated by a sovereign parliament.

She therefore turned the existing hierarchy with respect to representatives and electorate on its head and advocated the sovereignty of the people, something that should be realized by a parliament truly conforming to the citizens' will. In order to achieve this aim Macaulay recommended a number of reforms, most of which she justified in her historical writings as necessary for restoring the ancient rights of free Englishmen. She argued for the right of suffrage for all householders ("taken away by the disfranchising statute of Henry the Sixth"), the ballot, more equal representation, place bills, annual parliaments, and the abolition of rotten boroughs.[41]

Moreover, Macaulay interpreted the concept of independence in a truly radical way. She rejected any authority that might serve to circumscribe free thought. Thus, she was strictly against any established religion whatsoever because it inevitably led to "that resignation of private judgment, which is so favorable to civil tyranny."[42] She also condemned narrow religious beliefs because they made men mere instruments of the will of priests.[43] Similarly, she was strongly opposed to uncritically following any principle whatsoever. In her history of the seventeenth century Macaulay conceded that the king had all the precedents and laws on his side, but she nonetheless asked her readers to identify with those who adhered to the true spirit of the English constitution and recognized that custom might give "not only a legal, but a sacred and perpetual, establishment to

38 Macaulay, *Loose Remarks*, 24.
39 Cf. Macaulay, "An Address to the People of England, Scotland and Ireland on the Present Important Crisis of Affairs" (1775), in Smith, ed., *English Defenders*, 115–16.
40 Macaulay, "Address," 118.
41 Macaulay, *History*, 8:330. See also ibid., 1:60, 2:262–3, 406, 8:330–1; see also Macaulay, "On the English Constitution," *The Patriot*, vol. 1, no. 6, June 11, 1792, 207, and ibid., no. 7, June 26, 1792, 219.
42 Macaulay, *History*, 2:55; see also ibid., 2:54.
43 Macaulay, *History*, 3:253; see also ibid., 4:142: "In all the catalogue of human frailties, there are none which more corrupt the heart, or deprave the understanding, than the follies of religion."

tyranny."[44] Macaulay thus enlarged the concept of independence in a way that stressed the autonomy of the individual. Paradoxically enough, she used the authority of history to persuade her readers to reject all authority and rely only on their own judgment.

In her early work Macaulay also subscribed to those features of republicanism that have been described as nostalgic and backward-looking because they did not conform to contemporary economic conditions or popular values. She confirmed that the loss of liberty and eventual national ruin would follow the spread of luxury and recommended both agrarian and sumptuary laws as precautions.[45] Moreover, she fully accepted the harsh martial values of the republican tradition. She praised self-denial and "the exalted passions of sacrificing private views to public happiness,"[46] and she regarded war as desirable insofar as it hardened citizens and "produced a warlike spirit"[47] that enabled them to defend their liberties. Her whole history was written with the view to presenting "Patriots who have sacrificed their tender affections, their properties, their lives, to the interest of society"[48] as praiseworthy examples of desirable behavior. Her utter disregard of the values of sensibility at this early stage in her writing career also manifested itself in her opinion that it was a good thing to have miscreants sentenced to death: "A discipline thus severe and just, as it made the parliament terrible to their enemies, so it inspired their partisans with the utmost reverence and devotion."[49]

In sum, up to the 1770s Macaulay supported nearly all the tenets of republicanism, and both her historical and political works represented and justified republican values. Dealing with the seventeenth century in her famous *History of England* she held up examples of patriotic behavior, illustrated radical values, showed the success a determined resistance to the crown could have, and established a pattern of interpretation that could also be used to interpret political events in the late eighteenth century. Moreover, Macaulay formulated reforms that were allegedly necessary for restoring the ancient constitution, put forth an alternative republican model of political values and behavior, and provided radicals of the eighteenth century with a native tradition.

Her role as "female patriot" and her authority as the first radical historian of the eighteenth century earned her both praise and fame, but

44 Ibid., 4:38–9, 3:322–3n, 291. See also ibid., 3:33n., 1:xiv–xv.
45 Cf. ibid., 1:84, 3:187–8n; see also her *Loose Remarks*, 24–6.
46 Macaulay, *Loose Remarks*, 22.
47 Macaulay, *History*, 5:155; see also ibid., 2:215.   48 Ibid., 1:vii.
49 Ibid., 4:94.

apparently she was cut to the quick by criticism from representatives of the culture of sentiment. As she tells her readers in the preface to the sixth volume of her history, published in 1781 after a lapse of nine years, she had been accused of a lack of sympathy. From the mid-1770s on Macaulay tried to deflect this criticism in both word and deed. First, she moved from London to Bath to cure her "nervous disorders," which, for contemporaries steeped in the culture of sentiment, was a sure sign of the delicacy of her nerves and feelings. Second, she discontinued her work on a history of England in the seventeenth century to write a history of England in the eighteenth century in a style that conformed to fashionable polite values. In contrast to her former, scholarly history, which had extensive footnotes and long quotes, this new work had no notes and was written in episto-lary form,[50] employing this easy style to convey radical values. Macaulay's aim in writing this history was slightly different from her earlier historical work. In her account of the eighteenth century she concentrated on the growth of political corruption and the degeneracy of the times. She thus tried to persuade her contemporaries that reforms were absolutely necessary if the ruin of the nation was to be prevented. To mobilize broad support for political reforms her exposition focused on those points that radicals and the "country" opposition could agree on: repealing the septen-nial act, implementing place acts disabling crown officers from sitting in parliament, introducing a frugal style of government, reducing taxes, and repaying the public debt, the debt serving only the so-called "money'd interest" despised by both Tories and radicals. In 1778 Macaulay did not specify how often elections should be held; she also did not mention any reforms, such as the ballot or the extension of suffrage, which would have alienated the more moderate "country" opposition among her readership. In her history of the eighteenth century she thus put forth an agenda that one year later became the backbone of Christopher Wyvill's *Association Movement*. However, Macaulay's history was not a success. It was held in high esteem by radicals like Capel Lofft, but the general audience did not take to it — presumably because the attempt to blend polite style and traditional political values remained rather clumsy and because Macaulay's second marriage to William Graham, a Scottish

---

50 Catharine Macaulay, *The History of England from the Revolution to the Present Time, in a Series of Letters* (Bath, 1778). This work is usually criticized as being second rate at best; see, e.g., Marianne B. Geiger, "Mercy Otis Warren and Catharine Sawbridge Macaulay: Historians in the Transatlantic Republican Tradition (England)," Ph.D. diss., New York Unversity, 1986, 281, and Barbara B. Schnorrenberg, "An Opportunity Missed: Catharine Macaulay on the Revolution of 1688," *Studies in Eighteenth-Century Culture* 20 (1990): 233.

surgeon's mate more than twenty years younger than she, proved to be detrimental to her reputation.[51]

Despite this setback Macaulay did not abandon her attempt to combine republican and polite values. The last three volumes of her *History of England* are politically just as radical as her earlier work, condemning the Restoration as the "grand catastrophe" that "produced the return of national slavery."[52] At the same time, however, she refrained from commending harshness and martial values. In the preface to her sixth volume Macaulay even adopted the role of the tender and sympathetic patriot. On the one hand, she defended her earlier praise of those who risked their lives to further the liberty of their country; on the other hand, she firmly repudiated the accusation that she lacked humanity and even claimed that she had felt great sympathy for Charles I: "In this inquiry I was so far from feeling myself the bloody-minded Republican, as I have been termed by the butcherly writers of these days . . . that I shed many tears whilst I was writing his [Charles'] catastrophy."[53] Macaulay also began to evaluate behavior using the criterion of humanity. She even attributed politeness and sensitive dispositions to commonwealth men, claiming that they wanted to prevent the shedding of blood and tried to foster humanity.[54]

In her last political work, her pamphlet criticizing Burke's fatal *Reflections on the Revolution in France*, Macaulay also made use of the values of sensibility. In it she showed that she had lost none of her political sting; she even clarified former ambiguities when she flatly repudiated the authority of history as an important basis for legitimizing political reforms. What is more, she castigated the birthrights of freeborn Englishmen as arrogant and chauvinist pretensions because they denied the legitimate rights of all other countrymen. Her review of the possible legitimations of governments led her to conclude that all lawful political authority rested on the "unalienable and indefeasible rights of man."[55] The *"will of the people"*[56] was the only legitimate source of political authority. At the same time Macaulay made sure that her views no longer could be criticized for their alleged lack of feeling by supporting her defense of the French Revolution with argu-

51 Cf., e.g., Florence S. Boos and William Boos, "Catharine Macaulay: Historian and Political Reformer," *International Journal of Women's Studies* 3, no. 1 (1980): 53.
52 Cf. Macaulay, *History*, 5:321, 342.
53 Ibid., 6:xii; see also ibid., vii–xi.
54 Cf. ibid., 6:15–16, 351, 358, 7:214, 276, 355, 8:24–5, 205–6.
55 Catharine Macaulay, *Observations on the Reflections of the Right Hon. Edmund Burke, on the Revolution in France* (1790) (Boston, 1791), 38; see also ibid., 19, 38: the *"native* and *unalienable* rights of man." For her critique of the "boasted birthright of an Englishman," see ibid., 13.
56 Ibid., 39. Original emphasis.

ments based on the values of sentiment. She thus explained that the realization of natural rights in France could be prevented only through the "the effusion of *oceans* of blood,"[57] which no one with any degree of sympathy could wish for. She even avoided the republican term *public virtue* and instead claimed that it was "*liberal benevolence*, which . . . cheerfully sacrifices *a personal interest* to the *welfare* of the community."[58]

The influence of the culture of sensibility on Macaulay's thought is most obvious in her 1790 *Letters on Education.* This venture into educational theory did not, however, represent a withdrawal from politics; Macaulay had imbibed republican values and knew about the supreme political importance of the manners and morals of a nation. Her educational treatise was firmly based on Locke's epistemology. Macaulay repeated time and again that the senses were "the only inlets to human knowledge."[59] Education consisted "of all the impressions received through the organs of sense, from the hour of birth to the hour of death,"[60] and was of paramount importance to the formation of a pupil's character. She was thus able to argue that every passion or faculty lies latent in the human mind and can be strengthened only by the power of impressions and associations. The aims of her educational treatise combined elements of republicanism with the culture of sentiment: She wanted to form rules that prevented "the capricious tyranny of the passions" while aiming at refining and sensitizing the mind.[61]

Macaulay was conscious of the fact that no society had before attempted to combine both radical and sentimental values.[62] She nonetheless reviewed the systems of education of the ancient city-states in order to search for precedents for her new theory of education. In her chapters on Athens, Sparta, and Rome, she praised their realization of republican values but criticized their manners, which were too unrefined. She made quite clear that the only reason for admiring the ancients lay in their self-denying moderation and heroic patriotism.[63] On the whole she did not regard the ancient patriots as models to be emulated because they lacked benevolence. Indeed, their very virtues "were often at enmity with their humanity."[64] Although Macaulay adhered to the view that the spread of luxury had caused the fall of Rome, she offered a more positive evaluation of luxury than she had

---

57 Ibid., 37. Original emphasis.   58 Ibid., 16. Original emphasis.
59 Catharine Macaulay, *Letters on Education: With Observations on Religious and Metaphysical Subjects* (1790) (New York, 1974), 237; see also ibid., 163, 295.
60 Ibid., 274.   61 Ibid., i; see also ibid., iv, 425, 106, 422–3.
62 Cf. ibid., 250.   63 Cf. ibid., 248, 272.
64 Ibid., 240; see also 241, 251.

before. She acknowledged the possible relationship between luxury and refinement popularized by Scottish philosophers, and argued that the Romans were not as civilized as her own contemporaries, "for the privation of those luxuries which equally tend to corrupt and improve the mind, allowed them no means to acquire those graces and virtues which render the species objects of our admiration and esteem."[65] Thus, she conceded that there are two sorts of luxury, one of which "improved" and refined the human mind.

In contrast to the other English radicals who confined their advice on education to matters involving family, tutors, and schools, Macaulay based her recommendations on Locke's epistemology and the overall importance of impressions. In her discussion of "public education" she also concerned herself with architecture, gardening, and other ornamental arts that, in her opinion, were luxuries that might serve useful ends. She advocated the avoidance of experiences that might foster tendencies toward cruelty and instead the creation of circumstances that encouraged benevolence. She thus wanted to eliminate slaughterhouses and executions from public view and to encourage even poor people to cultivate small gardens.[66] Although she concentrated on experiences that allegedly foster sympathy, she did not forget her political agenda. She even argued that church pews should have no decorations that might "foster pride and servility" and thus were detrimental to the idea of political and religious equality.[67]

Macaulay's emphasis on sympathy was politically important. For her, the passing of laws favorable to sympathy would make coercive laws unnecessary because people governed by sympathy would perform "the duties of humanity" willingly.[68] Sympathy was thus a necessary component of responsible moral and political behavior.

However, Macaulay was not prepared to assign a subordinate role to reason as advocated by some Scottish philosophers. In her opinion reason was "always able to discern the moral difference of things."[69] She stressed again and again that there were immutable principles of virtue, independent of the changing manners and opinions of societies. It was therefore most important to develop the intellectual faculties of pupils to enable them to recognize those principles.[70]

---

65 Ibid., 239.   66 Cf. ibid., 276–81, 303–7.
67 Ibid., 333.   68 Ibid., 275–6.
69 Ibid., 193.
70 Cf., e.g., ibid., 49: "There is no cultivation which yields so promising a harvest as the cultivation of the understanding; . . . a mind, irradiated by the clear light of wisdom, must be equal to every task which reason imposes on it" (see also ibid., 23, 95).

In addition to sympathy and reason Macaulay thought that one tenet of republicanism was indispensable to responsible moral behavior. One aim of her educational treatise, therefore, was "to preserve as much as possible the independence of the mind."[71] In a letter titled *The Great Advantage of Inducing Habits of Independence in Children* Macaulay referred to the "blessings of liberty," which she wanted to secure by making her pupils independent.[72] For her, independence was of paramount importance because it prevented people from mindlessly following authority, which had nothing to do with truth. Moreover, she wanted to prevent the development of narrow-mindedness in her pupils and advised them to follow only those laws "which your enlightened reason dictates on a principle of conscience."[73] She even recommended that the scriptures should not be read before the age of twenty-one, by which time pupils had acquired critical faculties and independent minds. Although she granted that it might be wise to induce religious habits like praying earlier on, she was strictly against reading the Bible at an age when pupils were not yet able to evaluate its content and had to accept it as authority.[74] As to Macaulay's last reason for cultivating independence, she was well ahead of her time for she was one of the first in Britain to place value on originality. In contrast to many of her contemporaries, in 1790 Macaulay rejected authority because it inhibited original thought: "Opinions taken up on mere authority, must ever prevent original thinking, must stop the progress of improvement, and instead of producing rational agents, can only make man the mere ape of man."[75]

Macaulay's plan for education thus combined ideals of republicanism with the culture of sentiment. She sought to cultivate reason, independence, and sympathy as necessary prerequisites for responsible moral and thus political behavior. Macaulay also stressed that citizens must possess both private and public virtues to fulfill their political duties. In order to understand and, if necessary, criticize and resist political measures, citizens should be independent, rational, and virtuous: "The mere citizen will have learnt to obey the laws of his country, but he will never understand those principles on which all laws ought to be established; and without such an understanding, he can never be . . . truly moral; nor will he ever have any of that active wisdom which is necessary for co-operating in any plan of reformation."[76]

71 Ibid., 128.   72 Ibid., 66–8.
73 Ibid., 187–8; see also ibid., 127, 196.   74 Cf. ibid., 90, 134–9.
75 Ibid., 127; see also ibid., vi, 105. For the contemporary meaning of originality, see the OED and Jay Fliegelman, *Declaring Independence: Jefferson, Natural Language, and the Culture of Performance* (Stanford, Calif., 1993), 164–6.
76 Macaulay, *Letters on Education*, 198; see also ibid., 105, 139.

For Macaulay, as for Price, responsible political behavior was based on private morality. Macaulay thus modified her earlier opinions, which had been grounded solely on the tenets of republicanism. By 1790 she was convinced that citizens, in order to fulfill their duties, had to cultivate sympathy as well as achieve independence and develop their intellectual faculties. Independence and benevolence were essential components of informed political behavior.[77]

Macaulay's educational views can thus be read as complementary to her political writings. One might even claim that her work on education was meant to clear the ground for political change. In the late 1780s, when political reform movements stood little chance of success, it became more important to publish educational than political treatises. Because Macaulay believed, with Joseph Priestley, that public opinion was the basis for all political reform, it was first of all necessary to prepare the minds of the people, to make them want to throw off their shackles.[78] Macaulay did not want to produce "republican machines" who thought that they belonged to their country; she wanted her pupils to become autonomous human beings able to reach independent moral and political decisions. Thus, her treatise on education is ultimately a deeply political work.

Moreover, I argue that her educational tract shows her concern for the position of women in society and is in fact a rare combination of the values of sentiment, republicanism, and feminism. To claim Macaulay's importance as a precursor of feminism may seem rather farfetched. Susan Staves has argued that Macaulay's republicanism ultimately neglected the rights of women.[79] Staves's judgment must be taken with a grain of salt, however, because she discusses only the few remarks about women in Macaulay's historical and political writings; she does not take into account Macaulay's educational treatise. This is unfortunate for two reasons: First, in the writings that are predominantly influenced by republicanism, Macaulay projects a rather ambivalent attitude toward women. For instance, she praises one

77 See ibid., 112. Benevolence was of central importance both in the culture of sentiment and in Macaulay's treatise on education. I have not stressed that aspect of her work because benevolence was held to be not only the consequence of sympathy but also the most important ideal in eighteenth-century Britain. For Price's view of the necessity of private morality in citizens, see Richard Price, *A Discourse on the Love of Our Country, Delivered on November 4, 1789* (London, 1789), 43.

78 For Macaulay's opinion, see the diary of Sylas Neville, Apr. 30, 1768; quoted in G. M. Ditchfield, "Some Literary and Political Views of Catharine Macaulay," *American Notes and Queries* 12 (1974): 73; for Priestley, see "A Political Dialogue on the General Principles of Government" (1791), in John T. Rutt, ed., *The Theological and Miscellaneous Works of Joseph Priestley* (1817–1832), 25 vols. (New York, 1972), 25:107.

79 Cf. Susan Staves, "'The Liberty of the She-Subject of England': Rights Rhetoric and the Female Thucydides," *Cardozo Studies in Law and Literature* 1 (1989): 180.

petition of women in support of parliament and derides another petition by women "clamour[ing]" for peace, and even argues that parliament was justified in having them dispersed by means of arms.[80] In her historical writings Macaulay's attitude toward women is subordinated to the overall political aim of her work. Second, leaving out her educational treatise results in a one-sided account at best because Macaulay believed in the political importance of education.

One can take an observation by Mary Wollstonecraft as a starting point for a reappraisal of Macaulay's opinions on women. Wollstonecraft not only highly praised Macaulay; she even wrote her a letter saying "You are the only female writer who I coincide in opinion with respecting the rank our sex ought to endeavour to attain in the world."[81] I do not want to deny the differences between Macaulay's and Wollstonecraft's feminism, but Wollstonecraft certainly was not wide of the mark when she thought that her views and those of Macaulay on female education and the social position of women were remarkably similar.

Macaulay used Locke's epistemology for her own specific ends when she claimed that there were no innate differences between the sexes. Because Locke had shown that because there are no innate ideas, there could be no natural female characteristics either: "as the organs of sense are the same in both sexes, and consequently their perceptions, this difference which exists between them, can only arise from a different combination of their ideas."[82] Because she was convinced that there is "*No characteristic Difference in Sex,*" Macaulay emphasized that she only used the masculine pronoun in her educational work for stylistic reasons and that all her rules of education applied to both boys and girls.[83] Although she conceded that the customs of Europe should be taken into account in such things as reserving the rougher sports for boys, she set great store in a firm and vigorous constitution in women, who should do anything but conform to Burke's ideal of a "lisping" and "tottering" beauty. Because she wanted boys and girls to develop all their faculties she recommended that they should

---

80 Cf. Macaulay, *History*, 3:186–8 and 4:30. Staves, "She-Subject," 168–9, cites only one of these petitions and concludes that Macaulay principally supported political action by women.
81 Mary Wollstonecraft, Dec. 1790, quoted in Bridget Hill, "The Links Between Mary Wollstonecraft and Catharine Macaulay: New Evidence," *Women's History Review* 4, no. 2 (1995): 177. See also Mary Wollstonecraft, *A Vindication of the Rights of Woman* (1791), ed. Ulrich H. Hardt (Troy, N.Y., 1982), 170, 226.
82 Macaulay, *Letters on Education*, 179.
83 Cf. ibid., 203, 142, 62. Original emphasis. Florence S. Boos, "Catharine Macaulay's Letters on Education (1790): An Early Feminist Polemic," *University of Michigan Papers in Women's Studies* 2 (1976): 65, claims that Macaulay's denial of innate differences between the sexes was unique.

be educated together. Macaulay differed from most of her contemporaries
in that she wanted to educate boys and girls on a strictly equal basis:
"Confine not the education of your daughters to what is regarded as the
ornamental parts of it, nor deny the graces to your sons."[84] Men should be
just as tender, affectionate, sympathetic, and benevolent as women, and
females should be just as rational and independent as men. This aim was
not only founded on the fundamental similarity of the sexes but also sub-
stantiated by the fact that the immutable principles of virtue were the same
for men and women, and that both sexes should be enabled to lead a virtuous life to prepare themselves for heavenly judgment: "There is but one
rule of right for the conduct of all rational beings; consequently . . . true
virtue in one sex must be equally so in the other."[85] Macaulay's description of her ideal female pupil as a "careless, modest beauty, grave, manly,
noble, full of strength and majesty" demonstrates how radically she wanted
to transcend the popular gender roles of her time.[86] Macaulay went even
further than Wollstonecraft when she claimed that girls should not be
taught any virtue that was relevant only to their own sex. Whereas
Wollstonecraft wanted to use the power of existing customs to instill
chastity in girls, Macaulay was strictly against teaching anything on the
grounds of authority only. Her pupils were always to act according to
their own consciences.[87]

The contemporary differences between men and women contradicted
her thesis of the natural similarity of the sexes, and Macaulay gave a balanced evaluation of the reasons accounting for the subordination of
women. She referred to history and argued that in former times men abused
their bodily strength "to destroy all the natural rights of the female species,
and to reduce them to a state of abject slavery."[88] Both sexes then persisted
in upholding the resulting complementary distribution of rights and duties
between men and women, men because it was very flattering to them and
women because they had learnt to derive all their self-esteem from the

84 Macaulay, *Letters on Education*, 47–8, 50. This was taken over by Wollstonecraft; cf. *Vindication of the
Rights of Woman*, 100–1, 333, 349–50. For Burke's ideal, see "A Philosophical Enquiry into the
Origin of Our Ideas of the Sublime and Beautiful" (1757), in *The Works of Edmund Burke*, 6 vols.
(London, 1894–1900), 1:129.
85 Macaulay, *Letters on Education*, 201; see also ibid., 105, 139.
86 Ibid., 221. Most writers, such as James Fordyce and Lord Kames, had an abhorrence of "manly"
women.
87 Cf. Macaulay, *Letters on Education*, 212, 220. Macaulay also denounced the double standard, which
to her mind resulted from the fact that chastity had been regarded as the property of men; see ibid.,
220. For Wollstonecraft's view on chastity, see Wollstonecraft, "Review of Catharine Macaulay's
Letters on Education," in Janet Todd, ed., *A Wollstonecraft Anthology* (Cambridge, 1989), 116.
88 Macaulay, *Letters on Education*, 206.

admiration of men, and therefore counterfeited weakness and other allegedly female characteristics. For women, this hypocrisy was a kind of self-preservation because they had been taught to avoid reason and independence, and their only way to get a husband was by using their personal charms. Thus, women could have power only if they debased themselves. Educated to become coquettes, girls learned to give up all their virtues. Consequently, the "education of women . . . is precisely that which must necessarily tend to corrupt and debilitate both the powers of mind and body."[89] For Macaulay the many faults and weaknesses of women in the late eighteenth century were entirely the result of their education and their status in society, which denied them their rights and made them dependent on men.[90]

In her educational treatise Macaulay thus put forth a powerful criticism of the subordination of women. She used republican and sentimental values to convince her readers that both men and women would be happier and more virtuous if they enjoyed the same rights. First, she appealed to both the sentimental abhorrence of hypocrisy and coquettishness and the appreciation of a happy domestic life to criticize the status quo. She argued that men would be happier if they had educated wives with whom they could share their rational and refined pleasures.[91] Second, she used all the republican arguments against slavery, tyranny, and the debilitating consequences of dependence in support of her view that men and women should be treated as equals. Although she refrained from asking for definite legislative reforms, Macaulay deplored the dependence and powerlessness of women in much the same terms she employed in her historical and political writings: She denounced the tyranny of husbands and the corresponding slavery of wives, regretted that women were forced to delight in the few prerogatives they had by tyrannizing their suitors, and lamented the fact that women lacked both civil and political rights, and were thus denied their natural rights: "For with a total and absolute exclusion of every political right to the sex in general, married women, whose situation demands a particular indulgence, have hardly a civil right to save them from the grossest injuries."[92] She even enlisted divine support for her view that the subjection of women should be revoked: "So little did a wise and just Providence intend to make the condition of slavery an unalterable law of

89 Ibid., 205, 207–8, 211, 213.
90 See ibid., 202, 209, 214. Macaulay's criticism of the conduct and attitudes of women was never so harsh as Wollstonecraft's.
91 See ibid., 207. This was a common argument by feminists at the time.
92 Ibid., 206–12.

female nature, that in the same proportion as the male sex have consulted the interest of their own happiness, they have relaxed in their tyranny over women."[93] Thus, the nature of men and women, their rational interests and happiness, and the will of God all required that men and women should enjoy the same rights. For these reasons and because that was the only way to encourage virtue and pave the way for the happiness of men and women, it was necessary to educate both sexes on an equal basis. Men should be taught to recognize the value of an equal partnership, and women should learn to give up their indirect influence and precarious power in exchange for rational privileges.

Macaulay's educational views logically lead to the conclusion that both sexes should have equal rights. In an inconspicuous way that may have proved less repellent to contemporary readers than more partisan and antagonistic writing, Macaulay succeeded in arguing that the subjection of women should be abandoned because it was detrimental to female virtue, to the happiness of both sexes, and even to the progress and improvement of society. Macaulay's *Letters on Education*, which contained many of the ideas Wollstonecraft later put forth in her less coherent and more partisan and uncompromising *Vindication of the Rights of Woman*, can thus arguably be read as a trailblazing feminist work.

In summary, one can say that the particuliarities of Macaulay's republicanism consist mainly in a modification of republican values that made them more attractive to a late-eighteenth-century audience and her use of republican ideas to criticize the position of women in society. At the time, both were as remarkable as they were unusual. Perhaps being a woman made it easier for Macaulay to adjust her republicanism to fashionable sentimental values and apply republican and humane ideals to the education of women. After all, sensibility, sympathy, affections, and polite manners were allegedly more akin to females than to men. Moreover, Macaulay had nothing to lose by adopting sentimental values and neglecting some of the harsher republican virtues, which were irrelevant to women anyway. For male radicals, adopting sentimental values might have exposed them to the charge of being effeminate.

Being a woman certainly made Macaulay more aware of the sorry state of women's rights than any male author would have been. Indeed, it was hardly possible to be less aware of female rights than contemporary male radicals were. John Cartwright, for instance, could barely conceal his contempt when he rejected the claim of John Wesley and Josiah Tucker that

93 Ibid., 206–7.

the radicals' principles involving natural rights logically implied political rights for women.[94] Even Price, whose ethical theory was ahead of its time and who valued humane values more than other radicals, did not seem to notice that his criticism of denying Americans their rights might apply just as well to denying the rights of women: "But alas! it often happens in the *Political World* as it does in *Religion*, that the people who cry out most vehemently for Liberty to themselves are the most unwilling to grant it to others."[95] This reluctance is perhaps to be expected: The radicals rejected and questioned so many prevalent beliefs that it is not surprising they did not question their own position in relation to their wives.[96] Macaulay, however, took the bull by the horns: After she had adopted the role of the female patriot instructing her countrymen on their political rights and being a "simon-pure" republican for a decade, she was willing to take up the values of sentiment in her political work and employed both republicanism and sentiment as bases for the improvement of the position of women in society.

94 John Cartwright, *The Legislative Rights of the Commonalty Vindicated; Or Take Your Choice!* (1776), 2d ed. (London, 1777), 46–7.
95 Richard Price, *Observations on the Nature of Civil Liberty* (London, 1776), 92–3.
96 It should not be ignored, however, that Macaulay was less willing than radicals like Burgh or Priestley to recognize the rights of the lower middle classes. Although she was less strict in her later work, Macaulay wanted to keep the social hierarchy with respect to the middle and lower classes intact.

6

Between Liberalism and Republicanism: "Manners" in the Political Thought of Mercy Otis Warren

ROSEMARIE ZAGARRI

I

Historians have recently declared a truce in the debate concerning the relative influence of liberalism and republicanism during the revolutionary era of American history. James T. Kloppenberg, Isaac Kramnick, John Murrin, and Daniel T. Rodgers, among others, have concluded that neither liberalism nor republicanism dominated early American political thought.[1] Both are, in fact, more productively seen as fluid discourses rather than as fixed ideologies. As Forrest McDonald puts it, eighteenth-century Americans were "politically multilingual, able to speak in the diverse idioms of Locke, the classical republicans, Hume, and many others."[2] These divergent discourses ebbed and flowed over time and were strategically employed to meet the needs of various situations and events.

The new synthesis tends to assume that the discourses coexisted as complementary ideals. However, liberalism and republicanism (particularly classical republicanism) offer two different and at times contradictory visions of the individual, society, and the public good. Self-interest, for example, can conflict with one's ability to sacrifice for the common good. An assertion of individual rights and liberties can undermine an organic sense of

---

1 James T. Kloppenberg, "The Virtues of Liberalism: Christianity, Republicanism, and Ethics in Early American Political Discourse," *Journal of American History* 74 (June 1987): 9–33; Isaac Kramnick, "'The Great National Discussion': The Discourse of Politics in 1787," in Isaac Kramnick, *Republicanism and Bourgeois Radicalism: Political Ideology in Late Eighteenth-Century England and America* (Ithaca, N.Y., 1990), 260–88; John Murrin, "Can Liberals Be Patriots? Natural Right, Virtue, and Moral Sense in the America of George Mason and Thomas Jefferson," in Robert P. Davidow, ed., *Natural Rights and Natural Law: The Legacy of George Mason* (Fairfax, Va., 1986), 35–65; Daniel T. Rodgers, "Republicanism: The Career of a Concept," *Journal of American History* 79 (June 1992): 11–38.
2 Forrest McDonald, "The Intellectual World of the Founding Fathers," in Forrest McDonald, *Requiem: Variations on Eighteenth-Century Themes* (Lawrence, Kans., 1988), 9.

113

community. A belief in social equality challenges the presumption of hierarchy. How did people in early America reconcile these contradictions?

One American thinker who grappled with this tension was Mercy Otis Warren. In numerous plays, poems, satires, and in her magisterial three-volume *History of the Rise, Progress, and Termination of the American Revolution*, Warren articulated a vision of society that was simultaneously liberal and classically republican.[3] She expressed both a staunch dedication to the ideal of civic virtue and an unwavering commitment to civil liberties, a belief in the common good along with support for the pursuit of individual self-interest. Linking these two discourses was the concept of "manners." Like other eighteenth-century political thinkers Warren understood manners to mean something more than proper rules of etiquette or correct modes of social deportment. For her, manners referred to an internalized set of beliefs that regulate social behavior – the norms that produce sociability, benevolence, and civic virtue. If Americans practiced appropriate manners, according to Warren, then they could pursue their own interests as well as serve the common good. Manners thus eased the tensions between the individualistic thrust of liberalism and the communal impulse of classical republicanism.

Warren also employed the concept of manners for another purpose. Women, political thinkers agreed, were uniquely qualified to inculcate good manners. If America needed republican manners, it would be women who would instill them. In Warren's usage, the concept of manners assumed a gendered function, allowing women to shape the character, strength, and tenor of the new republic.

II

Mercy Otis Warren was one of the few political thinkers of revolutionary America who was also a woman. The sister of James Otis, the patriot, she received an education that was far more substantial than that of most females of her time. With her brother she was tutored in the classics of Greek and Rome as well as Shakespeare, Milton, and Pope. This instruction initiated in Warren a lifelong fascination with the life of the mind in

---

3 Mercy Otis Warren, *The Plays and Poems of Mercy Otis Warren*, ed. Benjamin Franklin V (Delmar, N.Y., 1980); Mercy Otis Warren, *History of the Rise, Progress, and Termination of the American Revolution interspersed with Biographical, Political and Moral Observations*, ed. Lester H. Cohen, 2 vols. (1805; reprint, Indianapolis, 1988); A Columbian Patriot, "Observations on the New Constitution, and on the Federal and State Conventions" (1788), in Herbert J. Storing, ed., *The Complete Anti-Federalist*, 7 vols. (Chicago, 1981), 4:270–87.

general and with political ideas in particular. As his own political career evolved, her brother James corresponded with Warren and encouraged her interest in affairs of state. Her husband, James Warren, recognized his wife's literary talents and supported her decision, made at the behest of John Adams, to begin writing political satires in support of the patriotic cause.[4] Throughout her long life (1728–1814) Warren produced published works and private correspondence that reveal a sophisticated analysis of early American political ideas.

Beginning in 1772 Warren published a series of plays that reflected classical republican themes.[5] In these works she lambasted Massachusetts Governor Thomas Hutchinson's overweening ambition, attacked British conspiracies against American liberty, and called on Americans to display virtue in the face of vice. Her poems, printed in various newspapers, aroused patriotic sentiment and mobilized resistance against England. A 1775 poem, for example, contrasted the corruption of Britain, where "Virtue turn'd pale, and freedom left the isle," with the virtue of the colonists, who willingly "quitted plenty, luxury, and ease" for the sake of their country.[6] Yet she also knew American men and women were susceptible to failings of their own. "The selfish passions, and the mad'ning rage/ For pleasure's soft debilitating charms" could have diastrous results. "Our country bleeds," she lamented, "and bleeds at every pore."[7] Virtue, a quintessentially republican trait, lay at the heart of the republican experiment. "Empire decays when virtue's not the base," she wrote in her play *The Sack of Rome*, "And doom'd to perish when the parts corrupt."[8] Such sentiments have led historians to label Warren one of "the most extreme among the American admirers of classical republicanism."[9]

Yet a liberal concern for individual liberties and personal freedom also permeated her work. She respected what has been called "negative freedom" – the freedom to be left alone. "I am for every one, doing as they

---

4 Rosemarie Zagarri, *A Woman's Dilemma: Mercy Otis Warren and the American Revolution* (Wheeling, Ill., 1995), 12–16, 48–77.
5 The early plays were "The Adulateur" (1772), "The Defeat" (1773), "The Group" (1775), all in Warren, *Plays and Poems*.
6 "A Political Reverie" (1775), in ibid., 191–2.
7 "The Genius of America Weeping the Absurd Follies of the Day – Oct. 10, 1778," in ibid., 246.
8 "Sack of Rome" (1785), in ibid., 80.
9 Paul A. Rahe, *Republics Ancient and Modern: Classical Republicanism and the American Revolution* (Chapel Hill, N.C., 1992), 351. Historians have considered Warren's classical republicanism much more thoroughly than her liberalism. See also Lester H. Cohen, "Mercy Otis Warren: The Politics of Language and the Aesthetics of Self," *American Quarterly* 35 (1983): 494, 497; Lester H. Cohen, "Explaining the Revolution: Ideology and Ethics in Mercy Otis Warren's Historical Theory," *William and Mary Quarterly* 37 (Apr. 1980): 200–18; Linda K. Kerber, "The Republican Ideology of the Revolutionary Generation," *American Quarterly* 37 (fall 1985): 483.

like," she told her son in 1797, "if not inconsistent with good morals or good manners."[10] To this end, Warren frequently returned to the issue of civil liberties. She saw Governor Hutchinson and the British as deliberately setting out to "quench the generous flame, the ardent love/ Of liberty in Servia's freeborn sons." By "destroy[ing] their boasted rights" Britain would, in effect, make the Americans into "slaves."[11] With the coming of war Americans fought to protect "the rights of men, the privileges of Englishmen, and the claim of Americans."[12]

After independence Warren sensed other threats to individual liberties. For one, the failure of the U.S. Constitution to include a Bill of Rights exposed the people to "future innovations" that would undermine their freedom.[13] The new, powerful centralized government would almost certainly find ways to chip away at cherished freedoms, including freedom of speech and trial by jury. As the only woman to speak out in the Constitutional debate (albeit pseudonymously as the "Columbian Patriot"), Warren took seriously her task of defending "the glorious fabric of liberty."[14] After ratification there were new enemies of freedom: The Federalists of the 1790s were, in her view, nothing less than "monarchists" obsessed with personal aggrandizement at the expense of the common good.[15] Only popular vigilance and constitutional limitations on the government's power could protect the people's rights.

Throughout her works Warren's commitment to liberalism existed, without apparent contradiction, alongside her support of classical republican ideals. The absence of tension reflects, in part, the fact that eighteenth-century Americans did not reify liberalism and republicanism the way contemporary historians have. They drew selectively and eclectically from a variety of intellectual sources. Describing the principles that animated the American Revolution, for example, Warren cited the works of what are today labeled "classical republican" authors, such as Milton and Harrington, in the same sentence that she mentioned the prototypical liberal, John Locke. "These were the opinions," she said in her *History of*

---

10 Mercy Otis Warren to James Warren Jr., June 4, 1797, Mercy Warren papers, Letterbook, 233 (reel 1, microfilm ed.), Massachusetts Historical Society, Boston. For a description of "negative freedom," see J. H. Hexter, "Republic, Virtue, Liberty, and the Political Universe of J. G. A. Pocock," in J. H. Hexter, *On Historians: Reappraisals of Some of the Masters of Modern History* (Cambridge, Mass., 1979), 301.
11 "The Adulateur," in Warren, *Plays and Poems*, 19.
12 *History of the Rise, Progress, and Termination of the American Revolution*, 2:630.
13 Ibid., 2:659.
14 A Columbian Patriot, "Observations on the New Constitution," in Storing, ed., *Complete Anti-Federalist*, 4:151–61.
15 *History of the Rise, Progress, and Termination of the American Revolution*, 2:663.

the Rise, Progress, and Termination of the American Revolution, "of Ludlow and Sydney, of Milton and Harrington: These were the principles defended by the pen of the learned, enlightened, and renowned Locke; and even Judge Blackstone, in his excellent commentaries on the laws of England."[16] There was another reason for the lack of tension, however. In Warren's thought the concept of "manners" mediated between liberal and classical republican discourses.

Warren derived her understanding of manners from her reading of Montesquieu and the thinkers of the Scottish Enlightenment. In *The Spirit of Laws* Montesquieu differentiated among manners, laws, and customs. "Manners and customs," he noted, "are those habits which are not established by the laws, either because they were not able, or were not willing to establish them." Whereas custom directed exterior behavior, manners related to "interior conduct."[17] Francis Hutcheson, David Hume, Adam Smith, and Lord Kames broadened and deepened the meaning of the term. As the Scots saw it, manners both refined and cultivated the moral sense and helped reconcile the individual with the duties of citizenship. Although related to virtue and morality, manners differed from them, comprising a form of social affectation that bound society together as a cohesive whole. "The laws of good manners," said Hume, were "a kind of lesser morality calculated for the ease of company and conversation."[18] Manners encouraged what Smith called "sympathy," a sense of empathy or benevolence toward other members of society.[19]

Whereas virtue was most appropriate to ancient polities, manners expressed an ethic more suitable in a modern, commercial society.[20] "Commerce," observed William Robertson, "softens and polishes the manners of men. It unites them, by one of the strongest of all ties, the desire of supplying their mutual wants."[21] Polished manners greased the wheels of social

---

16 Ibid., 2:630.
17 Charles Louis de Secondat, Baron de Montesquieu, *The Spirit of Laws*, ed. David Wallace Carrithers (1748; reprint, Berkeley, Calif., 1977), 294.
18 David Hume, "Of Political Society," in *Hume's Political Discourses*, ed. William Bell Robertson (1752; reprint, London, 1908), 250.
19 Adam Smith, *The Theory of Moral Sentiments; or, An Essay Towards an Analysis of the Principles by which Men Naturally Judge Concerning Conduct and Character, First of Their Neighbours, and then of Themselves* (1759; reprint, London, 1812), 385.
20 J. G. A. Pocock, "Virtues, Rights, and Manners: A Model for Historians of Political Thought" and "The Mobility of Property and the Rise of Eighteenth-century Sociology," both in J. G. A. Pocock, *Virtue, Commerce, and History: Essays on Political Thought and History, Chiefly in the Eighteenth Century* (Cambridge, 1985), 48–50, 117–23; Gordon S. Wood, *The Radicalism of the American Revolution* (New York, 1991), 213–25.
21 William Robertson, *The Progress of Society in Europe: A Historical Outline from the Subversion of the Roman Empire to the Beginning of the Sixteenth Century*, ed. and introd. Felix Gilbert (1769; reprint, Chicago, 1972), 67.

interaction and lessened social discord. According to the *New York Magazine*, the growing refinement of manners "promote[d] a mutual respect and
attention among the different classes of our citizens"; it enabled them to
"mutually sympathize with each other."[22] Such behavior contributed to the
overall harmony of society. "True and genuine politeness," claimed the *Rural
Repository*, "consists in our habitual regard for the feelings of others, and
will never stoop to the meanness of intentional offence."[23] Whereas ancient
polities demanded that their citizens bear arms for the common good,
commercial societies demanded something less drastic, a spirit of benevolence toward others.

Manners also provided the discipline that formed the foundation of the
social order and created norms that were, according to Edmund Burke, "of
more importance than law." "Manners," he said, "are what vex or soothe,
corrupt or purify, exalt or debase, barbarize or refine us, by a constant,
steady, uniform and insensible operation, like the air we breathe."[24] Manners
gave society its distinctive character. In a speech to the Massachusetts legislature Governor Caleb Strong argued, "We are generally apt to ascribe
too much to the efficacy of Laws and Government, as if they alone could
secure the happiness of the people; but no laws will be sufficient to counteract the influence of manners which are corrupted by vice and volup-
tuousness."[25] Government could do only so much; manners did the rest. If
the people's manners decayed, so would society.

Having absorbed Enlightenment notions, Warren integrated the concept
of manners into her own writing. She saw a distinctive brand of American
manners as the basis for the American character. At its core was a dedication to industry, thrift, and frugality. The availability of land, lack of feudal
tenure, and willingness of Americans to work hard produced, according to
Warren, a general "equality of condition" and "simplicity of manners."[26]
Other circumstances nurtured these values. Lacking a hereditary nobility,
America had escaped the pernicious influence of aristocrats who introduced superfluous wants or invidious distinctions into society. Americans

22 "On Refinement of Manners," *The New-York Magazine; or, Literary Repository* (July 1791), 406. For
   an analysis of the class dimensions of manners, see Vera Nünning, "From 'Honour' to 'Honest': The
   Invention of the (Superiority of the) Middling Ranks in Eighteenth-Century England," *Journal for
   the Study of British Cultures* 2 (1995): 19–41.
23 "Communications. – No. IX," *Rural Repository* (Hudson, N.Y.), Dec. 25, 1824, 1:116.
24 Edmund Burke, "Letters on a Regicide Peace" (1796), cited in Daniel Walker Howe, *The Political
   Culture of the American Whigs* (Chicago, 1979), 236.
25 "Speech," *Mercury and New-England Palladium* (Boston), Jan. 21, 1806.
26 *History of the Rise, Progress, and Termination of the American Revolution*, 1:14.

were satisfied, Warren claimed, with "a due mean between profusion and parsimony."[27]

Yet American "simplicity of manners" also faced significant challenges.[28] As Americans prospered, they lost some of their healthy sense of restraint. In her 1779 poem titled *Simplicity*, Warren observed:

> Each improvement on the Author's plan,
> Adds new inquietudes to restless man.
> As from simplicity he deviates,
> Fancy, prolific, endless wants creates;
> Creates new wishes, foreign to the soul,
> Ten thousand passions all the mind control.[29]

In the prerevolutionary years Warren had come to believe that the British had devised a plot to corrupt American manners. After the Coercive Acts, "The people trembled for their liberties, the merchant for his interest, the tories for their place, the whigs for their country, and the virtuous for the manners of society."[30] At the same time Warren hoped that manners would provide the means of resistance. Their simplicity would unite Americans in the face of moral turpitude and generate the vigor necessary to vanquish Britain.

Over the course of the Revolution, Warren became convinced that war itself was deleterious to good manners. "A state of war has ever been deemed unfavourable to virtue," she wrote to John Adams in 1778. "But such a total change of manners in so short a period, I believe was never known in the history of man. Rapacity and profusion, pride and servility, and almost every vice is contrasted in the same heart."[31] Warren eventually concluded that Americans themselves were their own worst enemy. Writing to Catharine Macaulay in 1789 she moaned, "We are too poor for Monarchy – too wise for Despotism, and too dissipated, selfish, and extravagant for Republicanism."[32] In Warren's scheme, self-indulgence and "intoxicated ambition" produced a "degenerate, servile race of beings" who

---

27 "Oeconomy," in "Alphabet for Marcia" (n.d), Mercy Warren papers, box 1, Massachusetts Historical Society.

28 *History of the Rise, Progress, and Termination of the American Revolution*, 2:644.

29 "Simplicity" (1779), in Warren, *Plays and Poems*, 232.

30 *History of the Rise, Progress, and Termination of the American Revolution*, 1:87.

31 Mercy Warren to John Adams, Oct. 15, 1778, in Massachusetts Historical Society, ed., *Warren-Adams Letters, Being Chiefly a Correspondence Among John Adams, Samuel Adams, and James Warren*, 2 vols. (Boston, 1917), 2:54.

32 Mercy Otis Warren to Catharine Macaulay, July 1789, Mercy Warren papers, Letterbook, 28 (reel 1, microfilm ed.), Massachusetts Historical Society.

were unfit for self-government.[33] By contrast, true freedom meant personal autonomy, as expressed in a simplicity of manners.

By the end of the 1790s, as she wrote the last chapter of her *History of the Rise, Progress, and Termination of the American Revolution,* Warren sensed that American manners faced a new challenge, in the form of an influx of foreigners into the country. Like many other members of the founding generation Warren feared that foreign immigrants did not share the attitudes, habits, or opinions that would nurture republican government. Abandoning any guise of historical objectivity, she urged her readers to shield themselves from these insidious influences: "Let not the frivolity of the domestic taste of the children of Columbia," she declared, "nor the examples of strangers of high or low degree, that may intermix among them, or the imposing attitude of distant nations, or the machinations of the bloody tyrants of Europe . . . rob them of their character, their morals, their religion, or their liberty."[34] A reassertion of good American manners, especially simplicity, would counteract the threat.

Good manners were particularly crucial in a republic. In a monarchy the crown set the tone of government and acted as the ultimate guarantor of the people's rights and liberties. In a republic, however, the people were the font of government and the protectors of their own liberties. Warren, like Edmund Burke, seemed to believe that manners were as important as laws. In the *History of the Rise, Progress, and Termination of the American Revolution* Warren attributed a quote to Montesquieu that read, "A violation of manners has destroyed more states than the infraction of laws."[35] In her view a successful regime depended not simply on the formal structure of government but on the people's shared values, internalized self-restraint, and voluntary obedience of the laws. "A deterioration in the people's manners," Warren warned, "weakens the sinews of the state."[36] Bad manners, including indolence, licentiousness, selfishness, and aristocratic pretension, could undermine republican government. Good manners would sustain both the letter and spirit of the law.

Manners would also temper the individualistic impulses unleashed with the growth of commerce. Despite its benefits, commerce, as Warren saw it, introduced greater opportunities for luxury, acquisitiveness, and "the Rest-

---

33 *History of the Rise, Progress, and Termination of the American Revolution,* 2:646.

34 Ibid., 2:687.

35 Ibid., 2:686, 687n. The editor, Lester H. Cohen, observes that whereas Warren attributed the quotation to Montesquieu, he cannot locate its source. Montesquieu does discuss "the reciprocal influence of laws and manners" in Book XIX.

36 Ibid., 2:646. The source of this quote is not identified, either by Warren or Cohen.

less pursuit of objects seldom attainable."[37] Good manners would prevent commercial success from becoming unbridled consumption. "I think he who aids in setting bounds to our wishes, governing our appetites, and checking the excrescences of imagination," Warren told her son, "may do more service to mankind than those who condemn the progress of industry."[38] Simplicity and benevolence would modulate the pursuit of individual self-interest and prevent one person's rights from infringing on another's. "What is generally called politeness is but the imitation of what we ought to be: civil, kind & attentive, but never servilely complaisant."[39] Manners thus prevented freedom from becoming license.

Warren's use of the concept of manners provided the conceptual link between republican virtue and liberal self-interest. As the glue of public affection that held society together, manners would prevent individualism from becoming excessive self-indulgence. Rights would include obligations toward the community, not just freedom from interference. As the public dimension of private virtue, its dictates would compel individuals to moderate the pursuit of their own interests and encourage respect for others. In Warren's view, manners, virtue, and rights were complementary characteristics, all crucial to the success of a modern republic.

Warren's emphasis on manners had further significance: It allowed her to find a place for women in republican government and society. Throughout her works Warren drew on the four-stage theory of history in analyzing the evolution of societies. Widely known and accepted in the eighteenth century,[40] this theory postulated that each society progressed over time through discernible phases of development, from savagery to civilization. In the movement from the hunter stage to the pastoral, to the agricultural, to the mercantile, trade expanded and society attained greater levels of leisure and material comfort. "The style of manners which takes place in a nation," commented Smith, "may commonly upon the whole be said to be that which is most suitable to its situation. Hardiness is the character most suitable to the circumstances of a savage; sensibility to those of one who lives in a very civilized society."[41] Manners thus reflected a society's level of social development.

---

37 Mercy Warren to John Adams, Apr. 27, 1785, in Massachusetts Historical Society, ed., *Warren-Adams Letters*, 2:252.
38 Mercy Otis Warren to Winslow Warren, Nov. 29, 1784, Mercy Warren papers, Letterbook, 306 (reel 1, microfilm ed.), Massachusetts Historical Society.
39 "Alphabet for Marcia" (n.d.), Mercy Warren papers, box 1, Massachusetts Historical Society.
40 Ronald L. Meek, *Social Science and the Ignoble Savage* (Cambridge, 1976), 31–6, 76–91, 99–209; Rosemarie Zagarri, "Morals, Manners, and the Republican Mother," *American Quarterly* 44 (June 1992): 192–215.
41 Smith, *Theory of Moral Sentiments*, 365.

Not incidentally, the status of women improved as society progressed.
Women occupied a dual role in this theory: They reflected society's degree
of civilization and moved the community further in that direction. Women,
it was believed, refined and polished the manners of men. At each stage they
softened men's passions, moderated their brutality, and turned their minds
to more genteel endeavors. The more highly developed a society, the more
civilized its men and the more elevated its women. "Women came to be
regarded," Lord Kames remarked, "in proportion as national manners
refined."[42] By the fourth stage, the mercantile, women were treated as men's
"equals" – as friends and companions rather than slaves or concubines. In
"refined and polished nations," commented John Millar, women were "entitled to the same freedom [with men], upon account of those agreeable qualities they possess, and the rank and dignity which they hold as members of
society."[43] Although equality, in this sense, did not encompass the right to
vote or hold public office, it did result in a new kind of social equality.

Despite its limitations, the four-stage theory along with the concept of
manners enabled Warren to conceive of a place for women in the
American republic. Through their influence over manners women gave
society its tone and character, and shaped the behavior that existed outside
of written laws and formal political institutions. Women's actions could
create a virtuous, obedient citizenry – or produce a selfish, decadent mob.
"The men possess the more ostensible powers of making and executing
the laws," wrote James Tilton. "The women, in every free country, have an
absolute control of manners: and it is confessed, that in a republic, manners
are of equal importance with laws."[44] Warren clearly understood the significance of this role. "I think we lessen the dignity of our own sex," she
told her niece, "when we accede to the opinion that our deportment indi-
vidually, is of little consequence to the world: The first rudiments of education are planted by the feminine hand, and . . . the early traits are seldom
eradicated from the breasts of those who must tread the stage and regulate
both the political and religious affairs of human life."[45] Women thus, in a
sense, determined the success or failure of the republican experiment.

---

42 Lord Kames (Henry Home), *Six Sketches on the History of Man*, abridged ed. (Philadelphia, 1776),
   235.
43 John Millar, "The Origin of the Distinction of Ranks; or, An Inquiry into the Circumstances Which
   Give Rise to Influence and Authority in Different Members of Society" (1771), in William C.
   Lehmann, ed., *John Millar of Glasgow, 1735–1801* (New York, 1979), 225.
44 James Tilton, M.D., "An Oration, pronounced on the 5th July, 1790," *Universal Asylum & Columbian
   Magazine* 5 (Dec. 1790): 372.
45 Mercy Otis Warren to Sally Sever, July 20, 1784, Mercy Warren papers, Letterbook, 466 (reel 1,
   microfilm ed.), Massachusetts Historical Society.

When a young woman complained that a man had denigrated the female intellect, she responded by affirming women's "appointed subordination" to men. Gender roles existed, she suggested, "perhaps for the sake of order in families." Yet she did not leave her answer at that. Her attention to extrapolitical norms of behavior allowed her to envision a social order in which gender distinctions were irrelevant. With proper education, she insisted, women no longer would be considered inferior to men. "Let us by no means acknowledge such an inferiority as would check the ardour of our endeavors, to equal in all mental accomplishments the most masculine heights."[46] Warren conceived of society as a meritocracy in which neither wealth nor lineage, nor sex determined one's social status. These beliefs gave her confidence in a gender-blind future. "When these temporary distinctions subside," she asserted, "virtue alone will be the test of rank."[47] Warren's only proviso concerned the locus of women's political activity. She preferred that women exercise their influence through "the soft whisper of private friendship" rather than in public arenas. As long as one's views were "just and honorary," Warren told Catherine Macaulay, it was "immaterial" whether men or women expressed them.[48] Through their influence on society's manners women would come to occupy a place of honor, merit, and equality in the American polity. They themselves would be the living mediators between liberalism and republicanism.

III

Warren was not the only person, not even the only woman, to explore the connections between republicanism and liberalism. Her friend Macaulay attempted to find her own resolution to the problem.[49] Her solution, as Vera Nünning suggests elsewhere in this book, was to invoke concepts that had their intellectual origins in many of the same Enlightenment treatises that Warren drew on. Like Warren, Macaulay modified the harsh strictures of classical republicanism by suggesting that citizens cultivate sympathy and politeness rather than the strict martial virtues of ancient times. Like Warren, Macaulay believed that republican values, rightly understood, enhanced women's status and created opportunities for women to make a

---

46 Mercy Otis Warren to a very young lady, n.d., Mercy Warren papers, Letterbook, 114–15 (reel 1, microfilm ed.), Massachusetts Historical Society.
47 Ibid., 115.
48 Mercy Otis Warren to Catharine Macaulay, Dec. 29, 1774, Mercy Warren papers, Letterbook, 6 (reel 1, microfilm ed.), Massachusetts Historical Society.
49 Zagarri, *Woman's Dilemma*, 54–5, 84, 90; Bridget Hill, *The Republican Virago: The Life and Times of Catharine Macaulay, Historian* (Oxford, 1992), 124–8.

contribution to the polity. Although neither Warren nor Macaulay conceived of women as voting citizens, they both believed women did have an important role to play as educated wives and mothers. Thus, in attempting to reconcile the tensions between liberalism and republicanism, both authors inadvertently found a back door to an eighteenth-century brand of feminism.

Warren's use of the concept of manners represented an ambitious attempt to come to terms with the contradictory strains of liberalism and republicanism in early American political thought. In her view, manners mediated between rights and virtues by inculcating a social ethic that would balance individual rights with social responsibilities. Not incidentally the concept also allowed her to envision a place for women. Appropriate manners, then, provided one key to the success of the republican experiment. Ardent Republican that she was, Warren surely would have seconded what her hero, Thomas Jefferson, observed: "It is the manners and spirit of a people which preserve a republic in vigor. A degeneracy in these is a canker which soon eats to the heart of its laws and constitution."[50]

---

50 Thomas Jefferson, *Notes on the State of Virginia*, ed. Thomas Perkins Abernethy (1785; reprint, New York, 1964), query no. 19, p. 158. For discussions of civility and manners in a contemporary republic, see Stephen L. Carter, *Civility: Manners, Morals and the Etiquette of Democracy* (New York, 1998), and Willard Gaylin and Bruce Jennings, *The Perversion of Autonomy: The Proper Uses of Coercion and Constraints in a Liberal Society* (New York, 1996).

The Transition from
Republicanism to Liberalism

7

The Liberal and Democratic Republicanism of the First American State Constitutions, 1776–1780

WILLI PAUL ADAMS

AMERICAN REPUBLICANISM IN THE CONTEXT OF EUROPEAN LIBERALISM

Why investigate the first American state constitutions for their republican, liberal, and democratic content? Because, together with the Declaration of Independence, they most authentically document the irreversible American commitment to republicanism in 1776. We have no more authoritative statement of the initial American variant of republican government. After a decade of public claims to their rights within the British Empire and over a year after the beginning of armed resistance, the world was given notice by rebellious American colonial political leaders that the extant governments were no longer effective. Within little more than a decade these constitutions became the foundation for a further step of nation building: for the replacement of the Articles of Confederation by the Constitution of the United States, for the evolution from *Staatenbund* (federation of states) to *Bundesstaat* (federal state). The Federal Constitution of 1787–91 built on and fulfilled the goals of 1776 to the degree that Southern regional interests permitted. Many of the political institutions and procedures agreed on in the Federal Constitution were derived from or written in reaction to previous experiences with state constitutions.[1]

---

1 Donald Lutz, "The State Constitutional Pedigree of the U.S. Bill of Rights," *Publius* 22 (1992): 19–45; Willi Paul Adams, "The State Constitutions as Analogy and Precedent," in A. E. Dick Howard, ed., *The United States Constitution: Roots, Rights, and Responsibilities* (Washington, D.C., 1992), 3–22. Bernard Bailyn emphasizes the evolutionary continuity of constitutional thought and practice from resistance to independence and from state constitution making to the 1791 Bill of Rights. See Bailyn's postscript, "Fulfillment: A Commentary on the Constitution," in Bernard Bailyn, *Ideological Origins of the American Revolution*, enlarged ed. (1967; reprint, Cambridge, Mass., 1992). Cf. Willi Paul Adams, *The First American Constitutions: Republican Ideology and the Meaning of the State Constitutions in the Revolutionary Era*, expanded ed. (1980; reprint, Madison, Wis., 2000), chap. 15.

Only after the successful establishment of a relatively powerful American state was republican, popular, or democratic government – all three terms were used at the time – perceived in Europe as a fundamental challenge to the dominant traditional combination of aristocracy and monarchy. As the German historian Leopold von Ranke explained in a fascinating series of private lectures he gave before the monarchical ruler of Bavaria after the failed revolutions of 1848:

By abandoning English constitutionalism and creating a new republic based on the rights of the individual, the North Americans introduced a new force in the world. Ideas spread most rapidly when they have found adequate concrete expression. Thus republicanism entered our Romanic/Germanic world. . . . Up to this point, the conviction had prevailed in Europe that monarchy best served the interests of the nation. Now the idea spread that the nation should govern itself. But only after a state had actually been formed on the basis of the theory of representation did the full significance of this idea become clear. All later revolutionary movements have this same goal. . . . This was the complete reversal of a principle. Until then, a king who ruled by the grace of God had been the center around which everything turned. Now the idea emerged that power should come from below. . . . These two principles are like two opposite poles, and it is the conflict between them that determines the course of the modern world. In Europe the conflict between them had not yet taken on concrete form; with the French Revolution it did.[2]

What Ranke rightly assessed as "the complete reversal of a principle" began when emigrated Europeans fought their motherland's colonial rule and put essential ideas of the Enlightenment into practice. The experiment in real life caught the attention of European courtiers as well as *philosophes* and, in profound if difficult-to-document ways, stimulated the cause of intellectual enlightenment and political liberalism in Europe.[3]

Thus, American republicanism played a crucial role in the development of European liberalism, and academic discourse as well as political debate during the nineteenth and early twentieth centuries recognized this historical significance of American republicanism as part of the great struggle for power that Ranke referred to in 1854: The struggle, since the seventeenth century, of the rising bourgeois middle class for a government responsive to its needs, against the traditional secular and clerical authori-

---

2 My translation from Leopold von Ranke, *Über die Epochen der neueren Geschichte: Historisch-kritische Ausgabe*, ed. Theodor Schieder and Helmut Berding (Munich, 1971), 415–17.
3 Peter Gay concluded in his comparative essay on the Enlightenment: "America became the model for Europeans of good hope – living, heartening proof that men had a capacity for growth, that reason and humanity could become governing rather than merely critical principles" (Peter Gay, "Enlightenment," in C. Vann Woodward, ed., *The Comparative Approach to American History* [New York, 1968], 36, 41).

ties who served the needs of only a privileged segment of the population.[4] The American political scientist Louis Hartz in the 1950s also placed his interpretation of the American Revolution squarely in the transatlantic world of the Enlightenment and early liberalism, if only to point out the difference the absence of European feudal institutions made in colonial and postcolonial America. Hartz's often caricatured interpretation is no disembodied history of ideas; rather, it is driven by comparisons of European and American socioeconomic conditions.[5]

More recent interpretations of the intellectual history of the American Revolution have neglected this wider context in favor of an internal American protonational discourse analysis that divides the American Whig ideology of 1776 into an admirable republican strain and a somehow less admirable liberal element. Historians J. G. A. Pocock, Gordon S. Wood, and others saw an initial communal and virtuous type of republicanism superseded by an individualistic, competitive, and market-oriented Lockean liberalism.[6]

In reality, when it came to drafting state constitutions in 1776, there was no coherent theory of a specifically American "republican" or "liberal" government to be put into practice, only English Whig theory of constitutional or free government – adapted to colonial American circumstances.

4 British political scientist Harold Laski recorded this tradition in his sketch of "The Rise of Liberalism" for the introductory section of Edwin Seligman, ed., *Encyclopedia of the Social Sciences*, 15 vols. (New York, 1930), 1:103–24; he drew a line from Locke's justification of Parliament's victory over monarchical absolutism in 1688 to twentieth-century liberalism via its American incarnation.
5 Louis Hartz, "American Political Thought and the American Revolution," *American Political Science Review* 46 (1952): 339–41; Louis Hartz, *The Liberal Tradition in America: An interpretation of American Political Thought Since the Revolution* (New York, 1955). Hartz's intentions, weaknesses, and strengths are discussed by Marvin Meyers, Leonard Krieger, and Harry Jaffa, with Hartz's reply in *Comparative Studies in Society and History* 5 (1962–3): 261–84, 365–77.
6 Gordon S. Wood's influential *The Creation of the American Republic* (Chapel Hill, N.C., 1969) traces the great distance that American constitution makers traveled, from a virtue-based republican idealism in 1776 to more realistic modern interest group politics as expressed by the federal constitution of 1787. J. G. A. Pocock emphasizes elements of Machiavellian civic humanism in American rhetoric in *The Machiavellian Moment: Florentine Political Thought and the Atlantic Tradition* (Princeton, N.J., 1975), where he states "the confrontation of virtue with corruption constitutes the Machiavellian Moment" (546). Critic Daniel T. Rodgers provides a revealing thumbnail sketch of the false dualism in his *Contested Truths: Key Words in American Politics Since Independence* (New York, 1987), 9. The historiography is fully elucidated in Rodgers's "Republicanism: The Career of a Concept," *Journal of American History* 79 (1992): 11–38. Bailyn, who is sometimes erroneously cited as an authority on that flawed dichotomy, recently concluded in a tone of exasperation that the thinking of the Federalist leaders in the ratification debates of 1787–8 could not be understood in those terms at all. See Bailyn, *Ideological Origins*, 351–2. Michael P. Zuckert demonstrates Pocock's confusion of issues on the level of political theory or philosophy and problems of political science or practice in his *Natural Rights and the New Republicanism* (Princeton, N.J., 1994), 165, passim. A thorough engagement with Pocock's thesis and a convincing reminder of the shaping forces of the early modern English market economy and early capitalism on American "liberalism" broadly defined is provided in Joyce Appleby, *Liberalism and Republicanism in the Historical Imagination* (Cambridge, Mass., 1992).

Nor was there a clearly defined set of institutions, a generally accepted model of republican government, for the advocates of American independence to establish. What came to be the American form of republican federal government evolved under the pressure of events between 1774 and 1791. After a transitory period of government by committees on the local level and a loose continental coordination, the Continental Congress, in its de facto declaration of independence on May 15, 1776, urged the surviving legislative assemblies or new revolutionary conventions of the thirteen rebelling colonies to act on the premise that henceforth all powers of government should be "exerted under the authority of the people of the colonies" as expressed in "full and free representation."[7] What this meant in practice was to be decided by each state's revolutionary activists. The proposal of a model constitution drafted by the Continental Congress for adoption by each state found little support. From 1776 to the end of the war, eleven states wrote one or two constitutions; six of them included a separate text called a declaration of rights. (Connecticut and Rhode Island modified their colonial charters only slightly and governed by them until 1818 and 1842, respectively.)[8]

The period of experimentation came to a provisional end only with the power-sharing agreement reached behind closed doors in Philadelphia in the summer of 1787 by the delegates of the twelve states whose political elites were ready to take the final step from a confederation of states to a federal nation. The subsequent election of delegates to the state ratifying conventions and their deliberations and decisions in 1788 provided a bold new way to put the Enlightenment ideal of popular sovereignty into practice.[9]

THE VOCABULARY OF 1776: "REPUBLICAN" AND "DEMOCRAT"
AS SYNONYMS

A close look at the public debates surrounding the writing of the first state constitutions does not suggest a systematic distinction between "republican" versus "democratic" ideas or institutions. The violent rejection of kingly, aristocratic, and colonial government in 1775–81 aimed at a new type of "popular government" – called "republican" or "democratic" by contemporaries – which henceforth evolved without another revolution-

---

7 Worthington Chauncey Ford, ed., *Journals of the Continental Congress, 1774–1789*, 34 vols. (New York, 1968), 4:357–8.

8 Adams, *First American Constitutions*, chaps. 1–3.

9 Jürgen Heideking, *Die Verfassung vor dem Richterstuhl: Vorgeschichte und Ratifizierung der amerikanischen Verfassung 1787–1791* (Berlin, 1988).

ary break into the type of American democracy based on manhood suffrage that Alexis de Tocqueville came to observe in 1831.[10]

The definitions of "republic," "republican government," and "democracy" were not determined by an American philosopher's treatise on government. Only in the debate over independence did "republican" begin to change from a defamatory cliché, used by Loyalists to stigmatize critics of the British constitution, to the positive term that evoked patriotic identification with the new order.[11] The first radical rejection of the British constitution in favor of independence and republicanism was published by Thomas Paine anonymously in January 1776. *Common Sense* rejected monarchy in any form, even the post-1688 British type of "mixed government." To single out one family from the rest of the community and to invest it with a hereditary claim to rule seemed incompatible with legitimate government. Republican and monarchical principles were mutually exclusive because a community of equals had no place for a monarch, and thus the division of mankind into kings and subjects was arbitrary. Paine advocated republican government not only as the natural government of the long distant past but also as the form of government of the future, something modern that Americans could realize as soon as they turned their backs on the bankrupt monarchical systems of Europe. At some point in the past, Paine granted, the House of Commons had guaranteed the famous English liberties and had therefore once justly been called "the republican part of the constitution." But now these "republican virtues" were lost, and the government of Britain was just as monarchical as those of Spain and France.[12]

Paine did not use the terms "democracy" or "democratic" in *Common Sense*. He also drew no distinction between limited and absolute monarchies but rather condemned all forms of monarchical rule.[13] Similarly, the much less inflammatory John Adams, in his pamphlet of *Thoughts on*

10 Gordon S. Wood, *The Radicalism of the American Revolution* (New York, 1992), 95. In his *Rebels and Democrats: The Struggle for Equal Political Rights and Majority Rule during the American Revolution* (Chapel Hill, N.C., 1955) Elisha P. Douglass investigated the strength of the more or less "popular" or "democratic" group or party and the would-be "aristocratic" party in the power struggles in the newly independent states without taking recourse to the rigid republican/liberal opposition.

11 Examples are cited in Willi Paul Adams, "Republicanism in Political Rhetoric before 1776," *Political Science Quarterly* 85 (1979): 397–421. See also the contributions by Caroline Robbins, Pauline Maier and Jack P. Greene in *Library of Congress Symposia on the American Revolution*, vol. 1: *The Development of a Revolutionary Mentality: Papers* (Washington, D.C., 1972).

12 Thomas Paine, *Common Sense*, ed. Isaac Kramnick (Harmondsworth, U.K., 1976), 81, passim.

13 In 1792 Paine differentiated between "republic" and "democracy" in the second part of his *Rights of Man*, ed. Henry Collins (Harmondsworth, U.K., 1969), pt. 2, chap. 3: "Of the Old and New Systems of Government." He called the American system of government "the only real republic in character and in practice that now exists" because it "is wholly on the system of representation" (200).

Government published in March 1776, avoided using the terms "democracy" and "democratic" and offered no explication of the traditional terminology concerning forms of government. But it is not at all evident that he had in mind a rigorous distinction between a republic and a democracy. Not until a decade later, when the Federal constitution was discussed, did Adams publicly reject the interchangeable use of "republican" and "democratic" government.[14]

There is ample proof of the synonymous use of "democratic" and "republican" during the War for Independence. In May 1776 Patrick Henry called himself "a Democrat on the plan of our admired friend, J. Adams." A few weeks later Richard Henry Lee approvingly described the constitution that was taking shape in Virginia as "very much of the democratic kind." In July 1776 Samuel Adams agreed with a correspondent that "the Soul or Spirit of Democracy" was "virtue." An unidentified "Spartanus," who developed his view of the new order in the *New York Journal* in June 1776, took for granted that New York would have to become "a proper Democracy." In August 1776 the *Maryland Gazette* called for the introduction of that most just of all governmental forms, a "well regulated democracy." The county convention of Mecklenburg in North Carolina demanded in November 1776 that the new constitution be "a simple Democracy or as near it as possible." In May 1777 Alexander Hamilton spoke positively of the New York constitution as "a representative democracy."[15]

An equal number of instances could be cited for when "republic," "republican," and "republicanism" were used for the same phenomenon. The *Providence Gazette* published an essay in August 1777 on different forms of government, and by its definition of democracy it acknowledged the interchangeability of "democracy" and "republican government" in current American usage: "By a *democracy* is meant that form of government where the highest power of making laws is lodged in the common people, or persons chosen from them. This is what by some is called a republic, a com-

---

14 John Adams, "Thoughts on Government," in Charles Francis Adams, ed., *The Works of John Adams*, 10 vols. (Boston, 1850–6), 4:193–209.
15 Patrick Henry to R. H. Lee, May 20, 1776, quoted in H. J. Eckenrode, *The Revolution in Virginia* (Boston, 1916), 162; R. H. Lee to Charles Lee, June 29, 1776, in James Curtis Ballagh, ed., *The Letters of Richard Henry Lee*, 2 vols. (New York, 1911), 1:203; Samuel Adams to Benjamin Kent, in Harry Alonzo Cushing, ed., *The Writings of Samuel Adams*, 4 vols. (New York, 1904), 3:305; "Spartanus," using the title "The Interest of America – Letter III," *New York Journal*, June 20, 1776, in *American Archives*, 4th ser., 6:994; *Maryland Gazette*, Aug. 15, 1776; William L. Saunders, ed., *The Colonial Records of North Carolina*, 10 vols. (Raleigh, N.C., 1886–90), 10:870a; Alexander Hamilton to Gouverneur Morris, May 19, 1777, in Harold C. Syrett and Jacob E. Cooke, eds., *The Papers of Alexander Hamilton*, 27 vols. (New York, 1961), 1:255.

monwealth, or free state, and seems so the most agreeable to *natural right and liberty*."[16] In May 1776 an anonymous article in the *Virginia Gazette* defended republican government with the observation that the English constitution had simply proven to be unsuitable for America. Genoa, Holland, Lucca, Switzerland, and Venice provided imperfect models of republican government, but in America there would arise the "best republicks, upon the best terms that ever came to the lot of any people."[17]

Only among the cautious Whig leaders of Essex County in Massachusetts does one find a public statement distinguishing democratic from republican government, at least by implication. Their extensive, well-reasoned comments on the unsatisfactory 1778 draft of the Massachusetts constitution listed as possible forms of government "despotic government," "monarchy," and "a republican form," obviously following Montesquieu. Anyone in Massachusetts who seriously proposed a "despotic government," the town delegates of Essex declared, insulted the people; and anyone who considered "monarchy" would be hissed off the stage. Only "republican government" was compatible with the desires of Americans. In its ideal form it should incorporate both aristocratic and democratic elements: "Among gentlemen of education, fortune and leisure, we shall find the largest number of men, possessed of wisdom, learning, and a firmness and consistency of character. . . . Among the bulk of people, we shall find the greatest share of political honesty, probity, and a regard to the interest of the whole. . . . The former are called the excellencies that result from the aristocracy; the latter, those that result from a democracy."[18] This usage subordinates "democracy" to the more encompassing category of "republican government" by limiting its meaning to the plebiscitarian element.[19]

REPUBLICAN AND DEMOCRATIC PRINCIPLES

Only in postmortem analysis does it make sense to systematically distinguish "democratic" or "republican" from "liberal" elements in the early state constitutions. Thus, in retrospect, I propose the following definitions:

16 *Providence Gazette*, Aug. 9, 1777.   17 Purdie's *Virginia Gazette*, May 17, 1776.
18 Oscar Handlin and Mary Handlin, eds., *The Popular Sources of Political Authority: Documents on the Massachusetts Constitution of 1780* (Cambridge, Mass., 1966), 330, 334–5.
19 See the history of the term *Demokratie* in Otto Brunner, Werner Conze, and Reinhart Koselleck, eds., *Geschichtliche Grundbegriffe: Historisches Lexikon zur politisch-sozialen Sprache in Deutschland*, 9 vols. (Stuttgart, 1972–97), 1:821–99. This article fails to record the usage documented here and, accordingly, needs to be corrected on 847 and 855; the article by Wolfgang Mager on the term *Republik* includes American usage (5:590–5).

Republican is any form of government without a monarch or a legally privileged aristocracy;

Republican or *democratic* are those rules and institutions that aim at putting into
practice their principles of popular sovereignty, the equality of all citizens,
and the precedence of the common good over private interests;

Democratic are elements that extend participation in political decision making
as voters or office holders to an ever greater part of the population;

Liberal are those qualities of the civic culture that check the exercise of political power by constitutional arrangements in order to protect individual rights
and interests, specifically those connected with holding private property and
producing, buying, and selling.

All these structural elements are present in the first state constitutions. They
appear explicitly or implicitly in the following contexts: when the source
of the new governments' legitimacy is stated; when the great goals of the
new governments are named, that is, securing the common good as well
as private interests, protecting the liberty and equality of the (still restricted
but potentially open) citizenry; when the modes of political representation
and the functioning of the new governments are regulated.

In the American colonies as well as in Europe, the core idea of republicanism was popular sovereignty, that is, the derivation of legitimate government not from a ruler's divine right but from the consent of the
governed. Popular sovereignty is the fundamental principle of Western
democracy. The Declaration of Independence appealed to this principle in
justifying the claim of the Continental Congress to speak for a new nation.
The state constitutions codified the idea at the level at which citizens com-
municate among themselves: "All power is vested in, and consequently
derived from, the people; . . . magistrates are their trustees and servants, and
at all time amenable to them," proclaimed the Virginia Declaration of
Rights even before the Declaration of Independence, in June 1776.[20]
Delaware's constitution, the first to be adopted after independence had been
declared, was particularly clear: "All Government of right originates from
the people, is founded in Compact only, and instituted solely for the Good
of the Whole." Therefore, "Persons instrusted with the legislative and executive Powers are the trustees and Servants of the Public, and as such
accountable for their Conduct."[21] The Massachusetts Declaration of Rights
of 1780, drafted by John Adams, combined in one sentence the principle
of popular sovereignty and the burning issue of distributing powers
between the states and a joint federal government: "The people of this

---

20 Francis N. Thorpe, ed., *The Federal and State Constitutions* (Washington, D.C., 1909), 7:3813.
21 Quoted in Adams, *First American Constitutions*, 136.

Commonwealth have the sole and exclusive right of governing themselves as a free, sovereign, and independent state; and do, and forever hereafter shall, exercise and enjoy every power, jurisdiction, and right, which is not, or may not hereafter, be by them expressly delegated to the United States of America, in Congress assembled."[22]

This conviction united the victorious American Whigs of 1776. After a decade of intense public debate among the major mainland colonies and the crown and parliament, and after one year of warfare, the principle of popular sovereignty was written into the first American constitutions as a matter of course, as the protocol of a concluded revolution. No longer at issue among the constitution drafters of 1776 was the principle of popular sovereignty itself but the degree of its implementation. In Adams's words: "It is certain, in theory, that the only moral foundation of government is the consent of the people. But to what an extent shall we carry this principle?"[23] Adams's skeptical undertone was typical for the decision makers of 1776. We encounter the same clarity of conception in the passages on popular sovereignty that characterize the statements relating to the common good and the duty of the good, "virtuous" citizen to subordinate his personal interests should the functioning or fate of the republic require it.

The proponents of independence in 1776 were not idealists who expected their fellow citizens to behave like members of a sectarian commune who renounce private property and other personal interests in the service of their small *res publica*. On the contrary, the revolutionaries expected their new form of popular self-government to serve their interests as well as the common or public good better than imperial government by a king-in-parliament had done. They knew that kingless government could fail: The collapse of Oliver Cromwell's Commonwealth dramatized the inadequacy of a government based on religious zeal and the harsh subordination of individual interests to collective ideals. Over a century of economic development, with nearly global trade and a much heralded population growth, had made Britain's North American coast part of the rapidly modernizing North Atlantic economy. In 1776 the merchants, gentleman farmers, lawyers, doctors, ministers, teachers, and printers of Boston and New York, Philadelphia and Charleston knew themselves to be part of this world. Republican government was to serve economic expansion, not the return to the quiet world of an isolated Puritan or Pietist-Quaker commonwealth.

22 Robert J. Taylor, ed., *Massachusetts: Colony to Commonwealth* (Chapel Hill, N.C., 1961), 129.
23 John Adams to James Sullivan, May 26, 1776, in Adams, ed., *Works of John Adams*, 9:375.

In the discussions that took place during the framing of the state constitutions, conflict between different interest groups was taken for granted, and government was organized to mediate the differences, not eliminate them. Virginia's bill of rights held up the common good as the compass to guide all governmental action: "Government is, or ought to be, instituted for the common benefit, protection, and security of the people, nation, or community; of all the various modes and forms of government, that is best which is capable of producing the greatest degree of happiness and safety."[24] Pennsylvania's Declaration of Rights followed Virginia's wording and defined the criteria of good government as the "common benefit, protection and security of the people, nation or community." Good government was inconsistent with "the particular emolument or advantage of any single man, family, or set of men, who are part only of that community."[25]

The idea of a common or public good was publicly discussed in language taken from the world of commerce. A Philadelphia pamphlet published in 1777 explained: "Public good is, as it were, a common bank, in which every individual has his respective share; and consequently whatever damage that sustains, the individuals unavoidably partake of the calamity."[26] This image was sufficiently ambiguous to reflect American reality accurately. It assumed a fundamental community of interests; that is why they submitted to the general terms of doing business. The analogy also allowed for the potentially conflicting interests among competing customers as a normal situation in human affairs. In real political life from 1776 on, the legislative assemblies were to provide the decision-making arena for negotiating conflicts of interest. In the fierce debate over Pennsylvania's unicameral legislature the advocates of a single powerful chamber and their opponents took conflicting interests for granted. The unicameralists feared that in a bicameral legislature one chamber would be dominated by "landed interests" and the other by "commercial interests." "To say, there ought to be two houses, because there are two sorts of interest, is the very reason why there ought to be but one, and that one to consist of every sort."[27]

The drafters of the constitution shared David Hume's pessimistic view of human nature. Alexander Hamilton, for one, subscribed to Hume's idea that private interest was the average person's strongest motivation. In 1775 Hamilton quoted Hume verbatim:

---

24 Thorpe, ed., *Federal and State Constitutions*, 7:3813.
25 Ibid., 5:3082–3.
26 John Hurt, *The Love of Our Country* (Philadelphia, 1777), 10.
27 Anonymous, *Four Letters on Interesting Subjects* (Philadelphia, 1776), 20; see Douglas Arnold, *A Republican Revolution: Ideology and Politics in Pennsylvania, 1776–1790* (New York, 1989), on the fierce struggle over constitutional reform in Pennsylvania.

In contriving any system of government, and fixing the several checks and controuls of the constitution, every man ought to be supposed a knave; and to have no other end in all his actions, but private interest. By this interest, we must govern him, and by means of it, make him co-operate to public good, notwithstanding his insatiable avarice and ambition.[28]

The state constitutions of 1776 took the frailties of human nature into account and did not call for a new Adam with the special virtues of a revolutionary *citoyen*. There was no need to develop a realistic "liberal" assessment of human nature in the decade after 1776.

This pessimistic view of human nature was quite compatible with the constitutional guarantees of equal rights to all citizens. "That all men are created equal" was a logical a priori article of the Whig contractual model of the ideal relationship between the individual and society. As such, equal rights and equal opportunity became guiding values of American republicanism. With these words, English subjects in America rejected their unequal status as colonials in the empire. The state delegates assembled in the Continental Congress on July 4, 1776, did not call for leveling inequalities in status and wealth and did not advocate unqualified manhood suffrage. However, American reformers in various fields (including the opponents of slavery and of property qualifications for voting) demanded fulfillment of the founders' principal commitment to citizen equality.

The three pre-1781 state constitutions that speak explicitly of equality do so in the same logical context as the Declaration of Independence, that is, when they mention the partners of the imaginary social contract that underlies legitimate government. Virginia's Declaration of Rights was the first to proclaim "All men are by nature equally free and independent, and have certain inherent rights, of which, when they enter into a state of society, they cannot, by any compact, deprive or divest their posterity." Pennsylvania's bill of rights used almost the same words, whereas Massachusetts changed the wording slightly, without apparent difference in meaning, to "All men are born free and equal."[29]

The Virginia slaveholders who voted for the equality clause in their bill of rights were no hypocrites. In their thoroughly racist, male-dominated, patrician model of Virginia society, the decision-making citizenry simply did not include blacks, white women, indentured servants and apprentices, or propertyless white men (unless their fathers were freeholders). None of

---

28 Syrett and Cooke, eds., *Papers of Alexander Hamilton*, 1:95. On Hamilton's pessimistic view of human nature, see Gerald Stourzh, *Alexander Hamilton and the Idea of Republican Government* (Stanford, Calif., 1970), chap. 3.

29 Thorpe, ed., *Federal and State Constitutions*, 1889, 3082, 3813.

the first state constitutions abolished slavery. Only the as-yet-unrecognized
territory of Vermont outlawed slavery.

The Green Mountain Boys were not the only Americans during the War
of Independence to recognize the dynamics of equality as encompassing
all men. The town meeting of Hardwick, Massachusetts, voted 68 to 10 in
1780 to demand (unsuccessfully) the rewriting of the first article in the
Massachusetts Declaration of Rights to read: "All men, whites and blacks,
are born free and equal."[30] Only a small minority of Americans shared
this ideal of equal political rights for all (adult men) in 1776. The Federal
Constitution of 1787–91 remained silent on the issue, and even the
more modest "equal protection of the law" clause was not written into the
Constitution until 1868, by way of the Fourteenth Amendment.

Agreeing on and proclaiming these republican principles in 1776 was
no end in itself. The next stop was the crafting of institutions and opera-
tive rules. Organizing "popular consent and popular control" of government was the main task of the state constitutions.[31] To the extent that they
achieved this goal, it represented a major step in the evolution of American democracy.

Electing representatives and thereby delegating authority had been an
obviously successful part of colonial self-government. That profound experience could not possibly have been upset in 1776 by a wave of emotional
majoritarian republicanism. The state constitutions no longer had to justify
the principle of representation. It was part and parcel of American republicanism long before James Madison wedded both terms in the tenth *Federalist* article. Alexander Hamilton articulated a consensus when, in 1777,
he characterized New York's constitution as a "representative democracy"
that will serve the state well: "A representative democracy, where the right
of elections is well secured and regulated and the exercise of the legislative, executive and judiciary authorities, is vested in select persons, chosen
really and not nominally by the people, will in my opinion be most likely
to be happy, regular and durable."[32]

At issue was not the principle but its application to changing local circumstances, that is, the allotment of more seats in the legislature to the
expanding frontier regions, to the disadvantage of the coastal settlements.
Writing new constitutions was an opportunity to correct injustices that in
many instances had been under discussion for many years. In Virginia the

---

30 See town meeting resolve of May 25, 1780, in Handlin and Handlin, eds., *Popular Sources*, 830.
31 Donald S. Lutz, *Popular Consent and Popular Control: Whig Political Theory in the Early State Constitutions* (Baton Rouge, La., 1980).
32 May 19, 1777, in Syrett and Cooke, eds., *Papers of Alexander Hamilton*, 1:255.

tidewater counties were powerful enough to insist on the old principle of
two representatives per county – to the disadvantage of the growing pied-
mont population. In Pennsylvania, however, the system was made fairer
through a redistribution roughly in line with population growth. Massachusetts also proved to be flexible and revised the system. Of the 266
representatives, Boston was allowed twelve (up from four); small towns sent
only one delegate. Calls for an even fairer distribution of seats by a formula
that combined a region's number of inhabitants with the amount of taxes
paid into the state coffers went unheeded.[33] Ever since, the simple number
of inhabitants has been the yardstick of American courts when they
examine the constitutionality of voting districts.

The delegation of authority to legislators and executive officers was tempered by the short duration of their appointments. All state constitutions
prescribed short terms of office as a precaution against the misuse of power.
Representatives, senators, councilors, and the governor of Massachusetts, to
mention an extreme example, were all to serve for one year only. Other
constitutions added rules restricting re-election in order to strengthen the
old republican principle of rotation in office.[34]

LIBERAL CHECKS ON POWER

What accounted for the long-range success of republican government in
the United States was an exercise in moderation. Neither the state constitutions nor the Federal Constitution declared the will of the new sovereign, the people, to be absolute. Republicanism in America was not carried
to its Puritan or Jacobin extreme.[35] Popular government in America, since
1776, has been restrained by "unalienable" rights of the individual, an idea
we have come to call the core value of liberalism.

An important step in safeguarding citizens' rights was the clear distinction of regular legislation from the fundamental rules of lawmaking itself
that were written down in a constitution and could not be changed by
the legislature. This modern concept of a republican constitution evolved
during the drafting of the American state constitutions between 1776
and 1780. The first constitutions were still drafted by the revolutionary

33 Adams, *First American Constitutions*, 236–9.
34 See table of terms of office varying from one to five years in Adams, *First American Constiutions*, 245.
35 On the contrast to the French republicans see Horst Dippel, "The Changing Idea of Popular Sovereignty in Early American Constitutionalism: Breaking away from European Patterns," *Journal of the Early Republic* 16 (1996): 32–3.

legislatures and voted into existence after three readings like ordinary laws. But in May 1776 the town meeting of Pittsfield, Massachusetts, demanded popular ratification: "A Representative Body may form, but cannot impose said fundamental Constitution upon a people. . . . It must be the Approbation of the Majority which gives Life and being to it."[36] The new procedure was put into practice only after five years of debate and experiment, when in 1780 a presumed majority of town meetings approved the constitution of Massachusetts that had been drafted by a specially elected constitutional convention.[37] When the time came for constitution writing on the federal level the concept of a written constitution as paramount law and practical experience with organizing the people's constituent power were already at hand.[38]

Constitution making was not understood by the republicans of the first hour as a one-time act of a "law giver" in the mode of their college Latin book heroes Solon and Lycurgus. All state constitutions modestly and realistically prescribed various sorts of amending procedures. Only the later importance of judicial review as a means of de facto constitutional amendment was not foreseen in 1776, but its development by judicial activism was made possible by the new American concept of a constitution as fundamental law.[39]

The separation of powers in the state constitutions documents the extent to which the majoritarian-democratic impulse was checked by the liberal distrust of power and a skeptical view of human nature. The argument was cogently summed up in the *Pennsylvania Evening Post* in March 1776 by a question-and-answer piece written in the Whig language of "mixed government":

Q. Why would you have your government so mixed?
A. Because the experience of ages has proved that mixed governments are the best.
Q. Simplicity is amiable and convenient in most things, why not in government?
A. Human nature is such, that it renders simple government destructive, and makes it necessary to place one power over against another to balance its weight.[40]

36 Taylor, ed., *Massachusetts*, 27–8.
37 The preserved town meeting returns are edited in Handlin and Handlin, eds., *Popular Sources*, 473–930.
38 Gerald Stourzh, " 'Constitution': Changing Meanings of the Term from the Early 17th to the Late 18th Century," in Terence Ball and J. G. A. Pocock, eds., *Conceptual Change and the Constitution* (Lawrence, Kans., 1988). Donald S. Lutz, *The Origins of American Constitutionalism* (Baton Rouge, La., 1988), chap. 8.
39 Dippel, "Changing Idea of Popular Sovereignty."
40 *Pennsylvania Evening Post*, Mar. 16, 1776. It was in this tradition that James Madison declared in *Federalist* No. 51: "Ambition must be made to counteract ambition."

Learned references to the reigning model of Newtonian physics supported commonsense psychology: A society's equilibrium and harmony could be stabilized by balancing one political force with a countervailing force.[41]

Because the colonial assemblies had for decades insisted on being the local version of Parliament, bicameral legislatures became the norm in 1776. The new republican names "Senate" and "House of Representatives" designated traditional Whig institutions. In the absence of an aristocracy in the European sense, candidates for the senate in most states had to own more property and be older than representatives and voters. Even the one-chamber legislature that Pennsylvania was used to was changed to the regular two-chamber parliament by 1790, but not without a fierce rhetorical and political struggle.[42]

Virginia's was the first republican constitution since the *Instrument of Government*, under which Britain had been governed from 1653 to 1657, to include the principle of the separation of powers in express terms: "The legislative, executive and judiciary departments shall be separate and distinct, so that neither exercise the powers properly belonging to the other: nor shall any person exercise the powers of more than one of them at the same time." This rule did not allow the governor to be a member of the legislature; the framework was laid in 1776 for the American style of presidential government on the federal level.

All states gave the republican governor an essential role in lawmaking, in some cases even strongly reminiscent of the royal governor's veto power. No Swiss-style plural executive was instituted in 1776. The colonial precedent of a powerful single-person executive did not so much frighten as inspire the constitution writers on the state level. The federal presidency, drafted in 1787, was a governorship writ large. (Four states called their governor "president.") In Massachusetts in 1780 the office of governor was continued under the traditional title and with the formal address "His Excellency." His veto power could be overridden by a two-thirds majority in senate and house. To avoid corruption by patronage he was to appoint judges, sheriffs, and other paid officeholders only "with the advice and consent" of a nine-man council, to be elected jointly by house and senate. This procedure clearly prefigured the watchdog function invested in the U.S. Senate in 1787.

Legal institutions, procedures, and doctrine were least affected by new republican values. Many of the American revolutionaries were English

---

41 Richard Striner, "Political Newtonianism: The Cosmic Model of Politics in Europe and America," *William and Mary Quarterly*, 3d ser., 52 (1995): 583–608.
42 Arnold, *Republican Revolution*.

lawyers. The only law they knew was the Common Law and English constitutional jurisprudence. One change, however, was easy to make: Most
full-time judges were to hold office "during good behaviour" (no longer
"during the king's pleasure"), which meant for life – unless insanity, alco-
holism, or criminal behavior led the legislature to impeach and remove
them from public office.

The state constitutions codified rights that hosts of English Whig lawyers
and writers had discussed since Sir Edward Coke drafted the Petition of
Right of 1628. It was not a question of the colonists having read John
Locke's *Treatise of Government*. How many colonists had read Locke did not
matter; they participated in the entire political culture that was based on
natural-rights thinking. In the colonies, as in England, hundreds of pamphlets and thousands of speeches, charges to juries, political sermons, and
anonymous newspaper essays discussed political issues in terms of the subjects' rights and the government's authority.

In this discourse any government's very reason for being was the protection of inalienable rights, of which the Declaration of Independence
named "life, liberty, and the pursuit of happiness." Virginia's Declaration of
Rights explained these "inherent rights" as "the enjoyment of life and
liberty, with the means of acquiring and possessing property, and pursuing
and obtaining happiness and safety." Virginia did not invoke divine authority, in contrast to "nature's God" invoked in the Declaration of Independence. Delaware briefly named "Life, Liberty and Property." The
Declaration of Rights of the Commonwealth of Massachusetts listed the
right of "seeking and obtaining . . . safety and happiness," guaranteed
the liberty of the press, and reserved to the people the "unalienable . . .
right to institute government and to reform, alter, or totally change the
same." But "the people" – presumably the majority of the adult men qualified to vote – were not to be all-powerful. In the preceding public debate
a group of moderate Republicans in Essex County had justified its demand
for a detailed bill of rights with the conviction that even "the supreme
power is limited, and cannot control the unalienable rights of mankind."[43]

Freedom of religion was inherent in the logic of radical Whig thought,
but in 1776 the political will to separate governmental authority and private
religious faith was not yet strong enough in all states. Massachusetts granted
freedom of worship but did not separate state and churches. The voters of
Massachusetts were the slowest to demand neutrality of their state government in its relations to all religious groups. Until 1833, Massachusetts

---

43 Essex result in Handlin and Handlin, eds., *Popular Sources*, 330–2.

privileged the Congregational churches by raising a tax exclusively for their benefit. Five states did abolish the privileged status of the Anglican church with their first constitutions. Rhode Island had forbidden the establishment of an official church ever since it received its charter in 1663.[44] Virginia passed the Act for Establishing Religious Freedom in 1786. Only with great effort did Thomas Jefferson and James Madison convince enough voters and representatives that "religious liberty" is one of "the natural rights of mankind."[45]

There was no explicitly republican political economy that needed codifying in the first constitutions. The safety of private property from arbitrary governmental requisition was part of the Whig culture that colonial Englishmen shared with all inhabitants of the realm. James Harrington, more than any other republican writer well known in the colonies and in seventeenth- and eighteenth-century England, had emphasized the necessary connection between the ownership of land and the distribution of political power. A political order was stable only when both overlapped. Nothing could have sounded more plausible to land-hungry colonists whose ideal of economic security was ownership of the family farm or plantation. Adams invoked Harrington's authority in 1776: "Harrington has shown that power always follows property. This I believe to be as infallible a maxim in politics, as that action and reaction are equal, is in mechanics."[46] But the American republicans followed Harrington only so far. To check the human passion for acquiring unlimited private wealth, Harrington also proposed the limitation of private property by an "agrarian" law. This the constitution writers of 1776 did not accept. The idea did make its way into the draft of Pennsylvania's bill of rights, which was published as a broadside and contained the clause: "An enormous Proportion of Property rested in a few Individuals is dangerous to the Rights, and destructive of the Common Happiness of Mankind; and therefore every free State hath a Right by its Laws to discourage the Possession of such Property."[47] Even Pennsylvania's revolutionary legislature, which was ready to experiment with a unicameral system, rejected this restrictive republican idea in the wide-open American setting. So much for those who try to find civic humanist frugality and fear of corruption by wealth in 1776 Pennsylvania.

44 John K. Wilson, "Religion Under the State Constitutions, 1776–1800," *Journal of Church and State* 32 (1990): 753–73.
45 "An Act for Establishing Religious Freedom," Jan. 16, 1786, reprinted in Henry Steele Commager, ed., *Documents of American History*, 7th ed. (New York, 1963), 125–6.
46 Adams ed., *Works of John Adams*, 9:376–7.
47 "Essay of a Declaration of Rights," undated broadside in the broadsides collection of the Historical Society of Pennsylvania, Philadelphia.

In reality, the acquisition of property was nothing to be ashamed of for Christians who took seriously the biblical injunction "Replenish the Earth and subdue it." English Whigs understood this command not as a license for a small group of privileged families to rule but applied it to the acquisition of property by "the people," as Locke put it in §25 of the *Second Treatise of Government.*

Jefferson's "pursuit of happiness" included Locke's broadly conceived acquisition of property. The property clauses in the first declarations of rights prove that in 1776 "happiness" and "property" were so closely connected with each other that naming one sufficed to invoke both. Virginia, Pennsylvania, and Massachusetts listed the freedom to acquire property among the precontract "inalienable" rights and included "happiness" and "safety" in the same sentence.

This is not to deny that many Americans also felt unsettled by the transition to early industrialization and that for some the language of civic humanism, as transmitted through the English Harringtonians, provided some of the rhetoric to deplore civic corruption through wealth.[48] This past-oriented element of American republicanism played its role in the revolutionary and early national periods, but only as the occasional sting of conscience. The impulse to modernize – that is, to expand agriculture and manufacturing to the advantage of the growing middle classes and to open the political process to their participation – was overpowering.

Property ownership as a precondition for voting was challenged by few Americans in 1776. Before 1800 the majority of white adults probably accepted graded property qualifications for voters and candidates, just as they accepted restricting the vote to men.

The dominant view in 1776 took the ownership of property as an indicator of personal independence as well as of a binding commitment to the fate of the community – both desirable qualities in those who shared in governing the town, colony, or state. Virginia's Declaration of Rights made the right to vote dependent on a "permanent common interest with, and attachment to the community." Implementation of this principle was left to the legislature, which meant that the 1769 election law remained in force: electors of the House of Representatives had to own at least a freehold of 25 acres or a town lot with a 12-by-12-foot house on it or a freehold of 50 acres without a dwelling. In Pennsylvania the July 1776 election of the Provincial Convention was considered special because it was to draft

---

48 Joyce Appleby, *Liberalism and Republicanism in the Historical Imagination* (Cambridge, Mass., 1992), chap. 3: "Modernization Theory and Anglo-American Social Theories."

and ratify a new constitution. The revolutionary preparatory committee therefore decided to extend the franchise and the right to be a candidate to include all adult militia members. The Pennsylvania constitution was not so inclusive and restricted the right to vote to taxpayers and the adult sons of freeholders, which in effect meant the male heads of households. In Massachusetts a laundry list of property qualifications for voters (an estate worth 60 pounds sterling) and candidates for the House (an estate worth 200 pounds), the Senate (an estate worth 600 pounds), and the governorship (an estate worth 1000 pounds) was written into the constitution. Only in Vermont was every adult male given the right to vote.[49] Weighting votes in proportion to taxes paid was not discussed as an option.

The restrictive effect of property qualifications varied over time and between regions, and has not yet been precisely measured. A summary of informed guesses by Chilton Williamson assumes that around 1780 the property clauses by and large denied the vote in elections to their state legislatures to between a quarter and one-half of the white male adults.[50]

No new consensus on property qualifications for voters and candidates for public office developed in the following decade. The drafters of the national constitution agreed only to be silent about property qualifications for federal office holders. Setting qualifications for their electors they left to the state legislatures – another one of the great compromises of 1787. Since irresistible economic growth and expansion of the nation's territory was expected, property qualifications for voting and office holding were accepted until they were phased out as unnecessary in the 1820s.

CONCLUSIONS

The first state constitutions document a pragmatic type of political thinking and institution building, various elements of which we can label republican, democratic, or liberal. The constitution writers built on their knowledge of and in many cases their personal experience with the colonial assemblies. Given popular sovereignty as the only remaining rationale of legitimate government in the newly independent states and given the largely middle-class nature of white American society, the new kingless regime, stabilized by the Federal Constitution of 1787–91, successfully combined the republican principle of popular sovereignty and democratic

49 Peter Force, ed., *American Archives*, 4th ser., 7:553; Adams, *First American Constitutions*, 196, 295, 300.
50 Chilton Williamson, *American Suffrage: From Property to Democracy, 1760–1860* (Princeton, N.J., 1960); Adams, *First American Constitutions*, 198–207.

participatory practices with the liberal protection of individual freedoms and rights.

Between 1765 and 1830 European settlers in certain parts of North America proved capable of organizing their political decision making in a comparatively inclusive – free, democratic, republican, liberal – way, whereas during the same period most Europeans at home failed to do so. Imperial government was replaced in the thirteen rebelling colonies by republican authorities simultaneously on local, state, and federal levels. Hence, American federalism, from the beginning, was not bedeviled by the postabsolutist notion of monolithic national sovereignty that contributed to the failure of the French Revolution and to other failures in the painful growth of liberalism in Europe. Breaking with the one-power-center concept of sovereignty was a precondition for an effective national government in 1787–91, which in turn proved the viability of republicanism as the fundamental logic and institutional framework for the government of a large territory with an economically and culturally diverse population.

8

Bennington and the Green Mountain Boys: The Emergence of Liberal Democracy in Vermont, 1760–1850

ROBERT E. SHALHOPE

For some time now historians and political theorists have been actively engaged in a search for the origins of liberal America. Ironically, they have discovered that throughout the nineteenth century, a time in which the United States became one of the most liberal societies in the world, no clear, sustaining ideology of liberalism ever emerged. Even after British devotees of Adam Smith and Jeremy Bentham fashioned a powerful liberal ideology in England, Americans continued to view themselves as republicans. Republicanism – a familiar ideology permeating all walks of life – continued to shape the attitudes of Americans; it provided them with meaning and identity in their lives. Liberalism – an unarticulated behavioral pattern more than a sharply delineated mode of thought – unconsciously shaped their daily activities. Thus, most Americans clung to a harmonious, communal view of themselves and their society even while behaving in a materialistic, competitive manner.

Because of this stubborn affinity for republicanism, the liberal, democratic society that emerged in nineteenth-century America became a paradoxical blend of the traditional and the modern. Caught up in market forces over which they had little control and, perhaps, even less understanding, Americans obstinately attempted to understand their changing world in familiar terms. More often than not the socioeconomic transformations taking place throughout American society – increasingly complex and quite often confusing – gave rise to unintended consequences. Perhaps nowhere was this more true than in Bennington, Vermont. There, between 1760 and 1850, three distinct strains of republicanism vied for dominance. Out of this dialectic among the egalitarian communalism of Strict Congregationalists, the democratic individualism of Green Mountain Boys, and the hierarchical elitism of Federalist gentlemen emerged an entirely new political culture: a liberal democracy. None of the participants in this process anticipated such a result. Indeed, none of them fully comprehended what they had created. But then, few, if any, of these individuals ever completely understood how they and their society had changed over the years.

This chapter provides an account of these changes and the manner in which the townspeople of Bennington responded to them. As such it is a part of the larger story not only of the origins of liberal America but of the significance of that cultural form for American society today.

This story begins with the struggles that took place throughout the 1770s on the New Hampshire Grants (present-day Vermont) between settlers holding land titles from the governor of New Hampshire and others with New York titles to the same property.[1] During this time Ethan Allen published a number of essays that became the foundation of subsequent political thought in Bennington.[2] In these publications Allen provided a detailed exposition of a struggle between a small faction of aristocratic gentlemen and an entire community of hardworking farmers. He developed an ideological perspective based on an egalitarian society of independent landholders. Slowly he began to articulate a position – a yeoman persuasion – that validated the efforts of ordinary citizens.

Even at this time, though, Allen's egalitarianism faced determined resistance in Vermont because of striking demographic changes taking place throughout the state. Migrants from centers of Old Light strength in eastern Massachusetts and western Connecticut came to Vermont in such numbers that they overwhelmed New Light majorities in some townships and seriously contested their control in many others. In addition, this tide of immigration brought an influx of gentlemen. Many were college-educated lawyers; all firmly believed in a traditional social and political order in which common people exhibited an unquestioning deference and respect toward their "superiors." These gentlemen and the Old Light migrants viewed the egalitarian attitudes of the New Lights and Green Mountain Boys – the very men who had defied New York authority, supported the Revolution, and created an independent state – with utter disdain. Town after town in Vermont became fractured by a struggle between residents' conflicting cultural values.

---

1 For the clearest analysis of the birth of Vermont, see Matt Bushnell Jones, *Vermont in the Making, 1750–1777* (Cambridge, Mass., 1939).
2 See particularly "Lover of Truth and Reason," Connecticut *Courant*, Mar. 31, 1772; "Friend to Liberty and Property," Connecticut *Courant*, Apr. 28, 1772; and *A Brief Narrative of the Proceedings of the Government of New York* (Hartford, Conn., 1774).

Bennington did not escape such a confrontation. Whether by accident, circumstance, or design, the settlement pattern in Bennington village assumed clear cultural manifestations by the late 1770s. Those committed to the values of a simple agrarian life of rough equality established themselves in the "Up-Hill" section of the village known as Courthouse Hill; more cosmopolitan, genteel families resided in the "Down-Hill" area commonly referred to as Meetinghouse Hill.[3] Samuel Robinson, Stephen Fay, and John Fassett – the town's original Strict Congregational founders – lived uphill; an influx of recent migrants – young gentlemen such as Isaac Tichenor, Colonel Nathaniel Brush, Colonel Joseph Farnsworth, and Noah Smith – settled in the downhill region. These men, together with Elijah and Eldad Dewey, sons of the town's first minister, formed the core of Meetinghouse Hill society.

Political tensions that developed in Bennington and throughout Vermont during the 1780s reflected these cultural divisions.[4] Vermonters divided their loyalties between a faction composed of common, ordinary citizens and one made up of cosmopolitan, genteel individuals. Thomas Chittenden, an egalitarian farmer, and Matthew Lyon, once an indentured servant, led the former, which had controlled the government of the state from its inception in 1777. However, a faction led by Tichenor and Nathaniel Chipman, college-educated gentlemen and trained attorneys, gradually began to gain power within the government.

Following Vermont's entrance into the Union on February 18, 1791, these same groups continued to vie with each other for social and political dominance within Bennington and throughout the state. After statehood, though, the battle lines became ever more sharply drawn and the conflict increasingly bitter. During this time the tension between those espousing a simple, egalitarian communalism and those committed to a more cosmopolitan, hierarchical perception of society continued to increase. Finally, in the fall of 1797 – following Chittenden's death in August of that year – Tichenor succeeded in being elected governor of Vermont. For their part, though, the citizens of Bennington voted overwhelmingly against Tichenor in every election.

Such stubborn opposition to Tichenor sprang from a dogged loyalty on the part of most Bennington freemen to an egalitarian heritage rooted not only in the original foundations of the town and its Strict Congregational

3 *Index to the Contents of The Vermont Historical Gazetteer*, ed. Abbie M. Hemenway (Rutland, Vt., 1923), v, 29–31.
4 For a succinct analysis of politics in Vermont during this period, see Aleine Austin, *Matthew Lyon: "New Man" of the Democratic Revolution, 1749–1822* (University Park, Pa., 1981).

church but also in the struggle against Yorker aristocrats that had united the New Lights and Green Mountain Boys. During the Revolution, Allen had grafted an exaltation of the ordinary yeoman to this opposition to aristocracy – an exaltation that became ingrained in the thought and language of Robinson, Nathan Clark, Fassett, and other leaders of the Revolutionary movement within Bennington. Following Chittenden's death, Lyon became both the lightning rod for these populist emotions and the principal spokesman of the emergent yeoman ethic. He constantly pitted independent, hardworking producers against idle, unproductive members of society. In this way he helped mold commonly held, yet seemingly inchoate convictions – beliefs that had long seemed too instinctive and their outward manifestations, too occasional, scattered, and ephemeral to assume the strength of a coherent belief system – into a powerful social and political ideology.

For their part, downhill leaders, who were by this time proud to call themselves Federalists, supported a social ideal that stressed stability, harmony, dependence, and the common good.[5] More than anything else, they identified with established authority emanating from a hierarchical social and political order. They esteemed their "betters" and felt obliged to guide and direct those "inferior" to themselves. They considered a stable, structured society to be an anchor of security and identity in a rapidly changing, chaotic world. They remained very much aware of inequalities in society and intended to maintain a governing elite, supported by the votes of the people, by strengthening traditional habits and customs of deference through family, church, and energetic government.

Given such intense beliefs, the fierce partisanship affecting state and national politics throughout the 1790s permeated Bennington's annual town meetings and election days. Political excitement in the village was not, however, limited to these occasions; the partisanship on these days paled in comparison to that manifested at the annual commemorations of July 4 and August 16, when the townspeople celebrated national independence and the victory at Bennington in 1777. Emotions became so strident on these occasions that the two parties had to stage separate celebrations. Naturally, the party faithful took the opportunity not only to praise the principles of their own cause but to impugn those of their opponents.

---

5 For insight into Federalist beliefs, see David H. Fischer, *The Revolution of American Conservatism: The Federalist Party in the Era of Jeffersonian Democracy* (New York, 1965), and James M. Banner Jr., *To the Hartford Convention: The Federalists and the Origins of Party Politics in Massachusetts, 1789–1815* (New York, 1970).

Whereas Federalist gatherings, with their emphasis on an organic society based on order and hierarchy, were generally simple and decorous, Republican celebrations tended to be larger and more exuberant affairs. Over the years Bennington Republicans toasted hundreds of principles, ideals, and individuals at their annual celebrations. They did, however, repeat particular toasts in one form or another at nearly every gathering. Certain concepts – republicanism, equality, democracy, American womanhood, agriculture, and domestic manufacturing – assumed a profound saliency for them. It was the figure of the independent yeoman, however, that dominated their public declarations of faith. "Democratic Farmer" declared that the confrontation between Federalists and Republicans was essentially "a conspiracy of the *indolent* against the *industrious*."[6] Americans were divided into two classes: "those who gain a livelihood by their own industry and those who get it by art or strategem, . . . by what is commonly called head work." Farmers, mechanics, and manufacturers made up the first class; judges, lawyers, priests, and merchants comprised the second. The merchants were the most insidious. By manipulating prices, credit, and the flow of goods, they were able to exploit the industrious farmer. By running hardworking people into debt and then holding them to the letter of the law, merchants supported a whole cadre of lawyers, sheriffs, and judges – men who "live by the sweat of your brows, and ride in their carriages, and strut and puff about the street, and call you the vulgar and rabble."[7] These observations of "Farmer" revealed the essential core of Republican thought in Bennington: a belief that America's productive classes were locked in a struggle for survival against idle nonproducers.

Bennington's Republicans thought that the answer to the machinations of the merchants was local manufacturing, whether in the home or in the mills beginning to appear along the Walloomsac River and its tributaries. Their own spinning wheels would free farm families from dependence on the foreign goods sold by local merchants, whereas new woolen mills not only provided a market for farmer's wool but produced cloth that further released them from the grasp of merchants. Republicans thereby recognized a dynamic relationship between manufacturing and the independence of the yeoman. It was for this reason that they toasted domestic manufactures as well as agriculture at their annual holidays. Indeed, they often combined the two by celebrating "Agriculture and Manufactures – one in political sympathies."[8]

6 *Vermont Gazette* (Bennington), Aug. 22, 1808.
7 *Green Mountain Farmer* (Bennington), June 3, 1811.
8 *Vermont Gazette*, Aug. 22, 1808.

Like their fellow countrymen, Republicans in Bennington gained increased precision of language and greater clarity of thought regarding the condition of American society from prominent Republican newspapers, such as the Philadelphia *Aurora* and the *National Intelligencer*, which local subscribers circulated among their fellow townsmen.[9] In this way Bennington's uphill people integrated their own thoughts, feelings, and circumstances with those of Republicans throughout the nation, thereby unself-consciously assimilating a powerful social ideology – Jeffersonian-Republicanism – that gave increased meaning and legitimacy to their own yeoman persuasion.

The Jeffersonian concepts absorbed by Bennington Republicans rested on Revolutionary principles long familiar to the great bulk of Americans.[10] These ideas integrated a strong commitment to John Locke's insistence on the protection of property and the good of the people as the only legitimate end of government with a libertarian fear of power and the enslavement of the people at the hands of corrupt officeholders. Believing that industrious, self-reliant citizens represented the natural economy of America, Jeffersonians made the commercial prosperity of ordinary individuals the primary economic base for a democratic, progressive nation.

Jeffersonian-Republicanism thus integrated the virtuous yeoman ideal of classical republicanism with Adam Smith's concept of the self-interested individual to form a radical new moral theory of government and society. Fragmenting society into its individual human components, it endowed each with a fundamental economic character and a natural capacity for personal autonomy. Equally significant, its proponents invested the independent producer with the moral qualities long associated with the virtuous citizen extolled by classical republicanism.

Once the principal beliefs of Jeffersonian-Republicanism had been thoroughly absorbed by Bennington Republicans, their own yeoman persuasion finally assumed the character of a coherent social philosophy. Having achieved legitimacy through association with similar ideas being articulated by an increasingly powerful national movement, its primary concepts took on a life of their own with the potential to shape thought and social behavior. Ironically, at the very time that the persuasion assumed such power, its

9 See, e.g., the Harwood diary, entries for Apr. 24, June 22, July 15, 1807. This diary is in the Bennington Museum, Bennington, Vermont.
10 For Jeffersonian-Republican thought, see John Zvesper, *Political Philosophy and Rhetoric: A Study of the Origins of American Party Politics* (New York, 1977); Lance Banning, *The Jeffersonian Persuasion: Evolution of Party Ideology* (Ithaca, N.Y., 1978); Drew McCoy, *The Elusive Republic: Political Economy in Jeffersonian America* (Chapel Hill, N.C., 1980); and Joyce Appleby, *Capitalism and a New Social Order: The Republican Vision of the 1790s* (New York, 1984).

major proponents were no longer yeomen. Men such as David Robinson Jr., O. C. Merrill, Jonathan Robinson, and David Fay had long since become commercial farmers or professionals. These uphill leaders clung to their yeoman beliefs long after such concepts had been drained of all social and economic reality. Their language became increasingly disembodied from a rapidly changing social reality. Their cries of equality, their salutes to the independent yeoman, the "Goddess of Liberty," and the "American fair," became ever more insistent at the very time that they restricted women to a limited economic and political sphere and created an increasingly stratified commercial society. Their ideology, however, allowed – even impelled – them to view themselves as committed to equality and communal wellbeing as they were actively creating a competitive, materialistic, and highly structured society. The result was a violent war of words with their Federalist counterparts, men whom they identified as the preeminent threat to yeoman independence and equality.

This war of words became increasingly vitriolic. In Bennington, unlike the rest of the nation, the triumph of Thomas Jefferson in 1800 did not inaugurate an era of Republican ascendancy and Federalist decline. Indeed, the War of 1812 brought significant political changes to Bennington. Opposed to the war and frustrated with commercial restrictions imposed on them by the Republican administration in Washington, a majority of voters in Vermont turned to the Federalist party. As in other townships throughout Vermont, the initial signs of Federalist success in Bennington appeared simultaneously with the outbreak of war in 1812. In September of that year voters elected Elijah Dewey to the General Assembly.[11] Then, at the annual town meeting the following year they elected Tichenor as moderator, Aaron Robinson as clerk, and five other Federalists as selectmen.[12] Dewey subsequently gained re-election to the General Assembly at the freeman's meeting on September 7, 1813. Far more important, though, is that at that meeting a majority of Bennington's freemen – for the first time in the town's history – cast their ballots for the Federalist candidate for governor.[13] This was a crushing blow to local Republicans. Even more upsetting was the identity of the successful gubernatorial candidate – Martin Chittenden. That old Tom Chittenden's son had "embibed the poison of aristocracy" by becoming a Federalist had long troubled Bennington Republicans;[14] for him to be elected governor, however, particularly with the aid of Bennington voters, was even more disturbing. It was an ominous sign of the times.

11 Bennington town records, book B, Sept. 3, 1812.
12 Ibid., Mar. 31, 1813.   13 Ibid., Sept. 7, 1813.
14 See particularly, the *Vermont Gazette*, Apr. 21, 1806.

Chittenden's election was indeed a precursor of things to come. In 1816 and again in 1817 voters in Bennington supported the Federalist candidate for governor. In addition, throughout the war and its immediate aftermath (1813–19), the town chose a Federalist four times for the Vermont Assembly. It sent a Republican only twice. During these years Bennington Federalists also dominated town offices, choosing the moderator of the annual town meeting and all the selectmen every year between 1812 and 1820.

Clearly, Federalism in Bennington – unlike Federalism at the state and national levels – was not dying out. It had not simply experienced a brief resuscitation during the War of 1812; rather, it enjoyed bountiful good health quite apart from the special circumstances of that conflict.[15] The reasons for this lay deeply embedded in the culture and political economy of Bennington. The prolonged life of Federalism in Bennington did not involve the persistence of a political party nearly so much as it did the perseverance of cultural attitudes that predated the existence of party. The cosmopolitan beliefs of Bennington's downhill residents were the stuff of which Federalism was made. More important, the economic and demographic forces that lay behind the ascendancy of the downhill people in Bennington during the first two decades of the nineteenth century accelerated rapidly in the postwar years. As the economic and social structure of the town became increasingly stratified, the power of the old agricultural interests weakened considerably. Conversely, as economic activity in Bennington became more and more commercialized – as growing numbers of people shifted from a subsistence to a market focus – the power and influence of local merchants grew ever stronger.[16] This was particularly true during the years following the Embargo of 1807 – a time when Moses Robinson Jr., Dewey, Jonathan Hunt, Micah J. Lyman, Lyman Patchin, and Noadiah Swift provided much needed stability to the merchant community in Bennington. These men – Federalists all – emerged from the War of 1812 firmly in control of local trade. Indeed, the authority of the downhill people in Bennington had never been so pervasive as it was during the years following the War of 1812.

This expansion of power naturally exacerbated existing tensions between uphill and downhill leaders; and yet these tensions did not prevent members

15 For insight into the manner in which the war served the Federalist cause in Vermont, see Chilton Williamson, *Vermont in Quandary: 1763–1825* (Montpelier, Vt., 1949), 258–76; John Duffy, "Broadside Illustrations of the Jeffersonian-Federalist Conflict in Vermont, 1809–1816," *Vermont History* 49 (1981): 209–22; and Edward Brynn, "Patterns of Dissent: Vermont's Opposition to the War of 1812," *Vermont History* 40 (1972): 10–27.
16 For an analysis of the manner in which local merchants extended their influence over the rural economy, see Christopher Clark, *The Roots of Rural Capitalism: Western Massachusetts, 1780–1860* (Ithaca, N.Y., 1990), 156–91.

of the separate factions from agreeing on economic matters. In fact, uphill and downhill leaders joined together at a meeting of farmers, manufacturers, and mechanics held at the courthouse on January 10, 1823, to discuss the economic future of their town. David Robinson Jr. served as secretary for the group, and the twenty-man committee chosen to draft resolutions included Merrill, Moses Robinson Jr., Stebbins Walbridge, and Stephen Hinsdill.[17] Perfect unanimity characterized this committee's deliberations; its report, delivered at an adjourned meeting a week later, expressed a consensus that pervaded not only the committee but all the participants at the convention. Their demand that Congress pass higher tariffs in order to protect home manufacturing rested on the belief that agriculture and manufacturing shared inseparable interests.[18] Their memorial to Congress stoutly maintained that "the union of manufactures and agriculture, has invariably increased commerce, and been the fountain of national prosperity, wealth, knowledge and distinction." Only a stronger tariff policy could guarantee the future of such a union. Realizing this, "the *cultivators of the soil* require the measure."[19]

That committee members such as Hinsdill, Walbridge, and Erwin Safford should conflate the interests of farmers and manufacturers in order to support high tariffs was not at all surprising. They operated flourishing woolen and cotton factories. It was not these men, however, who most passionately linked agriculture and manufacturing. Uphill leaders had been offering a single toast to "Agriculture, Commerce, and Manufacturers" at their July 4 and August 16 celebrations for years.[20] And Merrill gladly joined Hinsdill and others at a convention of wool growers and manufacturers when they sent a memorial to Congress proclaiming that "the union and mutual cooperation of manufacturing and agricultural industry and enterprize, have invariably been the source of positive national wealth, resources, knowledge & distinction."[21] Indeed, Bennington's most outspoken critic of the downhill gentry was also the town's foremost champion of farmers, manufacturers, and high tariffs. This critic, known to us only as "Z," repeatedly contended that "all classes of society" subsisted on the "hard-earned labours of the FARMER." And yet the very people whom farmers "clothe and feed, have at all times tried to disgrace their calling, and tax their industry."[22] Those exploiting farmers included lawyers, merchants, ministers, and politicians, but, importantly, not manufacturers. Manufacturers held the key to the independence and

---

17 *Vermont Gazette*, Jan. 13, 1824.   18 Ibid., Jan. 27, 1824.
19 Ibid., Feb. 3, 1824.
20 See, e.g., ibid., July 8, 1817; Aug. 26, 1823; July 13, 1824.
21 Ibid., Jan. 9, 1827.
22 Ibid., Mar. 26, 1822. For other letters by "Z," see ibid., Apr. 16, May 14, July 23, Sept. 24, 1824; June 21, July 26, 1825.

prosperity of agriculture. Farmers relied on the local markets that domestic manufacturers provided. These manufacturers, in turn, had to be protected from unfair foreign competition if they were to survive. Farmers therefore had to "encourage our own mechanicks and manufacturers," they had to "assist one another as brethren" if they were to prosper.[23]

Thus, in their exaltation of the farmer's independence – traditionally believed to be a vital element in the preservation of a republican social order in America – "Z" and his uphill colleagues inextricably linked the farmer with the manufacturer. In the process they quite unself-consciously integrated the yeoman persuasion of Ethan Allen with the Christian capitalism of Stephen Hinsdill.[24] As a result, they helped ensure that manufacturing entrepreneurs like Hinsdill shared with tillers of the soil the mantle of republicanism's independent citizen.[25]

Such beliefs on the part of uphill leaders revealed that common ground did in fact exist with their longtime opponents. This became readily apparent on September 15, 1832, when prominent members of the community, drawing their authority from an eighteenth-century state law allowing residents of a town to form a religious society in order to create a tax-supported church, formed the Congregational Society of Bennington. This new organization collapsed the traditional distinction between church and society that had characterized Bennington's church since its founding and placed complete control of the affairs of the old First Church in the hands of the society. The initial meeting of the society – restricted to those individuals willing to be taxed up to $50 annually – elected Tichenor president, Noadiah Swift vice president, Heman Swift treasurer, and Hinsdill to the board of trustees. These men served with the full approval of David Robinson and his uphill supporters.[26]

By forming the Congregational Society, leaders of the uphill and downhill factions in Bennington closed ranks to keep control of the church from passing into the hands of the nearly 300 new converts who had joined the church as a result of revivals that had swept through Bennington during

23 Ibid., Apr. 16, 1822.
24 This is the term Anthony F. C. Wallace employs in his study of the mill villages in Rockdale, Pennsylvania, which were remarkably similar to those of Bennington. Anthony F. C. Wallace, *Rockdale: The Growth of an American Village in the Early Industrial Revolution* (New York, 1978).
25 For a discussion of this phenomenon from a national perspective, see Rowland Berthoff, "Independence and Attachment, Virtue and Interest: From Republican Citizen to Free Enterpriser, 1787–1837," in Richard Bushman et al., *Uprooted Americans: Essays to Honor Oscar Handlin* (Boston, 1979), 99–124.
26 The minutes of the Congregational Society include the articles of the society and a list of all members. These minutes are in the papers of old First Church, Bennington Museum, Bennington, Vermont.

the previous six years. Membership in the church no longer carried with it the right to an equal vote in all decisions concerning it. Fundamental decisions regarding Bennington's church had been taken out of the hands of church members altogether. Whether they would admit it or not, members of the Congregational Society abandoned the traditional principles of equality and democracy on which the First Church had rested for so many years. Not to have done so would have meant surrendering control to the common working people of Bennington, who now comprised the majority of the church's membership.

Bennington's leading citizens presented the same united front in regard to public education. Whenever they gathered to celebrate Independence Day or the Battle of Bennington they invariably toasted common schools. They lauded "common education" as the "life of Liberty . . . the moral, and sure defence, against the enemies of freedom."[27] In such encomiums common schools constituted the very "life and happiness of society, the only safeguard of Republican Government."[28] And yet Bennington's principal leaders sent their own children to the town's private academies. They also steadfastly refused to distribute the proceeds of the town's school fund to the district schools. Had they done so, students attending these schools would not have been responsible for any fees whatsoever, and the children of families working in Bennington's mills would have been able to attend. Instead, led by their most prominent citizens, the townspeople of Bennington repeatedly voted to keep the school fund intact, to allow it to accumulate and to accrue interest.[29] Thus, unfortunately for the majority of citizens, town leaders simultaneously glorified and demeaned common schools.

A similar dynamic shaped the relationship between Bennington and its poor. Town leaders were as quick to attack imprisonment for debt as they were to laud common schools. The *Gazette*, which opened its pages to discussions of the matter, considered imprisonment of debtors an "unequal and an unjust tax" that "visits the poor" while "the rich are exempt."[30] Because imprisonment for debt was state law, its abolition did not rest with the citizens of Bennington. Still, unlike their behavior regarding tariffs to protect local manufactories, they did not gather in conventions to memorialize Congress or their state legislature on the subject. Neither did they instruct their representatives to broach the topic; consequently, none ever

27 *Vermont Gazette*, Aug. 21, 1827.   28 Ibid., Aug. 26, 1828.
29 The Harwood diary contains excellent discussions of these votes. See, e.g., entries for Apr. 1, 1831; Mar. 6, 1834; Mar. 29, 1837.
30 *Vermont Gazette*, Sept. 23, 1823.

did. Local authorities did, however, have the power to deal with poor people living within their own township. But here, too, just as in the case of common education, a contradiction existed between the language and the actions of Bennington's leaders. The town had a real opportunity to promote the yeoman independence these men extolled. It might have followed the suggestion of its pastor and purchased a farm where the town's poor could work off their debts.[31] Under this plan, the profits of the farm accrued to the town, and the poor gained an opportunity to work their way out of poverty. Instead, following the advice of their most influential citizens, voters routinely chose to follow custom: Town authorities auctioned off Bennington's poor to the highest bidders at annual public vendues.[32] Thus, private individuals, not the community, profited from the labor of the poor, who remained bound by debt.

Slowly, then, the intense factionalism that divided Bennington for so long began to fade. Uphill and downhill leaders began to find common ground; quite unself-consciously they moved toward a consensus on a variety of cultural issues. Such a union gave them tremendous influence and authority in the township. So powerful was their position that any challenge to their leadership would have had to come from outside the community. The death of William Morgan in neighboring New York in the summer of 1826 and the subsequent rise of the Antimasonic movement triggered just such a threat. By focusing its attacks on "village aristocracy" Antimasonry spread rapidly but unevenly across the state. It did particularly well in areas experiencing decline.[33]

The initial reaction in Bennington to the emergence of Antimasonry was calm and reasonable. By the time John C. Haswell took over as editor of the *Gazette* in January 1832, however, local suspicions of Antimasonry had been reified into political certainties. Haswell was convinced that the "enlightened yeomanry" of Vermont would soon unmask the "shallow and rotten hearted pretensions" of Antimasonic leaders. These men cared little about Masonry; they simply made it a "cat's paw to obtain office, office, office!"[34] Haswell finally delivered his most damning opinion: "Federalism under the garb of Anti-masonry has crawled up under their wings and has sucked their very life blood."[35]

31 Harwood diary, entry for Mar. 31, 1833.
32 For examples of these discussions, see ibid., entries for Mar. 25, 1835, and Mar. 29, 1837.
33 Paul Goodman, *Towards a Christian Republic: Antimasonry and the Great Transition in New England, 1826–1836* (New York, 1988), 122–9.
34 *Vermont Gazette*, June 11, 1833.   35 Ibid., Apr. 16, 1833.

If Haswell feared an Antimasonic insurgency in Bennington, he need not have been concerned. Both the uphill and downhill leadership were solidly against the movement, which, as a result, failed miserably within the township. Like other successful commercial centers in the state – towns in which well-entrenched elites had emerged within an increasingly stratified social and economic environment – the "village aristocracy" held firm in Bennington.[36]

At the same time that uphill and downhill leaders were closing ranks against Antimasonry, though, they vigorously attacked one another over other political issues affecting state and nation. This intense partisanship resulted from the political alliances that formed in Bennington following Andrew Jackson's election as president in 1828. Uphill leaders became ardent followers of the "Old Hero" and his Democratic Party, whereas the leadership of the downhill community fervently supported Jackson's opponents, the National Republicans. These political divisions seemed entirely appropriate. The egalitarian rhetoric of the Jacksonians resonated with the yeoman persuasion cherished by uphill leaders; so, too, did the Jacksonian emphasis on republicanism and the party's laissez faire social and economic attitudes. If the uphill leaders' intense localism and desire for individual autonomy drew them to the Democratic Party, the cosmopolitanism of the downhill leadership, as well as a belief in moral suasion that emanated from their more organic view of society, led the downhill community to support the National Republicans. In the absence of any new frame of reference, the power of the old political beliefs to influence the townspeople's thoughts and actions remained as strong as ever.

Actually, the exigencies of the national political dialog placed Bennington's uphill leaders in an increasingly tenuous position. Previous to Jackson's election they had supported banking, internal improvements, manufactures, high tariffs, and even the "American System" as essential for the growth and prosperity of their community.[37] During the 1830s, however, these principles became the stock in trade of the Whigs – the party label assumed by National Republicans in the 1830s. This left the uphill people in Bennington with little more than rhetorical issues stemming from their emotional attachment to the Jacksonian attack on aristocracy. Thus, when a convention of Bennington County Whigs called on the "yeomanry of the country"

---

36 Goodman, *Towards a Christian Republic*, 128–9, 282n28.
37 For editorials in favor of these principles, see the *Vermont Gazette*, Jan. 17, 24, Nov. 7, Dec. 26, 1826; Jan. 9, Oct. 16, 1827; Apr. 8, May 27, 1828.

to oppose Jackson's veto of the Bank of the United States, the editor of the *Gazette* labeled this assembly a collection of the "rich gentry" of the county.[38] The *Gazette's* Democratic editor grew increasingly shrill; in his opinion, Whigs in Vermont had to be voted out of power because they "have shingled the State over with BANKS AND CORPORATIONS, which, like putrid canker sores, are gnawing upon the vitals of the body politic – consuming the wages of Labor, eating up the profits of Industry, and making THE RICH RICHER and THE POOR POORER."[39]

Bennington Whigs became embroiled in the passions of the day. Caught up in the rhetorical warfare raging throughout the state and the nation, a convention of Bennington County Whigs declared that it was the duty of all freemen in the county "professing the Whig principles of the revolution" to "resist the introduction into this state of the office holder's system of politics." All true Whigs must oppose the effort to "perpetuate the principles of Gen. Jackson" – to "fasten upon the country the despotism of a party, having for its object, not 'the benefit of the governed,' but 'the spoils of victory.'"[40]

Despite all Democratic efforts the election of 1840 confirmed what had been apparent for some time: The town of Bennington and the state of Vermont had become bastions of Whig strength. Although there was no doubt of Whig dominance in Bennington, by 1840, however, the party itself had changed. The Bennington Whigs who celebrated William Henry Harrison's victory were far different from the town's National Republicans who had supported John Quincy Adams over a decade before: Hinsdill and a good many other downhill leaders had moved away; Tichenor, Aaron Robinson, Dewey, and Moses Robinson Jr. had died. In their absence the moral authoritarianism and elitism of the party gave way before the more utilitarian perspective of men such as Hiland Hall and Hiram Harwood, second-generation residents who had been raised ardent Jeffersonian Republicans. The democratic capitalism of Hall, rather than the cosmopolitan elitism of Tichenor or Aaron Robinson, permeated the language of these new Whigs.

Hall considered himself a man of the people, a true Jeffersonian. He invariably emphasized traditional values, such as the "vigilance of freemen," as the primary means to retain a republican government and society.[41] In

---

38 "Things, Which Every National Republican Must Believe," ibid, Aug. 28, 1832.
39 Ibid., Sept. 3, 1839.
40 *The Vermonter* (Bennington), July 21, 1835. A single issue of this paper is in the Hiland Hall papers, Park-McCullough House, North Bennington, Vermont.
41 Draft of a speech in the Hiland Hall papers.

Congress he lauded the "purely republican" habits of Vermonters, the way they judged governmental actions in "accordance with their republican principles." It was just such principles as these that caused the people of Vermont to oppose measures that promoted "the aristocratical accumulation and transmission of wealth in particular families."[42]

To emphasize his own opposition to "aristocracy" Hall associated himself with the egalitarian tradition of Ethan Allen and the Green Mountain Boys. On July 4, 1840, while introducing Daniel Webster to the Stratton Mountain convention, Hall skillfully linked the Whigs' campaign symbol of the log cabin with "the names & deeds of our Chittenden, our Allens, our Warner and of all those who as the fathers of our state we love dearest & prize highest." Then, in a burst of passion, he exclaimed that any "son of the Green Mountains who would discard the log cabin as an unfit emblem of his patriotism & love of liberty, would voluntarily dishonor the memory of his fathers & shake hands with the slanderer of the mother that bore him."[43]

Bennington's Democrats were not to be outdone. They, too, praised the sovereignty of the people, lauded the egalitarian values of the Green Mountain Boys, and attacked the aristocracy. Haswell wondered in the *Gazette* what had become of "that sterling independence, that abhorrence and detestation of tyranny, exhibited by our forefathers?" Was it possible, he asked, that "descendants of Ethan Allen, and his copatriots should have become so debased, so servile, as to cringe and fawn around the palace of a monied aristocrat?"[44] In another attack on Vermont's Whig congressmen, the fiery editor asked if it were "possible that the enlightened Green Mountain Boys can approve of the conduct of the Bank?"[45] David Robinson Jr., Merrill, and John S. Robinson also spoke passionately against the "monied power." They, too, saw the "great conflict between the democracy and monied interests of the country." They, too, warned the townspeople of Bennington against being "robbed of your birthrights by a monied aristocracy."[46] For these men nothing could be clearer: The Democratic Party represented "Equal Rights and Privileges" for all citizens, whereas Whigs fostered wealth and special privilege for the few at the expense of the many.[47]

The similarity between Whig and Democratic appeals revealed the emergence of a new political culture in Bennington. No longer did the

42 *Register of Debates in Congress*, 1st sess., 23d Congress, X, pt. III, 3948–9.
43 Hiland Hall's address to the Stratton Mountain convention, Hiland Hall papers.
44 *Vermont Gazette*, Mar. 25, 1834. 45 Ibid,. Aug. 12, 1834.
46 Ibid., July 31, 1840. 47 Ibid., Aug. 20, 1839.

dialectic between uphill egalitarianism and downhill elitism shape the town's political dialog. Now both parties espoused the democratic ethos of the uphill community. Whig and Democratic leaders alike championed the ideals of equality, opportunity, individualism, and free enterprise. In essence, these men competed with one another in their efforts to embrace the yeoman persuasion of Ethan Allen. By so doing – and by attacking one another as enemies of the yeoman – they obscured the similarity of their own social and economic interests.

The triumph of the yeoman persuasion in Bennington was, however, more symbolic than real; it represented a victory of rhetoric over reality. Far from being an egalitarian community, Bennington had become a hierarchically structured, economically stratified town, a town in which the extremes of inequality increased with each passing decade. A core of relatively affluent families controlled a disproportionate share of the land, power, and wealth in the town, whereas great numbers of landless poor passed through the area during any single year.[48] By 1840 two distinct populations – one stable and the other highly mobile – simultaneously resided within the town limits at any given time.[49] Bennington had become a town in which the great majority of its inhabitants – transient day laborers, tenant farmers, and mill workers – enjoyed very little of the equality or the opportunity being praised so ardently by Whigs and Democrats alike.

That Bennington was not a community of equals – that some residents had a great deal more than others – did not particularly disturb the town's Whig or Democratic leaders. Inequality seemed quite natural to them. Their equanimity stemmed from the yeoman image they embraced so passionately – an image that had undergone subtle transformations since Ethan Allen and the Green Mountain Boys thwarted New York authority over a half-century earlier. Then, the figure of the yeoman symbolized equality, the displacement of an aristocratic society of special privilege with an open, competitive one composed of common citizens. By the 1840s, however, the image of the yeoman had become far more libertarian. The attacks made by Lyon, Chittenden, and others on artificial

48 By 1820 the top 10 percent of the population in Bennington owned well over one-third of the town's wealth. This income distribution grew increasingly more skewed with the passage of time. See Bennington rate lists, 1785, 1820 and Census lists, 1850, 1860. Of the wills probated during the 1840s, the richest 10 percent accounted for over 40 percent of the town's wealth. See Bennington probate records, vols. 18–22, Bennington, Vermont.
49 Persistence rates for heads of household in Bennington from 1790 to 1850 were 39 percent, 46 percent, 37 percent, 48 percent, 40 percent, 34 percent, and 33 percent, respectively. In 1850 – the first year in which all inhabitants rather than just heads of household were listed – the persistence rate for those who were not heads of household was 23 percent.

barriers to equality had not led to social or material equality. Instead, their principles eventually supported the idea that every man should enjoy equal opportunities to establish superiority over his competitors. The egalitarian ethos underlying their actions had gradually been transmuted into a belief system that not only justified inequality but embraced it as morally acceptable.

Far from diminishing or eliminating inequalities in their society, the yeoman persuasion espoused by Hall, David Robinson Jr., and others helped perpetuate them. It was not that these men lacked Ethan Allen's deep commitment to equality; they embraced the concept with identical fervor. Equality to them, however, meant equality of opportunity, and equality of opportunity presumed a vast array of differences in talents and abilities. If some prospered while others failed, it was only because they worked harder or had greater ability than their less successful colleagues. All that was required of any society was fairness; each person must have an equal chance to compete with all others. Where such equality of opportunity existed, effort and talent would naturally create distinct differences in social status. In a truly free society, then, inequality was not only legitimate, it was ethically justifiable.

To believe otherwise was to doubt the validity of the yeoman persuasion itself – to doubt the individual initiative, personal autonomy, and free enterprise on which a truly republican society rested. None of Bennington's political leaders raised such a doubt. How could they? To doubt these principles was to doubt the very meaning and purpose of their own lives. It was little wonder, then, that they accepted without reflection the premise that Bennington actually was a fair and open society. The town's Whig and Democratic leaders never doubted that the son of a tenant farmer or a mill hand had the same opportunity to make something of himself as one of their own children. After all, these people had access to the town's common schools, were free to vote in town meetings, and could find gainful employment on their farms or in their factories. Consequently, the emphasis on an independent yeomanry remained; the town's leaders continued to trumpet the principles of liberal individualism. As the social and economic stratification of the town intensified, so, too, did the fervor with which its most prominent residents glorified ideals such as initiative, individualism, personal freedom, and independence. From their perspective, moreover, individual freedom and choice characterized the community because every citizen of Bennington enjoyed the same social and economic opportunities. Ordinary folk had only to apply themselves; self-discipline and hard work would bring sure rewards.

Over time, then, the egalitarian community envisioned by Bennington's New Light founders had become a liberal democracy – materialistic, utilitarian, aggressively individualistic, and inequitable. Under the pressure of rapidly changing socioeconomic conditions the independent yeomen, the sturdy mainstays of an egalitarian communalism, gradually underwent a subtle transmutation into the ambitious, self-made men who set themselves against neighbors and community alike. Simultaneously, however, the yeoman persuasion persisted; it continued to foster a rhetoric of selfless virtue that obscured the direction in which Bennington society was moving. By promoting the desire for unrestrained enterprise indirectly through an appeal to popular virtue – the reification of an independent yeomanry – Bennington's Whig and Democratic leaders helped produce a society of capitalists oblivious to the spirit of their own enterprise. Thus were they able to define their purpose as the promotion of traditional communal values while actually hurling themselves into the desperate pursuit of individual material gain. Over the years Samuel Robinson's independent yeoman had become Hall's democratic capitalist. Yet few in Bennington perceived the difference. Such was the strength and power of the yeoman persuasion that, like a veil, it obscured all actions or circumstances that might contradict it. As a result, Bennington's town leaders drew a reassuring sense of self-satisfaction and personal accomplishment from the belief that they had succeeded in an open, fluid environment in which every citizen enjoyed the same opportunity for social advancement and economic independence. Quite unreflectively, Bennington Whigs and Democrats alike had become firm advocates of liberal democracy.

9

The Birth of American Liberalism: New York, 1820–1860

JAMES A. HENRETTA

Ideology is not self-implementing. Although Lockean liberal ideas of natural rights and representative government filtered into Britain's North American colonies, they did not significantly affect the existing system of politics. Nor, in New York, did the libertarian and egalitarian principles of the American Revolution overthrow the traditional ruling elite of merchants and landlords. The New York Constitution of 1777 was a conservative republican document that preserved traditional property qualifications for voting and legally protected the huge estates of the Hudson River gentry.[1] Moreover, after 1790 New York, along with other American state governments, adopted neomercantilist policies designed to enhance the republican "common-wealth," largely ignoring the liberal principles of political economy advanced by Adam Smith. Liberalism – as a functioning system of government, economic policy, and cultural ideals – emerged in New York State only in the mid-nineteenth century as newly emergent social groups – professional party politicians, rural smallholders, and an entrepreneurial urban bourgeoisie – seized control of the political system.

MARTIN VAN BUREN AND THE POLITICAL REVOLUTION OF 1821

The architect of liberalism in New York State was Martin Van Buren (1782–1862). To his admirers Van Buren was "Little Van," a "Little Magician" with great personal charm and political skills; to his enemies he was "an artful, cunning, intriguing, selfish lawyer" concerned only with "office

---

1 Edward Countryman, *People in Revolution: Political Society and the American Revolution in New York, 1760–1790* (Baltimore, 1981).

and money.["2] In truth, Van Buren was a complex man whose bourgeois skills and ambition – hard work, rational calculation, and disciplined self-control – propelled him into the first ranks of American public life. Beginning as a state senator (1812–20) and the state's attorney general (1815–19), Van Buren turned the "Bucktail" Republicans into a disciplined political party that secured his election as United States senator (1821–8) and governor of New York (1829). Then, as the prime strategist of the coalition of the "plain republicans" of the North and the planters of the South that swept Andrew Jackson into the presidency, the New Yorker assumed high national positions, serving as secretary of state (1829–31), vice president (1833–7), and the eighth president of the United States (1837–41).

It was a remarkable ascent for a diminutive provincial lad whose father was an ordinary farmer–turned–tavern keeper. Born in 1782 in Kinderhook, Columbia County, on the east bank of the Hudson River, Van Buren grew up among white tenant farmers and smallholders who were dominated by a powerful landed gentry, led by the Livingston and Van Ness clans. Shamed as a young man by the refusal of Peter Van Ness to converse with him in public, Van Buren developed a complex relationship with members of that powerful family of notables. He relied on them to get a start in the world, mastering the law as a clerk in the New York City office of William P. Van Ness but then repudiating their tutelage and going his own way – becoming a skilled politician and legal advocate for the land rights of the tenants and yeomen of Columbia County. Thirty years later Little Van declared his social equality with his onetime patrons, buying Peter Van Ness's mansion and making it his country estate.

This quest for respectability – nay, gentility – was one of the defining features of Van Buren's life. While a young senator in Washington, he chose to share quarters with Federalists from distinguished families: Rufus King, Harrison Gray Otis, and Stephen Van Rensselaer, the greatest landowner in New York. To bolster his standing among such men Van Buren dressed meticulously and entertained in a lavish fashion. Later, as secretary of state, complained a critic, he threw "aristocratic" parties and showed scant "taste for republican habits."[3] A self-made professional lawyer and politician, Van Buren nonetheless measured his success in terms of a once-dominant and still-powerful gentry ethos.

2 Quoted in Robert V. Remini, *Martin Van Buren and the Making of the Democratic Party* (New York, 1959), 2; see also John Niven, *Martin Van Buren: The Romantic Age of American Politics* (New York, 1983), 5, 358.
3 Donald B. Cole, *Martin Van Buren and the American Political System* (Princeton, N.J., 1984), 190, 224; John C. Fitzpatrick, ed., *The Autobiography of Martin Van Buren* (Washington, D.C., 1920), 445–500; Niven, *Martin Van Buren*, 159–63.

Van Buren's social mobility was hard won, the product of decades of hard work and political innovation. Traditionally, New York's gentry families had managed elections by building up a local "interest": lending money to smallholding farmers, buying supplies from storekeepers and artisans, and treating their workers or tenants to rum at election time. They also "made" votes by giving propertyless tenants temporary titles to plots of land. "In the single town of Gallatin," Van Buren reported in 1810, "Robert LeRoy Livingston this morning admitted to me that he had made 190 [voters]."[4]

To win entry into this system of gentry politics, Van Buren became the client first of DeWitt Clinton, the Federalist candidate for president in 1811, and then of Governor Daniel L. Tompkins, a Jeffersonian who eventually became vice president under James Monroe. In 1811, with Clinton's backing and the votes of yeomen and tenant farmers, Van Buren – not yet 30 – won election as one of New York's eight state senators. But Little Van had no wish to be the dependent "tool" either of a leading notable or a fickle electorate. At first tentatively and then with greater assurance, he set about creating a new political order. First, he attacked the underlying premises of notable politics, repudiating traditional "classical republican" ideology, which disparaged political parties. Instead, he celebrated parties for checking both the government's "disposition to abuse power" and "the passions, the ambition, and the usurpations" of reckless political leaders.[5] Then, to provide himself with the economic means to compete with the notables, Van Buren set about building a disciplined party that could capture political office and then systematically use the resources of government – the "spoils" of public offices and legislative favors – to solidify its power and implement its policies.

Between 1817 and 1821 Little Van forged the Bucktail Republicans of New York into a coherent political force. Assisted by established men – Benjamin Knower, a hat and woolen manufacturer, Churchill Cambreleng, a prosperous New York City merchant, and lawyer Samuel Talbott – Van Buren recruited into the party a cadre of men much like himself, self-made professionals who came from middling families. Benjamin Butler was the son of a tavern keeper; William Marcy and Silas Wright grew up on farms in Western Massachusetts; all were lawyers with political ambitions. Two other key Bucktails, Edwin Croswell and Azariah Flagg, were aspiring journalists. Members of a new breed of bourgeois Americans who pursued

---

4 Quoted in Dixon Ryan Fox, *The Decline of the Aristocracy in the Politics of New York, 1801–1840*, ed. Robert V. Remini (New York, 1965), 146; Alan Taylor, "'The Art of Hook and Snivey': Political Culture in Upstate New York During the 1790s," *Journal of American History* 79 (Mar. 1993): 1371–98.
5 Quoted in Cole, *Martin Van Buren and the American Political System*, 96.

careers "open to talent," the Van Burenites styled themselves "the plain Republicans of the north" and took as their prime opponents the haughty notables of New York's ancien régime.[6]

Van Buren's personal confrontation with one such notable, DeWitt Clinton, precipitated a political revolution in the early 1820s. Clinton came from one of New York's great political families. Tall, handsome, self-assured, and college educated, he was everything that Van Buren was not, and he knew it, condescendingly referring to "the Van Burens and other would-be great men of the day."[7] Moreover, Clinton held different principles. Unlike Little Van, who consistently opposed the multiplication of charters to banks and other corporations, Clinton was a neomercantilist who advocated government support for economic development. Indeed, Clinton won four terms as governor of New York by promoting the Erie Canal and using construction contracts and canal jobs to build a powerful statewide political interest.[8]

To Van Buren, Clinton's personal arrogance and economic agenda made him a dangerous man. Using the popular rhetoric of internal improvements, the governor was extracting taxes from the people and using them to enrich wealthy Federalist canal contractors and land speculators. Risking his political career, Van Buren decided to oppose the popular chief executive, underwriting the purchase of the Albany *Argus* and using it to drum up the vote for his Bucktail faction. In the hotly contested election of 1820 Clinton hung on to the governorship, but the Bucktails took control of the assembly and the Council of Appointment, which disbursed over 6,000 government jobs and 8,000 militia posts. The Bucktail-dominated council immediately ousted all the top officers of the state – treasurer, comptroller, attorney general, all the chief militia officers, and eleven county sheriffs – and then methodically sifted through the remaining posts, ruthlessly removing Federalists and Clintonians. In their places the council named the leading Bucktails in each county to prestigious positions as judges (a total of 260 posts), justices of the peace (2,550 posts), and clerks, surrogates, or sheriffs (156 posts). Rank-and-file party members snapped up other fee-paying positions as coroners (630), masters in chancery (519), commissioners to acknowledge deeds (1,136), and nearly a thousand other minor legal offices.

6 On the Regency, see Cole, *Martin Van Buren and the American Political System*, 92–5.
7 Quoted in Niven, *Martin Van Buren*, 304, and 64, 68, 84. See also Fox, *Decline of the Aristocracy*, 154–6, 201.
8 Cole, *Martin Van Buren and the American Political System*, 86; Craig Hanyan with Mary Hanyan, "De Witt Clinton and the People's Men: Leadership and Purpose in an Early American Reform Movement, 1822–1826," *Mid-America* 73 (Apr.–July 1991): 87–114; Howard Lee McBain, *DeWitt Clinton and the Origin of the Spoils System in New York* (New York, 1907; reprint, 1967).

Almost overnight positions carrying salaries and fees worth $1 million changed hands.[9] Capping off this lucrative offensive, the assembly elected Van Buren to the United States Senate. State patronage rather than inherited privilege had become the driving force of New York's government.

Symbolizing this political revolution, the New York assembly condemned the customary pageantry surrounding the governor's opening speech to the legislature as one of the "remnants of royalty" and refused to offer the usual formal answer.[10] It then responded to public sentiment by voting to convene a convention to revise the Constitution of 1777, now widely attacked because of its centralizing and undemocratic character. The convention quickly threw out provisions that had restricted voting rights to £20 freeholders in assembly elections and £100 freeholders in contests for the governor and the senate, a rule that had excluded 40 percent of the adult men in the state.[11]

Federalists such as Chancellor James Kent stoutly defended the traditional restrictions on the franchise. "Society is an association for the protection of property as well as of life," Kent told the convention, "and the individual who contributes only one cent to the common stock, ought not to have the same power and influence . . . as he who contributes his thousands." "In England," replied David Buel Jr., a radical Bucktail, "they have their three estates, here there is but one estate – the people."[12] For his part, Van Buren repudiated both the elitist Federalists and the "mad-cap" democrats who advocated universal white male suffrage. In good bourgeois fashion Van Buren linked rights to responsibilities, arguing that the vote should be restricted to men who paid taxes. More radical Bucktails proceeded to define taxpayer suffrage in broad terms so that it included men who served in the militia or worked on the public roads. Consequently, the New York Constitution of 1821 replaced a "republican" definition of citizenship based on property ownership with a "liberal" conception based on the legal autonomy of the individual.

The convention also addressed the issue of patronage, which many New Yorkers believed was too extensive and too centralized. This question

---

9 "Civil Appointments Under the Council of Appointment," in N. Carter and W. Stone, eds., *Reports and Proceedings of the Convention of 1821* (Albany, N.Y., 1821), 161–2.
10 Quoted in Fox, *Decline of the Aristocracy*, 231.
11 Chilton Williamson, *American Suffrage: From Property to Democracy, 1760–1860* (Princeton, N.J., 1960), 195–207.
12 For quotations, Carter, *Proceedings*, 221 (Kent), 243 (Buel); Van Buren quoted in Dixon Ryan Fox, *Decline of the Aristocracy*, 240; Cole, *Martin Van Buren and the American Political System*, 72–3; Van Buren to John A. King, Oct. 28, 1821, in Charles R. King, ed., *The Life and Correspondence of Rufus King*, 6 vols. (New York, 1894–1900), 6:422.

created a dilemma for Van Buren: To maintain the strength of his Bucktail party he needed access to state jobs, but many rural Bucktails wanted more elective positions and local control of appointments. Acceding to this sentiment, Van Buren supported the abolition of the Council of Appointment and threw "home to the people" the election of about 8,000 militia posts, most of which were honorific.[13] However, as chair of the convention's committee on appointments, he proposed that 3,000 fee-bearing posts be controlled by the legislature and that the 2,500 justices of the peace (positions that were worth as much as $5,000 per year in fees) be appointed by the governor. To justify this centralization of patronage Van Buren redefined republicanism as "party" government. Like James Madison, Van Buren argued that "parties would always exist" and (going beyond Madison, who largely ignored patronage in *The Federalist*) that "they would consult their interests in the selection of candidates for public places." The political use of governmental posts was fair, Van Buren suggested, for it "would operate sometimes in favour of one party, and sometimes of another." It was efficient because it encouraged purposeful and responsible government. And it was democratic: "That the majority should govern was a fundamental maxim in all free governments."[14] However, most of the delegates were localists, not rising party politicians; in their minds majority rule meant local control. Consequently, the new Constitution decreed that sheriffs would be elected by county voters, whereas justices of the peace would be appointed by a committee of locally elected supervisors and centrally appointed county court judges.

Van Buren's political innovations and the Constitution of 1821 had created a new political regime: The old "republican" regime of notables had given way to "party" government on the state level and to a more democratic system in the towns and counties. The result was apparent to Alexis de Tocqueville, who visited the state in the late 1820s. Because New York's landed gentry no longer could "occupy in public [affairs] a position equivalent to what they hold in private life," Tocqueville wrote in *Democracy in America* (1835), they had retreated from the political world and now constituted merely "a private society in the state."[15] New York's political revolution of 1820–1 had placed the public world of government and law in the hands of rural smallholders and rising bourgeois politicians.

---

13 Carter, *Proceedings*, 262.   14 Ibid., 341, 353–4.
15 Quoted in Fox, *Decline of the Aristocracy*, 41; see also Martin Bruegel, "Unrest: Manorial Society and the Market in the Hudson Valley, 1780–1850," *Journal of American History* 84 (Mar. 1996): 1393–424.

POLITICAL ECONOMY: THE EMERGENCE OF THE
CLASSICAL LIBERAL STATE

The pursuit of power involved policy as well as patronage, and a key issue was the role of government in two areas of economic life: banking and internal improvements. In 1804 the New York legislature restricted the right to issue bank notes to state-chartered banking corporations, and by 1810 it had chartered ten commercial banks. In 1811, following the demise of the First Bank of the United States, merchants and manufacturers flooded the state legislature with petitions requesting additional banking charters. The legislators quickly obliged, granting five charters, but they required the new banks either to pay a monetary bonus to the state government or allow it to subscribe to shares of their stock. By 1819 the legislature had approved another twenty-three charters, and the state government owned nearly $1 million in shares of various banks.[16]

Van Buren was "always opposed to the multiplication of banks," as he noted in his autobiography, because he feared that business interests would corrupt representative government.[17] More often than not entrepreneurs bought the votes of key legislators by offering them free shares of bank stock. Once in business, many bankers made unsecured loans to directors and other "insiders" or issued bank notes far in excess of their paid-up capital. Both practices led to banking failures, with innocent investors or noteholders bearing much of the loss. To protect the public, in 1817 Van Buren used his authority as attorney general to take legal measures against the Utica Insurance Company, which was acting as a bank by circulating paper notes in the form of loans for business transactions.[18] The Panic of 1819 seemed to vindicate Van Buren's cry for financial caution because a dozen New York banks failed or teetered on the brink of bankruptcy. Seizing the moment, he tried to control excessive issues of bank notes by placing a tax on them. When the legislature rejected that proposal Van Buren used his influence at the Constitutional Convention to secure the insertion of a clause requiring a two-thirds legislative majority for bank charters.

While Van Buren served in the U.S. Senate during the 1820s his associates in New York – now known as the Albany Regency – continued the

---

16 Don C. Sowers, *The Financial History of New York State from 1789 to 1910* (New York, 1914), 48–50, chap. 4.
17 Fitzpatrick, ed., *Autobiography*, 36; Niven, *Martin Van Buren*, 302–5.
18 Jerome Mushkat and Joseph G. Raybeck, *Martin Van Buren: Law, Politics, and the Shaping of Republican Ideology* (Dekalb, Ill., 1977), 113–15, 125–6.

struggle to regulate the state's banks. In 1827 the Regency won the enactment of a statute that limited a bank's notes to three times its actual capital, prohibited excessive loans to directors, and specified 6 percent as the
maximum rate of interest on short-term loans.[19] Following his election
as governor in 1829 Van Buren again took personal charge of banking
reform, quickly winning legislative approval for a state-supervised banking
network: the New York Safety Fund.

The New York Safety Fund became the prototype of the regulatory
system in the American liberal state by blending private ownership with
public supervision. Under the Safety Fund, New York's banks remained
capitalist institutions, independent, privately owned, and profit-seeking.
However, the Safety Fund banks were regulated by a state-appointed board
of commissioners that had the authority to limit the issuance of notes and
prohibit certain types of investments. Moreover, the legislation required
banks to contribute 3 percent of their capital to the Safety Fund, which
would reimburse noteholders with claims against a failed bank. Here,
in rudimentary form, were two central institutional features of modern
American banking: a government-mandated but banker-managed regulatory apparatus (implemented nationally in 1914 in the Federal Reserve
System) and a compulsory insurance system to protect noteholders and
depositors (provided nationally in 1933 by the Federal Deposit Insurance
Corporation).[20]

This struggle over banking underlined a sharp political division over
issues of economic policy. On the one side stood Van Buren and his Bucktail Republicans, the forerunners of Jacksonian Democracy; advocates of
Adam Smith's political economy of classical liberalism, they opposed most
state assistance to special interests and advocated balanced budgets. On the
other side stood Clinton and his followers, many of them future Whigs;
neomercantilists, they had risen to power because of their unstinting promotion of the Erie Canal and their support for development-minded
government policies.

As internal improvements became a burning political issue during the
1820s and 1830s Clinton endorsed Henry Clay's American System, which
called for a federally financed network of roads and canals. Conversely, Van
Buren adopted "the doctrines of the Jefferson School," voting against

---

19 Sowers, *Financial History*, 48–50; Cole, *Martin Van Buren and the American Political System*, 28.
20 Charles W. Calomiris and Charles M. Kahan, "The Efficiency of Self-Regulated Payments Systems:
     Learning from the Suffolk System," National Bureau of Economic Research, *Working Paper no.
     5442*, examines the free enterprise alternative, the New England Suffolk System. Sowers, *Financial
     History*, chap. 4, traces the history of the Safety Fund.

federal subsidies and gradually forming a philosophy of limited government from which he never wavered. "The framers of our excellent Constitution," Van Buren would tell a Special Session of Congress at the height of the Panic of 1837, "wisely judged that the less government interferes with private pursuits the better for the general prosperity."[21]

As Van Buren advanced a Jeffersonian – and a classical liberal – conception of the role of the national government in Washington, the Albany Regency – led now by Silas Wright and Michael Hoffman – pursued similar policies in New York. Like many other Regency leaders, Hoffman came from a modest background and had risen through his own skills. The son of an immigrant German father and a native-born Protestant Irish mother, he first trained as a doctor and then in 1813 became a lawyer, establishing his practice in Herkimer, a small town in east-central New York. There he rose through the ranks of the Bucktails and in 1824 became the party's candidate for Congress. Winning election four times, he served in the House of Representatives from 1825 to 1833.[22]

When Hoffman returned to New York in 1833 the state stood at a fiscal crossroads. The legislature had not imposed a tax on property or auction sales for six years; instead, it met the modest administrative costs of state government by using the income from invested state funds. But this system of finance was on its last legs: Yielding to regional political interests, legislatures had committed the state to borrowing large sums of money to build an elaborate system of waterways connecting remote farming areas to the profitable Erie Canal. Hoffman predicted the inevitable result: a "deficit in the revenues of this state" because "for the future ten years the canals will be a drain on the Treasury if the interest on the debt be regarded as a current expense."[23]

Silas Wright, who served as the state's comptroller from 1828 to 1833, had foreseen this result but had not been able to secure legislative support for a small tax on property. He therefore met the annual deficits by depleting the state's investment funds and adding to the long-term debt – which had increased to $8.1 million by the time he left office. Building more canals without imposing taxes, Hoffman warned Flagg, the new comptroller, would result in a perpetual "British debt" – against which American Patriots, Antifederalists, and Jeffersonians had warned – and eventually "the

21 Van Buren quoted in Remini, *Van Buren and the Democratic Party*, 124; Irving J. Sloan, ed., *Martin Van Buren . . . Documents* (Dobbs Ferry, N.Y., 1969), 52.
22 On Hoffman, see James A. Henretta, "The Strange Birth of Liberal America: Michael Hoffman and the New York Constitution of 1846," *New York History* 77 (Apr. 1996): 151–76.
23 Hoffman to Flagg, Nov. 20, 1833, Flagg papers, New York Public Library (hereafter NYPL).

deadly and unyielding grasp of merciless taxation." But the legislators continued their spendthrift ways. Using logrolling tactics to secure legislative
majorities, both Whig and Democratic members of the assembly gratified
local and regional interests by building more canals and voting a $3 million
loan to the New York and Erie Railroad. When Flagg left office in 1839,
in the midst of the six-year long recession sparked by the Panic of 1837,
the state's debt had risen to $14 million.[24]

The worst was yet to come. During the next four years, Whig governor
William H. Seward and a Whig-dominated legislature raised the state debt
to $27 million by further expanding the canal system. The Whigs' deficit
spending was deliberate, designed to maintain employment and, as Samuel
Ruggles, a leading Whig, put it, to perfect the new "systems of inter-
communication" that were tying together "the whole northern part of the
continent." With Seward, as with Clinton, neomercantilism was in the
saddle. But now the government's finances were in disarray, with the value
of New York State bonds dropping precipitously; a $100 bond paying 6
percent interest fetched only $75. "The folly of man," Hoffman wrote sor-
rowfully to Wright at the close of 1841, "has created *impossibilities* and
Deficit."[25]

For the next five years public finance dominated the politics of New
York and prompted a split in the Democratic Party. On one side of this
schism stood the "Hunkers," status quo politicians who supported canal
construction, albeit on a modest scale, and who, their critics charged, "hun-
kered" after the spoils of office. Arrayed on the opposite side were Hoffman
and his friends, the core of Van Buren's Albany Regency. These radicals,
their opponents claimed, would destroy the state in the cause of reform,
and they labeled them "Barnburners," drawing on the ethnically charged
joke about New York's Dutch farmers who were said to burn down their
barns to kill the rats.[26]

The Barnburners' assault on Whig and Hunker policies played on several
intellectual themes. From the Jeffersonian past came the admonition that
each generation must control its own destiny. The various American state
governments had violated this principle, Barnburner Samuel Young
declared, by running up hundreds of millions in debt, and thereby appropriating "the toil of subsequent generations to glut the hungry cravings of

24 Hoffman to Flagg, Nov. 30, 1833, Flagg papers, NYPL; John Arthur Garraty, *Silas Wright* (New York,
   1949), 78–9; L. Ray Gunn, *The Decline of Authority: Public Economic Policy and Political Development
   in New York State, 1800–1860* (Ithaca, N.Y., 1989).
25 Ruggles quoted in Gunn, *Decline*, 146–9; Hoffman to Wright, Dec. 6, 1841, Flagg papers, NYPL;
   Herbert D. Donovan, *The Barnburners* (New York, 1925), 22–5.
26 Quoted in Donovan, *Barnburners*, 33.

this [one]; to eat the bread of unborn children." A related refrain reflected the Jacksonian premise of equal rights – that governments should not favor some men over others. A Barnburner newspaper, the Albany *Atlas*, condemned "the whole vile progeny of class legislation . . . the chartered monopolies, artificial credit system, fraudulent paper currencies, the perpetual taxation of public debt," and vowed to work to eliminate those political abuses.[27]

Most important, the Barnburners mounted a critique of nineteenth-century representative government. The problem, they argued, was not only that cowardly legislators created debts without imposing taxes to pay for them but also that elected officials arbitrarily took the property of some citizens and gave it to others. As Hoffman put it, lobbyists and logrolling promoted policies "that under the pretence of public works equally useful to all and charging all with taxes . . . have authorized such [projects] as are only beneficial to certain *districts* and *persons*." This use of the general taxing power evaded local responsibility for local improvements, Hoffman suggested, violating the principle "asserted and most ably maintained by Adam Smith in his Wealth of Nations Book 5 – Part 3 – Article 1."[28]

"What can save the State?" Hoffman asked rhetorically. The most obvious answer – and the most traditional – was simple retrenchment: "reform all useless offices – reduce salaries pay & emoluments to the lowest rates since 1830 – cease expenditures." But to pay the state's debts would require a new source of income, and, as a committed Jeffersonian, Hoffman rejected out of hand a bailout by the federal government – a plan then being discussed in Congress for the "Distribution of the proceeds of the Public Lands" among the various states. He maintained that the only moral solution to New York's debt crisis would be a "bearable" state levy, preferably "a suitable tax on the Luxuries of the rich."[29] But most Whigs and Hunker Democrats rejected a luxury tax. So too did many Barnburners: Standing for equal rights and a "neutral" state, they opposed legislation that consciously redistributed wealth either through subsidies or taxation.

Consequently, the Stop and Tax Movement that Hoffman led in 1842 resulted in both a moratorium on canal construction and the enactment of a regressive general property tax, a one-mill levy on real estate and personal effects. The results of these twin measures were dramatic. Within six

27 Young quoted in Gunn, *Decline*, 152–3; *Atlas* quoted in Gunn, "The Crisis of Distributive Politics," in William Pencak and Conrad Edick Wright, eds., *New York and the Rise of American Capitalism* (New York, 1989), 185.
28 Hoffman to Flagg, Aug. 9, 1842, Flagg papers, NYPL.
29 Hoffman to Wright, Dec. 6, 1841, Dix papers, Columbia University Library; Hoffman to Flagg, Nov. 24, 1842, Oct. 15, 1842, Flagg Papers, NYPL.

months, as construction expenses ended and taxes replenished the General and Canal Funds, the state's 6 percent bonds were trading at par, bringing substantial profits to speculators and recouping the paper losses of bankers in Albany, New York City, and London. Political exactions from smallholders had secured the investments of foreign and domestic capitalists – a social outcome that Hoffman viewed with dismay even as he welcomed the restored fiscal health of the state. But would it last? Despite Hoffman's pleas, the legislature refused to pass legislation that would require popular approval – through mandatory referenda – for future state indebtedness.[30]

In response to this rebuff Hoffman and the Barnburners campaigned for a new state constitutional convention, embarking on a movement for reform that would significantly alter the course of American history. The first victory came in 1845, when the voters authorized a new convention. When the convention convened in 1846, the state's debt, present and future, formed the core of its agenda. The delegates debated the issue for ten days, longer than any other matter. First they took up the existing debt, some $25 million, with an additional $13 million in interest payable by maturity. For his part, Hoffman rejected a permanent debt, what he called "the British system of . . . paying the interest and making the debt and drain for interest, perpetual." The Barnburner leader also rejected Whig and Hunker schemes to spend a portion of current revenues for canal extension and improvement, thereby delaying liquidation of the debt to 1883. Warning that competition from railroads and water routes through other states would soon cut the revenues of the Erie Canal, Hoffman won approval for a plan that would use canal income to liquidate the debt completely by 1865. In twenty years New York would be its own master.[31]

The issue of future debts was more bitterly contested, for it raised issues of constitutional principle as well as fiscal responsibility. Hoffman's plan would prohibit the state from extending loans or credit to private individuals or corporations and limit future state debts to $1 million, except as funded by specific taxes approved in a popular referendum. Whig delegates strongly opposed these restrictions on constitutional grounds, arguing that mandatory popular referenda on major state expenditures would change "our representative government into a democracy."[32]

---

30 See Gunn, "Distributive Politics," 192–3; Donovan, *Barnburners*, 44.
31 For the debates, see William G. Bishop and William H. Attree, *Report of the Debates and Proceedings of the Convention* (Albany, N.Y., 1846), 843–952, and the appendix, 1083–123; Hoffman speech, Sept. 11, ibid., 1083–90.
32 Remarks of Bascom, Sept. 22, 1846, Bishop, *Report*, 188.

The Barnburners' reply articulated a new – and decidedly "liberal" – constitutional theory for the American states. Existing fundamental law in New York and other states, complained Churchill Cambreleng, gave "the supreme legislative power of the State to the Legislature – unrestricted and unlimited." And what, he asked, "has been the consequence? . . . a legislative despotism." To constrain the power of the legislature and protect the liberty and property of citizens, Hoffman argued, the state's constitution should declare "that all powers not granted to the legislature are the residuary, reserved powers of the people, not to be exercised unless they make an express grant of them." In particular, Hoffman "did not want this tax-creating power left with the legislature." From bitter experience in the assembly he knew "what the power of corrupt lobby black-legs could do. . . . We will not trust the legislature with the power of creating indefinite mortgages on the people's property."[33]

Other delegates wanted even more restrictions on the government's authority. Embracing the emergent ideology of a laissez faire state, merchants, lawyers, and bankers from New York City urged the convention to diminish the extent of the state's traditional "police powers" by abolishing all offices for "inspecting any merchandise, produce, manufacture, or commodity whatever." Rejecting the neomercantilist policies of Clinton and the deficit financing of Seward, they also proposed to exclude the state from any role in economic development. "It is not the business of government to become a competitor with individuals in any branch of industry or of enterprise," declared George Shepard of New York City, offering an amendment prohibiting the state from contracting any debts. The "sole object" of government, Shepard maintained, was "to afford political protection to mankind in their lawful pursuits."[34]

Just as Hoffman wished to safeguard the property of rural smallholders and other ordinary citizens, so Shepard and other bourgeois liberals wanted to ensure that public expenditures would not deplete the wealth of urban capitalists. "For the legislature to assume to dispose the credit of the state," declared William Cullen Bryant, the influential editor of the New York *Evening Post*, "is to assume the control of property and credit of every individual citizen, and for any number of years." Thirty-one delegates supported Shepard's plan to ban all debts, and when his amendment failed (31 to 73) they joined with the Barnburners to approve Hoffman's plan to place strict

33 Remarks of Cambreleng, July 23, 1846, Hoffman, June 8, and Hoffman, Sept. 22, in Bishop and Attree, *Report*, 58, 403–4, 946.
34 Shepard, Sept. 22, 1946, in Bishop, *Report*, 512, 949–50.

constitutional limits on state indebtedness (by a margin of 72 to 36) and to create an elective judiciary to enforce them.[35]

"Every State in this Union" would follow New York's example, Hoffman told the delegates, and he was not mistaken. By the time of the Civil War most state constitutions imposed strict limits on indebtedness and mandated the popular election of judges. Empowered by direct election by the sovereign people, state judges began striking down more and more legislation on constitutional grounds, including spending bills that violated mandated debt limits.[36] Hoffman and his Barnburner colleagues had given constitutional form to Jacksonian principles of democracy and Smithian principles of economy, making them enduring features of American state governments. On both the state and national levels the ideology and institutions of the expansive republican commonwealth were giving way to those of the classical liberal state.

THE TRIUMPH OF BOURGEOIS PROPERTY RIGHTS

As a fiscal document the Constitution of 1846 was the work of smallholder farmers and bourgeois liberals who wanted low taxes and an end to state subsidies to entrepreneurs. As a political document the Constitution had a democratic populist thrust, greatly increasing the proportion of elected state and local offices and attacking the waning power of the landed notables. Just as the Bucktail revolution of 1820–1 diminished the political power of the gentry, so the Barnburner revolution of 1846 attacked the economic foundations of their seigneurial regime.

For more than a century Hudson Valley tenants had protested against landlord rule. In the 1740s and again in the 1760s German tenants and migrant farmers from New England rebelled against the feudal aspects of their leases and demanded fee-simple ownership. During the Revolution the conservative-led Patriot government seized the estates of some Hudson Valley loyalists and sold them at auction. But it opposed land redistribution, and the state constitution of 1777 explicitly guaranteed the legality of pre-revolutionary land grants. Finally, in 1787 the state legislature

---

35 Votes, 950; Hoffman, Sept. 23, 957 in Bishop, *Report*, 950, 957; Gunn, *Decline*, 184–9.
36 Hoffman, Aug. 18 and Sept. 23, 1946, Bishop, *Report*, 672–3, 957; Cambreleng, Oct. 9, 1846, ibid., 1080; Kermit L. Hall, "The Judiciary on Trial: State Constitutional Reform and the Rise of an Elected Judiciary, 1846–1860," *Historian* 44 (May 1983): 340–67; William E. Nelson, "Changing Conceptions of Judicial Review: The Evolution of Constitutional Theory in the States, 1790–1860," *University of Pennsylvania Law Review*, 120 (1972); Edwin S. Corwin, "The Extension of Judicial Review in New York, 1783–1905," *Michigan Law Review* 15 (Feb. 1917): esp. 284–5.

addressed the antirepublican character of the manorial regime, ending feudal obligations and banning all feudal tenures.

The great notable families – the Van Rensselaers, the Livingstons, the Schuylers, and the Kings, among others – found new, contractual ways to maintain their manorial estates. The landlords transferred land to tenants (and their heirs and assigns forever) under contracts of incomplete sale. These contracts required payment of a yearly rent of 10 to 15 bushels of winter wheat (worth about $30); reserved wood, mineral, and timber rights for the landlord; and stipulated that tenants provide a few days of personal service on the landlord's estate. More important, the agreements allowed the tenant to sell only the contract of incomplete sale (not the property itself) and permitted the landlord to claim one-quarter of the sales price (or reclaim full title to the farm by paying three-quarters of the market price). This quasi-feudalistic system preserved the massive estates of the landlords and brought them a steady income from their rents, timber rights, and quarter-sales. The annual rent roll for the 3,063 farms on Rensselaer-wyck, which embraced all of Albany and Rensselaer counties and part of Columbia county, was more than $100,000 (about $2 million today).[37]

The new leases prompted a new wave of tenant unrest. During the 1790s tenants on the Livingston and Van Rensselaer estates in Columbia County refused to pay rent and, disguising themselves as Indians, blocked the sale of properties seized for nonpayment. After Governor John Jay used the militia to put down the uprising, unrest simmered below the surface, particularly in upland regions where hundreds of tenant families eked out a bare subsistence and sought a society of egalitarian simplicity. "No man must be permitted . . . to own more than one house, and that one he himself must occupy," an antirent mass meeting in this region would declare in the 1840s.[38]

By that time upland tenants and their landlords were locked in a bitter struggle set off by the death in 1839 of Stephen Van Rensselaer III, the "Good Patroon." At the time of his death, the Good Patroon's tenants owed him some $400,000 in back rents, and he owed his creditors roughly the same amount. To balance the books and preserve the estate, Van Rensselaer's heirs sued to collect overdue rents. Tenants in the isolated Helderburg townships in western Albany County refused to pay unless they received new leases that eliminated quarter-sales and permitted tenants to buy their farms for two dollars an acre. This offer was fair, the tenants insisted, because

---

37 Breugel, "Manorial Society," 1393–415.
38 Quoted in ibid., 1421.

the landlords could invest the funds at 6 percent interest and receive a return that was equal to the annual rent. Determined to remain masters of their ancestral estates, Van Rensselaer's heirs and other landlords rejected this proposal, sparking a new wave of antirent agitation and "Indian" resistance.[39]

For the first time in this long struggle the political climate of the 1840s gave some hope to the tenantry. Even as Whig Governor William H. Seward sent in the state militia to maintain order, he condemned the leasehold tenure system as "oppressive, anti-republican, and degrading," and asked the legislature to intervene. Many legislators were of two minds, wanting to assist the tenants but unwilling to attack the property rights of the landlords. Only a minority of legislators favored proposals that would have tested the landlords' ancient titles in court or used the state's power of eminent domain to force sales at fixed prices.[40] When legislatively mandated mediation failed, tenant farmers in a dozen counties organized Equal Rights Anti-Rent associations and refused to pay rent. And when sheriffs tried to seize and sell their property, the farmers donned calico robes and Indian disguises and resisted by force.

As the Democratic candidate for governor in 1844 Barnburner Silas Wright took a strong stand against antirentism. Ignoring the Anti-Renters' social goal of joining ranks of the "virtuous and independent yeomanry," Wright condemned their challenge to "the right of the landlord to claim and collect rents." Nor was legislative intervention possible; as Wright wrote to his longtime associate Michael Hoffman, "the Constitution of the United States explicitly banned the State from passing any law 'impairing the obligations of contracts.'" In the end Wright dismissed the Anti-Renter position as "wholly indefensible constitutionally, legally, and morally." Hoffman was no less critical of the tenants: They "shriek for their share of the Spoils to be granted to them by special laws."[41]

Following his election Wright unleashed a full-scale campaign against Anti-Rentism, stationing a large force of state militia in the town of Hudson, banning the use of Indian disguises, and dispatching Attorney General John Van Buren, the son of the former president, to prosecute "Big Thunder" Smith A. Boughton, an Anti-Rent leader. For its part, the Democrat-controlled assembly rejected Anti-Renter proposals to eliminate

---

39 Henry Christman, *Tin Horns and Calico: A Decisive Episode in the Emergence of Democracy* (1945; reprint, Cornwallville, N.Y., 1978), chaps. 1–2.
40 Christman, *Tin Horns and Calico*, 39.
41 Wright to Flagg, Sept. 25, 1844, Flagg papers, NYPL; Garraty, *Wright*, 356–61; David M. Ellis, *Landlords and Farmers in the Hudson-Mohawk Region* (Ithaca, N.Y., 1946), 246–88; Hoffman to Flagg, Dec. 27, 1844, and Mar. 25, 1845, Flagg papers, NYPL.

landlords as judges in rent cases or to tax their rents and other reservations, branding such proposals as "special and class legislation."[42] The commitment of the leading Barnburners to the sanctity of contracts and the ideology of equal rights outweighed whatever sympathy they might have had for Anti-Renters as aspiring yeomen.

Still, Wright was an astute politician. Looking forward to the election of 1846, the governor called for the appointment of an assembly committee to address the issue of quasi-feudal tenures and used his influence to secure the appointment of Samuel J. Tilden to lead it. Tilden was a radical Jacksonian lawyer who, like Van Buren, hailed from landlord-dominated Columbia County; in 1838 he had assailed the "capitalists and landed proprietors" of England for wielding "the whole political power of the State for their own benefit." Personally hostile to a land monopoly, whether in England or New York, Tilden wrote a report that condemned "the restraints on alienation" in the Hudson Valley leases; they inhibited the "free exchange of the lands" and "the opportunities of enterprise." He proposed to limit all future agricultural leases to ten years and, more radically, to break up the present estates at the deaths of their present owners "by the exercise of the unquestionable power of the Legislature over the statutes of devise and descents." Although the Senate balked at this forthright attack on inheritances, the legislature enacted bills taxing the landlords' income from extended leases and banning the forced sale of property for nonpayment of rent.[43]

Tilden's classical liberal values informed the Constitution of 1846, which transformed manorial land into a marketable commodity. The constitution abolished "all feudal tenures of every description, with all their incidents"; limited leases of agricultural land to twelve years; and prohibited quarter-sales and other restraints on land transfers. In subsequent court cases New York judges upheld provisions for quarter-sales in leases drawn up before 1787 (when the legislature banned feudal restraints) and also allowed landlords to collect the rents specified in incomplete contracts of sale. However,

42 Christman, *Tin Horns and Calico*, 220–7, 254–60. Although Mushkat and Raybeck (*Martin Van Buren*, passim) celebrate Martin Van Buren as the advocate of tenants' rights, they admit that he never directly attacked the leasehold system, either in court cases or as a state senator. Consequently the actions of his protégés, Governor Wright and Attorney General John Van Buren, in the Anti-Rent controversy are not at all surprising. Moreover, Mushkat and Raybeck exaggerate the impact of Republican ideology on the elder Van Buren's legal practice and use of legal doctrines. As a skilled lawyer Van Buren tried to win his clients' cases and to do so used whichever doctrines worked best.
43 Christman, *Tin Horns and Calico*, 254–5; Robert Kelley, *The Transatlantic Persuasion: The Liberal-Democratic Mind in the Age of Gladstone* (New York, 1969), 256–60; Ellis, *Farmers and Landlords*, 227–32.

many owners decided to settle with their tenants, converting their leases into freehold mortgages; within a generation, only 2,100 of 12,300 farms in three Anti-Rent counties remained under lease.[44]

In the countryside of New York, bourgeois property rights were now in the ascendancy. When John Van Buren returned to the fray he was more aggressive as the advocate of yeoman and tenant rights and fee-simple ownership than his father had been; seigneurial landlords "act as clogs on industry, [and] are in conflict with the spirit and genius of our institutions," Van Buren argued in a case against the Livingston Manor. The bourgeois ethic of the father had come to fruition in the political rhetoric of the son – who was now a leader in the Free Soil movement. For John Van Buren and the other Free Soilers, the decline of the landed gentry of New York was merely a prelude to ending the expansionist dreams of the planter aristocracy of the South.

As rural smallholders and urban liberals finally eclipsed the landed gentry of the Hudson Valley, they were themselves challenged by proletarians from the immigrant districts of New York City. Between 1830 and 1845 the Irish and German population of the great metropolis on the Hudson had increased dramatically from 9 percent to 35 percent of the city's population, and the spread of capitalist enterprises had turned nearly 70 percent of the workforce into wage laborers. By 1855 the ethnic and economic divisions in the city were still more pronounced – half the population was foreign born, only 40 percent of the electorate owned land or taxable property, and the top 4 percent of the residents owned 70 percent of the wealth. No laboring man "can be a freeman, under the present state of society," declared Mike Walsh, a leader of the city's Irish workers. "He must be a humble slave of capital."[45]

New York City had become a class-divided society and a polity dominated by party machines and ethnic voters. Well into the 1820s wealthy men had filled many municipal offices, winning election because of their social status and active roles as dispensers of charity and sponsors of volunteer fire companies. Then professional politicians took over municipal government, using the public budget to provide aid to constituents and jobs to party workers. By 1840 the number of patronage positions in New York City had soared to nearly 2,000; the jobs and contracts dispensed by the street commissioner alone were worth $2 million a year. As municipal

44 Christman, *Tin Horns and Calico*, 293–303.
45 Walsh quoted in Sean Wilentz, *Chants Democratic: New York City and the Rise of the American Working Class, 1788–1850* (New York, 1984), 332; Amy Bridges, *A City in the Republic: Antebellum New York and the Origins of Machine Politics* (Ithaca, N.Y., 1987), 46.

governments spent more – on social services, superfluous workers, and corrupt contractors – their debts grew dramatically. In 1844 Hoffman raised the alarm, warning that the "insidious destructive" debts incurred by municipal bodies – "cities, counties, towns, villages and school districts" – might soon total more than the debt of the state government.[46]

Democratic and Whig politicians generally downplayed the issue of the debt of New York City and avoided confrontations on class-related disputes that might shake their grip on power. Thus they resisted the demands of social reformers and immigrant leaders for municipal ordinances to regulate the design and construction of tenement buildings; opposed Catholics, Methodists, and Baptists who wanted greater power in the Presbyterian- and Episcopalian-dominated Public School Society; and avoided the debate over temperance. But issues of ethnicity, culture, and class moved relentlessly toward the center of the political stage. In 1844 the American Republican Party swept to victory in the city elections, mobilizing native-born artisans, professionals, and small proprietors by campaigning on the issues of patriotism and temperance. In May 1849 class tensions again came to the fore when a bloody riot at the elite Astor Place Theater between Irish "Bowery Boys" and the police took dozens of lives. As the Philadelphia *Public Ledger* remarked, the riot etched into popular consciousness "a feeling to which this community has been a stranger – an opposition of classes – the rich and the poor."[47]

Immigration, capitalist wage labor, and political democracy had finally produced the volatile mix that New York conservatives had feared for more than a generation. During the debate over extension of the franchise at the Constitutional Convention of 1821, Federalist Elisha Williams had warned the delegates that soon "the needy shall be excited to ask for a *division* of your property; as they now ask for the right of governing it." That time had come. To pay for patronage and municipal projects, party politicians raided the treasury, raising the city's debt to $31 million by the early 1850s. As their real estate taxes rose, the minority of New Yorkers who paid them organized in protest. "Free men will not much longer put up with the robbery, the corruption, the infamy which have disgraced city government," Simeon Chittenden declared at a taxpayers' meeting. During the election of 1853 Chittenden and other prominent lawyers and

46 Amy Bridges, "Rethinking the Origins of Machine Politics," in John Hull Mollenkopf, ed., *Power, Culture, and Place: Essays on New York City* (New York, 1988), 51–60; Hoffman to Flagg, Sept. 1844, Flagg papers, NYPL.
47 *Ledger* quoted in Peter G. Buckley, "Culture, Class, and Place in Antebellum New York," in Mollenkopf, ed., *Power, Culture, and Place*, 43.

businessmen organized the City Reform movement. Although the reformers lacked the numbers to win control of city government, their movement
alarmed party politicians. To defuse the fiscal revolt and head off class conflict, Democratic politicians provided temporary tax relief to property
owners by issuing revenue-anticipation bonds; in 1856, these bonds covered
no less than 47 percent of New York City's annual expenditures, whereas
taxes covered a mere 32 percent.[48] Once an instrument for economic development and regional logrolling, deficit financing had become a device for
muting social conflict and maintaining the power of party machines.

Fiscal wizardry did not eliminate the dangerous issue of class. In 1854
and again in 1856, Fernando Wood, an equal rights advocate who had
become a millionaire through land speculation, won election as New York's
mayor, capturing 33 percent and 44 percent of the vote, respectively, in
closely contested four-way races. To bolster his standing among immigrant
wage workers, Wood responded to the recession of 1857 by proposing an
unprecedented public works project. He asked the Common Council to
issue city bonds (at 7 percent, redeemable in 50 years) and use the proceeds to hire unemployed laborers to open new streets, build Central Park,
and improve the Croton Water Works. Asserting that "those who produce
everything get nothing, and those who produce nothing get everything,"
the mayor warned of class warfare if his plan were not implemented. John
Bigelow, who had replaced Bryant as editor of the laissez faire New York
Evening Post, bitterly attacked Wood's welfare program, and John Van Buren
denounced Wood's inflammatory rhetoric as "a demagogical attempt to
array the poor against the rich, which resulted in mobs and rioting." Indeed,
unemployed workers marched on City Hall, prompting federal authorities
to dispatch troops to protect the New York customs house and armory.
Class warfare had come to democratic America, an English visitor noted,
as "bands of men paraded in a menacing manner through the streets of the
city demanding work and bread."[49]

By weakening the economic foundation of the liberal bourgeois order
the recession had created a major social crisis. The market and "private
capital" had not provided employment for "thousands of idle workmen,"
charged radical labor leader William West. "When famine stares fifty thousand workmen in the face," reiterated the *Irish News*, it was no time to be

48 Williams quoted in Marvin Meyer, *The Jacksonian Persuasion: Politics and Belief* (New York, 1957),
   241; Bridges, *City in the Republic*, 134–9.
49 Jerome Mushkat, *Fernando Wood: A Political Biography* (Kent, Ohio, 1990), chap. 5; Margaret Clapp,
   Forgotten First Citizen: John Bigelow (New York, 1947), 35–7, 134–7; Bridges, "Machine Politics,"
   61–3.

"quoting Adam Smith or any other politico-economical old fogy." New York's bourgeoisie and rural smallholders refused to be intimidated. Rejecting Wood's employment scheme as "one of the most monstrous doctrines ever broached in revolutionary France," state politicians and local reformers launched their own two-pronged assault on New York City and its problems. A newly elected Republican state government attacked the political leverage of immigrant workers, imposing a new municipal charter that cut the powers of the city government and limited the control of the mayor over contracts and the major centers of patronage: the almshouse, the board of education, and the fire and health departments. Equally important, new legislation replaced the Municipal Police with a new Metropolitan Force, managed by a state-appointed control board, and placed responsibility for the construction and operation of Central Park in another state-named board. Ousted by party machines from elected offices over the previous decades, New York's men of wealth and status now reappeared on the political scene, running state-appointed administrative bodies. Allied by the late 1850s with ex-Whigs and urban capitalists in the newly formed Republican Party, rural smallholders and their Regency and Barnburner political leaders stood forth as the advocates of bourgeois property. The "plain republicans" of New York had vanquished the manorial lords of the Hudson Valley and abandoned their historic alliance with the slave-owning gentry of the South. Making common cause with property-owning urban artisans who had embraced the Equal Rights Party in the 1830s, they prepared to do battle with those at both ends of American society: the immigrant "wage slaves" of the North and the masters of African-American slaves in the South. Classical liberalism had come to New York.

10

Republicanism, Liberalism, and Market Society: Party Formation and Party Ideology in Germany and the United States, c. 1825–1850

PAUL NOLTE

Republicanism and liberalism were born as ideas – or rather, as complex webs of ideas – that began to attract people of the privileged classes in the early modern era. But they eventually succeeded in deeply penetrating Western societies and political systems only after they turned into parties: Political ideologies crystallized as, or allied themselves to, social networks and movements that, in a more or less formalized structure, strove for power and in that quest competed with other ideological movements. Whereas previous historical scholarship on party formation had concerned itself either with the history of ideas alone or with the emergence and mechanisms of party organization in what could be called an institutional approach – a tendency particularly strong in Germany but also present in the United States – recent research in both countries has focused on the complex and fascinating links between ideology and political structure.[1]

From the vantage point of intellectual history, for example, it turned out that ideologies such as liberalism or republicanism were not neatly defined concepts that moved through history and were affixed to organizations in a wholesale manner, but rather consisted of a fluid pool of arguments and discourses that were used under certain circumstances, adapted to specific needs and conditions. Liberalism and republicanism thus appear as "languages" of social and political movements, offering explanations for change,

---

1 See the historiographical overview by Elisabeth Fehrenbach, "Die Anfänge der Parteiengeschichtsforschung in Deutschland," in Herbert Ludat and Rainer Christoph Schwinges, eds., *Politik, Gesellschaft, Geschichtsschreibung: Giessener Festgabe für Frantisek Graus zum 60. Geburtstag* (Cologne, 1982), 403–26.

outlets for anxiety, and legitimation for the claim to political power.[2] More often than not, elements from both the liberal and republican languages popped up in the "liberal," "republican," or "radical" parties.[3]

From the point of view of social history, however, there had always existed an interest in the social foundation of political parties and in the linkages between ideology and economic interest. More recently, though, social historians have shifted their attention toward the structure of politics in a broader societal context; they have sought the mechanisms and foundations of partisan politics in society at large as well as in particular groups, classes, or milieus. Edward Countryman's masterly study of society and politics in revolutionary New York is a good example of this approach.[4] In this new sociocultural perspective, social and intellectual history have begun to move toward each other and indeed to overlap. For the history of political parties and political ideologies, more specifically, the concepts of "political culture" and of a "political culture of partisanship" have proven very successful, providing a connection between the formation of liberal and republican ideologies, on the one hand, and the social foundations of political processes, on the other.[5]

Recent historiographical trends such as those on both sides of the Atlantic seem to facilitate a comparison of what otherwise, and within the respective older frameworks of interpretation, would almost seem incomparable. It thus may very well be that the stories of two "exceptionalisms" in the early nineteenth century dissolve and a historiographical framework

2 This concept has been developed and used extensively in the work of J. G. A. Pocock. See, e.g., his "Introduction: The State of the Art," in J. G. A. Pocock, *Virtue, Commerce, and History: Essays on Political Thought and History, Chiefly in the Eighteenth Century* (New York, 1985), 1–34; "The Concept of Language and the métier d'historien: Some Considerations on Practice," in Anthony Pagden, ed., *The Languages of Political Theory in Early Modern Europe* (Cambridge, 1987), 19–38; and, of course, *The Machiavellian Moment: Florentine Political Thought and the Atlantic Republican Tradition* (Princeton, N.J., 1975).

3 This corresponds to a tendency in recent research to dissolve somewhat the rigidity of the labels "republican" and "liberal," and of historiographical "republicans" and "liberals" moving toward each other. See, e.g., Joyce Appleby, *Liberalism and Republicanism in the Historical Imagination* (Cambridge, Mass., 1992).

4 Edward Countryman, *A People in Revolution: The American Revolution and Political Society in New York, 1760–1790* (Baltimore, 1981). I have tried to pursue a somewhat similar approach in examining early nineteenth-century liberalism, republicanism, and party formation in the German Southwest: Paul Nolte, *Gemeindebürgertum und Liberalismus in Baden 1800–1850: Tradition – Radikalismus – Republik* (Göttingen, 1994).

5 The – admittedly often diffuse – concept of "political culture" has been of enormous importance, I believe, in restructuring in the past two decades American political history from the colonial through the early republican periods; I am thinking, e.g., of the work of scholars such as Jack Greene, Edward Countryman, Richard Beeman, Daniel Walker Howe, or John Brooke. There is an interesting parallel in German history and political science with its recent attempt at reestablishing the concept of *Politische Kultur;* for an overview, see Karl Rohe, "Politische Kultur und ihre Analyse," *Historische Zeitschrift* 250 (1990): 321–46.

for assessing structural similarities between Germany and the United States (without neglecting the differences) emerges. First, the surge of research on republicanism, liberalism, and radical ideologies has already highlighted the international, transatlantic aspects of political discourse and political culture in the late eighteenth and early nineteenth centuries. This has especially been the case with regard to North America and Britain or France, and less so for America and Germany.[6] Second, the notion of a "market revolution" as a transforming agent of the early American republic, a concept that has become enormously influential since the mid-1980s, might prove a suitable frame for an interpretation of the indisputably profound economic and cultural changes in the German *Vormärz* as well. And third, mostly through local and regional studies on elections, ideology, and popular culture in the past decade or so, strong currents of party formation in German society in the sense of a partisan political culture have been recovered that can be compared to parallel processes in the United States.[7]

All that can be offered here is a tentative sketch of a framework, a concept, and arguments that hopefully demonstrate where further research could move from here. In the first section the impact of the economic and cultural changes wrought by the "market revolution" in the early nineteenth century in both countries is considered. The next two sections discuss different aspects of the two-party systems and the role of republicanism and liberalism within them: first, the social mechanisms of partisan politics, with special emphasis on the community level of the political process; and second, the problem of liberal and republican party ideology during that time. From there, a suggestion for an overall understanding of the similarities, and differences, of liberal parties in Germany and the United States emerges.

COMMERCE AND CULTURE: THE IMPACT OF THE "MARKET REVOLUTION"

It had long been a cornerstone of nineteenth-century historiography that the Industrial Revolution suddenly and sweepingly transformed Western economies and societies, turning agrarian, premodern landscapes into busy

6 Cf. Horst Dippel, *Germany and the American Revolution, 1770–1800: A Sociohistorical Investigation of Late Eighteenth-Century Political Thinking* (Wiesbaden, 1978).
7 See, e.g., Christoph Hauser, *Anfänge bürgerlicher Organisation: Philhellenismus und Frühliberalismus in Südwestdeutschland* (Göttingen, 1990); Nolte, *Gemeindebürgertum*; Jonathan Sperber, *Rhineland Radicals: The Democratic Movement and the Revolution of 1848/49* (Princeton, N.J., 1991); Karl H. Wegert, *German Radicals Confront the Common People: Revolutionary Politics and Popular Politics, 1789–1849* (Mainz, 1992).

hives of urban machine production and farmers into workers. In the past fifteen years or so, however, the historical understanding of the fundamental processes of socioeconomic modernization has changed dramatically – certainly in America, if perhaps to a lesser degree in Germany. Rather than focusing on the steam engine and heavy industry and their impact in a relatively short time span, historians now look at broader processes of economic change, at "commercialization," patterns of consumption, and market formation. Beyond the expansion in themes and topics of economic history, the cultural implications of this transformation have become a favorite issue for historical research and interpretation. Through this "culturalization" of economic processes a door has opened for a fresh look at the origins and determining factors of political development, of political attitudes, ideologies, and behavior, in the period of the market revolution.[8]

In American history, the very term *market revolution* has figured prominently in the last decade and has even begun to serve as the conceptual core for new syntheses of the Jacksonian era as a whole,[9] or of Jacksonian politics and party conflict in particular.[10] Drawing on older concepts such as the transportation revolution, historians have begun to reconsider the boom in the construction of canals, roads, and railroads, and they have studied the consequences of this rapidly expanding web of trade routes for the integration of all sorts of "producers" into the mechanisms of markets. Extending a discussion that originally started as a controversy on eighteenth-century agrarian history, they have traced the complex processes, mainly in the Northeast and the old Northwest, by which the subsistence-type family farm adopted new techniques of labor employment, production, marketing techniques, and through this, new horizons of cultural self-definition.[11]

The market approach, with its emphasis on the links between the cultural and the socioeconomic spheres, also provided a means for

---

8 For a summary and critical analysis of these trends in American historiography, see Paul Nolte, "Der Markt und seine Kultur – ein neues Paradigma der amerikanischen Geschichte?" *Historische Zeitschrift* 264 (1997): 329–60.

9 Charles G. Sellers, *The Market Revolution: Jacksonian America, 1815–1846* (New York, 1991). For this and the following, see Paul Nolte, "Der Durchbruch der amerikanischen Marktgesellschaft: Wirtschaft, Politik und Kultur in der frühen Republik," *Historische Zeitschrift* 259 (1994): 695–716.

10 Harry L. Watson, *Liberty and Power: The Politics of Jacksonian America* (New York, 1990).

11 The best monograph on this in my opinion is Christopher Clark, *The Roots of Rural Capitalism: Western Massachusetts, 1780–1860* (Ithaca, N.Y., 1990). Central to the discussion is James A. Henretta, "Families and Farms: Mentalité in Preindustrial America," *William and Mary Quarterly* 35 (1978): 3–32. For a more recent overview of the debate, see Allan Kulikoff, "Households and Markets: Toward a New Synthesis of American Agrarian History," *William and Mary Quarterly* 50 (1993): 342–55.

reintegrating the history of early nineteenth-century politics and ideology and for rescuing it from one-dimensional interpretations: Because both the "social control" paradigm of the history of the evangelical and reform movements and the "ethnocultural" reading of the second party system have proven unsatisfactory,[12] we have now come to see those two most important organized social mass movements in early nineteenth-century American history as expressions of strains and conflicts caused by the upheavals of the "market transformation" of American society, conflicts in which issues of class and social inequality, culture and religion, political ideas and ideologies overlapped and were, moreover, shaped by particular local and regional traditions or structures of power. "Essentially," Sean Wilentz summed up his interpretation of the origins of the Democratic Party, "Jacksonianism developed as an expression of the fears and aspirations of those petty producers and workers threatened by commercialization, as well as of voters in outlying areas not yet integrated into the market revolution."[13] The Whigs, however, coalesced in their "desire for orderly and regulated consolidation of the market revolution."[14]

In Germany matters seem to be more complex, or at any rate more historiographically diffuse, because the paradigm shift from "industrialism" to "market" has not yet advanced so far and so systematically as in the United States. The old orthodoxy, including its belief in a plain and simple relationship among industrialization, liberalism, and bourgeois groups, has collapsed, but a new paradigm for interpreting the connections between liberalism, the middle classes, and economic issues has not yet been fully established. Still, in much recent research there has been a tendency to view industrial development as a regional process developing over a long period of time and involving more than the factory production of capital goods.[15] The general types of Germany's regional economies in many ways resembled regional differentiation in the United States: Regions of agrarian staple production under coercive labor systems in Eastern Prussia were, in the first half of the nineteenth century, slowly developing markets for the

---

12 For a critique of the once influential concept of "social control," see Lawrence Frederick Kohl, "The Concept of Social Control and the History of Jacksonian America," *Journal of the Early Republic* 5 (1985): 21–34; but see also Daniel Walker Howe's important article on "The Evangelical Movement and Political Culture in the North During the Second Party System," *Journal of American History* 77 (1991): 1216–39.
13 Sean Wilentz, "Society, Politics, and the Market Revolution, 1815–1848," in Eric Foner, ed., *The New American History* (Philadelphia, 1990), 65. See also Sean Wilentz, "On Class and Politics in Jacksonian America," in Stanley I. Kutler and Stanley N. Katz, eds., *The Promise of American History: Progress and Prospects* (Baltimore, 1982), 45–63.
14 Wilentz, "Society, Politics, and the Market Revolution," 66.
15 See Sidney Pollard, ed., *Region und Industrialisierung* (Göttingen, 1980).

internal exchange of goods and services; there were the prominent industrial cores in the Rhineland and Westphalia; and there existed, for example, in the German Southwest, areas of mixed family farming and an established artisan and small business economy – every one of them breeding a somewhat different variant of liberal politics and ideology. In any case, the eighteenth-century tradition of a commercial middle class of wholesale traders and entrepreneurs figured prominently in the beginnings of both industrialization and political liberalism.[16] In an effort very similar to that in American history, historians of nineteenth-century Germany have demonstrated the importance of artisans and artisanal traditions, instead of the "classical" industrial workers, in economic transformations, thereby also calling attention to the roles of the artisans and small businessmen in local politics and culture before the 1850s.[17]

Moreover, the concept of a "market revolution" would suggest that very familiar topics of the German *Vormärz* history can be seen in a new light: The construction of railroads starting in the late 1830s or the heated conflicts over the formation and boundaries of the Deutsche Zollverein, the Prussian-led tariff union established in 1835, may then appear less as objective necessities of economic development, or as a first step toward Germany's political unification a generation later, and much more as facets of a broader commercial and cultural transformation that also took a prominent place in political discourse and party politics. The attitude of German liberals toward this transformation, it has turned out, was deeply ambivalent; although the liberty of trade and commerce was laden with hopes and aspirations, anxieties about the dangers of poverty or the loss of the agrarian foundations of society as a consequence of the industrial system were also widespread. Different from those in the United States, however, the political leaders, the state governments and bureaucracies, were almost unanimously in favor of internal improvements, whether railroads were built directly by the states, as in the Southern states, or whether they were considered private businesses, as in Prussia. Given the strong mercantilist traditions in Germany, no political leader could be expected

16 This role of the *Handelsbürgertum* (merchant middle class) has been demonstrated by Lothar Gall in *Bürgertum in Deutschland* (Berlin, 1989); see also Lothar Gall, ed., *Stadt und Bürgertum im Umbruch von der traditionalen zur modernen Gesellschaft* (Munich, 1993). An important case study on Rhenish industrialization and middle-class discourse on commercial development is Rudolf Boch, *Grenzenloses Wachstum? Das rheinische Wirtschaftsbürgertum und seine Industrialisierungsdebatte 1814–1857* (Göttingen, 1991).
17 For this trend, see Jürgen Kocka, "Traditionsbindung und Klassenbildung: Zum sozialhistorischen Ort der frühen deutschen Arbeiterbewegung," *Historische Zeitschrift* 243 (1986): 333–76; Friedrich Lenger, "Die handwerkliche Phase der Arbeiterbewegung in England, Frankreich, Deutschland und den USA – Plädoyer für einen Vergleich," *Geschichte und Gesellschaft* 13 (1987): 232–43.

to stand against state support for internal developments, much less to try to veto them.

These fundamental transformations could not leave people's culture, behavior, and political responses untouched on both sides of the Atlantic. Despite the enormous differences in political culture and political systems that had evolved since the early modern era, then, the impact of the market revolution posed similar challenges in the two countries. Both Germans and Americans had to deal in very similar ways with the problems of trade and tariff in the face of British competition; both had to come to terms with increasing social inequality that, in their perception, threatened to destroy a stable and morally balanced society; both had to weigh for themselves the pros and cons of venturing into the new market systems instead of staying within the boundaries of family, guild, or community. From these choices, though not from them alone, cultural and political options emerged that in turn left their imprint on the party systems – on two-party systems conspicuously developing at the same time.

"THE ART OF HOOK AND SNIVEY": THE MECHANISMS OF PARTISAN POLITICS

Germany and the United States in the decades around 1830–40 could both be called political societies in transition. They were in the midst of a communication revolution, triggered by the construction of canals (in the United States) and, a short while later and even more important, of railroads. People traveled more, news could spread faster, and spatial horizons for common people widened beyond the bounds of the local community.[18] Whereas newspapers in America had already played an important role in the shaping of partisan coalitions during the Revolution, the German states, despite the limits set by occasionally very harsh censorship, witnessed an explosion of local and regional papers that opened their pages for the discussion of community and state politics.

In both societies, moreover, the early decades of the nineteenth century were, generally speaking, a period of rapid suffrage extensions in America and even more so in Germany. Here, the terms of the reform period settlement had left the largest German state, Prussia, without a constitution and state parliament, but some Southwestern states had established *Landtage* (state assemblies) based on relatively broad male suffrage – although

---

18 For intriguing perspectives on this, see Richard D. Brown, *Knowledge Is Power: The Diffusion of Information in Early America, 1700–1865* (New York, 1989). Unfortunately, there is no comparable book for German history.

property qualifications continued to exist everywhere – and during the *Vormärz* developed a vibrant parliamentary culture. Similar to developments in Germany, the legal extension of suffrage in the United States preceded the development of the second party system by some years; in the decade between 1815 and the corrupt bargain election of 1824, almost all states dropped property requirements and thus introduced universal white male suffrage.[19]

Finally, though most elusive: In Germany as in the United States, traditional, eighteenth-century relations between the "better sort" and the "common people" rapidly disintegrated. This process, again, had developed more continuously in America since the Revolution or, perhaps, the Great Awakening,[20] and by 1830 it had transformed urban as well as small-town frontier America[21] into societies of independent (white male) individuals, where social prestige did not automatically translate into political influence on the laboring classes. However (unlike late-nineteenth-century "mass society," in which the "island communities" had vanished[22]) communities or small, regional networks of prestige and influence persisted, and members of the older genteel classes together with a new class of businessmen could still expect to be the natural political leaders, although they now had to compete for the consent of followers within a framework of partisan politics. Contrary to eighteenth-century politics, they now had to offer their followers something – possibly material rewards – in return for their support.

This transitory stage in the process of the decline of deference and the rise of individualism was also the mark of *Vormärz* and revolutionary Germany. Later, more suddenly than in the United States, and probably more shocking in the experience of contemporaries, the corporate order of estates stemming from the late medieval and early modern eras dissolved under pressure of both bureaucratic attacks on its legal foundations and the economic changes, particularly the beginnings of factory work and the growth of the new underclass of "pauperism."[23] As in the United States,

19 A classical account is Chilton Williamson, *American Suffrage: From Property to Democracy, 1760–1860* (Princeton, N.J., 1960).
20 See Rhys Isaac, *The Transformation of Virginia, 1740–1790* (Chapel Hill, N.C., 1981); for a similar argument concerning the revolutionary and early national periods, see Gordon S. Wood, *The Radicalism of the American Revolution* (New York, 1992).
21 Now probably the best case study: Alan Taylor, *William Cooper's Town: Power and Persuasion on the Frontier of the Early American Republic* (New York, 1996).
22 Robert H. Wiebe, *The Search for Order, 1877–1920* (New York, 1967).
23 A classic and still important account is Werner Conze, "Vom 'Pöbel' zum 'Proletariat': Sozialgeschichtliche Voraussetzungen für den Sozialismus in Deutschland," in Hans-Ulrich Wehler, ed., *Moderne deutsche Sozialgeschichte* (Königstein, 1981), 111–36. The best case study to consider

the orders of prestige and hierarchy on the community level continued to work for the most part, but they had to be filled with new contents and new patterns of legitimation; and wherever legal participation rights were opened up, elite families now had to compete for influence and majorities.

With this general framework in mind, let us now take a brief comparative look at some of the more important media of liberal partisan politics: at elections and campaigning; at the relationship between elite and followers; and at the role of clubs and associations. Finally, the gender-specific aspects of these two early nineteenth-century political cultures demand some consideration.

Elections made up the very center of partisan politics in both countries. At a time when parties were not yet strictly organized "machines" with a formal, and perhaps bureaucratic, leadership, one could even say that parties only came into full public existence at election time. However, in Germany as well as in the United States these were not rare occasions: Given the full scale of representative politics from the community or ward level to state and national politics, and the generally shorter terms of office, the particular political mobilization of electioneering could sometimes become an almost permanent condition. The basic methods and styles of campaigning were very similar in both countries, although they could differ from region to region or from state to state.[24] Newspaper propaganda started a long time before election day, and the rival parties often made use of different local papers that were known to support a specific party label. On the local level, county conventions or *Gemeindeversammlungen* convened for the nomination of candidates or for the purpose of making a party ticket the local elite had previously agreed on known to the electorate. To vote for party tickets instead of particular, "honorable" persons was familiar to both Germans and Americans in the 1840s – although perhaps a more established practice in the United States – whereas the influence of notable

---

this, especially the complex interplay of legal-bureaucratic and socioeconomic factors in the modernization of the "Ständegesellschaft," remains Reinhart Koselleck, *Preussen zwischen Reform und Revolution: Allgemeines Landrecht, Verwaltung und soziale Bewegung von 1791 bis 1848* (Stuttgart, 1967).

24 For the following, I have drawn especially on Harry L. Watson, *Jacksonian Politics and Community Conflict: The Emergence of the Second Party System in Cumberland County, North Carolina* (Chapel Hill, N.C., 1981); J. Mills Thornton, III, *Politics and Power in a Slave Society: Alabama, 1800–1860* (Baton Rouge, La., 1978), for the American case; for Germany, cf. Manfred Hörner, *Die Wahlen zur badischen zweiten Kammer im Vormärz (1819–1847)* (Göttingen, 1987); Paul Nolte, "Parteien und Propaganda im Vormärz: Die schwierigen Anfänge staatlicher Meinungslenkung in einer politisierten Gesellschaft," in Ute Daniel and Wolfram Siemann, eds., *Propaganda: Meinungskampf, Verführung und politische Sinnstiftung (1789–1989)* (Frankfurt am Main, 1994), 83–100; Nolte, *Gemeindebürgertum*, chaps. 2, 4.

individuals had not completely vanished, and they occasionally were elected against the prevailing party tide.

The most conspicuous element of electioneering in both countries, however, may well have been the "illegal" recruitment of voters by partisan politicians as a matter of course. Americans were used to the "art of hook and snivey," of trickery and deceit in election campaigns, at least since the first party system,[25] but it reached a new dimension with the political style of the second party system. Germans had to "learn" those tricky mechanisms of early democratic politics; they proved to be quick learners because family influence, bribery, and corruption had been an element of local politics in the early modern, prepartisan era as well. Candidates and local partisan leaders in both countries gave liquor or wine to the voters to "persuade" them. Both Germans and Americans knew the practice of packing the opposition party's meetings during a campaign, a practice that often ended in turmoil and sometimes in a fight.[26] Campaigning, in other words, was an activity that stretched far beyond the political sphere proper and invaded the whole of community life; it made use of patterns of community power and influence, and vigorously demanded partisanship from everyone entitled to vote. Although it is certainly true that some of the spectacular campaigning techniques in America were freely borrowed from the revival preachers of the evangelical movement, they also closely resembled the mechanisms of electioneering in Germany – and possibly elsewhere – where this religious movement was unknown.[27]

Party systems in both countries depended on a complex web of relations between party elites and followers, between activists and "just voters." The transitional stage of early-nineteenth-century society again shaped those relations: In oral societies, personal communication, personal acquaintance, and sympathy were prime factors in determining partisan allegiance, whereas the new means of communication, such as the railroads, opened up the possibility for candidates or officeholders to travel, visit their electorate, and strengthen personal bonds of mutual obligation.[28] The candidate coming into a village or small town had the chance to build up party loyalty on the periphery and to build for himself a network of acquaintances, where the local party leader basked in the reflected glory of putting this respected person up for a night or two in his house, thus securing

25 Alan Taylor, "'The Art of Hook and Snivey': Political Culture in Upstate New York During the 1790s," *Journal of American History* 79 (1993): 1371–96.
26 Thornton, *Politics and Power*, 155; Nolte, "Parteien und Propaganda."
27 Howe, "Evangelical Movement," 1231.
28 Nolte, *Gemeindebürgertum*, 171–88; Thornton, *Politics and Power*, 156.

respect, influence, and possibly votes in his own community. These were at the same time "egalitarian procedures"[29] and subtle affirmations of hierarchy and power in the community and party network. As an additional element of public politics, festivals and parades were widely used instruments in both countries for assembling a party's followers and bringing them in contact with the party leaders, and for fostering a sense of identity and togetherness among them.[30]

Clubs and associations figured as important elements of partisan political culture in both countries; they lent stability and permanence to an otherwise loosely structured party system. With all due caution, political or semipolitical clubs seem to have had a somewhat greater influence in liberal partisan politics in Germany than in the United States, where the more formalized structure of election politics – with a quickly developing pattern of primaries, party conventions, and so forth – retained predominance. Although research on German liberalism has long tended to overestimate the role of political clubs (*Vereine*) during the *Vormärz* while neglecting the more informal mechanisms described above, it remains true that particular German traditions fostered the centrality of associations in public social life.[31] "Enlightened" associations established by the upper classes before or around 1800 could later turn political and broaden their social base; the middle classes in the 1830s built their own clubs on the model of those associations, clubs that increasingly became instruments of local partisan politics. However, the corporate traditions in Germany often worked toward a gradual transformation of older civic associations into liberal political clubs. Although the vast majority of partisan political clubs remained local and separated, some wider networks of liberal clubs were established, such as the Press- und Vaterlandsverein (Press and Fatherland Society) in the wake of the liberal Hambach festival of 1832,[32] or the statewide or even

29 Robert H. Wiebe, *Self-Rule: A Cultural History of American Democracy* (Chicago, 1995), 74; Wiebe here gives a description of these "egalitarian procedures" in the political culture of the Second Party system that very much resembles German practices at the same time.

30 On Germany, see Manfred Hettling and Paul Nolte, eds., *Bürgerliche Feste: Symbolische Formen politischen Handelns im 19. Jahrhundert* (Göttingen, 1993); and several articles in Dieter Düding et al., eds., *Öffentliche Festkultur: Politische Feste in Deutschland von der Aufklärung bis zum Ersten Weltkrieg* (Reinbek bei Hamburg, 1988); on the United States, see Mary Ryan, "The American Parade: Representations of the Nineteenth-Century Social Order," in Lynn Hunt, ed., *The New Cultural History* (Berkeley, Calif., 1989), 131–53. See also Jürgen Heideking's chapter in this book.

31 Thomas Nipperdey, "Verein als soziale Struktur in Deutschland im späten 18. und frühen 19. Jahrhundert," in Thomas Nipperdey, *Gesellschaft, Kultur, Theorie* (Göttingen, 1976), 174–205; important in its focus on the community level is Eberhard Illner, *Bürgerliche Organisierung in Elberfeld 1775–1850* (Neustadt a.d. Aisch, 1982).

32 See Cornelia Foerster, *Der Press- und Vaterlandsverein von 1832/33: Sozialstruktur und Organisationsformen der bürgerlichen Bewegung in der Zeit des Hambacher Festes* (Trier, 1982).

national organizations of liberal and republican clubs in the revolution of 1848–9.[33] In the United States, associational life in the era of the second party system developed outside the partisan political realm in a stricter sense; rather it grew out of the cultural movements of the era – however heavily they overlapped with partisan politics. Antimasonry and abolitionism, temperance, poor relief, and religion: These were the well-known areas of the reformers' "benevolent empire" in which public associations blossomed.[34]

These last remarks, in the context of American historiography, hint at the gender-specific aspects of the German and American party systems. Both, at their core, were parts of male political culture, not only because women were not entitled to vote but also because gender had become, or was about to become, the single most important criterion for political participation. In the United States a complex system of gradation of political rights had been supplanted by a clear dichotomy based on race and sex.[35] In Germany many of the older gradations based on rank and estate had been abolished during the *Vormärz*; property qualifications, however, were still widespread and often replaced the "natural" aristocracy with what liberal and radical critics called an "aristocracy of money." Still, partisan politics bore the deep imprint of the male social and public world, an imprint that immediately becomes obvious in the centrality of the tavern or *Wirtshaus* in early liberal partisan politics.[36] Those patterns of male behavior were a mark of the second party system, too, but it seems as though American women were more successful in building up a public sphere of their own in their "female dominion of reform" than were their German contemporaries, although research in this area in Germany still lags behind.[37]

In sum, both Germany and the United States in the 1830s and 1840s were characterized by the powerful emergence of a partisan political culture

33 Dieter Langewiesche, "Die Anfänge der deutschen Parteien: Partei, Fraktion und Verein in der Revolution von 1848/49," *Geschichte und Gesellschaft* 4 (1978): 324–61; Wolfram Siemann, *Die deutsche Revolution 1848/49* (Frankfurt am Main, 1985), 90–114; the most detailed regional study now is Michael Wettengel, *Die Revolution von 1848/49 im Rhein-Main-Raum: Politische Vereine und Revolutionsalltag im Grossherzogtum Hessen, Herzogtum Nassau und in der Freien Stadt Frankfurt* (Wiesbaden, 1989).

34 See Mary Ryan, *Cradle of the Middle Class: The Family in Oneida County, 1790–1865* (New York, 1981); for the general context, see Ronald G. Walters, *American Reformers, 1815–1860* (New York, 1978).

35 Watson, *Liberty and Power*, 52–3.   36 Nolte, *Gemeindebürgertum*, 171–2.

37 On the United States, see Ryan, *Cradle of the Middle Class*, and Mary Ryan, *Women in Public: Between Banners and Ballots, 1825–1880* (Baltimore, 1991); on Germany, see Sylvia Paletschek, *Frauen und Dissens: Frauen im Deutschkatholizismus und in den freien Gemeinden 1841–1852* (Göttingen, 1990). This important study suggests that, very much as in the United States, German women during that time built up their "public sphere" chiefly through cultural and religious movements that were closely related to politics, but at the same time set apart from the male realm of partisan and election politics.

shaped by similar conditions of communication and social relations in the two countries. It would be reasonable to assume that those conditions not only left their mark on political behavior but also on the shaping of political belief systems and ideologies.

In both the United States and Germany, historians during the past few years have rediscovered the significance of broad ideological frameworks and of sociopolitical belief systems for the processes of party formation, for the functioning of partisan politics, and, not least, for the contemporaries' self-understanding of their place in a changing society and in a system of contested politics. The disregard for Jacksonian party ideology as mere rhetoric or cant has given way to a new perspective that underscores the deep sincerity in the ideological content of partisan politics in the 1830s and 1840s, a sincerity based both on the vividness of eighteenth-century republicanism and on the fundamental choices confronting people in the face of the "Market Revolution."[38]

In quasi analogy to American history, though not so fully developed as there, questions have been asked in Germany about eighteenth-century traditions of what used to be regarded as "modern" liberal thought – traditions pointing to the Enlightenment; to patriarchal notions of order, hierarchy, and liberty in an estate society; or to classical republican concepts of virtue and citizenship that made their way into the language and beliefs of townspeople between the 1830s and the revolution of 1848.[39] At the same time, problems of economic ideology, much longer neglected by German historiography than in Britain or America, have been discussed in relation to the formation of a bourgeoisie or of bureaucratic-liberal concepts of commercial development;[40] and it is now acknowledged – although not yet researched in a satisfactory way – that visions of economic order

---

38 Watson, *Liberty and Power*; Wilentz, "Society, Politics, and the Market Revolution"; Howe, "Evangelical Movement"; for a critical assessment, see Lawrence Frederick Kohl, "Republicanism Meets the Market Revolution," *Reviews in American History* 19 (1991): 188–93.

39 Extremely influential in the German discussion: Lothar Gall, "Liberalismus und 'bürgerliche Gesellschaft': Zu Charakter und Entwicklung der liberalen Bewegung in Deutschland," *Historische Zeitschrift* 220 (1975): 324–56; see also Paul Nolte, "Bürgerideal, Gemeinde und Republik: 'Klassischer Republikanismus' im frühen deutschen Liberalismus," *Historische Zeitschrift* 254 (1992): 609–56; Paul Nolte, "Der südwestdeutsche Frühliberalismus in der Kontinuität der Frühen Neuzeit," *Geschichte in Wissenschaft und Unterricht* 43 (1992): 743–56.

40 See Boch, *Grenzenloses Wachstum*; for the economic discourse in Prussian bureaucratic liberalism, see Barbara Vogel, *Allgemeine Gewerbefreiheit: Die Reformpolitik des preussischen Staatskanzlers Hardenberg (1810–1820)* (Göttingen, 1983).

and commercial development were important factors in the shaping of liberal ideology.

The terms of the current debate thus look very favorable for a comparison of liberal and republican party ideologies in the first half of the nineteenth century, and the issue certainly deserves more than the following brief remarks that focus on three central and interrelated problems: the attitudes toward central government; the attitudes toward market society and internal improvements; and the perceptions and visions of social order and inequality. All three have been identified by recent research as being of crucial importance for liberal and republican ideologies in both *Vormärz* Germany and Jacksonian America.

The controversy over the legitimate functions of government, and of the federal government in particular, was in many respects at the heart of the political conflicts in which the second party system was forged. Although Jackson eventually did not identify with the states' rights position during the Nullification Crisis, it was clear, as Harry Watson has summed up, "that the great states'-rights battles of the early Jackson administration had been settled in favor of those who opposed the federal power to promote industrialization, urbanization, and economic innovation."[41] Continuing the Jeffersonian contention that "the best government is that which governs least," Jackson in 1831–2 established a firm record of resistance against governmental support for economic improvement measures that proved to be very popular with segments of the American people. Following the first round of Jacksonian policies against internal improvements – with the tariff debates and the Maysville veto as important steps – at the beginning of Jackson's second term the "war" against the Second Bank of the United States definitively forged the Democratic coalition and gave rise to the emergence of the Whig party from the remnants of the National Republicans, and thus to the clear-cut political boundaries in the formation of the second party system. The issue of government intervention and states' rights – also closely related to the slavery question – remained important, but it carried within it the seeds of internal party controversy and sectional conflict, a problem that, not accidentally, caused the eventual downfall of the second party system. Different from Germany, as we shall see, economic issues in America have come to be seen as the prime integrators of parties and the single most important factor in determining party allegiance during the 1830s and 1840s.

41 Watson, *Liberty and Power*, 129.

In the quarrels over issues of economic order and development, and over the government's role in them, fundamental anxieties and visions about the social order were brought to the fore. In his famous Bank Veto message of July 10, 1832, Jackson rose in defense of the "humble members of society – the farmers, mechanics, and laborers" and their "right to complain of the justice of their Government," while at the same time dismissing the attempts by the "rich and powerful" to secure special protection by law in order to get even richer.[42] This was not the language of class struggle but of a radical egalitarianism that wished to establish a solid, middle-class prosperity for all independent (that is, nonslave) Americans, whereas the Whigs, despite their general commitment to social equality, adhered to an "organic" vision of society willing to accept new social hierarchies resulting from the economic success of individuals. In language resembling eighteenth-century social thought, the Democrats were intent on fighting this "money aristocracy" in which they saw a betrayal of genuine American principles.[43] Their constituency feared increasing clefts in society as a result of market development, the expansion of banking and paper money, and the beginnings of industrialization.

The new interpretation of party ideology during the second party system has considerably enriched, and at the same time complicated, our understanding of what was "liberal" or "conservative," what was "traditional" or "modern" in the political goals and social visions of the Whig and Democratic parties. Indeed, those very categories have proven anachronistic (if often difficult to avoid) because both parties, and the cultural movements they represented, adhered to a particular blueprint of society and politics that included an inextricable mixture of anxiety and optimism and a deep ambivalence about progress and nostalgia. Although the Whigs were more often considered the party of progress, the Democrats often refuted history and claimed "the expansive future" to be their "arena."[44] And whereas the Democrats are rightly seen as more skeptical of economic development, Whigs also viewed commercial activity as "dangerous to the virtue of the generation exposed to it."[45] This is not to say, however, that the two parties were nonideological or interchangeable in their programs and cultural appeals. On the contrary, within the contemporary horizon of

42 James D. Richardson, ed., *The Messages and Papers of the Presidents, 1789–1902,* 11 vols. (Washington, D.C., 1904), 2:590.
43 For a typical Democratic attack on the "money aristocracy," see "Thoughts on the Times," *Democratic Review* 6 (Dec. 1839): 449–62.
44 "The Great Nation of Futurity," *Democratic Review* 6 (Dec. 1839): 427.
45 See, e.g., "Influence of the Trading Spirit upon the Social and Moral Life of America," *American (Whig) Review* 1 (Jan. 1845): 95.

ideology and cultural belief systems they offered clearly distinguishable alternatives that were particularly effective in drawing lines of partisan affiliation on the community level and against the background of its specific conflicts.[46]

The problem of liberal ideology may look even more twisted and complicated in Germany because the "Whig" and the "Democratic" tradition were both, for most of the time and in most areas, represented under a common "liberal" party label, although they may still be distinguished as different ideological and cultural threads. Together with the obvious importance of bureaucratic liberalism in both Prussia and the Southwestern states, this has sometimes obscured the fact that liberal party formation outside the government or government-related groups was strongly fueled by resentment against the central government. On the local level a "liberal" faction in community politics often emerged in opposition to encroachment of the state bureaucracy on affairs increasingly considered part of an autonomous sphere of citizens' politics.[47] This resentment was nourished by a long tradition of resistance and skepticism in popular culture in the face of the expanding absolutist and bureaucratic state. Liberalism, in other words, provided a tool and a suitable language to give a new political meaning to an old conflict. Similarly to the Jacksonian republican tradition in America, small town German liberals believed that central authority had to be reduced to a minimum; liberty was believed to be found in the greatest possible freedom from intervening efforts of a central bureaucracy.

In Prussia, the largest and most heterogeneous German state by far, a different form of antigovernment attitude was introduced through the integration of new provinces after the Vienna Congress: In the Rhineland, in particular, liberalism became an expression of its claim to autonomy from the conservative Berlin government, a conflict further intensified by religious overtones: The Catholic Rhinelanders fought against the Protestant Prussian bureaucracy.[48] Generally, it can be said that during the *Vormärz* (liberal) parties in Germany, as long as they actually embodied part of society, almost always stood in opposition to government authority. Only

---

46 See Howe, "The Evangelical Movement," 1228; Watson, *Liberty and Power*, 237–9; Watson, *Jacksonian Politics*.

47 For details, see Nolte, *Gemeindebürgertum*, chap. 2; for the local processes of party formation, see also the fine case study by John R. Wilson, "Seedbed of Protest: Social Structure and Radical Politics in Ettlingen, Grand Duchy of Baden, 1815–1850," Ph.D. diss., The Johns Hopkins University, 1981.

48 Herbert Obenaus, "Region und politisches Interesse im Vormärzliberalismus Preussens," in Dieter Langewiesche, ed., *Liberalismus um 19. Jahrhundert* (Göttingen, 1988), 71–82; Elisabeth Fehrenbach, "Rheinischer Liberalismus und gesellschaftliche Verfassung," in Wolfgang Schieder, ed., *Liberalismus in der Gesellschaft des deutschen Vormärz* (Göttingen, 1983), 272–94.

shortly before the revolution of 1848, and as an eventual response to the growing radicalism within the liberal movement, were attempts at an organization of progovernment, conservative or conservative-liberal parties seriously undertaken and found response in a wider electorate.

As in the United States, the attitudes toward central government were related to liberal views of economic development. State protection for the eroding institutions of a corporate economy was welcome in the artisanal and petty-commercial milieu that formed a major hotbed of early German liberalism, and the principle of *Gewerbefreiheit* (freedom of trade) was seen as a potential danger not only to one's own business but to the structure of a well-ordered society as a whole.[49] What was worse, however, was state protection and financial support for the emerging industrial sector. When in the economic crisis of 1847, for example, three Baden factories demanded state support to secure their existence, small town liberals defending artisan and agrarian interests vigorously petitioned against such financial aid – the government was supposed to refrain from intervention in what was considered a "private matter."[50] But other liberals favored governmental help in this affair, using more modern arguments of social policy with regard to the 3,500 workers employed in the three factories. This was a typical conflict of the 1840s, and in many ways it resembled the American controversy between the Democrats and the Whigs over economic development and state support for internal improvements. In Germany, however, both positions were rooted in one single, liberal party, thus again and again provoking controversies between the "market" wing, which often included liberals in the state bureaucracies, and the petty-commercial "community" wing of liberalism which was more skeptical of rapid economic development and market integration.

Why did this conflict not break apart German liberalism? Why did it not become the core for the crystallization of two different parties as in the United States? There are at least two answers to these questions. First, despite their differences, liberals still had some common ground in their economic ideas and visions. Skeptics and supporters of state aid to the industrial economy, skeptics and supporters of a German tariff union, and artisans in the Southwest and bourgeois entrepreneurs in the Rhineland –

---

49 This is one of the most important results of the reinterpretation in the past two decades of early German liberalism. See, e.g., Helmut Sedatis, *Liberalismus und Handwerk in Südwestdeutschland* (Stuttgart, 1979); Heinz-Gerhard Haupt and Friedrich Lenger, "Liberalismus und Handwerk in Frankreich und Deutschland um die Mitte des 19. Jahrhunderts," in Langewiesche, ed., *Liberalismus*, 305–31.

50 See Nolte, *Gemeindebürgertum*, 289–90.

all adhered to a socioeconomic vision that regarded the English model of
a preponderance of industry as dangerous and favored instead a balanced
and slowly progressing economy in which family farming and artisanal
trades would retain their places and could still have a say in questions of
political economy.[51] Second, economic positions were important, and they
also framed an overall vision of social order and equality. But the prime
identity of a liberal consisted of a political rather than an economic con-
fession.[52] To put it in a somewhat oversimplified way: The overall structure
of the German *Vormärz* party system was not hammered out in the Bank
War or the economic crash of 1837 but in conflicts with monarchical
and bureaucratic authority over issues of political liberty, over demands
for freedom of the press or for representative government that had long
become unquestionable cornerstones of the political order in America.

The economic ideal of a simple market society was closely linked to a
social vision that Lothar Gall has aptly termed the *klassenlose Bürgergesellschaft* (classless civil society).[53] Industrial development and the unrestrained reign of capitalist market principles was feared because it would
destroy the *Mittelstand* – the healthy middle of society consisting of economically, and thus politically, independent citizens. The fear of increasing
social inequality as a result of capitalist development made German liberals, in much the same way as Jacksonians in America, advocates of an egalitarian order that equally condemned excessive wealth and excessive
poverty. Even liberals in the Rhineland, with its advanced commercialization, clung to a version of a utopia where rigid social classes did not exist
and every independent male would have an equal chance of participating in economic and political affairs.[54] As in America, the formation of
social classes was rejected in the traditional language of eighteenth-century
society which described bourgeois entrepreneurs as a new "aristocracy" of
money; and the radical, small town republicanism that emerged in the revolution of 1848–9 favored the republic as a system that would safeguard
society against the dangers of the moneyed aristocracy's political dominance
now associated with the political system of monarchy.[55]

51 This is argued very persuasively, e.g., by Hans-Werner Hahn, "Zwischen deutscher Handelsfreiheit
   und Sicherung landständischer Rechte: Der Liberalismus und die Gründung des Deutschen Zoll-
   vereins," in Schieder, ed., *Liberalismus*, 239–71. For the Rhenish bourgeoisie's early concepts of
   industrial development, see Boch, *Grenzenloses Wachstum*.
52 See, e.g., Karl Rohe, *Wahlen und Wählertraditionen in Deutschland: Kulturelle Grundlagen deutscher
   Parteien und Parteiensysteme im 19. und 20. Jahrhundert* (Frankfurt am Main, 1992), 43.
53 Gall, "Liberalismus und 'bürgerliche Gesellschaft.'"
54 See Fehrenbach, "Rheinischer Liberalismus und gesellschaftliche Verfassung."
55 See Nolte, *Gemeindebürgertum*, 209–23, 338–52.

It may seem surprising to see far-reaching similarities between the structures of political ideologies at large as well as affinities between certain,
very specific arguments – for example, on virtue and corruption or on
social order and inequality – in two countries that at the time were not
engaged in a particularly intense intellectual or political exchange. How
can we account for these similarities? Two explanations have already been
mentioned in this chapter and indeed stand at the core of its argument:
First, the decades under consideration here were marked by a strong presence of eighteenth-century traditions in the liberal and republican movements of both countries. They invoked a language of republican liberty that
had spread widely throughout the Atlantic world. Germany's political
and ideological traditions in the eighteenth century had to a large extent
been different, as we have seen, and the eighteenth-century heritage in
nineteenth-century liberalism and republicanism here was very much a
borrowed heritage, an "invention of tradition":[56] Its vision of the future
was based on a reading of German history that in turn had been soaked
in French and British thought since the late Enlightenment era.[57] Nevertheless, this cultural projection fitted genuine German traditions, such as
the town burghers' communal spirit or the widespread reservations against
the intrusion of a central government in local affairs. Second, the economic,
cultural, and social changes wrought by the market revolution in the early
to mid-nineteenth century were similar and demanded a decision by liberals and republicans about their stance on these fundamental challenges, a
decision that, again, could plausibly be justified in terms of an arsenal of
"classical republican" arguments readily at hand – or could be repudiated.
The linkage of both, the last revival of notions of classical republicanism in
the face of the market revolution, which characterized the 1830s and 1840s
in Germany as well as in the United States, provided for the particular partisan dynamics of that time in both countries.

But the parallels in the ideological frameworks of the second party
system in America and the German *Vormärz* may be carried a step further.
Party controversies in both countries essentially did not pit "liberals" against
"conservatives" but rather expressed a fundamental tension within the
liberal-republican tradition itself, a tension that may be described as the last
remnant of a "court versus country" conflict in eighteenth-century society

56 Eric Hobsbawm and Terence Ranger, eds., *The Invention of Tradition* (Cambridge, 1983).
57 For the important example of Montesquieu, see Rudolf Vierhaus, "Montesquieu in Deutschland:
Zur Geschichte seiner Wirkung als politischer Schriftsteller im 18. Jahrhundert," in Rudolf Vierhaus, *Deutschland im 18. Jahrhundert: Politische Verfassung, soziales Gefüge, geistige Bewegungen; Aus-
gewählte Aufsätze* (Göttingen, 1987), 9–32.

and political culture.[58] In the United States the Whig party, in the Hamiltonian tradition, represented the "court" interest, whereas the Democrats, in the tradition of a Jeffersonian social and economic vision,[59] represented the "country" interest, albeit the "country" during the presidency of Andrew Jackson had obviously come to central administrative power. In Germany the "country" interest, ideology, and language were represented in community liberalism, in liberal movements that originated in the small town environments of tradition-oriented petty producers, whereas the "court" interest found expression in bureaucratic liberalism and in parts of the middle class that were inclined to support industrialization, that preferred a national outlook, and that leaned toward the state, especially the nation-state.

However, it would be wrong, particularly in the case of Germany, to understand these two positions as strictly demarcated, hostile camps. Rather, they are better seen as two poles of a liberal continuum, as cultural options for understanding and dealing with the political, social, and economic transformations of the revolutionary century. Although German country liberalism was based more on the political core of the classical "country" ideology — opposition to central government and monarchical authority — American country liberalism rather leaned on its economic core — the principles of agrarianism and skepticism about quickly advancing commercial development. But both expressed a particular mixture of "nostalgia"[60] and social radicalism that was bound to disintegrate in the second half of the nineteenth century.

Early nineteenth-century party systems and their systems of belief and cultural persuasion that we call "liberalism" or "republicanism" in Germany as well as in the United States belonged to an era of transition and uncertainty. They were nourished in an environment of social and political mobilization, yet stayed firmly bound to the narrower horizons of localized communication and social relations. They prospered in an age of commercial spirit and economic expansion, and yet the limits to this development still allowed them to cling to notions of an egalitarian, preindustrial society of virtuous petty producers. When the social and economic changes after

---

58 Although this is a familiar, if controversial, concept for eighteenth- and early nineteenth-century American history, these categories have rarely been used as a conceptual framework for interpreting German political culture and for comparing it with other countries in an international or transatlantic context. See Nolte, "Der südwestdeutsche Frühliberalismus"; Nolte, *Gemeindebürgertum*.

59 See Joyce Appleby, *Capitalism and a New Social Order: The Republican Vision of the 1790s* (New York, 1984).

60 For this concept in relation to "Country ideology," see Isaac Kramnick, *Bolingbroke and His Circle: The Politics of Nostalgia in the Age of Walpole* (Cambridge, Mass., 1968).

the middle of the nineteenth century took on dimensions that blew up those visions and practices of a transitory society, the party systems and party ideologies built on them languished. In this perspective, both countries may not have been as "exceptional" as they believed and as many historians continue to believe. They may much more likely represent variations – unique variations, to be sure – in the broad transatlantic patterns of society and ideology in the revolutionary period of modern history between 1750 and 1850.

11

Festive Culture and National Identity in America and Germany, 1760–1860

JÜRGEN HEIDEKING

FESTIVE CULTURE AS A CREATIVE FORCE

During the past decade public festivals and civic celebrations have become a favorite topic of scholarly investigation and debate. This growing academic interest has certainly been stimulated by great commemorative events such as the bicentennials of the U.S. Constitution and the French Revolution, the 150th anniversary of the Hambach Festival, and the 500th anniversary of Columbus's first voyage to America. Another source of inspiration as well as anxiety has been the revival of the nation-state and nationalism in the wake of the Eastern European revolutions of 1989–90 and German reunification. These external political influences coincided with a new trend in the social and cultural sciences: Political and social scientists are studying ceremonies, cults, rituals, and symbols to gain insight into the popular reception of ideas and ideologies, into mechanisms of social integration and exclusion, and into processes of communication that shape the "public sphere" of modern societies. Anthropologists and cultural historians have asked questions about the genesis and development of mentalities and collective identities, about the forms and functions of "social memory," as well as about the importance of emotions, sacrality, and "transgressions" of established norms and rules. If perused in a more systematic and coordinated way, these two basic approaches – of the social and political sciences – could well complement and reinforce each other.[1] A relatively new discipline, cultural semiotics, which explains "culture" in terms of systems of signs and symbols, promises to lay the

---

1 Jürgen Kocka suggested this in "Faszination und Kritik: Bemerkungen aus der Perspektive eines Sozialhistorikers," in Etienne François, Hannes Siegrist, and Jakob Vogel, eds., *Nation und Emotion: Deutschland und Frankreich im Vergleich im 19. und 20. Jahrhundert* (Göttingen, 1995), 389–92.

foundation for such a synthesis. To analyze festive culture in this context would require a distinction among three different stages: the intended meaning of the celebration; the symbolic code that transports this meaning; and the reception by the broader public. It seems difficult, however, to move from impressive theoretical concepts to empirical research and readable publications.[2]

These problems notwithstanding, the discovery or rediscovery of festive culture has made clear that public celebrations constitute a fundamental aspect of social life and that they fulfill essential albeit ambivalent functions for every community. They guarantee as well as threaten the social order; they fuse the sacred and the profane; and they act as seismographs of the cohesion as well as the conflicts of social groups. The principal distinction between the traditional view and the contemporary debate seems to be a growing belief that celebrations do not just "reflect" social practices but that they possess the elemental power to create and "construct" (or "deconstruct") political concepts and cultural meaning. In this sense, festive culture is part of the historical process that shapes and transforms power relations, social structures, and popular mentalities.[3] By focusing on the question of national identity I attempt to put this new approach into a comparative perspective. A closer look at festive culture may help to clarify how Americans and Germans responded to three historical challenges: (1) the dissolution of the feudal order and the demand for political participation of larger sections of the population; (2) the transformation from predominantly agrarian to commercial, market-oriented societies, accompanied by the rise and differentiation of the urban middle class; and (3) the conflicting pressures of centralization and national integration on the one hand and localism, regionalism, and particularism on the other.

---

2 See Klaus P. Hansen, *Kultur und Kulturwissenschaft: Eine Einführung* (Tübingen, 1995).
3 Important recent contributions to the discussion of theoretical and methodological questions include Benedict Anderson, *Imagined Communities: Reflections on the Origin and Spread of Nationalism* (New York, 1985); Winfried Gebhardt, "Fest, Feier und Alltag: Über die gesellschaftliche Wirklichkeit des Menschen und ihre Deutung," Ph.D. diss., University of Tübingen, 1986; Aleida Assmann and Dietrich Harth, eds., *Mnemosyne: Formen und Funktionen der kulturellen Erinnerung* (Frankfurt am Main, 1991); Geneviève Fabre, "Lieux de fête et de commémoration," *Revue française d'etudes américaines* 51 (1992): 7–17; Manfred Hettling and Paul Nolte, "Bürgerliche Feste als symbolische Politik," in Manfred Hettling and Paul Nolte, eds., *Bürgerliche Feste: Symbolische Formen politischen Handelns im 19. Jahrhundert* (Göttingen, 1993), 7–36; Etienne François, Hannes Siegrist, and Jacob Vogel, "Die Nation: Vorstellungen, Inszenierungen, Emotionen," in François, *Nation und Emotion*, 13–35; Helmut Berding, ed., *Nationales Bewusstsein und kollektive Identität: Studien zur Entwicklung des kollektiven Bewusstsein in der Neuzeit* (Frankfurt am Main, 1994).

AMERICAN AND GERMAN FESTIVE CULTURES,
1760S TO 1820S

The Construction of Republican Festive Culture in the United States

The first wave of American public ceremonies, rituals, and celebrations in the 1760s and 1770s had a distinctly rebellious and subversive character, and these activities – Stamp Act demonstrations, boycotts, "Boston Massacre" commemorations, "Tea Parties," and so forth – contributed greatly to the disintegration and final collapse of British colonial authority. It has been argued that the colonists "celebrated themselves into an American future" and that these celebrations, effectively publicized by the patriot press, for the first time created a sense of common destiny and American identity.[4] The rituals, techniques, and symbols of these early manifestations of festive culture were largely borrowed from the English radical "plebeian" opposition, which had been particularly active around the middle of the eighteenth century. This anti-establishment, anti-authoritarian tendency became a constituent element of the new American festive culture, and it colored the first Independence Day celebrations on the Fourth of July. But, from the 1780s onward, it was overshadowed by a different version of civic republicanism that put more emphasis on order, self-discipline, regularity, and social harmony. The Grand Federal Processions of 1788, huge parades in several coastal cities from Boston to Charleston on the occasion of the ratification of the U.S. Constitution, must be understood as the ideal expression of this moderate, optimistic, and progressive republican spirit.[5] Preceding the famous French Revolutionary festivals by more than two years, these processions created an image of how the supporters of the

---

4 David Waldstreicher, "Rites of Rebellion, Rites of Assent: Celebrations, Print Culture, and the Origins of American Nationalism," *Journal of American History* 81 (1995): 37–61; Dirk Hoerder, *Crowd Action in Revolutionary Massachusetts, 1765–1780* (New York, 1977); Peter Shaw, *American Patriots and the Rituals of Revolution* (Cambridge, Mass., 1981); Paul A. Gilje, *Rioting in America* (Bloomington, Ind., 1996); see Jürgen Heideking, "Einheit aus Vielfalt: Die Entstehung des amerikanischen Nationalbewusstseins in der Revolutionsepoche 1760–1820," in Ulrich Herrmann, ed., *Volk–Nation–Vaterland* (Hamburg, 1996), 101–17.

5 For a detailed interpretation of the ratification celebrations, see Jürgen Heideking, *Die Verfassung vor dem Richterstuhl: Vorgeschichte und Ratifizierung der amerikanischen Verfassung 1787–1791* (Berlin, 1988), pt. 8:709–87; cf. Jürgen Heideking, "The Federal Processions of 1788 and the Origins of American Civil Religion," *Soundings* 77 (1994): 367–87; Jürgen Heideking, "Die Verfassungsfeiern von 1788: Das Ende der Amerikanischen Revolution und die Anfänge einer nationalen Festkultur in den Vereinigten Staaten," *Der Staat* 34 (1995): 391–413. Hans-Christoph Schröder takes a different view in "Der Pope's Day in Boston und die Verfassungsfeier in Philadelphia," in Uwe Schultz, ed., *Das Fest: Eine Kulturgeschichte von der Antike bis zur Gegenwart* (Munich, 1988), 244–57.

Constitution wanted to see themselves and wanted their society to be seen by the outside world.[6] The first procession in Boston in February 1788 seems to have been spontaneously organized by local artisans and mechanics, but the following events were thoroughly choreographed, sophisticated festivals sponsored by merchant associations and artisan guilds, involving the urban elite as well as the "middling sort" of people, and drawing tens of thousands of spectators. The climax was reached on July 4, 1788, when the people of Philadelphia combined the celebration of American independence with that of the Constitution.

Many elements of the parades – such as the ships carried through the streets and the floats on which artisans performed their various crafts – harkened back to European pageants, especially the annual Lord Mayor's Shows in London (which, in turn, had their roots in ceremonial practices of Renaissance Florence and Venice). On the whole, however, the federal processions were genuinely American productions that, for the first time, projected the concept of a sovereign, self-governing republican people onto the streets. The organizers and marchers made it visually clear that the Americans – in contrast to the "common man" in Europe – no longer contented themselves with a subservient, passive role but rather proudly staged their own public celebrations. By featuring a well-regulated column of up to 5,000 marchers divided into sections and subsections, the processions conveyed another important message: Although (or because) the new republican states comprising the American union lacked strong rulers and a formal hierarchy, they were orderly, harmonious, and interdependent communities bound together by patriotism, virtue, mutual affection, and benevolence. This sense of community was affirmed at the banquets in which thousands of participants joined at the end of the marches.

Explicitly and symbolically the processions made a variety of additional statements. Trade banners, emblems, and slogans proclaimed support for a new, more economically powerful federal government and demanded the protection of American producers against imports from Europe. On another level, the celebrations demonstrated a longing for an American cultural identity and a national consensus. This was underlined by the enthusiastic involvement of artists who produced decorations, drawings, poems, and songs; it also found expression in the symbolic interpretation of the course of American history as a linear progression from Columbus through the founding of the colonies to the Revolution and the Federal Constitu-

---

6 This fact has been overlooked by European scholars. See, e.g., the otherwise groundbreaking study of Mona Ozouf, *Festivals and the French Revolution* (Cambridge, 1988).

tion. In some places actors dressed as George Washington attempted to per-sonify the continuity of Revolution, War of Independence, and Constitution. The conviction expressed by some speakers that public celebrations would educate the younger generation and would help to make them good republican citizens reflected the didactic impetus of the Enlightenment and Rousseau's writings about national festivals. Finally, and perhaps most important, the processions endowed the new political system with moral dignity and religious legitimacy. The presence of members of the clergy (often including a Jewish rabbi) and the biblically inspired rhetoric created a sacral atmosphere, while symbolic and allegorical arrangements put the Constitution in a religious context by, for example, placing the document on the "altar of liberty" or in a "federal temple." Classical and Christian religious symbols – the temple, the altar, the "sacred flame" – came to be closely related to the new national symbols and insignia such as the flag and the American eagle. Here lie the origins of a secular "civil religion" that did not clash with the traditional experiences of Americans in their various denominations. Newspaper reports and private letters attest to the fact that the processions created a "solemn" atmosphere that deeply impressed marchers and spectators alike.[7] Trying to disrupt this festive mood could prove dangerous and costly: When a newspaper editor in New York, who opposed ratification, published an article ridiculing the parade, his shop was attacked and his printing press destroyed by an angry crowd.

Certainly, the processions of 1788 presented a partisan view of American politics and an idealized image of social reality: Antifederalist criticism of the Constitution was not allowed, and certain segments of the population – farmers, the "lower sort of people," free blacks, women – were either underrepresented or excluded. Women, for example, appeared only as allegorical figures (Columbia, Liberty, Justice, and so forth) or – dressed in long white robes – as symbols of purity and chastity. Nevertheless, it seems safe to say that the grand federal processions installed a new kind of republican

---

7 Commenting on the Philadelphia procession, Benjamin Rush wrote on July 9, 1788: "The triumphal car was truly sublime. It was raised above every other subject. The Constitution was carried by a law-officer, to denote the elevation of the government and of law and justice above everything else in the United States. . . . I do not believe that the Constitution was the offspring of inspiration, but I am perfectly satisfied that the Union of the States, in its *form* and *adoption*, is as much the work of divine providence as any of the miracles recorded in the old and new Testament were the effects of a divine power" (quoted in Merrill Jensen, ed., *Documentary History of the Ratification of the Constitution*, 18 vols. [Madison, Wis., 1976–97], 18:264, 266). See also Michael Kammen, *A Machine That Would Go of Itself: The Constitution in American Culture* (New York, 1986), 45; Laura Rigal, "'Raising the Roof': Authors, Spectators, and Artisans in the Grand Federal Procession of 1788," *Theatre Journal* 48 (1996): 253–77.

festive culture, a dynamic and nationalized version of the revolutionary ideology that particularly suited the practical needs and political aspirations of the urban middle class.

Although the federal processions of 1788 set precedents and served as models for public celebrations in the nineteenth century, the American festive culture never became monolithic.[8] This was partly due to the French Revolution, which radicalized the political discourse in the United States during the 1790s and fueled a debate between Federalists and Republicans over the "true republican way" of celebrating. In most cities the artisans, mechanics, and tradesmen shifted their allegiance to the Jeffersonian-Republicans and tried to preserve, if not the form, at least the spirit of the grand processions in the annual Fourth of July celebrations. Their preference for "sound republican simplicity," their Jacobinic toasts and radical songs, pointed to a more democratic style of politics and festive culture. The Federalists, on their part, began to put even more emphasis than before on the themes of order and stability. They did this in particular by moving George Washington, the war hero and first president, into the center of public ceremonial life. This tendency had already been apparent on the occasion of Washington's inauguration in March 1789, which capped a triumphal journey with enthusiastic receptions in several places from Virginia to New York. In the 1790s staunch Federalists obviously considered Washington's birthday on February 22 to be as important as Independence Day. In Washington's person they celebrated – with militia parades, processions of politicians and other dignitaries, speeches, and banquets – the ideal of virtuous, selfless leadership and the symbolic center of the Union. At the same time, Washington himself tried to embellish the presidency with some ceremonial splendor by staging levees and balls at his home in Philadelphia. He sought to strengthen the prestige of the federal government to keep the still fragile Union together. The Republican press, however, condemned the "cult of Washington" as well as the modest ceremonial pomp unfolding at the "republican court" as signs of monarchical corruption and violations of republican principles. Internal and external enemy images – "monocrats" versus "Jacobins"; the "atheistic" French versus the "reactionary" British – proliferated and found their way into the vocabulary of public events.[9]

8 Susan G. Davis, *Parades and Power: Street Theater in Nineteenth-Century Philadelphia* (Philadelphia, 1986), 117–25.
9 Cf. Simon P. Newman, "Principles or Men? George Washington and the Political Culture of National Leadership, 1776–1801," *Journal of the Early Republic* 12 (1992): 477–507; Simon P. Newman, *Parades and the Politics of the Street: Festive Culture in the Early American Republic* (Philadelphia,

The importance of these partisan contests over political symbols and rituals should not be exaggerated, however. Indeed, there existed divergent styles of festive culture and different opinions about "true republican" celebrations, but this phenomenon fit into a broader pattern of "conflict within consensus" that characterized the early national period.[10] The attitude toward the Constitution is a good example. Federalists and Republicans interpreted the text differently, but they both claimed to defend the Constitution against open attacks and subversion. The festive culture reflected and stabilized this basic consensus. Federalists preferred to celebrate the Constitution, whereas Republicans stressed the importance of the Declaration of Independence, but nobody tried in earnest to play the one founding document ideologically or symbolically against the other. When Washington died in 1799 the people of Philadelphia staged the largest public ceremony since the grand procession of 1788, with Federal and Republican militia corps joining in a common funeral parade. Under the presidencies of Thomas Jefferson and James Madison the celebration of Washington's birthday became less controversial than it had been during the first president's lifetime. In Boston, one of the last Federalist strongholds, followers of the two parties continued to celebrate the Fourth of July separately until 1817. The fiftieth anniversary of the Declaration of Independence ten years later was observed in "a climate of general good will," and most Americans interpreted the coincidental deaths of John Adams and Jefferson on July 4, 1826, as a providential sign confirming political reconciliation and national unity.[11]

The relative homogeneity of America's early national festive culture, which survived the political conflicts of the 1790s, was not threatened by undercurrents of resentment and protest on the margins of republican society. In the big cities and in some rural areas there existed – especially among laborers and blacks – alternative rituals and ceremonies that remained connected with the "plebian" culture of the colonial period or that had been adapted from African religious cults. They included "mock celebrations" that poked fun at local authorities, various forms of street

1997); Jürgen Heideking, "Das Englandbild in der nordamerikanischen Publizistik zur Zeit der Revolution," in Franz Bosbach, ed., *Feindbilder: Die Darstellung des Gegners in der politischen Publizistik des Mittelalters und der Neuzeit* (Cologne, 1992), 179–99; Joyce Appleby, "Radicalizing the War for Independence: American Responses to the French Revolution," *Amerikastudien/American Studies* 41 (1996): 7–16.

10 Kammen, *A Machine*, 29; cf. David Waldstreicher, *In the Midst of Perpetual Fetes: The Making of American Nationalism, 1776–1820* (Chapel Hill, N.C., 1997).

11 William H. Cohn, "Une fête nationale: le 4 juillet dans l'histoire américaine," *Cultures* 3 (1976): 147–63; Len Travers, *Celebrating the Fourth: Independence Day and the Rites of Nationalism in the Early Republic* (Amherst, Mass., 1997).

theater, and carnivallike practices such as the "mummeries" in Philadelphia. In the eyes of the majority, people involved in such activities lacked the "respectability" required for republican citizenship; expressions of "festive subcultures" could therefore be suppressed at any time if they seemed to endanger the public order.[12]

The basic republican consensus was strengthened by the War of 1812, which revived American nationalism and added some new symbols and commemorative dates to the repertoire of American festive culture: the – still unofficial – national anthem, the victorious battle of New Orleans, and the figure of Uncle Sam as the first personification of an American "national character." Since the Revolution a distinctive calendar of public ceremonial events had taken shape without central direction or planning. It encompassed annual national holidays (the Fourth of July and Washington's Birthday), important political events (the inauguration of a president, presidential visits), local holidays with national relevance (Evacuation Day in New York), the anniversaries of battles, and special days of fasting and prayer proclaimed by state governments and churches. Even free blacks paid tribute to the national culture by choosing the Fifth of July as an alternative "Independence Day" (later they added the anniversary of the abolition of slavery in the British Empire).

An innovation occurred in 1825 when the people of New York celebrated an achievement that resonated across the nation: The opening of the Erie Canal became the first economic event in United States history to be honored with a parade. This public festival was modeled after the federal processions of 1788, and it even outdid Philadelphia's splendid parade in honor of the visiting Marquis de Lafayette in 1824. The predominance of artisans and mechanics, the spirit of civic republicanism, and the ideal of a homogeneous, self-governing society connected this celebration with the past; the occasion, however, signaled the beginning of a new chapter in which American festive culture would adapt to rapid social and economic change.[13]

12 Shane White, "'It Was a Proud Day': African Americans, Festivals, and Parades in the North, 1741–1834," *Journal of American History* 81 (1994): 13–50; cf. Davis, *Parades and Power*, 73–112.
13 Cf. Mary P. Ryan, "The American Parade: Representations of Nineteenth-Century Social Order," in Lynn Hunt, ed., *The New Cultural History* (Berkeley, Calif., 1989), 131–53, esp. 135; Mary P. Ryan, *Women in Public: Between Banners and Ballots, 1825–1880* (Baltimore, 1990); Sean Wilentz, "Artisan Republican Festivals and the Rise of Class Conflict in New York City, 1788–1837," in Michael H. Frisch and Daniel J. Walkowitz, eds., *Working-Class America: Essays on Labor, Community, and American Society* (Urbana, Ill., 1983), 37–77, esp. 47–52.

The Failure of a National Holiday in Germany

In eighteenth-century Germany, Enlightenment ideas and the economic needs of courts and governments sparked a debate about religious and popular holidays. Reform-minded administrators criticized what they perceived as "festivals of immorality, wastefulness, and disorder," and they endeavored to create a "rational" festive culture marked by thrift and discipline. Proposals for instituting "national holidays" appeared for the first time around 1790 in the context of enlightened absolutism and financial rationalization. "National" did not mean "German" but still related to a specific state or territory whose population the reformers wanted to "integrate" by means of well-organized festivals.[14]

These efforts were interrupted by the French Revolution and the subsequent revolutionary wars, which brought many Germans in contact with French republican festive culture. Beginning in 1792 public celebrations "à la française" took place in the occupied and later annexed Rhineland. At first, some devoted German republicans participated willingly in propagating the goals and values of the Revolution, and the Rhenish population showed a measure of sympathy for these unfamiliar ceremonies that mixed formal acts of government and military parades with didactic street theater and more-or-less organized public rejoicing. But when the revolutionaries openly attacked the church, and when the celebrations became propaganda instruments of the French occupation regime, sympathy turned into mistrust, disaffection, and defiance. Instead of putting up open resistance, the people in the Rhenish towns and cities used the medieval tradition of carnival to ridicule the secular cult of reason and virtue. Even before Napoleon proclaimed the annexation of the left bank of the Rhine in 1801 the French festive calendar and republican civic culture had become hopelessly discredited in Germany.[15]

The new German festive culture that took shape during and immediately after the wars against Napoleon rejected the French revolutionary cult but at the same time borrowed from its forms and tried to assimilate some of its symbols. In October 1814, on the occasion of the first anniversary of the Battle of Leipzig, people all over Germany celebrated their first national

14 Paul Münch, "Fêtes pour le peuple, rien par le peuple: 'Öffentliche' Feste im Programm der Aufklärung," in Dieter Düding, Peter Friedemann, and Paul Münch, eds., *Öffentliche Festkultur: Politische Feste in Deutschland von der Aufkärung bis zum Ersten Weltkrieg* (Hamburg, 1988), 25–45, esp. 35–9.
15 Ottilie Dotzenrod, "Republikanische Feste im Rheinland zur Zeit der Französischen Revolution," in Düding, Friedemann, and Münch, eds., *Öffentliche Festkultur*, 46–66.

holiday.[16] Insofar as these ceremonies had the potential to serve as models for the future and to lay the foundation for a national festive culture, they can be seen in a light similar to that of the American federal processions of 1788. The celebrations had been prepared by a campaign in the press, especially by Ernst Moritz Arndt's pamphlet "Ein Wort über die Feier der Leipziger Schlacht," published in September 1814. He recommended that the Germans, instead of waiting until a nation-state had been established, should immediately organize national festivals ("teutsche Nationalfeste") to demonstrate their sense of belonging to one people and their yearning for national unity. The lack of any central coordination left room for spontaneity and variation. In most cases the initiative came from local dignitaries or clubs; civil servants, members of the clergy, professors, and teachers acted as organizers, and the character of the festivals was thoroughly bourgeois and middle class. The celebrations were intended as collective expressions of joy and gratitude for the liberation of the fatherland and as opportunities for fraternization across the political, geographical, social, and religious lines that separated the nation. This German nation was imagined as a harmonious community of rulers and people, based on the solidarity that the governing dynasties, the aristocracy, and the bourgeoisie supposedly had shown in the "war of liberation" against Napoleon. Therefore, any signs of opposition or protest were missing, and "liberty" meant first of all the absence of foreign oppression. Indirectly, however, demands for constitutions, civil rights, and political participation found expression in the heightened self-confidence of ordinary citizens.

Three major rituals dominated the activities on October 18 and 19, 1814: the citizens' processions that formed in the town centers and, under the ringing of church bells and the boom of militia cannons, marched to a nearby hill or open space; huge bonfires in the evening, accompanied by patriotic speeches, singing, and oath taking; and, the next morning, a common church service, followed by banquets and balls that continued well

16 Dieter Düding, "Das deutsche Nationalfest von 1814: Matrix der deutschen Nationalfeste im 19. Jahrhundert," in Düding, Friedemann, and Münch, eds., *Öffentliche Festkultur*, 67–88; cf. Dieter Düding, "Deutsche Nationalfeste im 19. Jahrhundert: Erscheinungsbild und politische Funktion," *Archiv für Kulturgeschichte* 69 (1987): 371–88. On early forms of German nationalism, see also the contributions of Monika Wagner, Ernst Weber, Jürgen Wilke, and Christof Römer in Ulrich Herrmann, ed., *Volk–Nation–Vaterland* (Hamburg, 1996). Cf. The general observations by Hans-Ulrich Wehler in the same volume: "Nationalismus, Nation und Nationalstaat in Deutschland seit dem ausgehenden 18. Jahrhundert," 269–78. An overall view is given by Hagen Schulze, *Der Weg zum Nationalstaat: Die deutsche Nationalbewegung vom 18. Jahrhundert bis zur Reichsgründung* (Munich, 1985); Elisabeth Fehrenbach, *Verfassungsstaat und Nationsbildung 1815–1871* (Munich, 1992); James J. Sheehan, *German History, 1770–1866* (Oxford, 1989). A review of recent literature is provided by Dieter Langewiesche, "Nation, Nationalismus, Nationalstaat: Forschungsstand und Forschungsperspektiven," *Neue politische Literatur* 40 (1995): 190–263.

into the night. In their formal structure and "liturgy" the celebrations mixed elements of traditional German *Volksfeste* and church holidays with those of the new American and French national festivals. In addition, the illuminations and fireworks staged in major cities were reminiscent of sumptuous court festivities or the splendid receptions of monarchs and princes.

If we look at the symbols, allegories, emblems, and so forth, and if we try to capture the atmosphere of the celebrations, three traits stand out: the importance attached to nature and history; the mutual reinforcement of religious and national sentiments; and the virulence against the French enemy image. The open air meetings, the bonfires on hills overlooking the countryside, and the use of oak leaves as a counterpart to the French cockade supported the romantic notion of a special German attachment to nature. At the same time, the patriotic rhetoric traced the national origins back to Germanic times, linking the Battle of Leipzig with Hermann's victory over the Romans. The strong religious component of the celebrations can be seen as a direct response to the French revolutionaries' efforts to supplant traditional Catholicism with a purely secular cult. The German patriots, on their part, freely mixed symbols and allegories taken from the pagan past (bonfires, oak leaves, Germania, Apollo, Pallas Athene) with those of the Christian present (altars, holy flames, and so forth). It was less the power of specific images than the fusion of the secular and the religious spheres – the combination of patriotic speeches and sermons, of "liberty songs" and chorales, of oaths and prayers – that produced the strong emotions, the tears, kisses, and cheers of joy, to which many observers and participants testified.

In marking the anniversary of the Völkerschlacht the celebrations also provided opportunities for directing negative emotions against a foreign enemy. The war years had already witnessed an outpouring of rabidly anti-French poetry, and the festivals continued the process of defining a German national identity by contrasting "good" German with "bad" French qualities. In this context, gender images played an important role: Whereas the French "national character" was regarded as "female" and effeminate, the (almost exclusively male) German patriots saw themselves as representatives of a "male" and virtuous nation. To a certain degree, the national holiday took on the form of an anti-French political demonstration. In speeches and drawings Napoleon was portrayed as the incarnation of evil, and in some places patriots burned him in effigy. Frequently, the bonfires were transformed into auto-da-fés, ritual burnings of French documents (the Code Napoleon, the Constitution of the Rheinbund), French weapons, and other insignia symbolizing "French oppression." Consciously or

220 Jürgen Heideking

unconsciously, the image of a foreign enemy was used to confirm the imagined "identity of interests" between rulers and ruled in Germany and to further national integration.[17]

The events of October 1814 probably are less important for what actually happened than for an assessment of "what could have been" under different political circumstances. The celebrations must be seen as the first signs of an authentic German national consciousness and as early manifestations of a bourgeois "public sphere" not opposed to the monarchical principle but capable of transforming the fragmented political landscape into a more open, participatory, and unified state system. That the German patriots expected their nation to occupy an exceptional position in the divine order of things and to fulfill a special mission did not distinguish them from nationalists in most other countries. The strong emotions and the exploitation of enemy images are conspicuous, but they cannot be seen as German peculiarities either.[18] In Germany, however, the development of an authentic national identity and a corresponding festive culture was made impossible by the outcome of the Congress of Vienna and by the tendency of the ruling classes to equate nationalism with revolutionary subversion.

For some years, the patriots continued to celebrate the anniversaries of the battles of Leipzig and of Belle Alliance (Waterloo), but their social base was shrinking, and they came into more and more conflict with the traditional authorities. In terms of ceremony and ritual, the Wartburgfest on October 18–19, 1817, was more or less a repetition of the first national festivals. Organized by students from several German universities, it added the black, red, and gold flag and the plain and simple "altteutsche Tracht" (traditional costume) – invented by Friedrich Ludwig Jahn's gymnasts – to the repertoire of national symbols. More important, the several hundred participants for the first time formulated political demands. Inspired by "the peoples' movements from the Netherlands to the Free States of North America," they discussed draft constitutions for a federated German monarchy as well as for a German republic. The *Grundsätze und Beschlüsse des 18. Oktobers*, which represented the majority opinion, have been called "the

17 Michael Jeismann, *Das Vaterland der Feinde: Studien zum nationalen Feindbegriff und Selbstverständnis in Deutschland und Frankreich 1792–1918* (Stuttgart, 1992).
18 See Reinhart Koselleck, "Volk, Nation, Nationalismus, Masse," in Otto Brunner, Werner Conze, and Reinhart Koselleck, eds., *Geschichtliche Grundbegriffe: Historisches Lexikon zur politisch-sozialen Sprache in Deutschland*, 9 vols. (Stuttgart, 1972–97), 7:141–431; Eric J. Hobsbawm, *Nationen und Nationalismus: Mythos und Realität seit 1780* (Frankfurt am Main, 1991); Benedict Anderson, *Die Erfindung der Nation: Zur Karriere eines erfolgreichen Konzepts* (Frankfurt am Main, 1993); William R. Hutchison and Hartmut Lehmann, eds., *Many Are Chosen: Divine Election and Western Nationalism* (Minneapolis, Minn., 1995).

first national-liberal party program."[19] The citizens of Eisenach joined the students, professors, and gymnasts (*Turner*) in a procession celebrating the national holiday and the three hundredth anniversary of the Reformation. Compared to 1814, the anti-French rhetoric was toned down considerably. Some anti-Semitic statements and the ceremonial burning of books and pamphlets, which allegedly favored feudalism and absolutism, provoked a srong (and mostly negative) public echo.

The Wartburgfest was followed by a cycle of government repression and student radicalization that made the continued celebration of national festivals impossible and drove the radical patriot movement underground. By 1820 it had become clear that the efforts to establish a permanent national holiday and to create a single nationalist style of public festivity had failed. Like the political landscape, German festive culture remained fragmented, and different festive traditions were carried on by the courts, the states, the churches, and the cities and towns. Increasing numbers of patriotic and liberal-minded citizens who sought alternatives joined local and regional associations (*Turner-, Sänger- und Schützenvereine*), which kept the national idea alive by celebrating their own festivals.

THE TRANSFORMATION OF FESTIVE CULTURE, 1820S TO 1860S

The Disintegration of Republican Festive Culture in the United States During the Antebellum Period

What happened to American festive culture in the era of the "market revolution"? To give a comprehensive answer to that question would require much more empirical research. From the existing literature one gets the impression that, during the antebellum period, the relatively homogeneous republican festive culture of the early nineteenth century dissolved into a variety of styles and practices. The pressures that contributed to this disintegration and transformation came from three different directions: (1) The growing complexity of American society, caused by rapid economic change, made it increasingly difficult to stage the harmonious civic celebrations typical of the early national period; (2) in a political climate shaped by democratization and party competition, public celebrations and festivals no longer acted as moderating forces but rather contributed to the

---

19 Peter Brandt, "Das studentische Wartburgfest vom 18./19. Oktober 1817," in Düding, Friedemann, Münch, eds., *Öffentliche Festkultur*, 89–112, esp. 104.

escalation of ideological and sectional conflicts; and (3) the mass immigration of the 1840s and 1850s produced ethnic tensions that could not be ameliorated by the traditional American festive culture.

After the opening of the Erie Canal in 1825 Americans became used to celebrating major economic achievements and technical breakthroughs. Spectacular public parades were held, for example, on the occasion of the completion of the Baltimore Railroad (1828), the opening of the Croton Reservoir in New York (1842), and the laying of the Atlantic cable (1858). However, the economic progress that received so much praise at the same time undermined republican festive culture. It became increasingly difficult to integrate the whole urban community into these parades or any other public festivals. The parades proved to be symbolic battlegrounds for the inclusion or exclusion of particular social groups, and they began to mirror the growing tensions between merchants and master artisans, on the one hand, and journeymen and laborers, on the other. Whereas the first group, according to Sean Wilentz, articulated "liberal doctrines on the necessity of self-interest and pursuit of individual gain," the second group defended the traditional "artisan republicanism" with its emphasis on mutuality, virtue, and commonwealth.[20] The parades and processions gradually lost their representative character. The urban elite more or less withdrew from communal events and found more congenial ways of celebrating economic progress and promoting their ideas in the organization of trade fairs and industrial expositions. At the opposite end of the social spectrum, the laborers and workers no longer regarded participation in the parades as their first priority. More and more often they staged separate demonstrations and parades, showing their class solidarity and making their demands and protests public.[21]

The national holidays were still observed, but the annual celebrations lost much of their authenticity and popular appeal. The official ceremonies acquired the character of uniform, mechanically observed rituals. In Philadelphia, as in many other places, Fourth of July parades degenerated into military spectacles, dominated by militias and marching bands. But even here conflicts surfaced between the volunteer militias, whose members could afford horses and colorful uniforms, and the regular militia companies, who often had to march in ordinary dress and without weapons.[22] Abraham Lincoln's wish, expressed in 1838, that the Americans might revive the spirit of the Declaration of Independence and create a "civic

20 Wilentz, "Artisan Republican Festivals," 52.
21 See Davis, Parades and Power, 113–54; Ryan, "American Parade," 138–41.
22 Davis, Parades and Power, 49–72.

religion" illustrates this loss of meaning and direction. The *Encyclopedia of American Social History* tells us that in the 1830s the Fourth of July even became "the butt of national ridicule" and famous for "the dullness of its soporific oratory."[23] As the generation of the founding fathers passed away, the Revolution acquired a mythical quality not connected to the practical problems of the day. Important anniversaries (George Washington's centennial birthday in 1832) and historic events (the French Revolution in 1830; Lafayette's death in 1834) generated more energy and emotions. Almost inevitably, however, these celebrations were drawn into the political battles of the time, especially the Nullification crisis and Andrew Jackson's "bank war." The antagonists did not hesitate to use them as platforms either for proclaiming the right of secession, for attacking the "monster bank" and its supporters, or for building up an anti-Jackson coalition.[24] This must be seen in the context of the general political polarization that helped to erode traditional festive practices and change the cultural climate of the United States. Fueled by the broadening franchise and the formation of popular parties, politics took on the dramatic functions that the old ceremonies and rituals no longer fulfilled. By participating in the election campaigns with their national conventions, mass rallies, processions, banners, emotionally charged appeals, songs, and so forth, the American voters celebrated, according to Richard P. McCormick, "a great democratic festival" and turned it into "a satisfying form of cultural expression."[25] This "new order of politics" stood in sharp contrast to the spirit of republican civic culture. On the one hand, the rise of popular parties certainly contributed to a nationalization of institutional forms and political styles; on the other hand, one must assume that the "dramatic" nature of party politics aggravated the crisis of the 1850s that led to the Civil War.[26]

23 Robert A. Orsi, "Parades, Holidays, and Public Rituals," in Mary Kupiec Cayton, Elliott J. Gorn, and Peter W. Williams, eds., *The Encyclopedia of American Social History*, 3 vols. (New York, 1993), 3:1918.
24 Examples are given in Davis, *Parades and Power*, 127–32; see Archie V. Huff, "The Eagle and the Vulture: Changing Attitudes Toward Nationalism in Fourth of July Orations Delivered in Charleston, 1778–1860," *South Atlantic Quarterly* 73 (1974): 10–22.
25 The year 1840 saw "the most spectacular campaign in which the whole nation had ever engaged . . . highly competitive party structures exerted every effort to arouse popular excitement . . . the voters were moved to identify strongly with the symbols, personalities, organizations, and myths that taken together constituted their party" (Richard P. McCormick, *The Second American Party System: Party Formation in the Jacksonian Era* [New York, 1966], 341–2, 350).
26 It might be argued that the patriotism generated by the Mexican-American War of 1846–8 contradicts this observation. There existed, however, some public opposition to the war, especially in New England; and immediately after the American victory various "conspiracy theories" that pitted the North against the South quickly gained ground.

The impact on American festive culture of mass immigration and various religious and secular reform movements needs to be investigated more thoroughly. Some local studies indicate that, in the 1840s, the participation of immigrants in parades and other public ceremonies became a point of debate and a source of conflict. In Philadelphia, anti-immigration protesters on the Fourth of July 1844 staged a "Grand Native American Procession," which provoked serious rioting.[27] Occasionally, immigrants were excluded from communal activities because of their low social status and/or their Catholic religion. In the 1850s the growing involvement of Irish and German Catholics in public festivities had a negative side effect: It accelerated the retreat of the elite and the upper middle class into a "private sphere," sheltered from intrusions by ordinary folks.[28] This, combined with nativist resistance, seems to have induced immigrant communities to organize their own parades and festivals – a tendency that reached its peak in the late nineteenth century and continues to the present.[29] Parallel to this growing awareness of ethnic identities, a number of reform movements, especially the Temperance movement and the Abolitionists, mobilized tens of thousands of Americans by adapting traditional festive forms such as parades and banquets, and by creating new rituals and symbols. In the western parts of the country religious revivals and camp meetings seem to have pushed secular forms of celebrations into the background.

By the eve of the Civil War the republican festive culture had given way to a diversity of cultural styles and ceremonial practices employed by different social groups, competing political parties, new ethnic and religious communities, and crusading reform movements to foster their own agendas. In view of the growing complexity of American society it was perhaps inevitable that festive culture now existed in a variety of forms; more serious was the fact that it lacked a common spirit and a common purpose. Under these circumstances, it could not act as an integrating, cohesive force; on the contrary, its symbolic and emotional power was used to intensify the conflicts over states' rights and slavery that tore the Union apart.

---

27 Davis, *Parades and Power*, 149–50.
28 Ryan, "American Parade," 145–7; Kathleen N. Conzen, "Ethnicity as Festive Culture: Nineteenth-Century German America on Parade," in Werner Sollors, ed., *The Invention of Ethnicity* (New York, 1989), 44–75.
29 Ramón A. Gutiérrez and Geneviève Fabre, eds., *Feasts and Celebrations in North American Ethnic Communities* (Albuquerque, N. M., 1995).

The Nationalization of Bourgeois Festive Culture in Germany

The American "civil society," from the beginning, practically coincided with the American "state" or the government(s) of the United States. In Germany, however, "civil society" developed slowly and haltingly in a process of emancipation from the sovereign representatives and institutions of the feudal, monarchical state. It articulated itself in the parliaments elected on the basis of the first state constitutions, in the (still controlled and censored) press, and – last but not least – in public celebrations and festivals. During the nineteenth century, therefore, German festive culture both reflected and influenced the relationship between the "state" and the emerging bourgeois "civil society."

In accordance with the political situation, festive culture remained highly diverse, fragmented, and particularistic. Yet, the changing nature of some festivals indicated that the traditional powers were ready or felt compelled to make concessions to the bourgeoisie and even to the common people. Good examples are the big public festivals in the southern states of Bavaria and Württemberg, the Oktoberfest in Munich, and the Cannstadt Vasen, which were instituted by government decrees in 1810 and 1818, respectively. In one sense, these events grew out of the Enlightenment debate over "rational" ways of celebrating. Both festivals were built around an agricultural state fair that aimed at educating the rural population and at raising the productivity of the state economy. In the early years these events were still divided between official ceremonies and separate days for popular entertainment and amusement. Gradually, however, urban citizens – merchants, manufacturers, professionals, artisans – began to play a more active, independent role, and the participation of ordinary people in parades and other public ceremonies grew. In Munich, the artists who planned and decorated the annual parades acted as if they were members of the aristocracy and the bourgeoisie. In this way, popular festive culture began to overshadow the more exclusive celebratory activities of the courts, and public festivals helped to foster a sense of Bavarian and Württembergian "state identity."[30] Similar tendencies can be observed in the smaller states and territories of southern and south-central Germany. In the Rhineland, carnival developed into a distinctive festive culture with regional variations. Although it made use of older forms of plebeian protest, it must be seen

---

30 Gerda Möhler, *Das Münchner Oktoberfest: Brauchformen des Volksfestes zwischen Aufklärung und Gegenwart* (Munich, 1980); see Wolfgang Hartmann, *Der historische Festzug: Seine Entstehung und Entwicklung im 19. und 20. Jahrhundert* (Munich, 1976), 19–22.

in the context of the emancipatory efforts of the bourgeoisie. By tem-
porarily breaking down class barriers carnival rituals helped to reduce social
distance and to strengthen the self-confidence of the urban middle class.
The annual carnival parades, which were held in Cologne and other
Rhenish cities starting in the 1820s, mocked courtly practices by imitating
royal "entrées" and triumphs – the solemn receptions and acclamations
given to rulers by their subjects.[31]

Despite all this fragmentation and particularism, the idea of national
unity formed the leitmotif of the bourgeois festive culture that developed
during the first half of the nineteenth century. The political nature and the
territorial borders of the envisioned nation-state remained unclear or disputed, but public celebrations became the preferred means to urge its creation and anticipate its existence.[32] There are three major forms of festivity
in which this nationalist spirit found expression: political festivals in the
tradition of 1814–17 (which always contained some oppositional or even
revolutionary potential); meetings of patriotic associations organized on a
local or regional level that, later on, launched into nationwide activity; and
festivals celebrated by German cities commemorating historic events or
honoring personalities of "national" importance.

The tradition of political holidays survived in the relatively liberal atmosphere of Southwest Germany, resurfacing in dramatic fashion at Hambach
in the Bavarian Palatinate in 1832 and making its final appearance in the
festivals of the 1848–9 revolution. Hambach was an expression of the general
unrest that gripped the German population in the aftermath of
the French revolution of 1830 and the Polish uprising against Russia. More
than 20,000 participants from various parts of Germany turned the
Hambacher Fest, officially organized to honor the Bavarian constitution,
into a powerful demonstration for basic democratic rights, especially
freedom of the press, and for national unity. Even today, the image of the
procession winding uphill to the castle ruin occupies a special place in
national memory. (The castle itself is a national monument and houses a
museum.) The patriotic speeches and songs, the freedom trees, the black,
red, and gold banners and cockades, and other popular symbols (pipes, hats,
and so forth) fused criticism of arbitrary, despotic government with appeals
to German solidarity and demands for a national constitution. At the same
time, the meeting opened a forum for political debate and served as a

31 Klaus Tenfelde, "Adventus: Zur historischen Ikonologie des Festzuges," *Historische Zeitschrift* 235
    (1982): 45–84.
32 Volker Sellin, "Nationalbewusstsein und Partikularismus in Deutschland im 19. Jahrhundert," in Jan
    Assmann and Tonio Hölscher, eds., *Kultur und Gedächtnis* (Frankfurt am Main, 1988), 241–64.

platform for influencing public opinion. Discussions on the castle revolved around the advantages and disadvantages of specific constitutional models for a German nation-state and even for a European confederation. Radical speakers proclaimed the sovereignty of the people, which had been realized in the United States, as the ideal toward which Germans should strive.[33]

Although the situation remained perfectly peaceful, the Bavarian authorities and most other governments of the German Confederation (Deutscher Bund) felt seriously challenged by the oppositional rhetoric as well as by the strong support the festival received from all classes of the population. The harsh measures taken against the organizers and the press prevented for many years the repetition of such open defiance of the existing order.[34] This did not mean, however, that public expressions of liberal ideals and sentiments became completely impossible. A different form of political festival was celebrated in the Grand Duchy of Baden on the occasion of the twenty-fifth anniversary of the state's constitution in 1843. This festival comprised multicelebrations, not organized centrally but observed statewide, based on the political-religious worship of the constitution: Like a church relic, its text was carried in solemn processions through towns and cities all over Baden. The ceremonies and public speeches conveyed a message tempered by a specific form of "communal liberalism" that had developed in southwest Germany after the late eighteenth century. In political and social terms, the festivals propagated the system of constitutional monarchy and the ideal of a "classless" but nevertheless clearly structured and well-regulated society. The cult of the constitution and the efforts to restrain social and political conflicts in the interest of communal harmony call to mind the early American version of republican festive culture. Moderation also prevailed with respect to national issues. Many speakers referred to a German nation, but the concept remained vague and did not necessarily encompass a nation-state. By solemnly confirming their state identity the people of Baden offered an idealized model of political and

---

33 See Helmut G. Haasis, *Volksfest, sozialer Protest und Verschwörung: 150 Jahre Hambacher Fest* (Heidelberg, 1981); Cornelia Foerster, "Das Hambacher Fest 1832: Volksfest und Nationalfest einer oppositionellen Massenbewegung," in Düding, Friedemann, and Münch, eds., *Öffentliche Festkultur*, 113–31. On origins and background, see Foerster, " 'Hoch lebe die Verfassung'? Die pfälzisschen Abgeordnetenfeste im Vormärz (1819–1846)," in Düding, Friedemann, and Münch, eds., *Öffentliche Festkultur*, 132–46; Wolfgang Schieder, "Der rheinpfälzische Liberalismus von 1832 als politische Protestbewegung," in Helmut Berding et al., ed., *Vom Staat des Ancien Régime zum modernen Parteienstaat: Festschrift für Theoder Schieder* (Munich, 1978), 169–95.

34 Further alarmed by the Frankfurter Wachensturm in April 1833, the Bavarian government sent troops to prevent a celebration of the anniversary of the Hambacher Fest. See Uta Jungmann, "Die blutigen Ereignisse am Hambacher Jahrestag 1833: Ein Beispiel für den Widerstreit von Obrigkeit und Bürgertum im Vormärz," *Jahrbuch der Hambach Gesellschaft* (1944–5): 123–46.

social order to the rest of the nation. Efforts to continue the constitutional festivals were hampered by growing political radicalism and partisan ideology that foreshadowed the deep conflicts of the 1848–9 revolution.[35]

The funeral parade for the victims of street fighting in Berlin in March 1848 is considered the most impressive and memorable celebration that occurred during the German revolution. Because of the omnipresence of national symbols and the heavy emphasis on patriotic sacrifice and national unity (embracing Protestants, Catholics, and Jews), the parade must be seen as a political demonstration. The religious, almost mystical sense of unity conjured up by the rituals and symbols contrasted with the social and political divisions that soon made themselves felt in Berlin, Prussia, and all over Germany.[36] The failure of the revolution sealed the fate of the political festival – at least in its oppositional, liberal-democratic, or radical-republican form.[37]

The association movement, which began during the Napoleonic Wars with the formation of *Turnervereine* (gymnastic associations), provided an alternative channel through which the bourgeoisie could express their nationalist sentiments and liberal convictions. Friedrich Ludwig Jahn's patriotic clubs fell victim to the repressive measures which followed the murder of Kotzebue in 1819, but on the eve of the revolution there again existed about 250 "unpolitical" *Turnervereine* numbering between 80,000 and 90,000 members, mostly from the middle class. The choral societies (*Männergesangsvereine*) originated in south-central Germany and in Switzerland. They grew even faster, boasting in 1847 more than 100,000 members organized in 1,100 clubs. *Schillervereine* (Schiller associations), which attracted many *Bildungsbürger* (educated citizenry), staged great festivals in their "strongholds" of Breslau, Dresden, and Stuttgart.[38]

During the *Vormärz* period the activities of these associations extended from the local to the regional and sometimes even to the national level. The climax was reached in 1847 with an Allgemein-deutsches Sängerfest

35 Paul Nolte, "Die badischen Verfassungsfeste im Vormärz: Liberalismus, Verfassungskultur und soziale Ordnung in den Gemeinden," in Hettling and Nolte, eds., *Bürgerliche Feste*, 63–94.
36 Manfred Hettling, "Das Begräbnis der Märzgefallenen 1848 in Berlin," in Hettling and Nolte, eds., *Bürgerliche Feste*, 95–123.
37 At many of the revolutionary festivals, "the common symbolism of the unity of the nation was used to express very different meanings with regard to the states . . . a common symbolic universe was interpreted in divisive and conflict-laden ways by different social, regional, and confessional groups, turning the representation of national unity into a vehicle for the expression of social, confessional, and political antagonizing" (Jonathan Sperber, "Festivals of National Unity in the German Revolution of 1848/49," *Past and Present* 136 [1992]: 114–38, esp. 137).
38 Dieter Düding, "Nationale Oppositionsfeste der Turner, Sänger und Schützen im 19. Jahrhundert," in Düding, Friedemann, and Münch, eds., *Öffentliche Festkultur*, 166–90.

(All–German Choral Festival) in Lübeck, attended by 1,100 members, and a Turnfest (Gymnastics Festival) in Heidelberg with 1,400 participants, mostly from southwest and south Germany. In both cities the local population enthusiastically supported the meetings and became part of the festive community. These and other festivals of gymnasts and choral societies transmitted a thinly veiled political message: They criticized German particularism, demanded constitutions and limited government, and even professed admiration for the principle of popular sovereignty. Processions, public singing, and mass gymnastics provided the opportunity to demonstrate order and self-discipline, to create an atmosphere of fraternity, and to pledge allegiance to national symbols (the flag, which had been officially banned in 1832, Hoffmann von Fallersleben's *Deutschlandlied*, and other patriotic songs).

The repressive climate of the 1850s severely limited the activities of the clubs, but they soon re-emerged, establishing interregional bonds and reaching new membership heights. In 1856 the Erste deutsche Sängerbundsfest (First German Choral Union Festival) took place in Dresden; three years later the *Schillervereine* elevated the festivals marking the 100th birthday of the poet into "a national dream of the birth of the second German Kaiserreich," and in 1860 the gymnasts celebrated their Erstes Allgemeines Turnfest (First General Gymnastics Festival) in Coburg.[39] Influenced by Swiss models, associations of sharpshooters (*Schützenvereine*) also adopted a freedom-loving patriotic attitude and joined gymnasts and choral societies in celebrating national festivals. In 1862 a delegation of German-American sharpshooters attended the first Allgemeine deutsche Schützenfest (All-German Festival of Riflemen) in Frankfurt am Main. These spectacular meetings of *Sänger, Turner,* and *Schützen* with up to 100,000 participants disseminated national-liberal sentiments and principles by demanding German unity and civil rights, favoring a *grossdeutsche Lösung* (greater Germany solution) over Prussian hegemony, and praising the examples of Switzerland and the United States. The fragile nature of the professed solidarity and fraternity was revealed in the late 1860s, when *Arbeitervereine* (workers' associations), which had attended the first national festivals, decided to withdraw and organize separate working-class festivities.

A different form of bourgeois mentality and festive culture manifested itself in the great public celebrations staged by German cities. Since medieval times the city had been at the center of bourgeois life and culture,

---

39 Rainer Noltenius, "Schiller als Heiland und Führer: Das Schillerfest 1859 als nationaler Traum von der Geburt des zweiten deutschen Kaiserreichs," in Düding, Friedemann, and Münch, eds., *Öffentliche Festkultur*, 237–58.

and the urban citizens had always struggled to retain some measure of autonomy and independence from the feudal powers. In the nineteenth century the bourgeoisie made use of public festivals to "manage" the social change caused by the expansion of markets and the rise of an industrial economy, as well as to "mediate" between the needs and aspirations of city, state, region, and nation. The celebrations with their magnificent parades and historic pageants served mainly two purposes: to confirm the ideal of a corporate, harmonious, and self-governing *Bürgergesellschaft* in spite of the growing tensions between various groups and classes of the urban population; and to integrate the city into wider regional and national networks without losing its sense of local pride and identity.[40]

From 1826 on, when the Franconian capital of Nuremberg celebrated its first *Volks-* and *Nationalfest* (Ethnic and National Festival), the *historischer Festzug* (historical pageant) developed into the archetypical form of bourgeois festive culture. Its model was "The Triumph of Emperor Maximilian," an early ideal pageant designed and illustrated (but not executed) by Maximilian himself and by prominent artists, first among them Albrecht Dürer.[41] But whereas this "triumph" of 1512 completely centered on the person of the ruler, the arrangement of the nineteenth-century parades emphasized the increasing importance and independence of the urban citizens. Highlights in the history of these events include celebrations in honor of Albrecht Dürer (Nuremberg, 1828 and 1853),[42] Johannes Gutenberg (Mainz and Frankfurt am Main, 1837–40),[43] and Martin Luther (Leipzig, 1830, 1868, and 1883);[44] the city anniversaries of Munich (1858) and Braunschweig (1861);[45] and several *Kölner Dombaufeste* (festivals celebrating the effort to complete the Cologne Cathedral) between 1842 and the opening of the "national" cathedral in 1880.[46] For all their diversity, these

---

40 The term *klassenlose Bürgergesellschaft* was coined by Lothar Gall in *Bürgertum in Deutschland* (Berlin, 1989). See Thomas Nipperdey, *Deutsche Geschichte 1800–1866: Bürgerwelt und starker Staat* (Munich, 1983); Dieter Langewiesche, "Reich, Nation und Staat in der jüngeren deutschen Geschichte," *Historische Zeitschrift* 254 (1992): 341–81.

41 Hartmann, "Der historische Festzug," 11–12. In the nineteenth century, the popularity of the historical pageants was not confined to Germany. Spectacular parades took place in a number of European countries, especially in the Netherlands, Belgium, and Switzerland.

42 Ibid., 23–7.

43 Jürgen Steen, "Vormärzliche Gutenbergfeste," in Düding, Friedemann, and Münch, eds., *Öffentliche Festkultur*, 147–65.

44 Johannes Burkhardt, "Reformations- und Lutherfeiern: Die Verbürgerlichung der reformatorischen Jubiläumskultur," in Düding, Friedemann, and Münch, eds., *Öffentliche Festkultur*, 212–36.

45 Hartmann, "Der historische Festzug," 27–31; Hans-Walter Schmuhl, "Die Tausendjahrfeier der Stadt Braunschweig im Jahr 1861: Zur Selbstinszenierung des städtischen Bürgertums," in Hettling and Nolte, eds., *Bürgerliche Feste*, 124–56.

46 Leo Haupts, "Die Kölner Dombaufeste 1842–1880 zwischen kirchlicher, bürgerlich-nationaler und dynastisch-höfischer Selbstdarstellung," in Düding, Friedemann, and Münch, eds., *Öffentliche Festkultur*, 191–211; see Hartmann, "Der historische Festzug," 37–41.

festivals displayed some important common traits. In the form of the parade, they portrayed the city as a naturally structured, corporate community of citizens (and sometimes, as in the case of Munich, as a community of court and bourgeoisie); they depicted an optimistic image of the economic and cultural achievements of the urban population; and they constructed a historical continuity from Germanic times and the medieval empires of Charlemagne and Barbarossa through the blossoming of city culture in the Renaissance period to the present "national awakening." This was done in an increasingly elaborate, scholarly, and aesthetic manner by employing archivists, artists, and historians in the preparation of the events and in the decoration of the floats and "living images." In the course of the nineteenth century, therefore, the historical pageants evolved into works of art, combining a sophisticated choreography with costumes "true to the original," with harmoniously arranged paintings, symbols, and allegories, and with illuminations and musical performances. Detailed reports in the press as well as specifically printed pamphlets and books intensified the desired effects. Everywhere, the organizers took great pains to avoid conflicts between local and regional allegiances, on the one hand, and the longing for national unity and German identity, on the other. By paying tribute to (bourgeois) "German heroes" such as Dürer, Gutenberg, and Luther, or by incorporating the history of a city into an unbroken chain of events from the mystical beginnings to the imagined "rebirth" of German nationhood, the pageants asserted the general equality of city, region, and nation. The *Dombaufeste* elevated the Cologne Cathedral to a national symbol. At the same time, the common effort to complete the building served as a symbol of reconciliation between the Catholic Rhineland and Protestant Prussia, and between church and state. Ideologically, these festivities differed markedly from the oppositional style developed by liberals and democrats. The German bourgeoisie was becoming less and less homogeneous, but its various groups and interests still found common ground in their desire for social stability and national unity.

CONCLUSIONS

The main argument here can be summed up in a paradox: The Americans celebrated their national holidays, but they did not cultivate and preserve a unifying festive culture; by contrast (not living in a nation-state), the German bourgeoisie – liberals, democrats, and conservatives in their own specific ways – used festivals and celebrations to "imagine" or "invent" a common history and to symbolically "construct" a German nation.

In Germany bourgeois festive culture began as an appeal of some patriotic intellectuals to the rulers and the people to strengthen national solidarity, which supposedly had existed during the Napoleonic Wars. When the rulers did not respond to the idea of a national holiday and even tried to suppress it, liberals and democrats used festive culture to oppose absolutism, feudalism, and particularism. From the 1830s on, "unpolitical" clubs and associations became the favorite vehicles to continue this tradition. A different form of festive culture developed in the German Southwest and in the cities, where the urban upper and middle classes succeeded in symbolically bridging the gap between rulers and subjects, between conflicting economic interests, and between local and national identities.

In the United States festive culture was part of the political process from the beginning. Since the 1790s a radical, anti-authoritarian, and egalitarian festive culture coexisted with a more conservative style that emphasized order, social stability, and national cohesion. After the War of 1812 both versions combined into one common, homogeneous republican festive culture. Soon, however, this harmony dissolved when competing political and social forces invented new ways of celebrating or imbued old forms with new meaning. In both Germany and the United States, therefore, festive culture contributed to the general political climate and emotional atmosphere that made possible the dramatic events of the 1860s. The Civil War, the Wars of German Unification (*Einigungskriege*), and the proclamation of the Kaiserreich in 1871, transformed American and German festive cultures: In both countries the spirit and the style of public celebration changed considerably during the final decades of the century.

If one tries to compare the manifestations of German and American festive culture during the first half of the nineteenth century, some general – and still tentative – observations can be made concerning similarities and differences. An important common characteristic is the decentralized nature of public celebrations in the United States and Germany. In both countries the initiative for festive activities usually came from local authorities or citizens' associations, not from governments. German political particularism allowed different regions – for example, the Southwest or Bavaria – to develop their own cultural styles. In a similar way, federalism seems to have fostered local initiative and regional diversity in the United States. The question of which way and to what extent American public celebrations differed from region to region needs to be investigated more systematically. Taking an inventory of American festive culture with its ceremonies, rituals, and symbols, and comparing the findings with research on European practices could be a task for future cultural historians.

In both Germany and the United States the city stood in the center of public celebrations. Only cities could mobilize the masses, raise the money, and make the technological expertise and artistic talent available that guaranteed impressive, spectacular events. To a large extent, therefore, festive culture was urban culture, although everywhere the majority of the population still lived in rural areas. On both sides of the Atlantic the public procession or parade became the metaphor of urban civil society, of a "city in action," a "people on the march" progressing economically and culturally toward a bright future. By participating in a parade the citizens were "observing themselves in the process of defining themselves";[47] parades allowed the urban upper and middle classes to celebrate their own growing importance and visually express their ideal of a well-ordered society and good government. It seems that this situation continued longer in Germany than in the United States, where the urban elite, beginning in the 1830s, tended to concede the streets to the lower classes and to regard parading as an affair for ordinary folks.

The "aura of the sacral," noticed by historians with respect to French revolutionary festivals, also permeated American and German public celebrations. In contrast to French festive culture, however, traditional religiosity was not replaced by a secular cult but rather became an integral part of new forms of "civil religion." In the United States and Germany, the support of the churches and the active cooperation of the clergy intensified the solemn character and emotional atmosphere of parades and other public festivities. Only the mechanical repetition of certain ceremonies and rituals could disrupt this aura of sacredness and turn solemn events into travesties.

Ideologically, both German and American festive cultures were progressive and future-oriented; however, in Germany nature and history received more attention and played a more important role. The integration of the scenery and the use of specific symbols – fire, oak leaves – were intended to express a German "national character" and German cultural identity, for example, by distinguishing German *Natürlichkeit* (naturalness) from French *Künstlichkeit* (artificiality). History, understood and explained as the collective experience of the German people, became the most important means to legitimize the quest for a nation-state. This cult of nature and history gave German festive culture a strong undercurrent of romanticism and mysticism; it is problematic, however, to draw a straight line from early nineteenth-century patriotic exaltations to Nazi propaganda spectacles

---

47 Kenneth Silverman, *A Cultural History of the American Revolution* (New York, 1987), 580.

in the 1930s.[48] The virulence against external-enemy images and of anti-Semitism seems to have decreased after 1820 until both phenomena resurfaced in the last decades of the century.

Americans put less emphasis on history and nature because for them the Revolution was the central source of legitimacy and because they did not feel an urgent need to define their "national character" by contrasting themselves with their neighbors.[49] The tendency to concentrate on economic development is reflected in the growing number of public festivals staged on the occasion of economic achievements. Fairly early, the enthusiasm for technological progress found expression in great exhibitions, which constituted a new dynamic element of American festive culture.[50] To a certain extent, similar efforts were undertaken in Germany, especially in connection with the construction of the railroads.[51] During the first half of the nineteenth century, however, the Industrial Revolution exerted only a moderate influence on German festive culture.

In the United States the combined forces of industrialization and democratization shaped an increasingly pluralistic and competitive social environment that found its counterpart in a diverse, fragmented festive culture. In Germany the pace of social and political change was considerably slower. Here, the bourgeoisie created a partly oppositional, partly homogenizing festive culture as a means to assert itself against the traditional authorities and to propagate its vision of a unified, economically progressive nation.

---

48 For a wide-ranging and differentiated interpretation, see George L. Mosse, *Die Nationalisierung der Massen: Von den Befreiungskriegen bis zum Dritten Reich* (Frankfurt am Main, 1976).

49 Michael Kammen, *A Season of Youth: The American Revolution and the Historical Imagination* (New York, 1978).

50 The year 1853 saw the opening of the New York Crystal Palace exposition, an event obviously inspired by the first world exposition in London in 1851. See Wilentz, "Artisan Republican Festivals," 57.

51 Gerhard Stahr, "Kommerzielle Interessen und provinzielles Selbstbewusstsein: Die Eröffnungsfeiern der Rheinischen Eisenbahn 1841 und 1843," in Hettling and Nolte, eds., *Bürgerliche Feste*, 37–62. The opening ceremonies of the railroad Köln–Aachen–Antwerpen were used by bourgeois business circles in the Rhineland to stress their cosmopolitan attitude and the good relations with the Western neighbors.

12

Charles Follen's View of Republicanism in Germany and the United States, 1815–1840

EDMUND SPEVACK

REPUBLICANISM IN GERMANY AND THE UNITED STATES: FOLLEN AS BRIDGE FIGURE

The two traditions of republicanism that took hold in Germany and the United States in the period from 1780 to 1840, as well as their patterns of historical development, show both similarities and major differences. The German tradition, much less known than its American counterpart, was recently summarized in a challenging article by Paul Nolte.[1] In particular, Nolte argues that republicanism in Germany could not make the transition from classical republicanism to a more modern form, like the development that took place during the American Revolution. From the beginning German republicanism was much more premodern, local, communal, and hostile to the development of a modern market economy. The political thought of the leading German political theorist, Carl von Rotteck, for example, shows that German republicanism made only a half-hearted attempt to embrace modern liberal politics and capitalist economic concepts. Thus, according to Nolte, German republicanism before 1840 initially existed more to preserve the old local, communal order than to aid the birth of a new, modern world. After the paradigm shift of the 1840s German republicanism did not become a strong independent movement, nor did it find a strong ally in a vibrant liberalism; rather, it was soon displaced by rivals such as socialism and conservatism, and its notions of local political community and congruent rather than competing economic interests were overtaken by modern social concepts, such as the class antagonism of industrialized society.

---

1 Paul Nolte, "Bürgerideal, Gemeinde und Republik: 'Klassischer Republikanismus' im frühen deutschen Liberalismus," *Historische Zeitschrift* 254 (1992): 609–56.

The American discussion was initiated by Bernard Bailyn and Gordon Wood, and subsequently challenged by J. G. A. Pocock.[2] The American Revolution in the late eighteenth century both brought to the fore and crystallized many aspects of republicanism, including the fear of corruption and luxury and the idea that virtue consists of sacrificing individual interests for the common good. Republicanism, according to Bailyn and Wood, was the revolutionary ideology of an entire generation of Americans, the core beliefs of which would come to affect many subsequent generations. Republicanism was a positive mood, originating in the English-speaking world and contributing to the political sphere the newly defined notion of "the public good." In contrast, Pocock's republicanism was born out of the pessimism and anxiety experienced in the Italian city-states of the Renaissance; even in the American case Pocock conceived of the rise of republicanism as a constant struggle against the degenerative forces of history.

Are the traditions of republicanism in Germany and the United States so different in nature that they have nothing in common? Both began with the realization that in a modern society power should originate not from above but from below, and both were firmly in favor of popular sovereignty. The belief in representative government brought with it the necessity of protecting the civil rights of the individual citizen from the power of the state; these concepts are found not only in the American Bill of Rights but also in the German constitution proposed by the Frankfurt constitutional assembly in 1848. Also relevant in both the early national United States and *Vormärz* Germany is the concept of the necessity of civic virtue, avoiding corruption and preventing too much power in too few hands. The United States had successfully converted to a liberal society with a market-based capitalist economy by the middle of the nineteenth century, but this transition was much more difficult and came much later in Germany.

One additional similarity between republicanism in Germany and the United States is the localistic outlook favored in both traditions during the late eighteenth century. A detailed description of the American Anti-Federalist position in 1787–8 was provided four decades ago by Cecilia Kenyon.[3] She discussed the Anti-Federalist criticism of the U.S. Constitution, which was seen as "aristocratic" and "antidemocratic." Following

2 See Daniel T. Rodgers, "Republicanism: The Career of a Concept," *Journal of American History* 79 (1992): 11–38.
3 Cecilia Kenyon, "Men of Little Faith: The Anti-Federalists on the Nature of Representative Government," *William and Mary Quarterly* 12 (1955): 3–43.

Rousseau, the Anti-Federalists believed that republican forms of government could survive only in small, localized geographic areas with homogeneous populations. Local interests should not be overruled by abstract national interests. Because the Anti-Federalists thought that it was human nature to abuse power, representation of the many by the few in the House of Representatives had to be very carefully structured to avoid oppressive government. Separation of powers had to be firmly established, as Montesquieu had suggested, and the power of the president and the Senate to collaborate had to be checked as much as possible. However, in the view of the Anti-Federalists "the people" themselves tended to be unstable and imprudent and could not be trusted to make sound decisions. The southwestern German republicanism that Nolte described contains similar elements of localism. Charles Follen (1796–1840), however, thought differently in both the German and the American contexts.

A close examination of Follen as a German-American bridge figure underscores the fact that, although differences in the German and American evolutions of republicanism before 1840 cannot be denied, the similarities are surprisingly strong.[4] Follen's political career, roughly from 1813 to 1840, shows that a German republican could swiftly and smoothly make the transition to the American scene. He was able to preserve his personal activist and cantankerous mentality, to recognize and set out to solve political problems that confronted society at large, and to tirelessly propagate his visions of perfecting the individual and serving the common good. When faced with entirely new social issues and political problems, this German lawyer and revolutionary, who had lived in exile in Switzerland, adapted to the society of New England and managed to preserve many of his central political beliefs and much of his ideological language. His main views hardly changed; rather, they were just applied to the new environment of New England.

Follen participated in the early German nationalist movement after 1813 and in the radical movement of 1815–19; he emigrated to Switzerland, living there from 1819 to 1824, and arrived in the United States at the end of 1824. His initial reaction to the United States as a "free state" in which all his political dreams had been fulfilled, and his later active political participation, support two hypotheses: first, that his own life formed a unity rather than a combination of two unrelated and fragmented parts, and second, that there were indeed direct and profound connections between

---

4 Edmund Spevack, *Charles Follen's Search for Nationality and Freedom: Germany and America, 1796–1840* (Cambridge, Mass., 1997).

Follen's political beliefs and actions in Europe, and those that he held and engaged in during the last fifteen years of his life in the United States.

In the German context Follen's political creed was further advanced and decidedly more radical than the mainstream communal republicanism of his time. Follen espoused several elements of German classical republicanism as characterized by Nolte, but his political positions in 1818 already had much in common with the unsuccessful German radicalism of the 1840s, beginning to be known as "the left." Follen's legalistic, narrow-minded, quarrelsome, and naively idealistic mentality (what Hartwig Brandt has called "his puritanical illiberalism")[5] fit almost perfectly into the reform activity taking place in contemporary New England; American reformers have often been described in similar terms.[6]

Central to Follen's personal belief system were the ideas of freedom and nationality, both very much associated with republicanism. The concept of freedom should be understood on several levels: the self-emancipation of the individual from outdated philosophical superstitions and a false political consciousness, and the rise of the individual as a citizen and free agent within a modern civil society as inspired by the American and French revolutions. The concept of freedom overlapped with Follen's view of nationalism, which called for the emancipation of nations from internal oppression and their transition to truly independent actors on the international stage. In both Germany and the United States, Follen participated in the debate over what the "nation" should be and how it should be defined. At the same time, and on both continents, he seemed obsessed with the republican opposition between freedom and liberation, on the one hand, and despotism or slavery, on the other. The means by which Follen hoped to achieve his goals are more problematic. Although this is difficult to prove using the existing sources, it can be assumed from circumstantial evidence that readiness to use violence for political change always remained at the core of Follen's beliefs, from the political assassinations of *Vormärz* Germany to the growing abolitionist radicalism of the antebellum United States.

After 1812 Americans, like the new nationalist forces in Germany, set out to define themselves as a nation. Key elements in this process included war (the Wars of Liberation in 1813 in Germany versus the War of 1812 in the United States); calls for cultural emancipation (in Germany,

5 Hartwig Brandt, ed., *Restauration und Frühliberalismus 1814–1840* (Darmstadt, 1979), 17.
6 See the description of William Lloyd Garrison in the biography by John Thomas, *The Liberator: William Lloyd Garrison, A Biography* (Boston, 1963).

loosening ties with France; in America, drawing away from Britain); and feverish reform activity concerned with the sort of social experimentation (abolitionism, temperance, religious revivals, utopian communities, women's rights) in which Follen would like to have engaged in his native Hesse, had this been politically possible. Although he always remained on the radical fringes wherever he lived, Follen brought to America certain aspects of German communal republicanism. At the same time he absorbed more modern forms, although he never became a modern liberal, and the rise of free market capitalism remained marginal in his political consciousness. Follen clearly can be seen as a rather left-wing, authoritarian republican in both the German and the American contexts. Follen never was a man of the moderate political mainstream; for much of his life he occupied the position of radical outsider.

In Germany, Switzerland, and America, Follen was above all a man of action, but it is easy to trace his life and thoughts. He left a great number of written records and vented his most important ideas in texts. Follen wrote essays and scholarly articles; he lectured, preached, and contributed to many journals. These texts have been preserved in five volumes, *The Works of Charles Follen*, edited by his American wife, Eliza Cabot Follen.[7] They have also been analyzed in some detail.

Radical Nationalism (1813–1824)

Follen's life can be divided into six major phases, each of which exhibits certain characteristics directly relevant to his development as a republican thinker and political agitator in three countries. The first phase is charac- terized by his attachment to the early forms of modern German national- ism in the early nineteenth century. This period includes his student life at Giessen, membership in the first *Burschenschaften* (fraternities), and partici- pation in the Wars of Liberation in 1813. His nationalism was inspired by German political figures and academics such as Friedrich Gottlieb Welcker, Ernst Moritz Arndt, Friedrich Ludwig Jahn, and Heinrich Luden. The "Germanism" (*Deutschtümelei*) practiced by the Giessen "Blacks" student

---

7 Eliza Lee Cabot, ed., *The Works of Charles Follen, with a Memoir of His Life*, 5 vols. (Boston, 1841). The first volume of this edition is a 600-page biography of Follen, based on his writings, diaries, and personal papers. A serious problem with researching him lies in the absence of unpublished archival materials. Whereas there is much circumstantial evidence in both German and American archives, the bulk of the actual Follen letters, diaries, and papers have been lost; it is not unlikely that they were destroyed by his devoted wife after she had completed her very favorable portrait in volume one of the *Works*. If a more complete set of Follen papers were available, a much sharper image of the man and his character would be achievable.

fraternity (Giessener Schwarzen) was ridiculed by writers as diverse as E. T. A. Hoffmann and Saul Ascher, and Follen did not engage in this type of political activity for very long. His absence from the Wartburg festival, organized by radical students in 1817, is one strong indication that Follen was already moving in a different, much more radical direction.

Follen's second phase of development, beginning in 1818, marked his turn toward revolutionary radicalism. His readiness to direct radical action may be seen in the legal advice he provided to Hessian communities when they were overburdened by taxes in 1818. More important, Follen's increasing involvement not only with nationalist students in Giessen but also with older and more politically mature Hessian revolutionaries, such as Friedrich Ludwig Weidig, Wilhelm Schulz, and Heinrich Karl Hofmann, is an indication of this activism. Follen also met members of the radical club known as the Darmstadt "Blacks" (Darmstädter Schwarzen), who, before 1820, participated in the *Adressenbewegung*, the agitation for a modern representative Hessian state constitution. After Follen's departure many of these individuals would go on to collaborate with the most famous figure of Hessian radicalism in the period, the playwright Georg Büchner. Follen's turn to radicalism was underscored by his move to Jena in 1818 and his leadership position among the Jena "Unconditionals" (Unbedingte). This small, close-knit group of revolutionaries took their inspiration from the principle of "conviction," as formulated by the Jena philosopher Jakob Friedrich Fries. Their aim was to destroy the German Confederation by individual terrorist attacks on its leading political and cultural figures. After the assassination of the conservative playwright August von Kotzebue (who had ridiculed the student movement in his writings and was seen as a supporter of political reaction) by Follen's protégé Carl Sand in 1819, the Carlsbad Decrees passed later that same year and the ensuing period of political repression known as the *Demagogenverfolgung* put an end to Follen's revolutionary activity within the German Confederation. By the time he fled to Switzerland in 1819, none of Follen's political associates in Jena had the slightest doubt that he was a "German devil" and a "bloody revolutionary."[8]

The third phase in Follen's life was his period of political exile in Switzerland. The significance of the exile experience for German republicans of those years cannot be overestimated. The University of Basel had become home to a great number of German political refugees, including

---

8 Robert Wesselhöft, *Teutsche Jugend in weiland Burschenschaften und Turngemeinden* (Magdeburg, 1928), 67–86.

such figures as Wilhelm Leberecht DeWette, Arnold Ruge, and Julius Fröbel, and Follen eventually found employment there. From the relative safety of Switzerland, Follen organized what was known as the *Jünglings-bund* (Youth League), a secret society of revolutionary students at universities throughout the German Confederation. Follen thus did not withdraw from active political agitation in exile, as did his brother August Follen (who escaped into a romantic obsession with medieval German culture); instead, he stepped up his subversive activities aimed at undermining Metternich's Restoration and the German Confederation.[9]

Follen was a highly prolific writer, and nearly all his writings survive in published form. The purpose here is to trace elements of republicanism throughout his publications. His first writings are his constitution of the *Giessener Schwarzen* student fraternity, published as the *Giessener Ehrenspiegel* (1816), and his defense of the new fraternity, titled *Beiträge zur Geschichte der teutschen Samtschulen seit dem Freiheitskriege* (written in 1816 and published in 1818).[10] In the *Ehrenspiegel* Follen laid out rules for the reform of German student life according to the principles of "honor, loyalty, and chastity." Duels were to be avoided, and a feeling of national belonging was to be encouraged. Sexual abstinence, "Christian uprightness," and personal integrity were the main demands Follen placed on the modern student. They were to be responsible citizens rather than public nuisances, and, by their behavior, were to foster the dream of a united Germany.

In *Teutsche Samtschulen* Follen not only defended the new student movement but also delivered radical statements about a new political order for Germany after 1815. A youth himself, he created a countermanifesto for the youth of his time and called on students to organize a "Christian-German free state," admonishing them not to remain satisfied with the external freedom resulting from the Wars of Liberation but to push further toward internal political freedom as well. "Freedom, equality, unity" was to be the slogan of a new student generation. Follen denounced the disciplinary measures initiated by university officials and made use of the dichotomy of "slavery" versus "freedom" when describing the situation of the students. The main goal was to "unite all Christian Germans in one great bond of conviction." Both documents show elements of classical German communal republicanism.

By 1818 Follen's concept of nationality was changing because he was drawing away from mainstream liberal academic sentiments. The main aim

9 Edmund Spevack, "August Adolf Ludwig Follen (1794–1855): Political Radicalism and Literary Romanticism in Germany and Switzerland," *Germanic Review* 71 (1996): 3–22.
10 Both tracts published in Carl Walbrach, ed., *Der Giessener Ehrenspiegel* (Frankfurt am Main, 1927).

of his new group, the Jena Unconditionals, was (as noted) to destroy the German Confederation, radicalize German nationalism, and ignite a social and political revolution. The most significant document proving that Follen had become a left-wing republican early on is the "Draft of the Constitution for a Future German Empire" ("Grundzüge für eine künftige teutsche Reichsverfassung"), which he wrote with the advice of his older brother August, in 1818–19.[11]

The "Draft of a Constitution" contained ideas as radical as they were utopian. Follen showed himself to be an unconditional Jacobin who would shy from no political means to realize his goals. Hartwig Brandt has remarked on Follen's "levelling rationality, puritanical illiberality, and Spartan attitude towards education."[12] Indeed, a rigidly authoritarian tone pervades the entire document. The ambiguity of derivation is striking: The "Draft" presents a mixture of French democratic and republican ideals derived from Rousseau, on the one hand, supplemented by native German traditions and the nationalistic ideas of Jahn, on the other. It shows not only Follen's idealism but also his personal toughness. The "Draft" begins with a definition of the *Volk* and the idea that the *Volk* require a *Reich*. All Germans are described as completely equal in their rights, and the legal omnipotence and exclusive power of the people is stressed. It calls for tight control over the salaries and terms of office of public officials, binding them to distinctly republican virtues. Follen called for a single German Christian state church, one sign of his illiberalism and his belief in religious coercion. He placed important emphasis on education: Children are to be taught both nationalism and equality early on. Soldiers are considered part of the *Volk*, not a separate group. He emphasized physical exercise to ready all citizens to defend the *Reich* against foreign aggressors, if necessary. Freedom of the press and of speech are universally granted. Estates function as sociological categories rather than as sources of social status and political power. Follen also proposed a modern system of administrative levels, with a king as the top official. Citizens receive rights exclusively from the state, and the individual freedom of the citizen is not as important as the welfare of the collective. Follen's "Draft" is progressive and authoritarian at the same time; it exhibits many elements of an authoritarian republicanism.

In 1819 Follen's brother August published the anthology of poetry titled *Freye Stimmen Frischer Jugend*, which contained several poems and songs by Follen.[13] These are mild compared with the text of Follen's radical revolu-

---

11 Published in Brandt, ed., *Restoration und Frühliberalismus.*
12 Ibid.
13 August Adolf Follen, *Freye Stimmen Frischer Jugend* (Jena, 1819).

tionary hymn, "The Great Song" ("*Das Grosse Lied*"), written in 1818.[14] This text reflected Follen's turn to violence and his participation in the activities of local Hessian revolutionaries. Three main themes dominate "The Great Song": raw appeals for violence and popular self-liberation from tyranny, mystical celebration of secret revolutionary groups, and prominent religious imagery and emotional rapture. It contains a blunt call for the uprising of poor Germans against their oppressors, the princes. Freedom is not to be peacefully awaited but fought for. According to Follen, the hour of world conflagration was approaching and would include major parts of Europe. Cataclysmic events would destroy the current social and political world order. The "Song" calls for Hessian peasants to save themselves through bloody revolution, an action compared, in the final stanza of the "Great Song," to the Christian concept of incarnation. Salvation, Follen argued, was available only at the price of violent revolution.

It is not hard to connect Follen's violent verses to the assassination of the playwright August von Kotzebue. There can be little doubt that he was at least indirectly responsible for the assassination. The murder, however, threatened the existence of modern German radicalism. Political reaction followed with the Carlsbad Decrees and the founding of the Mainz Central Investigation Commission, as well as with the Prussian persecution of political radicals (*Demogogen*) under police minister Albert von Kamptz.

When Follen fled to Switzerland in 1819 he did not give up his hopes for revolutionizing Germany. In his memoirs Follen's former friend and Jena roommate Ferdinand Wit von Dörring published a report, supposedly by Follen, evaluating the potential for revolutionary change within the German Confederation (*Bericht des Carl Follenius über die revolutionäre Stimmung in Deutschland*).[15] Although this document should be read with care, keeping in mind Wit von Dörring's bias against Follen, it probably genuinely represents Follen's political thought at the time. He wrote that one could no longer recognize the history of the German people in its current government. He included a utopian proposition for direct popular democracy and saw the Congress of Vienna as a betrayal, bringing with it the suppression of free speech, oppressive taxes, and false justice. The "martyrdom" of Sand was interpreted as one of the first political signs of hope. Sand was, for Follen, a representative of the people, and the police investigation of Sand was evil, arbitrary, and terrible. According to Follen, revolutionaries must destroy the current state by the "struggle of annihilation by individuals against other individuals." The entire political situation, he wrote, "points to a bloody

---

14 English version published in *Works*, 1:appendix.
15 Published in Ferdinand Wit von Dörring, *Fragmente aus meinem Leben und meiner Zeit* (Leipzig, 1827–30), 194–200.

future for Germany." He issued a call to arms to all who wanted to follow the path to revolution, expressing his readiness to struggle against the monarchical principle. In his professed willingness to sacrifice his own life, Follen did not show political realism; instead, he played into the hands of political repression by Metternich and the Restoration governments. Heinrich von Treitschke referred to him as a "German Robespierre," and his fellow student leader Robert Wesselhöft wrote: "He was a German devil. . . . Dr. Follen was a bloody revolutionary." Follen's tactic of "la guerre des individues" was seen by Ernst Rudolf Huber as harmful to the development of a successful German liberal movement.[16]

In Switzerland, Follen wrote two articles for the journal *Wissenschaftliche Zeitschrift*, published by professors at the University of Basel, titled "On the Destiny of Man" ("Über die Bestimmung des Menschen") and "On The Legal Teachings of Spinoza" ("Über die Rechtlehre des Spinoza").[17] He also conceived a major book titled *Das Naturrecht*, based on his lectures at Basel University, where natural law was still being taught. In "On the Destiny of Man" Follen outlined his own moral principles and discussed man's moral stature, conscience, self-control, and self-perception, the relationship between duty and individual needs, and liberation. Man possessed the attributes of conscience and *Gottgefühl* (divine inspiration), the ability to be religious. From self-control and self-perfection sprang human freedom. Man was to sacrifice his own well-being for the perfection and liberation of humanity. In history Follen saw a constant struggle between the principles of freedom and slavery. Man must continually opt for freedom and wipe out slavery from the earth. In his article on Spinoza, Follen aimed to demonstrate the validity and usefulness of natural law for the establishment of modern republican nation-states. Humans must pursue liberation. The best tool to achieve this objective was law. Humans could achieve freedom by collectivizing law in a social contract and then obeying it systematically. The ideal form of this would be *Volksherrschaft* (popular sovereignty). The rules of civil society were to be as similar as possible to natural law.

In addition to his plans for Germany Follen engaged in international revolutionary conspiracy, maintaining contact with well-known European radicals. By 1819 Follen's contacts in France included the Marquis de Lafayette, Victor Cousin, Benjamin Constant, and the radical lawyers Marc-René Voyer d'Argenson and Joseph Rey. He also continued to promote his

---

16 For an evaluation of Follen's role in German radicalism, see Spevack, *Charles Follen*, 82–5.
17 *Wissenschaftliche Zeitschrift, herausgegeben von Lehrern der Baseler Hochschule* (Basel, 1824), 4ff. and 56ff.

radical *Jünglingsbund* and when this league was exposed in 1824 Follen was forced to flee to America. His initial plans for his stay in America can be seen clearly in his memorandum "On the Founding of a German-American University,"[18] which proceeded from three main assumptions: Freedom of movement for radicals no longer existed in contemporary Germany; America offered a republican form of government and a free society that would grant protection to European refugees; and his emigration to America was only temporary – he assumed he would return to Germany once things had changed for the better. The memorandum proposed the founding of a separatist German institution of learning in the United States, which would form part of a "German Free State" to be inhabited by German political émigrés who would remain in America only until they could return to Germany and participate in a German (or even greater European) revolution. Follen's "university" was to function as a place in which German revolutionaries could gather and discuss the future, and ready themselves intellectually for their future roles. This plan was swiftly abandoned, however, indicating Follen's integration into American society and his eventual decision to remain in America for the duration of his life. Particularly after his marriage to an American woman from a prominent Boston family in 1828, Follen became increasingly Americanized and began to engage actively with specifically American political and social problems.

Carrying German Ideas to America (1824–1831)

The fourth phase of Follen's life began with his flight from Switzerland, which was about to extradite him to Prussia, and his arrival in the United States at the end of 1824. Follen was employed at Harvard University as a lecturer on German from 1825 until 1829 and then from 1830 to 1835 as the first-ever professor of German literature and language in the United States. He played a leading role in the popularization of German thought in New England. Because New Englanders were in the process of emancipating themselves from British cultural patterns, they sought alternative examples; Larzer Ziff has documented this process.[19] The longing for cultural emancipation can be seen in contemporary writings such as William Ellery Channing's "Remarks on a National Literature" and in Ralph Waldo Emerson's address, "The American Scholar." Follen was able to step into

18 Herman Haupt, "Denkschrift über die Gründung einer deutsch-amerikanischen Universität," *Deutsch-Amerikanische Geschichtsblätter* 22–3 (1922–3): 56–76.
19 Larzer Ziff, *Literary Democracy: The Declaration of Cultural Independence in America* (New York, 1981).

this vacuum and successfully introduce current elements of German literature, culture, philosophy, theology, and science into New England. It is
interesting to note the forms and aspects of German culture on which
Follen chose to focus: the plays of Schiller rather than those of Kotzebue,
the poetry of Körner, and the philosophy of Kant. Follen was thus responsible for importing the radical and republican elements of German culture
into New England. It is remarkable with how much interest these were
taken up by Americans such as Emerson and William Ellery Channing,
who became Follen's close friend.[20]

After his arrival in America, Follen's writing activity increased. His letters
to his family in Hesse, presenting his expectations of what America would
be like and his initial reactions to his new home country, are fascinating
documents of what this German republican expected to find in a land in
which all his dreams had supposedly been realized.[21] Follen's initial image
of America was extremely bright and hopeful. The diary that he kept on
the ship *Cadmus* during his voyage from Le Havre to Philadelphia in
December 1824 is only one example.[22] In it he expressed his wish to maintain his political commitment and to continue his struggle for freedom and
social justice. His diary and his early letters to his family illustrate his idealized images and hopes. Only after several years in the United States did
Follen revise this unrealistic view and begin to critique some of what he
saw as defects of American society, notably the slavery system. Later writings show his increased understanding of American realities and the imper-
fections of life in the United States.

Follen brought a specific view of German literature to New England in
a sizeable selection of German prose and poetry included in his *German
Reader* (first published in 1826, with many subsequent editions; it was
published with another work, *German Grammar*).[23] In 1829 he expressed
his views on world history in two reviews of works by the contemporary German historian Arnold Heeren.[24] This activity continued in his
"Inaugural Discourse," which he delivered in 1831,[25] after he had been
appointed professor at Harvard University. His *Lectures on Schiller* (delivered

---

20 Although there are no references to Follen in Emerson's journals of the period, it can be assumed
   that the two men knew each other personally. During the winter of 1828–9, Emerson and Follen
   competed for a job as assistant minister at the Old North Church in Boston, Emerson receiving
   74 and Follen 3 votes. It is also likely that Emerson heard Follen speak at the Harvard Divinity
   School, and that Emerson's liberal theological views were influenced by those of Follen. For details,
   see Henry Pochmann, *German Culture in America* (Madison, Wis., 1957), 119–20, 567n498–9.
21 Haupt, "Follen-Briefe," *Deutsch-Amerikanische Geschichtsblätter* 14 (1914): 7–83.
22 *Works*, 1:128.
23 Charles Follen, *German Reader* (Boston, 1826) and *German Grammar* (Boston, 1826).
24 Ibid., 5:99–124.   25 *Works*, 5:125–52.

in 1831–2)[26] were a continuation of his attempts to introduce Americans to those German literary figures of whom he approved politically.

In his review of Heeren, Follen spoke out against the propensity in contemporary historiography to exaggerate the merits or faults of individuals, religious organizations, political parties, and noble families. He believed Providence was guiding mankind toward freedom, happiness, and perfection. Every individual and nation was moving toward the goal of eventually attaining freedom and happiness. Follen remained critical, however, of Hegel's belief that world history unfolds according to preconceived rules. He called for an internal and external social history of nations. In his suggestions for an American national historiography Follen warned against overrating the role of history and tradition and becoming overly attached to the past. It was most important to look for the spirit of human improvement. America represented the highest point on Follen's scale of development because here individual liberty, popular sovereignty, and religious freedom had been realized.

Knowledge of German language and literature was extremely rare in New England before Follen published his *Reader* in 1826. All the included texts were by politically liberal writers, or at least by writers who had been adopted by the German left. From Luther to Schiller, here was a synopsis of the authors whom Follen favored. The writings of Herder, Lessing, Novalis, Herder, Schiller, and Wieland were all discussed and edited by Follen. Among the thinkers whom he chose to discuss in his "Inaugural Discourse" delivered at Harvard in 1831 were Fichte, Kant, Pufendorf, Savigny, and Thomasius. Follen applauded German attempts at emancipation from slavish imitation of French models, and he praised the recent revival of German literature at the hands of Madame de Staël. She had managed to win many admirers to German literature in her own country, including important intellectuals such as Cousin and Constant. Follen also mentioned the roles of Samuel Taylor Coleridge, Percy Bysshe Shelley, and Thomas Carlyle in transmitting German culture to English-speaking audiences. He called on New Englanders to turn to the study of German culture, literature, and philosophy.

In his *Lectures on Schiller* Follen introduced one of his favorite social and moral role models to an American audience. To him, Schiller was not only a superior poet, but he also espoused the sort of political and social issues with which Follen could identify. Schiller was thus at the same time both the perfect artist and the perfect morally engaged individual. Follen praised

26 Ibid., vol. 4.

what he described as Schiller's love of justice and freedom, his heroic resistance to every form of oppression, and his interest in religious problems. He considered his own life to be parallel to, and involved with, that of Schiller, who had, like Follen, stayed with the father of the poet Theodor Körner and taught as professor at the University of Jena. Follen and his generation of students had been enthralled by plays such as *Wilhelm Tell*, in which they recognized their own willingness to fight for the cause of freedom from any sort of oppression. Schiller was also important to this generation because of his positive attitude toward the reform of Christianity and his blending of religion with nationalist ideas.

The *Lectures on Moral Philosophy*, which Follen first delivered in Boston in 1830–1, were highly significant because they introduced the ideas of Kant to New England.[27] As Otto Dann shows in his chapter in this book, the political ideas of Kant were fundamental to German concepts of republicanism after 1780. Follen initiated the American reception of Kant's philosophy, including its relevance for political and social thought. Thus Kant's concepts gained intellectual acceptance in the United States, exerting influence on such leading figures as Emerson. Recent work on the significance of freedom in the thought of Kant provides circumstantial evidence that Follen could indeed glean much from Kant's philosophy. The British philosopher Henry Allison has dealt extensively with the important role Kant assigned to the concept of freedom in the following moral situations: the attainment of virtue and holiness, the fulfillment of duty, the curbing of radical evil, and the striving for moral self-perfection.[28] Allison's study shows that the problem solutions with which Follen concerned himself, and which he used to guide his own life, were available as blueprints in the writings of Kant.

Although he did not subscribe to Kant's idea of the "categorical imperative," Follen's own intellectual position of radical subjectivity and absolute adherence to individual conscience, which he had preached in Giessen and Jena, could not exist without confronting Kant and did not change during his time in America. In his *Lectures on Moral Philosophy* Follen reaffirmed one of his most basic principles: that the true meaning of life lay in "the conquest of the self" and the "striving for divine perfection."[29] The key philosopher of his time, Follen explicitly said, was Kant. Some of the most important passages of the lectures dealt with Kant's concept of duty and the functioning of the individual's conscience and moral decision making.

27 Ibid., vol. 3.
28 Henry E. Allison, *Kant's Theory of Freedom* (Cambridge, 1990).
29 *Works*, 3:1–17.

The individual was led by his own conviction and the guidance of reason. He was bound by a self-defined and socially defined duty, and by social responsibility. But Follen was also explicitly critical of some of Kant's teachings. Humans, according to Follen, should strive for a self-defined moral duty. Moral philosophy as a whole should be conceived as a "system of human perfection." Self-assigned duties could not be the same for all individuals; it was important, however, to speak not "the language of slaves" but rather that of free, responsible men. Although "moral inducements" for deviant persons were preferable to violent means, Follen still did not rule out the latter. If moral suasion failed, violent means would have to be used as a last resort. This discussion, reminiscent of Rousseau's phrase "forcing men to be free" in *The Social Contract*, could have been taken directly from Follen's constitution of 1818–19. The problem of violence and political coercion thus lingered without much modification throughout Follen's life, and it was clearly stated that violence had its place in his political and moral world.

Religion and Republicanism

The fifth phase of Follen's life is characterized by the great importance he attached – spiritually, philosophically, and socially – to religion. For Follen religion was always closely linked to social reform, primarily a tool for the moral and social regeneration of society. Follen was an ultra-liberal Protestant in the United States, belonging to the Unitarian church but espousing radical ideas even within this liberal denomination. In his sermons as a Unitarian minister he endorsed unpopular political causes, such as the antislavery movement; in his public lectures he chose to explore such controversial issues as pantheism and atheism.

Follen's three essays published under the title *On the Future State of Man* (1830) were highly philosophical.[30] They should be seen in the context of Follen's preoccupation with religion after the mid-1820s and his membership in the Unitarian church (he was ordained as a minister in that church in 1836). It is fascinating to see the intersection of German radicalism with American religion in the 1820s and 1830s in New England, the consequences of which were bound to be controversy and unrest.

Follen began the first essay by providing a historical sketch of how various cultures in world history answered the question of life after death.

---

30 Ibid., 5:3–98. Articles previously published in *Christian Examiner* 7 (Jan. 1830): 390–404; 8 (Mar. 1830): 115–32; 9 (July 1830): 265–93.

In the second essay he stated his own opinion of what a modern answer might entail. In the third he analyzed the "moral powers" of man that constituted his immortality. By moral powers Follen meant man's conscience and his free will. As opposed to animals, man had free choice. He could freely control his own life and could resist certain instincts that animals had to follow. Most important was man's ability to choose between "selfish and disinterested desires."[31] He could also listen to his conscience, a vital part of human existence that animals lack. Conscience and the possibility of truly moral and just action, Follen argued, would always survive in man. By touching on the issues of immortality and human morality as well as the ethical self-determination and potential self-perfection of each individual, Follen not only explained theological positions that had recently surfaced in Germany; he also directly intervened in the current theological discussion in America. What is more, he set forth a republican morality.

Follen's review of Constant's *De la Religion* (1832) showed that even in America he retained his interest in European politics.[32] In an effort to link religious with political principles Follen reviewed Constant's book for an American audience. He admired Constant's view of religion as a free, libertarian, and individualistic concept that would best thrive if interpreted by each individual for himself. Follen voiced his surprise that "a man who was known only as a politician, and as a general scholar, should appear before the world as the author of a theological work." Follen was particularly interested, however, in how political liberalism could be applied to religion and how religion and politics could interlock and aid each other. He offered the reader some of the strongest, most revealing statements about his own political beliefs, writing:

When the French Revolution stretched forth its spectral hand in the midst of the banquet hall of despotic Europe, her thousands of lords looked with trembling upon the bloody fingers, and not one of her political soothsayers had wisdom enough to read the mysterious hand-writing, or courage enough to make known the interpretation thereof. Indeed, the friends of freedom, not less than its enemies, saw with fear the first instinctive outbreakings of a spirit which seemed directed not only against the prevailing despotism, but against all social order, religion, civilization, and refinement. . . . True, this spirit of liberty has at times appeared as a destroying angel; but the angel has passed over the great interests and hopes of mankind, which have in the soul of man a safe habitation, secured by the pro-

31 Charles Follen, "On the Future State of Man, Third Essay," *Christian Examiner* 9 (July 1830): 265–8.
32 Charles Follen, "Benjamin Constant's Work on Religion," *American Quarterly Review* 11 (Mar. 1832), 103–20.

tecting hand of God. . . . It is despotism in every shape, persecuting or patronizing, destroying or corrupting, at which the finger of Providence is pointed.[33]

Arguing that "religion and liberty are not antagonistic, but kindred principles," Follen found in Constant's work a legitimization of his own viewpoint: He had come upon terms to justify his own combination of religion with political liberalism and reinforce his concept of a religion of spiritual emancipation and political liberation.

In his introduction to the *Franklin Lectures*, delivered in Boston in 1834 and directed to an audience of workers, Follen again addressed a variety of political and social issues, pulling together concepts of religion and social reform.[34] He commented on the changes in the American workplace due to the rise of industrialization: New machines had helped Americans to progress from a state of "chaos and barbarism" and advance from "savagery" to "civilization." Follen presented a strong argument that material progress was necessary, positive, unavoidable, and compatible with human happiness. However, there existed certain obstacles to progress that had to be overcome by all Americans. In a mode reminiscent of German communal republicanism, he denounced what he called an unhealthy "mercenary spirit" that could spread among workers and employers. He linked the concept of economic progress to religious themes and subsequently turned to a lengthy discussion of religion. Although contemporary religion contained many errors and falsehoods there did exist a "true religion" to which humans could adhere. All human creeds sprang from the universal human tendency to aspire to something infinite, unattainable by the ordinary exercise of our faculties. Religion was not stationary but progressive and was an expression of the ability of man to strive for his own infinite improvement. Follen declared religion to be useful to the modern working man, believing that "if American industry aspires for perfection, it must drink deep of the living waters of religion." Religion was not only the fulfillment of a basic, inborn human need; it also was necessary for self-improvement and for the progress of society.

In many of his lectures and publications of the time Follen took to exploring controversial margins of contemporary American theology, as seen in his essay "Religion and the Church" (1835),[35] his *Lectures on Infidelity* (1837),[36] the *Lectures on Pantheism* (1838–9),[37] and the many sermons that Follen delivered throughout the 1830s.[38] Religious reform remained

---

33 Follen, "Benjamin Constant's Work," 103–4.   34 *Works*, 5:228–53.
35 Ibid., 5:254–313.   36 See ibid., 1:446–9.
37 For details, see ibid., 1:501–5.   38 Ibid., vol. 2.

tied for Follen to social and political issues. In 1927 the intellectual historian Vernon L. Parrington commented ironically on the "Jacobin" elements in Bostonian religious reform movements of the 1830s; he saw the acts of reformers such as Follen first and foremost as a disguised form of European leftist radicalism.[39]

The essay "Religion and the Church" was indeed radical in that Follen once again spoke on behalf of freedom, in favor of a critical attitude toward accepted doctrines in religion and society. His appeal could not be to a large group of readers because he contradicted and denied what the great majority of them held to be true. Follen's statements were very much influenced by the climate of religious liberalism fostered by current theologians in Germany and Unitarians and Transcendentalists in the United States. Follen carefully avoided claiming the superiority of any particular religion, creed, or denomination; rather, he argued that all religions were valid in their own right and were an expression of something common to all humans, a longing for worship and communion with the force that had created the world and kept it in motion. Follen also presented an intimate insight into his own religious views and development. The main element of religion for him was the self-sacrifice of Jesus for mankind. Consequently, he had come to believe that an individual's sacrifice for humanity was the highest form of religious expression. Living in a universe run by universal laws and presenting a harmonious whole, man constantly progressed toward perfection, using science and skepticism as ways to test whether he was still following the right course.

Follen's *Lectures on Infidelity*, delivered in the spring of 1837 in New York, were immediately controversial, and in the winter of 1838–9 Follen once again became the object of suspicion and criticism when he read his *Lectures on the History of Pantheism* in Boston. The later 1830s in fact brought an American backlash against what was seen as the dangerous influence of German atheism and infidelity. Scholars such as Andrew Norton were active in a campaign to blame German theology for the increasing secularization of American society, and he attacked the influence of German liberal theology (traces of which could be found in Emerson's "Divinity School Address") in tracts such as his "The Latest Form of Infidelity" (1838).

Follen's ideas on the combination of religion and social reform can be seen in his many sermons. In the mid-1830s he preached on the Biblical passage "I have come not to destroy, but to fulfill." Follen discussed his own role as a religious man and reformer, stating that "the great object of change and reform is not change and reform, but to find the most perfect, and there-

---

39 Parrington quoted in Spevack, *Charles Follen*, 204–5.

fore most permanent form in law and religion, in science and art, in public and domestic life."[40] Follen also stressed the ever-changing character of religion, which, as other areas of human experience, should be adapted to the times. Religion was necessary to contribute to the cause of progress and to find a more perfect way of life for mankind. Follen decried forms of religion that promoted a withdrawal from worldly affairs; instead, true believers should actively engage in the liberation of man from social oppression.

Antislavery and Violence

The sixth and last phase of Follen's life was marked by his great devotion to the antislavery crusade in America. It is here that most of the main themes of Follen's life came to the fore clearly and unambiguously: the opposition of freedom and liberation to oppression and despotism; the belief that slavery in the American South was illegal and un-American; the idea that law was an instrument with which social ills could effectively be eliminated; and the clandestine and ambiguous personal relationship with political violence. The antiviolent stance of Follen's friend William Lloyd Garrison is well known. Although he became considerably more radical as time went on, publicly condemning the American Union and predicting that the United States would be "drenched in blood" if slavery were not immediately abolished, Garrison was violent only in his texts but never in person. In Follen's case, the situation is much more difficult to judge; it can be argued with some certainty, however, that had he not died in a tragic shipping accident in January 1840 he would have applauded the outbreak of the Civil War twenty years later. Although the evidence was glossed over by Eliza Follen in her biography and her edition of Follen's *Works*, there can be little doubt that the readiness to participate in political violence always remained part of Follen's left-wing republican identity, both in Europe and in the United States.

By the mid-1830s the antislavery movement had become Follen's main commitment. He wrote four major speeches and articles, including his "Address to the People of the United States on the Subject of Slavery" (1834);[41] his "Speech before the Massachusetts Antislavery Society" (1836);[42] "The Cause of Freedom in Our Country" (1836);[43] and "Antislavery Principles and Proceedings" (1838).[44] Furthermore, Follen

---

40 Ibid., 1:469–70.   41 Ibid., 5:189–227.

42 Ibid., 1:appendix 6, 627–33.

43 Charles Follen, "The Cause of Freedom in Our Country," *Quarterly Antislavery Magazine* 1–2 (Oct. 1835–July 1837), 61–73.

44 Charles Follen, "Antislavery Principles and Proceedings," *Christian Examiner* 25 (Nov. 1838): 238.

played an important role as an intermediary between the extremism of Garrison and the belated and moderate abolitionism of the Unitarian leader Channing.[45]

Follen's "Address," delivered in late May 1834, was his first major contribution on antislavery before a sizeable audience. He did not slander or indiscriminately attack slaveholders and their supporters; rather, he systematically dealt with the major political, moral, and economic issues of the controversy. This sort of treatment would, he thought, lead Americans to "confess and repair our wrongs" and "to act in obedience to the law of liberty which we have proclaimed." If the whole of American political behavior was to be meaningful and true to its own principles, slavery would have to be abolished immediately and completely. "Every Fourth of July," he argued, "is to us a day of exultation for what we have done, and a day of humiliation for what we have left undone." Follen saw enslaved blacks as American citizens who were being denied their full rights. Slaveholders, too, were being hurt by the unlawful and shameful practice of slavery. Immediate abolition would lead only to increased political stability, not instability. Follen cited the example of Haiti as one in which the abolition of slavery had led to the political stability and prosperity of this black-ruled autonomous state. Due to the violence there, however, this example was only partly appropriate.

Follen attacked slavery mainly on legal grounds, as contrary to the Declaration of Independence and the Constitution. Since slavery was thus unconstitutional Congress should acknowledge that fact and abolish it as swiftly as possible. The continued existence of slavery in the United States would lead to political instability and economic decline. In fact, Follen argued, open violence would be unavoidable in the long run if American decision makers were not true to their promise of freedom and democracy. According to Follen, the comparison with despotism and reactionary politics in Europe should make Americans realize which side they must be on: "The despotism which our forefathers could not bear in their native country, is expiring, and the sword of justice . . . has applied its exterminating edge to slavery."

Follen next spoke before the Massachusetts Antislavery Society in Boston on January 20, 1836. He said that the antislavery crusade was first and foremost one of "philanthropy, or love of man." Its followers must recognize that slaves were humans, as they themselves were, and endowed with the same rights and duties. Follen called on the abolitionists to help fulfill the principles of the Declaration of Independence and its provisions for uni-

---

45 Spevack, *Charles Follen*, 218–25.

versal legal equality and individual human rights. He advocated admitting black members to the Massachusetts Antislavery Society, and incidentally stated that foreigners, too, should have the same rights and duties as American members. Follen claimed that "our cause is the cause of man" and called for an international movement to abolish slavery and all other forms of political and legal oppression. Although Follen denounced the recent violence against abolitionists, he did argue in favor of the right of self-defense. Follen also advocated giving women an active role in the antislavery crusade. To abolish slavery, Americans must use all possible means and all channels of communication.

The essay "The Cause of Freedom in Our Country," published in October 1836, placed Follen's argument more narrowly into the American national context. He set out to examine critically how the principles of freedom and liberty had been realized and unrealized in the contemporary United States. He particularly contrasted liberty and oppression as polar opposites. Unfortunately, Follen found, in the United States "the worm of oppression is gnawing every fibre of the frame." In theory, America possessed all the attributes of a great nation, including great natural resources and wealth and a republican form of government; however, American resources were not being used effectively to protect freedom but in fact aided oppression. Slaveholders were marring the image of America as the land of freedom and justice. Slavery was "not just a local evil," but something that "infects the whole neighborhood, and aggravates every minor disorder in the body politic." If Americans allowed slavery to continue, so would prejudice against color and they would soon fall back into a state of feudalism, inequality and political privilege. The excessive greed of whites had led to the dehumanizing not only of American blacks but of native Americans, too. Follen called on the "friends of freedom" to unite in fighting "the enemy," who relied on racial and financial exploitation.

After protesting against the legislation known as the Gag Bill, passed by Congress in 1836, which hindered the effectiveness of abolitionist petitions, Follen published his article "Antislavery Principles and Proceedings" in November 1838. It provides an insight into the complex American antislavery movement and a synopsis of the debates within it: relations between the American Antislavery Society and local groups, the question of goals, the means to be used to achieve them, the "Gag Bill," and the connections between the American Antislavery Society and foreign antislavery groups. He advocated "moral action" and the tactics of persuasion; abolitionists had no intention of encouraging slaves to rebel. The experience of slave emancipation in the West Indies, Follen argued, was very positive and should be repeated in the United States where liberated blacks would be a great asset to their nation as free citizens. Finally, Follen argued, liberating the slaves would in fact bring great economic gain to former slaveholders.

Follen's last publication, an essay titled "Peace and War" (1839), summed up many of the political beliefs that he held as a mature man.[46] Above all, the essay once again brought out the question of violence, which had lingered beneath the surface of Follen's political thought and rhetoric wherever he went. Although his wife tried to cleanse her biography of Charles Follen of all elements of violence, they are visible (if unacknowledged) in Follen's behavior after the assassination of Kotzebue by Sand. By the time he became involved with the antislavery crusade, Follen was no longer a German revolutionary but an American reformer who sympathized with the work of the American Peace Society and the cause of pacifism; still, the question of the use of force occupied his mind as much as it had twenty years before. Evidently, the ideas espoused in the article "Antislavery Principles and Proceedings," written to please his abolitionist colleagues, were not satisfying to him as a final answer.

Follen searched the Bible, especially the episodes in the life of Jesus as recorded in the Gospels, for evidence on how a Christian was to relate to the question of armed struggle. Much in Christian teaching, he found, spoke against this, and the life of Jesus, Follen argued, signified the eventual prevalence of pacifist behavior over brute force. Yet Jesus had thrown the moneylenders out of the temple; Follen came to the conclusion that Jesus' teachings did not preclude securing the basic rights of man with the use of force. Follen therefore rejected complete abstinence from political violence. The rights of states and of individuals could be defended in a violent way if all other means failed. "Liberty is the only sure foundation of true peace," he argued, and it thus had to be defended at all costs. In the international realm, "just wars" had to be fought against "tyrants" seeking to deny the self-government of people within a nation. In the face of injustice and oppression, war became not only a right but in fact a duty for the victimized party. In the long run, the best solution to international conflict was to change entirely the internal political structures of as many nations as possible. Follen favored setting up an international Congress of Nations and a World Court. In the long run, the attainment of lasting world peace could be achieved only by "republicanizing the world." Americans should learn to bear arms and actively work to extend their own republican system to Europe and the rest of the world.[47]

---

46 *Works*, 5:314–73.   47 See Spevack, *Charles Follen*, 240.

A FINAL EVALUATION OF FOLLEN'S
VIEW OF REPUBLICANISM

Follen was what Nolte has referred to as a "dogmatic republican."[48] His initial anti-Napoleonic stance was typical of German republicans in the first decades of the nineteenth century. After 1815 German republicanism became an ingredient of the liberal nationalist fraction of the German political spectrum; after 1840 it became the province of the radical left. The necessity of individual self-perfection, as urged by Follen, and the possibility of positive social change through the use of law and moral reform were typical elements of republican conceptions of "virtue" and the "common good." Arguing for German national unification under a republican form of government, Follen epitomized the tension between the localized communal republicanism in southwestern Germany, on the one hand, and the quest for national belonging and political unity, on the other, a tension also felt among the American Anti-Federalists. There was, however, a more problematic flipside to Follen's personal and political being: He also advocated violent revolution in Germany and thus made himself an outsider in a nation that overwhelmingly rejected political violence. This fact made life in the German Confederation impossible for him. After his "*Grundzüge für eine künftige teutsche Reichsverfassung*" of 1818 Follen combined a devotion to freedom and liberation with a dangerous illiberalism and intolerance toward political enemies.

In America, after his emigration from Europe, Follen remained unusually radical. He was initially accepted by the social mainstream when he preached European forms of radical culture, politics, and theology to New Englanders. Later on, however, his vision of American politics and nationality was no longer shared by the majority of his new compatriots. Although he tried hard to become an American, Follen was once again ostracized from nearly all groups with which he came into contact, except those of the most ardent reformers, and was eventually able to live only on the fringes of American society. It was his zealous and unbending opposition to slavery that made him an outsider in New England. Follen was not able to accept the existence of slavery in a republic that he otherwise saw as nearly perfect in its political and social development. Antislavery and the constant conflict between freedom and enslavement thus became the core themes of Follen's republican crusade in America.

48 Nolte, "Bürgerideal, Gemeinde und Republik," 654.

The Logic of Liberalism

13

"The Right to Possess All the Faculties that God Has Given": Possessive Individualism, Slave Women, and Abolitionist Thought

AMY DRU STANLEY

I

The problem of possessive individualism haunts the study of American slavery and emancipation. It lies at the heart of the ambiguities of anti-slavery reform, distilling the moral questions involved in the transition from chattel slavery to free-market relations which was envisioned by abolition-ists. It marks the limits of an ideal of freedom defined by the negation of property in the persons of others. It lies as well at the heart of the per-plexities of liberalism as a theory of women's emancipation, distilling the contradiction between affirmations of universal human rights and assump-tions of sexual inequality based on immutable physical difference.[1]

This chapter reconsiders antislavery ideas of possessive individualism in light of the circumstances of enslaved and freedwomen. It explores diverg-ing notions of the relationship between theories of sex difference and the-ories of emancipation rooted in rights of proprietorship, foremost among them the right of self-ownership. My interpretation centers on antislavery rhetoric of the body. It focuses particularly on the complex ideological con-sequences of the use by abolitionists of the symbol of the suffering female slave to condemn self-dispossession. I argue that this symbolism – as it was handled by black, female antislavery thinkers – worked to disrupt rather than to validate the conventional categories of sex difference customarily associated with liberal beliefs. This chapter also addresses the rights con-sciousness of freedwomen; I argue that the right of self-ownership was of

---

1 See David Brion Davis, *The Problem of Slavery in the Age of Revolution 1770–1823* (Ithaca, N.Y., 1975); Thomas Bender, ed., *The Antislavery Debate: Capitalism and Abolitionism as a Problem in Historical Inter-pretation* (Berkeley, Calif., 1992); Carole Pateman, *The Sexual Contract* (Stanford, Calif., 1988).

no small importance. The glaring ideological limits, evasions, and contradictions of possessive individualism as an antislavery theory have been well
plumbed by historians.[2] But very little is known about how that theory
figured in the aspirations to freedom of black women. Exploring this body
of thought casts new light not only on constructions of liberalism but on
the meaning of freedom in the ages of slavery and of emancipation.

II

In an 1850 sermon on the "The Rights and Duties of Masters," James
Henley Thornwell, the South Carolina minister who was one of slavery's
most formidable defenders, decried the abolitionist theory that the slave
owner held property in the slave's limbs, organs, and soul. Arguing from
the standpoint of moral philosophy, Thornwell insisted that no human per-
sonality, not even the slave's, could be owned by another. The master was
entitled merely to labor (however forcibly it might be extracted), not to
the slave's person, which was understood as distinct from labor. Like the
free laborer, therefore, the slave remained essentially self-owning – in
Thornwell's words, the slave's body was "not mine, but his."[3]

Arguments such as Thornwell's cut to the heart of abolitionist faith. In
the eyes of virtually all antislavery advocates, self-ownership constituted the
taproot of freedom. For them, the defining sin of slavery was its denial of
property in the self. As Theodore Dwight Weld proclaimed in 1838, "SELF-
RIGHT is the *foundation* right – *the post in the middle*, to which all other
rights are fastened." The primacy of the conviction so unambivalently
announced by Weld is well documented in recent historical scholarship on
abolitionism. Less well known is how widely this conviction was espoused
beyond the circle of the movement's most famous spokesmen, uniting a
constituency cleft not only by disagreements over principles and tactics but
by differences of sex and race, as well. In 1838, for example, the Second
National Anti-Slavery Convention of American Women declared that

2 See Catherine Hall, "In the Name of Which Father," *International Labor and Working-Class History*
   41 (spring 1992): 23–8; Davis, *Slavery in the Age of Revolution*; Eric Foner, *Politics and Ideology in the
   Age of the Civil War* (New York, 1980), 57–76; Thomas C. Holt, *The Problem of Freedom: Race, Labor,
   and Politics in Jamaica and Britain, 1832–1938* (Baltimore, 1992); Julie Saville, *The Work of Reconstruction: From Slave to Wage Laborer in South Carolina, 1860–1870* (New York, 1994); C. B. Macpherson,
   The Political Theory of Possessive Individualism: Hobbes to Locke (Oxford, 1962); Evelyn Brooks Hig-
   ginbotham, "Beyond the Sound of Silence: Afro-American Women in History," *Gender & History* 1
   (spring 1989): 50–67.
3 James H. Thornwell, *The Rights and the Duties of Masters: A Sermon Preached at the Dedication of a
   Church, Erected in Charleston, S.C., for the Benefit and Instruction of the Coloured Population* (Charleston,
   S.C., 1850).

women had the authority to assert the core right of self-ownership on the slave's behalf, to ask whether a man's "bones and sinews shall be his own, or another's." Black abolitionists, born both free and slave, also adopted the rhetoric of possessive individualism, designating self-entitlement an indispensable aspect of liberty, although recognizing that it hardly toppled the barriers of racial prejudice or economic privilege. "Colored men and women" in Jamaica, wrote Nancy Prince, a free black born in Massachusetts, were "determined to possess themselves, and to possess property besides." Fugitive slaves advocated the right of self-sovereignty with particular fervor, perhaps born of experiencing its nullification. The former slave Samuel Ringgold Ward made the point succinctly in an 1850 speech: "This is the question, Whether a man has a right to himself."[4] To most abolitionists the conflict between fundamental rights and self-dispossession was a guiding assumption.

In exalting the inviolable right of self-ownership, antislavery advocates did not simply argue on the abstract plane of natural law; they turned to the body's palpable torments and reasoned in sensual, empirical ways. They compiled excruciating evidence of physical suffering, meant to incite a visceral response and play on the cult of feeling dominant in Victorian America. Abolitionists were by no means alone in deploying images of suffering bodies; the literature of antebellum humanitarian reform was stocked with them. Conceivably, even the most empathetic of white abolitionists might not have been able to exclude all traces of voyeurism from their representations of the suffering slave. For black abolitionists, however, these images may have represented not only the singular horrors of slavery but also the vulnerability to violence and coercion shared by all members of their race. Again and again, Frederick Douglass summoned his audience to feel the slave's pain as his back was "torn all to pieces . . . warm brine . . . poured into . . . bleeding wounds." In Douglass' metaphorical description of the destruction of slave marriages, the "hearts of husband and wife" were rent by slave dealers, "bleeding ligaments . . . which before constituted the twain one flesh." And the crimes of the domestic slave trade came alive through an inventory of marketable body parts. "At these auction-stands,"

---

4 Ronald G. Walters, "The Boundaries of Abolitionism," in Lewis Perry and Michael Fellman, eds., *Antislavery Reconsidered: New Perspectives on the Abolitionists* (Baton Rouge, La., 1979), 9; Elizabeth Cady Stanton et al., eds., *History of Woman Suffrage*, vol. 1: *1848–1861* (Rochester, N.Y., 1887), 339; Henry Louis Gates Jr., ed., *Collected Black Women's Narratives* (New York, 1988), 49–50; C. Peter Ripley, ed., *The Black Abolitionist Papers*, 5 vols. (Chapel Hill, N.C., 1985–92), 4:50. See also Jonathan A. Glickstein, " 'Poverty Is not Slavery': American Abolitionists and the Competitive Labor Market," in Perry and Fellman, eds., *Antislavery Reconsidered*, 195–218; Eric Foner, "The Meaning of Freedom in the Age of Emancipation," *Journal of American History* 81 (Sept. 1994): 435–60.

stated William Wells Brown, a leader of the black abolitionist movement, "bones, muscles, sinews, blood and nerves, of human beings, are sold."[5]

The bodily images reflect how seriously abolitionists took the corporeal dimension of the formal right of self-proprietorship, which they regarded as the only secure guarantee of personal autonomy. The obverse of the slave whose person was dismembered, through punishment and as a commodity, was the autonomous individual whose body was inviolate. Freedom, as Douglass curtly defined it, was "appropriating my own body to my use." Here abolitionism differed from other contemporary expressions of liberal thought in which the attributes of individualism characteristically implied a renunciation of bodily experience and the irrationality and carnality long associated with matters of the flesh. Rather than being unintelligible in terms of Enlightenment political theory, the body's claims were formulated by abolitionists in the classical, legal language of rights. To be sure, antislavery rendered freedom abstract by enshrining ownership of the self at the expense of an older republican emphasis on ownership of productive property. Notably, however, by conceiving free individuals (in contrast to slaves) as unmistakably embodied bearers of rights, abolitionists simultaneously rendered self-ownership concrete while suggesting a new moral and ideological framework for thinking about the vicissitudes of human bodies. By their lights, soul and body were inseverable; spirit could not be emancipated where flesh was bound.[6]

Above all, abolitionists focused their thought on the circumstances of the enslaved female body. In their eyes, the two sexes suffered incommensurately under slavery. They constantly stressed that for all the cruelty inflicted on male slaves, only the bondswoman endured sexual violence as well as bloody punishment and the terror of the auction block. As one

5 Letter to William Lloyd Garrison, *The Liberator*, Nov. 18, 1842, in Philip S. Foner, ed., *The Life and Writings of Frederick Douglass: Early Years, 1817–1849*, 5 vols. (New York, 1950), 1:108–9; William Wells Brown, "The American Slave-Trade," *Liberty Bell* (1848): 235–6. See Karen Halttunen, "Humanitarianism and the Pornography of Pain in Anglo-American Culture," *American Historical Review*, 100 (Apr. 1995): 303–34; Elizabeth B. Clark, "'The Sacred Rights of the Weak': Pain, Sympathy, the Culture of Individual Rights in Antebellum America," *Journal of American History* 82 (Sept. 1995): 463–93; Elizabeth Alexander, "'Can You Be BLACK and Look at This?': Reading the Rodney King Video(s)," *Public Culture* 7 (1994): 77–94.
6 Letter to William Lloyd Garrison, Nov. 18, 1842, 109. See Leonore Davidoff, "'Adam Spoke First and Named the Orders of the World': Masculine and Feminine Domains in History and Sociology," in Helen Corr and Lynn Jamieson, eds., *Politics of Everyday Life: Continuity and Change in Work and Family* (London, 1990), 229–55; Karen Sanchez-Eppler, *Touching Liberty: Abolition, Feminism, and the Politics of the Body* (Berkeley, Calif., 1993), 1–49. On the opposition between liberal theory and the circumstances of human embodiment, see Michel Foucault, *The History of Sexuality*, vol. 1: *An Introduction* (New York, 1978), esp. 145–59; Pateman, *Sexual Contract*, esp. 189–234; Lauren Berlant, "National Brands/National Body: Imitation of Life," in Bruce Robbins, ed., *The Phantom Public Sphere* (Minneapolis, 1993), 176–9.

writer observed, it was only in regard to female chattel that the master's lust swelled his sadism and greed, mingling "the effervescence of lewdness with the wantonness of ferocity."[7]

The flesh of female slaves thus took center stage in abolitionist propaganda. Within the broad antislavery repertoire of bodily metaphors, the predominant one was the scourged body of the bondswoman, an image that symbolized the slave's utter debasement. Even abolitionists left to private fantasy the master's rape of his female slaves, but they did not flinch from depicting other abuses that were disturbingly fraught with sexual meaning. In his autobiography, Douglass dwelt on the wounds of slave women, giving a detailed account of the punishment delivered by a jealous master on a female slave for daring to meet illicitly with her lover: "Esther's wrists were firmly tied. . . . Her back and shoulders were bare to the waist. Behind her stood old master, with cowskin in hand, preparing his barbarous work with all manner of harsh, coarse, and tantalizing epithets. The screams of his victim were most piercing. He was cruelly deliberate, and protracted the torture, as one who was delighted with the scene." Douglass recalled that while, as a young boy, watching the whipping of his cousin – "Her neck and shoulders were covered with scars . . . her face literally covered with blood" – he was first aroused to slavery's wickedness.[8]

In accounts tinged with eroticism, abolitionists evoked a corporeal slave economy diametrically opposed to the sexual order of a free society in which female purity was valued as a priceless possession. Witness after witness divulged the slave masters' "habit not only of stripping their female slaves of their clothing . . . but of subjecting their naked persons to the most minute and revolting inspection." Horror at such lewdly intimate practices of calculating profit drew together a diverse antislavery following – black and white, male and female, those born slave and freemen. Abolitionists joined in describing scenes that were all but pornographic, lingering particularly, as had Douglass, over the unclothed body of the female slave.

---

7 George Bourne, *Slavery Illustrated in Its Effects upon Woman and Domestic Society* (1837; reprint, Freeport, N.Y., 1972), 59. See also Jacqueline Jones, *Labor of Love, Labor of Sorrow: Black Women, Work, and the Family from Slavery to the Present* (New York, 1985); Deborah Gray White, *Ar'n't I a Woman: Female Slaves in the Plantation South* (New York, 1985); Elizabeth Fox-Genovese, *Within the Plantation Household: Black and White Women of the Old South* (Chapel Hill, N.C., 1988).

8 Frederick Douglass, *My Bondage and My Freedom* (1855; reprint, New York, 1969), 82, 84, 87–8. See also Jean Fagan Yellin, *Women and Sisters: The Antislavery Feminists in American Culture* (New Haven, Conn., 1989), 71–89; Hazel V. Carby, *Reconstructing Womanhood: The Emergence of the Afro-American Woman Novelist* (New York, 1987), 35; Hortense J. Spillers, "Mama's Baby, Papa's Maybe: An American Grammar Book," *diacritics* 17 (summer 1987): 65–81; Ann du Cille, "The Occult of True Black Womanhood: Critical Demeanor and Black Feminist Studies," *Signs* 19 (spring 1994): 591–629, at 592; Sanchez-Eppler, *Touching Liberty*, 22–3.

Routinely, they testified, she was put up for public exhibition as a commodity, entirely naked. The former slave Louisa Picquet recounted the procedure of her own sale at a public auction: "Whoever want to buy come and examine, and ask you whole lot of questions. They began to take the clothes off of me." According to Thomas Wentworth Higginson, when a female slave was put up for sale, slave traders bid buyers to *strip her naked and examine every inch of her.*[9]

Such sensationalized representations were no less potent in abolitionist polemics against slavery as an immoral system of labor and an illegitimate exercise of power. Jehiel Beman, a free black journeying for the first time in the South, recounted being stricken nearly speechless by the sight of "my sisters toiling, pitchfork and rake in hand, under the scorching rays of the sun . . . but little on the body . . . my feelings were such as I cannot describe. I tried to raise my cries to Heaven, but in this I was interrupted, for the flowing tear forced its way down my care-worn cheek." In language more matter-of-fact, but with clearly prurient undertones, the Yankee reformer Samuel Gridley Howe described a public whipping at a New Orleans slave prison: "There lay a black girl, flat upon her face on a board . . . a strap passed over the small of her back. . . . Below the strap she was entirely naked." Doubtless such reports touched a nerve in Northern audiences, though perhaps not always in the ways abolitionists may have intended.[10]

On the bodies of female slaves, therefore, abolitionists saw most spectacularly branded the crimes of slavery that accrued from treating human beings as property to be bought and sold. Notably, at the very moment blackface minstrel performances fetishized the bodies of mainly black men in a new form of commercial entertainment,[11] antislavery reformers called public attention, for expressly insurrectionary purposes, to the commodified bodies of female slaves. Dishonored, stripped bare, the bondswoman literally embodied the denial of property in the self, which for abolition-

---

9 Theodore Dwight Weld, *American Slavery as It Is: Testimony of a Thousand Witnesses* (New York, 1839), 154; H. Mattison, *Louisa Picquet, The Octaroon: A Tale of Southern Slave Life, Or Inside Views of Southern Domestic Life* (New York, 1861), in *Collected Black Women's Narratives,* 16; Higginson cited in Charles K. Whipple, *The Family Relation, as Affected by Slavery* (Cincinnati, 1858), 15. See Halttunen, "Pornography of Pain"; Darlene C. Hine and Kate Wittenstein, "Female Slave Resistance: The Economics of Sex," in Filomina C. Steady, ed., *Black Women Cross-Culturally* (Cambridge, Mass., 1981), 290–6.
10 Jehiel C. Beman to Joshua Leavitt, Aug. 10, 1844, in *Black Abolitionist Papers,* 3:451; Samuel Gridley Howe, "Scene in a Slave Prison," *Liberty Bell* (1843): 177.
11 See Eric Lott, *Love and Theft: Blackface Minstrelsy and the American Working Class* (New York, 1993), 111–22; David R. Roediger, *The Wages of Whiteness: Race and the Making of the American Working Class* (New York, 1991), esp. 121–2.

ists counted as the ultimate evil of slavery. In antislavery literature she stood (or usually lay prone) as the symbol of the dispossessed self, someone without rights, the paradigmatic chattel. Through her image abolitionists sanctified, by negation, the liberal ideal of self-ownership as the essence of freedom.

This method of reasoning had no precedent in the classical liberal thought of the seventeenth and eighteenth centuries, from which American abolitionists derived the main lineaments of their critique of slavery. Although contrasting freedom and bondage, Enlightenment writers certainly did not take the subjugation of slave women as a platform for asserting the fundamental rights of free men; it is doubtful that they even considered women within the category of autonomous, self-owning individuals.[12] For abolitionists, however, there was obvious utility in attacking the slave system on behalf of the female sex; indeed, diverse battles had long been rhetorically waged in the name of violated womanhood.

But for antislavery thinkers to anchor visions of freedom in the negative symbolism of the bondswoman's body was something new and full of ideological ambiguity. According to reigning cultural beliefs, the black woman's body represented the most degenerate example of both the alleged pathology of female sexuality and the alleged natural inferiority of the black race. This abject icon, however, became central to an antislavery politics of human emancipation. Since ancient times the idea of personal freedom had entailed the right to an inviolate body – but only for men. By defining freedom through the negative example of the female slave's physical subjection, abolitionists opened to question the right of women to own themselves. Volatile in its gender implications, the eroticized symbolism of antislavery held the potential to complicate the categories of sex difference embedded in classical liberalism and Victorian scientific theory, as well as in older intellectual traditions.[13]

12 See Amy Dru Stanley, *From Bondage to Contract: Wage Labor, Marriage, and the Market in the Age of Slave Emancipation* (New York, 1998), chap. 1; Pateman, *Sexual Contract.*
13 On antislavery feminism and the corporeal dimensions of individual sovereignty, see Sanchez-Eppler, *Touching Liberty*, 1–21; Ellen Carol DuBois, "Outgrowing the Compact of the Fathers: Equal Rights, Woman Suffrage, and the United States Constitution, 1820–1878," *Journal of American History* 74 (Dec. 1987): 856; Elizabeth B. Clark, "Self Ownership and the Political Theory of Elizabeth Cady Stanton," *Connecticut Law Review* 21 (1989): 905–41. On ancient formulations, see David M. Halperin, "The Democratic Body: Prostitution and Citizenship in Classical Athens," *Differences: A Journal of Feminist Cultural Studies* 2 (1990): 1–28. On subjection because of sex and race, see Lorraine Daston, "The Naturalized Female Intellect," *Science in Context* 2 (1992): 209–35; Sander L. Gilman "Black Bodies, White Bodies: Toward an Iconography of Female Sexuality in Late Nineteenth-Century Art, Medicine, and Literature," in Henry Louis Gates Jr., *"Race," Writing, and Difference* (Chicago, 1986), 223–61; Londa Schiebinger, *Nature's Body: Gender in the Making of Modern Science* (Boston, 1993), 115–83.

For most abolitionists that was hardly the intended outcome of their outcry against slavery. Virtually all of them foresaw emancipation as transforming chattel into self-proprietors: "righting the slave – restoring him to himself." But they differed over whether this form of deliverance would abolish distinctions based on sex as well as on race. At stake were opposing visions not only of possessive individualism but of the relationship between freedom and marriage.[14]

The dominant abolitionist position was that slave emancipation would convert freedmen alone into sovereign, self-owning individuals. Property in women would simply be conveyed from slaveholders to husbands. This conception recapitulated the gender rules of classical liberal theory, which defined men as masters of the household with proprietary rights to their dependent wives. With the abolition of the slave master's "prior right" the former bondsman would gain the birthright of all free men: title not only to himself but to his wife – to her person, labor, and sexuality. In an argument notably inconsistent with his commitment to women's rights and his opposition to restrictive gender distinctions, William Lloyd Garrison affirmed the sovereignty of husbands as a fundamental element of freedom. The freedman, he declared unequivocally, would be "master of his own person, of his wife." As masters at home, former bondsmen could lay claim to the chastity of black women violated under slavery.[15]

So entrenched, so authoritative was this definition of freedom that even leading female abolitionists who condemned patriarchal institutions employed its terms. In her 1836 *Appeal to the Christian Women of the South*, Angelina Grimke asserted the right of free women to combat slavery but at the same time rather contradictorily set forth only the manhood rights annulled by slavery. Slavery, she argued, "is a violation of the natural order of things." It "*robs the slave of all his rights* as a *man*." Slaves were "robbed of wages, wives, children." By the order of nature, therefore, the freedman's property in his wife would be as irrevocable as in his wages, whereas the freedwoman would become entitled to her husband's protection – a reciprocity of marriage rights denied to slaves. For the freedwoman, emancipation would lie not in rights of individual ownership, but rather in coverture – what one antislavery writer termed "*woman's grand shield,*

---

14 Editorial by Thomas Hamilton in *Black Abolitionist Papers*, 5:41. See also Ann du Cille, *The Coupling Convention: Sex, Text, and Tradition in Black Women's Fiction* (Oxford, 1993); Claudia Tate, *Domestic Allegories of Political Desire: The Black Heroine's Text at the Turn of the Century* (New York, 1992); Hazel Carby, "'On the Threshold of Woman's Era': Lynching, Empire, and Sexuality in Black Feminist Theory," in Gates, ed., *"Race," Writing, and Difference*, 315.

15 Bourne, *Slavery Illustrated*, 61, 121; *Liberator*, Dec. 7, 1855. See Stanley, *From Bondage to Contract*, chap. 1.

MATRIMONY."[16] Thus, freedom was interpreted as slavery's antithesis but according to the binary laws of gender.

This was not, however, the only abolitionist construction of the freedom entailed in "righting the slave" through restoring ownership of the self. A divergent strain of antislavery thought made subversive use of the figure of the bondswoman and of appeals grounded in the body to voice women's claim to the rights of possessive individualism. Emancipation was prophesied in terms not of marriage bonds but of female self-ownership. The symbolic power of the debased female body established the logic of personal sovereignty as a universal right, unqualified by sex difference. Even though this remained a recessive strain of abolitionism, it was not without highly articulate and influential exponents, particularly in the black antislavery community.

Foremost among them was Frances Ellen Watkins Harper, the most prominent black woman writer and orator of her generation. Contemporaries called her the "bronze muse" and recognized her as a "glorious speaker" – "one of the ablest advocates . . . of the slave." In an address to the annual meeting of the American Anti-Slavery Society in 1858, Harper set forth a heterodox vision of freedom. She invoked the accepted principle that the slave must be granted "the rights of a man," but she argued that the right of a man to himself must also belong to a woman.[17]

Eloquently fusing the rhetoric of possessive individualism with that of radical Christianity, Harper extended the scope of natural rights to guarantee women property in the self. She began by equating personal freedom with proprietary rights; she pointed out that the "bondman . . . does not own the humblest joint that does the feeblest services . . . that the slave mother who clasps her child . . . does not own it by right of possession." She then veered off in more radical ways as she spoke in the first person

16 Angelina E. Grimke, *Appeal to the Christian Women of the South* (New York, 1836), 24, 12; Bourne, *Slavery Illustrated*, 121. See also Catherine Hall, *White, Male, and Middle Class: Explorations in Feminism and History* (New York, 1992), 205–54.

17 Dorothy Sterling, ed., *We Are Your Sisters: Black Women in the Nineteenth Century* (New York, 1984), 160; William Still, *The Underground Rail Road: A Record of Facts, Authentic Narratives, Letters* (Philadelphia, 1872), 158, 758–61, 779; Frances Smith Foster, ed., *A Brighter Coming Day: A Frances Ellen Watkins Harper Reader* (New York, 1990), 5; *National Anti-Slavery Standard*, May 22, 1858. See Carby, *Reconstructing Womanhood*, 62–94; Bert J. Loewenberg and Ruth Bogin, eds., *Black Women in Nineteenth-Century American Life: Their Words, Their Thoughts, Their Feelings* (University Park, Pa., 1976), 243–51; Shirley Yee, *Black Women Abolitionists: A Study in Activism, 1828–1860* (Knoxville, Tenn., 1992), 112–35; Julie Winch, " 'You Have Talents – Only Cultivate Them': Black Female Literary Societies and the Abolitionist Crusade," and Anne M. Boylan, "Benevolence and Antislavery Activity among African American Women in New York and Boston, 1820–1840," both in Jean Fagan Yellin and John C. Van Horne, eds. *The Abolitionist Sisterhood: Women's Political Culture in Antebellum America* (Ithaca, N.Y., 1994), 101–37.

of her own individual rights. Although freeborn, she imagined herself as a fugitive slave brought to trial in the North. "To prove – what?" she demanded. "To prove whether I have a right to be a free woman or am rightfully the chattel of another; whether I have the right to possess all the faculties that God has given, or whether another has the right to buy and sell, exchange and barter that temple in which God enshrined my human soul."[18] Harper's vision of emancipation powerfully demonstrated the multivalence of the symbol of the female slave. For her, this symbol's antithesis was a freedwoman fully endowed with rights, whose body was as sacred as a holy shrine. Not only did her argument counterpose religious and market metaphors, it joined soul and body, thereby controverting the racist association of black women with the body's most squalid habits and carnal passions. Simultaneously, it represented the freedwoman as a sovereign, self-owning individual rather than as the object of her husband's property rights.

Harper herself did acquire a husband. But throughout her life she challenged the theory of marriage as a property relationship based on male domination and female dependence. Her poems and fiction writing repeatedly portrayed women who, as wives, lost neither their economic independence nor their independence of spirit. In a short story published in 1859 she expressly criticized coverture in language echoing the attack on chattel slavery. Marriage should not "be a matter of bargain and sale," the heroine declares. But the villain regards it "as the title-deed that gave him possession of the woman."[19] For Harper, the husband's claim to property in his wife violated inalienable right much as did the slave master's claim to his human chattel.

The pursuit of self-entitlement was also the central theme of Harriet Jacobs's slave narrative, *Incidents in the Life of a Slave Girl, Written by Herself,* a book promoted by leaders of the abolition movement. Unlike Harper's work, however, Jacobs's story of her own passage from slavery to freedom directly confronted the problem of sexual property in women. For Jacobs, freedom entailed self-ownership of a definitely sexual character. As a slave she chose to take a white lover rather than submit to her master's claims. Idealizing relations of voluntary exchange, and insisting on bodily auto-

---

18 *National Anti-Slavery Standard,* May 22, 1858.
19 Frances Ellen Watkins (Harper), "The Two Offers," *The Anglo-African Magazine* (Sept.–Oct. 1859): 288, 290. See, e.g., by Frances Ellen Watkins (Harper), *Sketches of Southern Life* (Philadelphia, 1893), 12–15, 19, 21; *Iola Leroy or Shadows Uplifted* (1893; reprint, Boston, 1987), 154–5, 172–3, 178, 205, 210, 242, 277. See also Frances Smith Foster, *Written by Herself: Literary Production by African-American Women, 1746–1892* (Bloomington, Ind., 1993), 88–93, 183–86; du Cille, *Coupling Convention,* 3–12, 32–4, 44–7; Barbara Christian, *Black Women Novelists: The Development of a Tradition, 1892–1976* (Westport, Conn., 1980), 3–29; Still, *Underground Rail Road,* 755–80.

nomy, she defended her desperate resort to illicit sexual relations as a matter of free contract. "It seems less degrading to give one's self, than to submit to compulsion," she wrote. "There is something akin to freedom in having a lover who has no control over you, except that which he gains by kindness and attachment." Jacobs refused to recognize herself as property, even to the extent of having her freedom bought, though eventually it was, against her will. For, she explained, as she became accustomed to the values of free society, the more intolerable she found even the most benevolent owner, implying that genuine freedom meant owning herself. "The more my mind had become enlightened, the more difficult it was for me to consider myself an article of property. . . . Being sold from one owner to another seemed too much like slavery." Jacobs did not directly protest the proprietary character of marriage, but, contrary to the prevailing view, she hardly assumed that the slaveholder's sexual rights should rightfully pass to a husband. Nor did she see marriage and freedom as one and the same. Rather, she counterposed them in a way that suggested their asymmetries, declaring at her narrative's close, "my story ends with freedom; not in the usual way, with marriage." Jacobs became a freedwoman but not a wife.[20]

Marriage had no place either in the contrast between freedom and slavery formulated by Sarah Parker Remond, a Yankee-born free black who was a popular abolitionist lecturer in both England and America. In her reworking of standard abolitionist themes, the description of the sexual abuse of female slaves culminated in an affirmation of a woman's right to be an autonomous, propertied individual. Addressing a London audience in 1859, she put the plight of slave women at the center of her appeal. As a British antislavery newspaper reported, she spoke as the representative of her own race but also "pleaded especially on behalf of her own sex." Like other abolitionists, she began by explaining that words failed to express the unique suffering of women on Southern plantations: "the unspeakable horrors," the "depth of the infamy into which they were plunged by the cruelty and licentiousness of their brutal masters."[21]

But the argument Remond went on to develop broke with formulaic expressions. She favorably compared the situation of poor English needle-women with the plight of American slave women. Evoking the misery of seamstresses made famous in the poem "Song of the Shirt," she acknowledged "the trials and toils of the women of England – how, in the language

20 Jacobs, *Incidents*, 55, 199, 201. See also Foster, *Written by Herself*, 95–116; Yellin, *Women and Sisters*, 87–96; Beth Maclay Doriani, "Black Womanhood in Nineteenth-Century America: Subversion and Self-Construction in Two Women's Autobiographies," *American Quarterly* 43 (June 1991): 199–222.
21 "Lectures on American Slavery," *Anti-Slavery Reporter*, July 1, 1859.

of Hood, they were made to 'Stitch, stitch, stitch,' till weariness and exhaustion overtook them." This was a common ploy of Remond's fellow Garrisonians: granting the degradation of wage laborers, only to assert their absolute elevation above chattel slaves. Even the worst-off hireling, went the usual argument, was a free man with a right to his wages and to own himself. But in speaking on women's behalf Remond altered the sex of the figures contrasted in this model of slavery and freedom – a change that radically transformed the antislavery tribute to possessive individualism. With regard to the needlewomen, she declared, "But there was this immeasurable difference between their condition and that of the slave-woman, that their persons were free and their progeny their own, while the slave-woman was the victim of the heartless lust of her master, and the children whom she bore were his property."[22] In Remond's exposition, the theory of self-ownership – freedom of one's person – not only embraced women but took on an explicitly sexual content. For her, the heart of the difference between slavery and freedom was not property in the laboring body but property in the sexual body. Children, not wages, were the fruits of the body's toil.

It is noteworthy that Remond contended that the progeny of free women were "their own." Her argument circumvented the claims of marriage, treating the rules of coverture as a dead letter, portraying free women's existing rights as greater than they actually were. She mentioned neither the duties nor rights of a husband or a father. Nor was female chastity an emblem of male honor. It was the needlewomen in their own right who owned – fee-simple – precisely that property possessed by slave masters in their women chattel. As Remond proclaimed, "their persons were free and their progeny their own," in contrast to the female slave who was the "victim of the heartless lust of her master" and whose children were "his property."[23] For Remond, free women's title to their children arose from the still more basic right of bodily freedom that was understood to hinge on self-ownership. Thus, her conception of personal autonomy was stamped with classical liberal doctrines of individual proprietorship. But in juxtaposing these doctrines to the antithetical symbol of the female slave, Remond constructed a theory of women's emancipation that subverted the very tradition of liberal individualism to which it was heir.

In recent historical scholarship the theory of female self-ownership has most commonly been identified with feminist reformers who were allied with abolitionism but whose primary cause was the women's movement.

22 Ibid. See also Stanley, *Bonds of Contract*, chap. 1.
23 "Lectures on American Slavery."

It is well known that advocates of women's rights adopted antislavery rhetoric – pairing women with slaves, and marriage with bondage – and that they viewed self-entitlement as a paramount concern. The "real question," as Lucy Stone wrote privately in 1856, was whether a wife had an "absolute right" to her "body, and its uses" – "Has woman a right to herself?" Stone confessed to being "not ready" to bring this momentous and sexually charged question before the public. But, in fact, it was already tacit in women's temperance reform and quite explicit in mounting feminist attacks on coverture, which, as Elizabeth Cady Stanton said, designated the wife's "person . . . the property of another." And by the postbellum era this question had come to dominate the politics of women's rights.[24]

But among the antislavery vanguard decades earlier, it was black women who most unequivocally asserted a woman's right to herself. Some of them had directly known the dominion of a slave master; most of them had never known dependence on a husband. Along with other abolitionists they assailed the subjection of female slaves and defended the liberty of free women to speak on their behalf. In their hands the symbol of the black woman came to represent not only the terrors of bondage but the rights of freedom. Their black abolitionist brethren did not directly engage the question, nor did they expressly defend or disown the prevailing abolitionist theory of the freedman as his wife's master.[25] But in affirming the right of the bondswoman to own herself – in disrupting any simple equation of marriage with freedom – black female thinkers recast the emancipatory potential of possessive individualism as a theory of slave liberation. It has recently been argued that the Western ideal of personal freedom was born in ancient times from the yearning of female slaves to negate their condition (women were the first to suffer mass enslavement) but that this ideal

24 Letter of Lucy Stone to Susan B. Anthony, Sept. 11, 1856, quoted in Blanche G. Hersh, *The Slavery of Sex: Feminist-Abolitionists in America* (Urbana, Ill., 1978), 66; Ellen Carol DuBois, ed., *Elizabeth Cady Stanton, Susan B. Anthony: Correspondence, Writings, Speeches* (New York, 1981), 48. See Clark, "Political Theory of Elizabeth Cady Stanton"; DuBois, "Outgrowing the Compact"; Linda Gordon, *Woman's Body, Woman's Right: A Social History of Birth Control in America* (New York, 1976), esp. 95–115.
25 See Foster, *Written by Herself*; Nell Irvin Painter, "Difference, Slavery, and Memory: Sojourner Truth in Feminist Abolitionism," in Yellin and Van Horne, eds. *Abolitionist Sisterhood*, 139–58; Nell Irvin Painter, *Sojourner Truth: A Life, a Symbol* (New York, 1996); Yee, *Black Women Abolitionists*, 136–54; Yellin, *Women and Sisters*, 77–96. On the ambiguities of black male abolitionists' views on female self-sovereignty, see James O. Horton, "Freedom's Yoke: Gender Conventions Among Antebellum Free Blacks," *Feminist Studies* 12 (spring 1986): 51–76; bell hooks, *Ain't I a Woman: Black Women and Feminism* (Boston, 1981); Julie Winch, *Philadelphia's Black Elite: Activism, Accommodation, and the Struggle for Autonomy, 1787–1848* (Philadelphia, 1988), 86; Rosalyn Terborg-Penn, "Black Male Perspectives on the Nineteenth-Century Woman," in Sharon Harley and Rosalyn Terborg-Penn, eds., *The Afro-American Woman: Struggles and Images* (Port Washington, N.Y., 1978), 28–42. The sources do not show that black male abolitionists expressly proclaimed free men's property in their wives.

was subsequently rediscovered and appropriated by male thinkers. If so, then black female abolitionists could be said to have reclaimed their rightful intellectual legacy.[26]

To their way of thinking, the autonomous, self-owning freedwoman would not be fenced off from the interdependencies of social relationships. Instead, she would take her place as an equal member of a community of rights-bearing individuals. Her ties to her children were categorically affirmed as a bond that was considered indispensable rather than contrary to personal autonomy, an extension of self-sovereignty claimed in the language of proprietorship. As the former slave Bethany Veney put it, in "my Northern home . . . I had the same right to myself that any other women had. No jailor could take me to prison, and sell me at auction to the highest bidder. My boy was my own, and no one could take him from me." However much feminists such as Stanton and Stone insisted that wife and husband must have equal legal rights to their children as well as to marital property, they were more inclined to imagine the essence of freedom in absolutely individual terms, as a solitary ideal. But a line of black female thinkers stretching from Remond to Anna Julia Cooper at the end of the nineteenth century did not conceptually sever property in the self from ownership of one's children. Like the rights consciousness of other subordinate groups, this creed of propertied individualism expressed a longing for both collective and personal emancipation, a release from the coercions of sex and race.[27]

In no single figure was the merger of black abolitionism and feminism more famously embodied than in the fugitive slave and itinerant preacher Sojourner Truth. Indeed, so well known are her ideas about her rights, her body, and her womanhood that they would almost be clichés – were they not so historically important. Speaking at an Ohio women's rights convention in 1851, Truth announced that man was "in a tight place, the poor slave is on him, woman is coming on him." Flaunting the strength of her

26 See Orlando Patterson, *Freedom in the Making of Western Culture*, Freedom, vol. 1 (New York, 1991), xv, 50–63, 78, 106–32; Gerda Lerner, *The Creation of Patriarchy* (New York, 1986), 77–100.
27 *The Narrative of Bethany Veney, a Slave Woman* (Worcester, Mass., 1889), in Gates, ed., *Collected Black Women's Narratives*. See also Wai-Chee Dimock, "Rightful Subjectivity," *Yale Journal of Criticism* 4 (1990): 25–51. For contrasting interpretations of possessive individualism as a theory of rights, see Hendrik Hartog, "The Constitution of Aspiration and 'The Rights That Belong to Us All,'" *Journal of American History* 74 (Dec. 1987): 1013–34; Eileen Boris, "Gender, Race, and Rights: Listening to Critical Race Theory," and "Response" by Melinda Chateauvert, both in *Journal of Women's History* 6 (summer 1994): 111–32; Ellen Carol DuBois, "Taking the Law into Our Own Hands: Bradwell, Minor, and Suffrage Militance in the 1870s," in Nancy A. Hewitt and Suzanne Lebsock, eds., *Visible Women: New Essays in American Activism* (Urbana, Ill., 1993). It is beyond the scope of this chapter to examine fully the differing feminist inflections of possessive individualism broached here, but I would caution that the distinction should not be pushed too far.

body to falsify assumptions about the natural incapacities of her sex and to justify "woman's rights," she said, "I have as much muscle as any man, and can do as much work as any man. I have plowed and reaped and chopped. . . . I can carry as much as any man, and can eat as much too." In the name of equal rights Truth reportedly exposed her body to public view, her arm in 1851 and then her breast in 1858. An ironic proof of her femininity, the display also parodied the slave auction.[28]

With respect to the intellectual tradition at issue here, Truth's importance lies not only in the fact that she spoke about rights through her body or that she was taken by her contemporaries to personify black antislavery feminism. She embodied as well the process by which the antislavery ideas of free black women in the North were transmitted to former slaves in the postbellum South. Truth worked with ex-slaves as an agent of the National Freedmen's Relief Association, and she broadcast her beliefs to them. "I . . . go around among the Freedmens camps," she stated in 1864. "They are all *delighted* to hear me talk." Something she might have talked about was her apprehension that freedom would remain unrealized: "Colored men will be masters over the women, and it will be just as bad as it was before. . . . I want women to have their rights." Perhaps she reiterated the themes of her famous speech of 1851, themes she sounded again and again over the years. "If I have to answer for the deeds done in my body just as much as a man, I have a right to have just as much as a man. . . . You [men] . . . think, like a slaveholder, that you own us. . . . I have pled with all the force I had that the day might come that the colored people might own their soul and body. Well, the day has come, although it came through blood. . . . We are now trying for liberty that requires no blood – that women shall have their rights."[29] Precisely what Truth said in the freedmen's camps went unrecorded, but plausibly she meditated there, as elsewhere, on the bodily dimensions of individual rights.

In the wake of slave emancipation, scores of other black female abolitionists besides Truth acted as ambassadors of freedom, traveling South to work as teachers and missionaries among the former slaves. Along with

---

28 Quotation from Nell Irvin Painter, "Representing Truth: Sojourner Truth's Knowing and Becoming Known," *Journal of American History* 81 (Sept. 1994): 489. On the complexities of Truth as historical figure and as symbol, see also Carleton Mabee, *Sojourner Truth: Slave, Prophet, Legend* (New York, 1993); Painter, *Sojourner Truth*, 121–31, 164–78, 258–80; Erlene Stetson and Linda David, *Glorying in Tribulation: The Lifework of Sojourner Truth* (East Lansing, Mich., 1994).

29 Sterling, *We Are Your Sisters*, 253; Stanton et al., eds., *History of Woman Suffrage*, 2:193–4, 224–5. See also Elizabeth Alexander, "'We Must Be about Our Father's Business': Anna Julia Cooper and the In-Corporation of the Nineteenth-Century African-American Woman Intellectual," *Signs* 20 (winter 1995): 336–56.

Bibles, clothing, and spelling books, they undoubtedly dispensed their views on female emancipation as well.

Frances Ellen Watkins Harper crisscrossed the South between 1867 and 1871, giving public lectures to former slaves and staying in their cabins. "How busy I am," she wrote from South Carolina in May 1867, "traveling, conversing, addressing day and Sunday schools." In some ways her efforts resembled those of Elizabeth Cady Stanton, who traversed the country during the same years campaigning for women's emancipation. Stanton met separately with small groups of white women to discuss the situation of women in marriage and sexual matters. Harper met alone with freedwomen, speaking out on the same issues. "Sometimes I speak twice a day," she wrote from rural Georgia. "Part of my lectures are given privately to women, and for them I never make any charge." These lectures expressed the complexities of her understanding of the link between freedom and marriage. On the one hand, Harper urged fidelity to marriage conventions as a mark of racial progress: "The colored man needs something more than a vote in his hand: He needs to know the value of home life; to rightly appreciate and value the marriage relation . . . to leave behind him the old shards and shells of slavery." But on the other hand, she taught that female subjection ran counter to a right valuing of marriage as a form of emancipation. "Part of the time I am preaching against men ill-treating their wives," she stated. "The condition of the women is not very enviable in some cases. They have had some of them a terribly hard time in Slavery, and their subjection has not ceased in freedom. . . . One man said of some women, that a man must leave them or whip them." By this time Harper had attended women's rights conventions and doubtless aimed to promote freedwomen's sense of their personal autonomy. Hearing such talk, meeting apart from their menfolk, some freedwomen might well have reached a greater consciousness of their right to themselves, one antagonistic to the doctrine of male masterhood.[30]

More cryptic were the remarks of Charlotte Forten, a black abolitionist who went south to teach freedpeople on the South Carolina Sea Islands. On witnessing the marriage ceremonies of former slaves, she wrote in her diary that she was "*truly* glad that the poor creatures are trying to live right and virtuous lives." But for herself, she confided in a later entry, "Think *I* sh'ld dread a funeral much less."[31] Was she thinking of the rule of cover-

30 Still, *Underground Rail Road*, 767, 770, 772–3, 777; Stanton et al., eds., *History of Woman Suffrage*, 2:178, 182–3.
31 Ray Allen Billington, ed., *The Journal of Charlotte Forton: A Free Negro in the Slave Era* (London, 1953), 153, 207.

ture that rendered the wife dead in the eyes of the law? Perhaps her ambivalence (inadvertently) colored the perceptions of the former slaves she
taught.

To suggest possible resonances between the ideas of reformers such as
Forten, Harper, and Truth and the beliefs and activities of freedwomen is
not to suppose that freedwomen were akin to blank tablets on which their
Yankee sisters wrote their own worldview wholesale. Rather, in the shaping
of freedwomen's complicated consciousness of their rights, one potent
source may have been the encounter with female abolitionists, particularly
of their own race, who were also apostles of feminism.[32]

That virtually no freedwomen possessed an education in classical liberal
theory is obvious. Yet their views in some cases had much in common with
liberal precepts. Based on evidence from the Freedmen's Bureau and other
sources, it is plain that many freedwomen strove to control their own
bodies, to possess their labor and its proceeds, and to enforce voluntary relations of exchange. Even as wives, within newfound bonds of marriage,
many saw themselves, at some level, as autonomous individuals vested with
rights of proprietorship. Mostly, as the legal documents attest, their rene-
gade views were expressed by acts rather than by words, and by negations
of their husbands' claims rather than by explicit assertions of positive individual rights. In the early years of emancipation freedwomen participated
actively in the mass politics of black communities, a form of public franchise that may have highlighted the private contradictions of wifely sub-
mission. Seeking to exercise the contract rights denied by coverture, some
freedwomen opposed their husbands signing labor agreements for them
and claimed title to their own wages. Others invoked their legal rights
within the marriage relation, suing their husbands to oblige them to fulfill
their half of the domestic bargain. Still others had their husbands arrested
for whipping them. Although they closely embraced the kin ties forged in
slavery, not all freedwomen willingly reckoned themselves tokens of their
menfolk's emancipation. For them, no less than for black men, freedom
heightened – or perhaps generated – a sense of their rights as both individuals and family members.[33]

32 See Patricia Hill Collins, "The Social Construction of Black Feminist Thought," *Signs* 14 (summer
    1989): 750.
33 See Eric Foner, *Reconstruction: America's Unfinished Revolution, 1863–1867* (New York, 1988), 88; Elsa
    Barkley Brown, "Negotiating and Transforming the Public Sphere: African American Political Life
    in the Transition from Slavery to Freedom," *Public Culture* 7 (1994): 107–46; Stanley, *From Bondage
    to Contract*, chap. 1; Victoria Bynum, "Reshaping the Bonds of Womanhood: Divorce in Recon-
    struction North Carolina," in Catherine Clinton and Nina Silber, eds., *Divided Houses: Gender and
    the Civil War* (New York, 1992), 330–2.

Paradoxically, at the very moment many freedmen were collectively invalidating self-ownership as a sufficient material basis for freedom, some of their wives were claiming a right to own themselves. Thus, a Georgia freedman in an 1876 divorce petition alleged that his wife defiantly declared, "I am my own woman and will do as I please." Perhaps this freedwoman translated unarticulated notions of bodily integrity and personal autonomy into a full-fledged assertion of self-entitlement. Or perhaps this was a stock complaint, formulaically invoked by husbands against wives, because the same phrase appeared in another divorce suit filed the same year in the same county.[34] However, even as a formula, the words suggest that freedwomen must somehow have transgressed by staking a claim to property in the self.

III

Abolitionism's recessive strain thus lived on in the minds of some freedwomen, though the extent to which its antebellum exponents planted it there is admittedly unclear. For those who espoused this logic, freedom could mean nothing less than purging sex difference from the ascendant abolitionist ideal of the emancipated slave: "He is free, and his own master, and can ask for no more."[35]

Recognizing these currents of thought runs against the grain of recent scholarship; historians have made much of black women's familial image of freedom and the collective nature of their values, at the expense of insight into their desires as possessive individuals. Black women (freedwomen especially), it is said, did not subscribe to modern notions of personal autonomy. Their rights claims were not animated by the self-interested tenets of liberal political economy or by the radical individualism of evangelical Christianity. Yet the evidence suggests otherwise. However intensely black women in the nineteenth century valued kinship bonds and strove for collective emancipation, they were also keenly aware of their rights as individuals – rights premised on possession of the self.[36]

34 Quotation in Bynum, "Reshaping the Bonds of Womanhood," in Clinton and Silber, eds., *Divided Houses*, 330, and Laura F. Edwards, "Sexual Violence, Gender, Reconstruction, and the Extension of Patriarchy in Granville County, North Carolina," *North Carolina Historical Review* 68 (July 1991): 255. For contending visions of the contours of freedom, see Saville, *Work of Reconstruction*; Foner, "Meaning of Freedom"; Leon F. Litwack, *Been in the Storm So Long: The Aftermath of Slavery* (New York, 1979).
35 Quoted in Foner, *Politics and Ideology*, 64.
36 On the view that black women in nineteenth-century America did not conceptualize freedom in terms of individual autonomy, see, e.g., Jones, *Labor of Love*, 58; Fox-Genovese, *Within the Plantation Household*, 372–96; Brown, "Negotiating and Transforming," esp. 124–5; Edwards, "Sexual

To acknowledge this intellectual tradition is scarcely to provide an uncritical celebration of the liberal theory of possessive individualism, which historically has obscured and legitimated the unfreedoms of market relations – an issue I have addressed elsewhere. Rather, I have undertaken to explore why, at a critical historical juncture, that theory provided a language for black women's aspirations to freedom. Its appeal derived not least from its negation of the domestic bonds that constituted chattel slavery and marriage as a similar, though not identical, property relationship: its negation of the status of being dispossessed. As the legal theorist Patricia Williams, herself a descendant of slaves, has written of individualistic rights rhetoric: "Where . . . one's experience is rooted . . . in *being* illegitimate, in being raped, and in the fear of being murdered, then the black adherence to a scheme of negative rights – to the self, to the sanctity of one's personal boundaries – makes sense."[37] The intellectual history studied here constitutes a crucial moment in the forging of that adherence.

That the ethos of self-ownership is closely linked to a cast of mind that reduces all human experience to the calculus of buying and selling remains indisputable. Admittedly, the difficulty lies in squaring the market's abstract values with the antislavery symbolism of bleeding, naked, black, female bodies. But to lose sight of the contradictory implications of the ideal of possessive individualism is to render its hegemony inexplicable. If the ideal of self-ownership had not carried such emancipatory power, it could not have disguised the existing coercions of free society.

Violence, Gender." However, the ambition of self proprietorship is intimately linked to what Hazel Carby has termed the desire at the turn of the century for "the uncolonized black female body"; see her "On the Threshold," 315.

37 Patricia Williams, "Alchemical Notes: Reconstructing Ideals from Deconstructed Rights," *Harvard Civil Rights-Civil Liberties Law Review* 22 (1987): 17. See Stanley, *Bonds of Contract*. For debates on rights talk, see Hartog, "Constitution of Aspiration"; Peter Gabel, "The Phenomenology of Rights-Consciousness and the Pact of the Withdrawn Selves," *Texas Law Review* 62 (May 1984): 1563–99; Mark Tushnet, "An Essay on Rights," ibid., 1363–1403; Frances Olsen, "Statutory Rape: A Feminist Critique of Rights," ibid., 387–432; Mark Tushnet, "Rights: An Essay in Informal Political Theory," *Politics and Society* 17 (1989): 403–51; Martha Minow, *Making All the Difference: Inclusion, Exclusion, and American Law* (Ithaca, N.Y., 1990).

14

Freedom of Contract and Freedom of Person: A Brief History of "Involuntary Servitude" in American Fundamental Law

ROBERT J. STEINFELD

Liberal ideas are normally taken to have played an important role in the development of free markets, and of free labor based on contract in those markets. A closer look at labor regimes in the nineteenth century, however, reveals that liberal commitments to freedom did not straightforwardly produce what we today would think of as free labor. Just as often they produced a form of coerced contractual labor. And this was quite simply because liberal commitments to freedom embraced a basic conflict between freedom of contract and freedom of person.

To the extent that one possessed absolute freedom of contract, one would have been free to contract away one's personal liberty. One would have been free to contract into slavery or bind one's labor irrevocably for long periods of time. To the extent that the state found it desirable to prevent this result, it could only do so by imposing limitations on the freedom of contract in the interest of preserving the freedom of persons.

Modern free labor is the result of just such a choice to restrict freedom of contract. Before this basic issue within liberalism was finally resolved in favor of freedom of person and against freedom of contract, many of the first market regimes based on free contract produced coerced contractual labor rather than free labor. In the first flourishing of free contract in the nineteenth century, lawmakers in many different countries seem to have believed that labor markets based on promises could only function properly if contracts could be rigorously enforced against workers. As a result they often gave employers harsh remedies for contract breach so that they could compel workers to perform their agreements.

In effect, these contract regimes allowed workers to bind their labor irrevocably for a time. They represented the expression of a kind of freedom of contract, the freedom to contract away part of one's freedom for a time. Only when this contractual freedom was limited by circumscribing the kinds of contract remedies employers enjoyed at law, or were permitted to induce workers to agree to in labor contracts, was modern free labor created. Modern free labor was not the product of liberal ideas as they were manifested in free markets but the product of a difficult political and moral resolution of fundamental dilemmas within liberalism itself.

Freedom of trade (*Gewerbefreiheit*) was introduced into Prussia by the Industrial Law (*Gewerbeordnung*) of 1845.[1] As part of this liberal, free-market reform, the relationships between masters and their journeymen in the artisanal sector, and factory workers and their employers in the expanding industrial sector, were made a matter of free contract.[2] For breach of these freely negotiated contracts, however, factory workers, journeymen, and other wage workers were subject to penal sanctions, including imprisonment. The law declared that "journeymen, helpers, and factory workers, who leave work without permission and without legal justification, or are guilty of shirking, or gross disobedience or insistent obstinacy, are to be punished by a fine of up to twenty thalers or imprisonment for up to fourteen days."[3] Penal sanctions for breach of contract by factory workers were later eliminated by the Industrial Law of 1869.[4]

It is interesting that Prussia was far from being alone in nineteenth-century Europe in imposing penal sanctions on wage workers for breach of contract. In England, which possessed the most advanced economy of this period, Parliament imposed even harsher penal sanctions on English wage workers who could be imprisoned for up to three months for quitting before the expiration of their contracts, for leaving work without permission, or for disobedience.[5] Between 1720 and 1843, during the same period in which free markets replaced the traditional economy, Parliament passed more than half a dozen statutes mandating penal sanctions for labor-contract breaches.[6] Between 1857 and 1875 about

---

1 *Gesetzsammlung für die Königlichen Preussischen Staaten 1845*, "Gewerbeordnung," 41–78 (hereafter *PGS*, 1845). Freedom of trade, however, was repealed four years later in 1849, and not reestablished in Prussia until the Industrial Law of 1869, enacted by the North German Confederation.
2 *PGS*, 1845, "Gewerbeordnung," §§ 134, 145.   3 *PGS*, 1845, "Gewerbeordnung," § 184.
4 *Bundesgesetzblatt des Norddeutschen Bundes, 1869*, "Gewerbeordnung," no. 26, 245–82, § 154.
5 See, e.g., 4 Geo. IV., c. 34, § III (1823). Until the last quarter of the nineteenth century it was common for English wage workers to serve either under contracts for a term or under contracts terminable only after some period of notice had been given. Employment at will was fairly unusual among skilled workers of the period.
6 Sidney Webb and Beatrice Webb, *The History of Trade Unionism* (London, 1956), 250–1n2.

10,000 workers per year were proceeded against in England for violating their labor agreements.[7]

In the twentieth century the criminal enforcement of labor contracts has come to be viewed as rendering such labor "coerced" or "involuntary." During the nineteenth century, however, that was far from being the view of many Europeans; from their standpoint free markets required reliable contract enforcement. Without reliable contract enforcement large-scale markets would not have been feasible.[8] As one historian recently observed,

it was not until the eighteenth century, in Western Europe, England, and North America, that societies first appeared whose economic systems depended on the expectation that most people, most of the time, were sufficiently conscience ridden (and certain of retribution) that they could be trusted to keep their promises. . . . Only to the extent that [the] norm [of promise keeping] prevails can economic affairs be based on nothing more authoritative than the obligation arising out of promises.

Both the growing force of the norm of promise keeping and its synchronization with the spread of market relations are clearly inscribed in the history of the law of contract. . . . For the first time the law strained to make promisors generally liable for whatever expectations their promises created. Never before had promises counted for so much in human affairs, and never before had the penalties for being short-willed and unreliable been so severe.[9]

Nineteenth-century European legal rules mandating penal sanctions for breach of labor contracts must be seen as part of the process by which freer markets were created. Large-scale free labor markets simply could not function properly unless labor contracts could be reliably enforced. But labor agreements, it was widely believed at the time, could not be reliably enforced against largely propertyless workers by means of monetary damages.[10] Penal sanctions represented, under the circumstances, nothing more than a remedy for breach of contract in situations where monetary damages could not be relied on. Such a remedy was thought to be an essential aspect of free contract in labor markets.

Not very much has been written explaining the abolition in 1869 of penal sanctions for breach of contract by factory workers in Germany, but in England the process has been described in detail. Organized labor

---

7 *Judicial Statistics, England and Wales, 1857–1875*, 19 vols. (London, 1858–76); see also Daphne Simon, "Master and Servant," in John Saville, ed., *Democracy and the Labour Movement* (London, 1954), 186n2.

8 Douglass C. North, *Institutions, Institutional Change, and Economic Performance* (Cambridge, 1990), 33–5.

9 Thomas Haskell, "Capitalism and the Humanitarian Sensibility, Part 2," *American Historical Review* 90 (1985): 553–5.

10 See, e.g., James Edward Davis, *The Master and Servant Act, 1867* (London, 1868), 7.

mounted a long campaign beginning in the early 1860s to have penal sanctions repealed. In 1875 Parliament finally responded to the growing power of labor by repealing the statutes. In England, labor prevailed in this campaign not only because of its growing electoral influence but also because its reinterpretation of penal sanctions came to be widely accepted in English culture, including English legal culture.[11] From an ordinary contract remedy entirely consistent with the liberal principle of free contract, penal sanctions began to be recharacterized as a remedy inconsistent with the liberal principle of equal treatment under the law. (It was not equally available to workers for employer contract breaches.)[12] Over the ensuing twenty-five years it came increasingly to be seen as a contract remedy that turned "contracts of service" into "contracts of slavery" and therefore became increasingly inconsistent with the long-standing liberal tradition that freedom of contract should not extend to contracts of slavery.[13]

It seems clear that many nineteenth-century Europeans drew the distinction between "free" and "coerced" labor differently than we do, but that that line began to be redrawn by the end of the nineteenth century. There is a very basic reason why the line between "voluntary free" labor and "involuntary coerced" labor has been drawn in different ways at different times. Nearly all forms of labor not performed for sheer pleasure can be characterized in either way. When we speak about most kinds of labor compulsion, we are talking about situations in which the compelled party is offered a choice between disagreeable alternatives and chooses the lesser evil.

This type of compulsion is present, for example, in both slavery and modern free wage labor. In slavery, labor normally is not elicited by directly imparting motion to a slave's limbs through overpowering physical force. It is compelled by forcing slaves to choose among very unpleasant options, for example, among death, dismemberment, torture, and endless confinement, on the one hand, or backbreaking physical labor, on the other. The labor of free wage workers is similarly elicited by offering workers a choice, for example, between life on an inadequate welfare stipend, on the one hand, or performing more or less unpleasant work for wages, on the other. In the case of both the slave and the free worker, the parties may be said to have been coerced into performing the labor or to have freely chosen the lesser evil. Either characterization is applicable. This is why some choices

---

11 The Second Reform Act, which was passed in 1867, extended the suffrage to many town artisans.
12 Frederic Harrison, "Tracts for Trade Unionists" in Edmund Frow and Michael Katanka, eds., *1868, Year of the Unions: A Documentary Survey* (New York, 1968), 141–2.
13 L. J. Fry in *De Francesco v. Barnum*, 45 chap., d. 430 (1890), 438.

among evils can be characterized as voluntary decisions, whereas other choices among evils can simultaneously be characterized as coerced. Where the line is drawn from a logical standpoint is arbitrary.

Needless to say, the choices presented in slavery are much harsher than the choices normally presented in free wage labor. We may rightly say, therefore, that the degree of coercion in one form is normally much greater than it is in the other, but there are no legal grounds for saying that the performance of labor in one case is coerced, whereas in the other it is voluntary. As a matter of logic we have to say either that both are involuntary to different degrees or that both involve the free choice of a lesser evil.

The judgment about where to draw the line separating voluntary from involuntary labor turns out not to be a judgment about where coercion begins or ends in labor relations, but rather a judgment about what kinds of hard choices we will allow some individuals to force other individuals to make as the latter decide whether to enter or leave a labor relation, and which kinds of hard choices we will not permit.

Judgments like these are equally involved in the modern definition of free labor and are inscribed in modern contract and constitutional law. The remedy of monetary damages for labor-contract breaches (which is permitted under modern law) will coerce workers into satisfying their labor agreements under certain circumstances. "[A]ny legal liability for breach of contract," Justice Oliver Wendell Holmes wrote, "is a disagreeable consequence which tends to make the contractor do as he said he would."[14] "In the case of a solvent person," the legal realist Robert Hale noted, "the motive for performing might often be the desire to escape pecuniary liability [for breach of contract]. If such desire is strong enough to make him render the services stipulated in his contract, then the law does compel performance and enforce the labor."[15]

It is only by ignoring the coercive effects of various pecuniary remedies for breach of contract that the modern definition (and law) of free labor is arrived at, in the same way that many nineteenth-century Europeans ignored the coercive effects of penal sanctions for breach of contract in their definition of free labor. The modern definition (and law) of free labor also ignores a range of other, so-called "economic" pressures that may compel workers to enter employment, to submit to discipline during employment, and to remain in employment.

14 *Bailey v. Alabama*, 219 U.S. 219 (1911), 246.
15 Robert L. Hale, *Freedom Through Law: Public Control of Private Governing Power* (New York, 1952), 191.

John Stuart Mill, writing a decade after the English Poor Law implemented a policy of less eligibility in the reforms of 1832, noted that free
wage workers could be expected to enter employment only in situations
in which the main alternative to employment was kept more disagreeable
than employment itself.

If the condition of a person receiving [poor] relief is made as eligible as that of
the labourer who supports himself by his own exertions . . . [it] would require
as its supplement an organized system of compulsion, for governing and setting
[people] to work. . . . But if, consistently with guaranteeing all persons against
absolute want, the condition of those who are supported by legal charity can be
kept considerably less desirable than the condition of those who find support for
themselves, none but beneficial consequences can arise.[16]

As in Europe, the modern American constitutional definition of free
labor was only arrived at after a long struggle over the precise line that
should separate the types of hard choices that would "coerce" the labor of
workers who confronted them from the types of hard choices that left
workers "free" to choose labor as the lesser evil.

American fundamental law on the subject of coerced labor can be traced
back to the language of the Northwest Ordinance enacted by Congress in
1787. It declared that "There shall be neither Slavery nor involuntary servitude in the [Northwest] territory otherwise than in the punishment of
crimes, whereof the party shall have been duly convicted."[17] The ordinance
applied to an area that encompasses the present-day states of Illinois,
Indiana, Michigan, Ohio, and Wisconsin. But the language of the ordinance
was later incorporated into the Thirteenth Amendment to the United States
Constitution, which abolished slavery and involuntary servitude throughout the nation.

It is primarily to the interpretation of the term *involuntary servitude*, first
in the ordinance and later in the Thirteenth Amendment, that we must turn
for an understanding of the changing definition of *free labor* in American fundamental law. As we examine these legal interpretations, however, we should
keep at least two things in mind. First, adult white indentured servants were
still being imported into the United States in 1787 and would continue to
be imported in significant numbers until 1820, and in smaller numbers until
at least 1830. It seems likely that the framers of the Northwest Ordinance
would have considered these contractual arrangements to be voluntary rather
than involuntary servitude, which the ordinance prohibited.

16 Mill, *Collected Works*, III (*Principles of Political Economy*) (Toronto, 1965), 961.
17 Northwest Ordinance of 1787, art. VI.

Second, unlike the situation in England and Prussia, these imported indentured servants were the only adult white workers subject at the time to penal sanctions for labor-contract breaches. The reasons for this development are a bit of a mystery, but we do know that it is traceable to the eighteenth century. Before 1700 statutes in a number of American colonies subjected "hired" workers to penal sanctions for breaches of contract. But over the course of that century these statutes began to disappear from the colonial codes, leaving immigrant indentured servants the only white adult contractual labor still subject to penal sanctions.

It was a struggle over the legality of indentured servitude under the provisions of the Northwest Ordinance that produced the first judicial interpretations of involuntary servitude. The southern border of the Northwest Territory was shared with areas in which slavery was entrenched and legal. When settlers from these areas began to arrive in the Northwest Territory, many brought slaves with them. Others believed it would be beneficial to the new territory to allow slaves to be imported. One expedient under which slaves were held in parts of the territory was to have them sign indentures committing them to twenty, forty, or more years of service, either before they were brought into the territory or after they arrived.

When the question of the legality of black indentured servitude was brought before the high courts of two of the states carved out of the territory, it produced two very different interpretations of precisely what practices were prohibited by the ban on involuntary servitude. In *Phoebe v. Jay*, decided in 1828, the Illinois Supreme Court framed the issue in terms of whether a laboring agreement had been entered into "voluntarily."[18] If it had, then legal enforcement of the resulting agreement through specific performance or penal sanctions did not transform the labor from voluntary to involuntary. The labor was "voluntary" because the worker had "voluntarily" agreed to perform it. All that was involved was the enforcement of a contract entered into freely.[19]

Given the long history of indentured servitude in this country and the common practice of penal sanctions to enforce labor contracts in Europe, the Illinois court's view of involuntary servitude was probably quite widely shared at the time. The Illinois ruling did leave unresolved the question of how harsh the terms of a "voluntary" labor agreement would have to be before the agreement would be considered a contract of slavery and be

---

18 1 Ill. (Breese) 268 (1828).
19 Ibid. See also, the concurring opinion of Justice Thomas in *Sarah, a woman of color v. Borders*, 4 Scam. 341 (Ill., 1843), 347.

rendered illegal by the absolute prohibition against slavery contained in the ordinance. But under the Illinois ruling any state of servitude short of outright slavery apparently could be entered into in conformity with the ordinance, as long as it was done voluntarily.

The Illinois court did, however, have to face the question of precisely what circumstances would render a decision to sign an indenture "involuntary" in the first place. In *Phoebe v. Jay* a black woman had signed an indenture to serve her master for forty years.[20] The indenture had been entered into pursuant to a statute that allowed slave masters to bring slaves into the territory but required that they bring the slave before a clerk of the court of common pleas within thirty days, "and in the presence of said clerk, the said owner or possessor shall determine and agree, to and with his or her negro or mulatto, upon the term of years which the said negro or mulatto will and shall serve his or her said owner or possessor."[21] If a black person refused to sign an indenture or to perform its terms, the master was authorized under the statute to return the person to the state in which he or she had been held as a slave.

The Illinois court entertained no doubt that the decision to sign an indenture made by a black person confronted with this set of choices must represent a coerced decision rather than the free choice of a lesser evil. "I conceive that it would be an insult to common sense," Justice Lockwood wrote for the court, "to contend that the negro, under the circumstances in which [s]he was placed, had any free agency. The only choice given [her] was a choice of evils."[22] What other hard choices might coerce a person into entering a labor relation involuntarily remained to be explored.

If in Illinois the specific enforcement of a forty-year labor agreement did not render the labor involuntary so long as it had been entered into voluntarily, such was not the case in Indiana. In 1821 the Indiana high court set aside the indenture of a black woman who, the court reported, had "voluntarily bound herself to serve . . . as an indented servant and housemaid for 20 years."[23] The court ruled that

while the [woman] remained in the service of the obligee without complaint, the law presumes that her service was voluntarily performed; but her application to the Circuit Court to be discharged from the custody of her master, establishes the fact that she is willing to serve no longer; and, while this state of the will appears, the law can not, by any possibility of intendment, presume that her service is voluntary. . . . The fact then is, that the appellant is in a state of involuntary

20 1 Ill. (Breese) 268 (1828).   21 Ibid., 269.
22 Ibid., 270.
23 *The Case of Mary Clark, a woman of color*, 1 Blackf.122 (Ind. 1821), 123.

servitude; and we are bound by the Constitution, the supreme law of the land, to discharge her therefrom.[24]

Under the Indiana ruling, labor became involuntary servitude the moment a person wanted to leave the relationship but was prevented from doing so by a judicial decree of specific performance or by bodily seizure by an employer. Here, the legal right to withdraw from the labor relationship at any time marked the boundary between free labor and involuntary servitude. The use of the legal remedies of specific performance or penal sanction to enforce even a voluntary labor agreement turned the labor into involuntary servitude. The issue implicitly left unresolved by the Indiana decision was whether a labor contract could be enforced through any legal remedy at all consistent with the proscription of involuntary servitude.

More fundamentally, the Indiana ruling brought to the surface a fundamental problem within liberal commitments to freedom, which contained a basic, unresolvable contradiction between commitments to liberty of person and commitments to liberty of contract. Liberty of person under the rule required that one's contractual liberty be restricted, insofar as one was no longer legally entitled to alienate one's labor irrevocably by contract.[25]

These opposing interpretive traditions persisted in American constitutional law throughout the nineteenth century. The United States Supreme Court, surprisingly, did not make a definitive choice between them until the twentieth century. This is not to say that both views enjoyed equal popularity in the wider culture. It is fair to say that throughout the North, labor practices and ideas conformed in the main to the view set forth by the Indiana court. With the complete disappearance of white immigrant indentured servitude in the 1830s the labor agreements of white adults were not subject to specific performance or to penal sanctions anywhere in the Northern states, with one significant exception discussed subsequently. But there were only a few court opinions inscribing this view into constitutional law. One was rendered by the Massachusetts Supreme Judicial Court in 1856.

In *Parsons v. Trask*, the Massachusetts Supreme Judicial Court held that a voluntary labor contract amounted to a species of servitude akin to slavery when a worker was not free to leave before its expiration and if the nature

---

24 Ibid., 126.
25 On this contradiction, see Guyora Binder, "Substantive Liberty and the Legacy of the Fuller Court," unpublished manuscript in author's possession, § VI. (30.); and Frank H. Knight, *Freedom & Reform: Essays in Economics and Social Philosophy* (New York, 1947; reprint, 1982), 78–9.

of the services and the place where they were to be performed were left to be determined unilaterally by the employer.[26]

Even the Civil War did not lay the interpretive question definitively to rest. The Thirteenth Amendment incorporated the language of the Northwest Ordinance but did not provide clarification. In 1867 Congress adopted the Indiana and Massachusetts interpretation of the term *involuntary servitude* in the Anti-Peonage Act it passed that year pursuant to the Thirteenth Amendment. The peonage statute that Congress enacted in 1867 reached a labor relationship that was often entered into voluntarily. But the statute had been drafted poorly and its language was ambiguous. More fundamentally, the interpretive question had not been definitively resolved. The U.S. Army and, in certain cases, agents of the Freedmen's Bureau, for example, could still believe that they were introducing a free labor system into the South after the war even as they went about specifically enforcing the labor contracts of former slaves who came under their jurisdiction.

The U.S. Supreme Court did not directly confront the issue until 1897, when a majority of the court adopted not the Indiana and Massachusetts interpretations of "involuntary servitude" as we might have expected but rather the Illinois reading. However, the Indiana view, which was to triumph in the twentieth century, survived in Justice Harlan's dissent. The case of *Robertson v. Baldwin* arose when several merchant mariners were arrested for deserting their ship in Oregon in breach of the contracts they had signed agreeing to perform the duties of seamen during the entire voyage. The men were arrested and held until the ship was ready to sail, and then they were placed on board against their wills. They refused to perform their duties, and when the ship returned to San Francisco they were arrested and charged with refusing to work in violation of a federal statute governing merchant seamen. They sued based on a writ of habeas corpus, asking that they be freed from their confinement, and argued that the federal statute under which they were being held violated the involuntary servitude provision of the Thirteenth Amendment.[27]

The court upheld the validity of the statute on two grounds. The first, broader ground is the more interesting one. The validity of this statute, Justice Brown wrote for the court,

depends upon the construction to be given to the term "involuntary servitude." *Does the epithet "involuntary" attach to the word "servitude" continuously, and make illegal*

---

26 *Parsons v. Trask*, 73 Mass. (7 Gray) 473 (1856), 478.
27 *Robertson v. Baldwin*, 165 U.S. 275 (1897), 280–1.

any service which becomes involuntary at any time during its existence; or does it attach only at the inception of the servitude, and characterize it as unlawful because unlawfully entered into? If the former be the true construction, then, no one, not even a soldier, sailor or apprentice, can surrender his liberty, even for a day; and the soldier may desert his regiment upon the eve of battle, or the sailor abandon his ship at any intermediate port or landing, or even in a storm at sea. . . . *If the latter, then an individual may, for a valuable consideration, contract for the surrender of his personal liberty for a definite time and for a recognized purpose, and subordinate his going and coming to the will of another during the continuance of the contract; – not that all such contracts would be lawful, but that a servitude which was knowingly and willingly entered into could not be termed involuntary.* Thus, if one should agree, for a yearly wage, to serve another in a particular capacity during his life, and never to leave his estate without his consent, the contract might not be enforceable for the want of a legal remedy, or might be void upon grounds of public policy, but the servitude could not be properly termed involuntary. Such agreements for a limited personal servitude at one time were very common in England [citing the 1823 English statute]. . . . The breach of a contract for personal service has not, however, been recognized in this country as involving a liability to criminal punishment, except in the case of soldiers, sailors and possibly some others, nor would public opinion tolerate a statute to that effect.[28]

The majority correctly saw that criminal punishment for labor-contract breaches was not nearly so anomalous as many people in the United States thought. It used English practice of the period as a way of vindicating its choice of freedom of contract over freedom of person, its resolution of that irresolvable dilemma within liberalism itself. The court's second ground was based on the opinion that "the [Thirteenth] amendment was not intended to introduce any novel doctrine with respect to certain descriptions of service which have always been treated as exceptional," merchant mariners constituting one of these exceptions.[29] In a blistering dissent, Justice Harlan offered this reply to the court's opinion: "The condition of one who contracts to render personal services in connection with the private business of another becomes a condition of involuntary servitude *from the moment he is compelled against his will* to continue in such service. . . . [T]o require him, against his will, to continue in the personal service of his master is to place him and keep him in a condition of involuntary servitude."[30] Harlan opined that

If congress under its power to regulate commerce with foreign nations and among the several states, can authorize the arrest of seamen who engaged to serve upon a private vessel, and compel him by force to return to the vessel and remain during the term for which he engaged, a similar rule may be prescribed as to employés

28 Emphasis added. Ibid.   29 Ibid., 282.
30 Emphasis added. Ibid., 301.

upon railroads and steamboats engaged in commerce among the states. . . . Again, as the legislatures of the States have all legislative power not prohibited to them . . . why may not the States, under the principles this day announced, compel all employés of railroads engaged in domestic commerce, and all domestic servants, and all employés in private establishments, within their respective limits, to remain with their employers during the terms for which they were severally engaged, under penalty of being arrested by some sheriff or constable, and forcibly returned to the service of their employers?[31]

Harlan, a Southerner himself, may well have realized that the majority's opinion could open the floodgates to this kind of legislation in the South. Immediately following the Civil War a number of Southern states had attempted to enact black codes that contained provisions, among others, for the criminal punishment of labor contract breaches. These were characterized in the North as attempts to reimpose slavery, and most of the codes were repealed or withdrawn, though some of these early laws survived.[32] With one eye on possible Northern reaction, in the 1880s Southerners began to fashion a new set of laws calling for criminal punishment, now, in most cases, not directly for breach of labor contracts but for acceptance of advances followed by failure to work out one's time. These so-called false pretense statutes proliferated in the 1880s and 1890s and were mainly used to compel black farm workers to perform their labor agreements. In agriculture, a reliable labor force was especially important. Entire crops might be lost if workers were not available at crucial times in the growing season. To ensure a reliable labor force, Southern landowners in this period typically signed black farm workers to year-long contracts. On signing, a landowner would advance a sum of money to a worker as a loan repayable by deductions from wages during the term. Under these false pretense statutes, if a worker left before completing the contract term and while still in debt to the landowner, he could be criminally prosecuted for committing a species of fraud and fined or imprisoned. Technically these prosecutions were for fraud and not for breach of a labor agreement, but in reality the statutes made it possible for landowners criminally to enforce the labor agreements of their black agricultural workers.

Under the logic of *Robertson v. Baldwin*, however, such subtlety would not be necessary. Southerners could feel free to attack the problem of labor contract enforcement directly.[33] Indeed, the majority's opinion echoed an

---

31 Ibid., 302–3.
32 William Cohen, *At Freedom's Edge: Black Mobility and the Southern White Quest for Racial Control, 1861–1915* (Baton Rouge, La., 1991), 28–37.
33 A number of Southern legislatures enacted these statutes as false pretense statutes in order to circumvent state constitutional restrictions on imprisonment for debt.

opinion delivered by the South Carolina Supreme Court not too many years earlier in *State v. Williams*, ruling that a South Carolina statute that provided directly for the criminal punishment of labor contract breaches did not violate the constitution's prohibition of involuntary servitude.

If the general assembly sees proper to make the violation of a particular species of civil contracts a criminal offence, we are unable to discover in the provisions of the constitution anything which forbids such legislation. No person is required to enter into such a contract unless he chooses to do so; and if he does so, he must take the consequences affixed by the law to the violation of a contract into which he has voluntarily entered. . . . We are unable to discover any feature of "involuntary servitude" in the matter. Everyone who undertakes to serve another in any capacity parts for a time with that absolute liberty which it is claimed that the constitution secures to all; but as he does this voluntarily, it cannot be properly said that he is deprived of any of his constitutional rights; and if he violates his undertaking he thereby of his own accord subjects himself to such punishment as the law making power may have seen fit to impose for such violation.[34]

The opinions in *Robertson v. Baldwin* and *State v. Williams* make apparent that the interpretive tradition developed in Illinois in the 1820s still possessed great vitality at the close of the nineteenth century, long after the Civil War. At the time *Robertson v. Baldwin* was decided in 1897 there were, in effect, two systems of contract law covering labor agreements in this country: The Southern one bore rough similarities to the contract system in effect in Prussia and England not too many years before. The Northern one, in which neither specific performance nor penal sanctions were available for labor contract breaches, had a long history and was supported by its own constitutional tradition that harkened back to a decision of the Indiana high court. Under these two constitutional traditions, both systems could make plausible arguments that they were free labor systems based on free contract.

The truth seems to have been that the majority in *Robertson v. Baldwin* did not believe their decision applied beyond the situation of merchant mariners. This is interesting in and of itself, given that *Robertson v. Baldwin* was brought before the Supreme Court as a test case mounted by the seamen's union.[35] The decision produced a strong reaction among organized seamen. As the *San Francisco Examiner* put it: "According to the highest tribunal which can pass on the matter, the difference between a deep-water sailor and a slave is $15 per month."[36] Union leaders immedi-

---

34 *State v. Williams*, 32 S.C. 123 (1889), 126.
35 Hyman Weintraub, *Andrew Furuseth, Emancipator of the Seamen* (Berkeley, Calif., 1959), 35.
36 Quoted in ibid.

ately launched a campaign in Congress to have the federal statute amended. Under intense pressure from the seamen's union, Congress did give the seamen half of what they had been lobbying for, amending the statute, but only eliminating criminal penalties for desertion in American ports; it retained criminal penalties for desertion in foreign ports.[37] The seamen's union continued to lobby Congress on and off for another decade before ultimately achieving its goal of having penal sanctions for breach of contract abolished. It was not until 1915 with the LaFollette Seamen's Act that Congress finally eliminated criminal penalties for desertion from private vessels.[38] By this time the seamen's victory was primarily symbolic, however, for shipowners had long since ceased to use penal sanctions to enforce the contracts of their sailors.

The seamen's union had continued to pursue its goal of eliminating penal sanctions for breach of contract even after the Supreme Court had begun to hand down its first peonage decisions. In *Clyatt v. United States* (1905), decided only eight years after *Robertson*, the court finally made a definitive choice between constitutional traditions, adopting the Indiana interpretation of the term "involuntary servitude." Justice David J. Brewer writing for the court, declared

> Peonage is sometimes classified as voluntary or involuntary, but this implies simply a difference in the mode of origin, but none in the character of the servitude. The one exists where the debtor voluntarily contracts to enter the service of his creditor. The other is forced upon the debtor by some provision of law. But peonage, however created, is compulsory service, involuntary servitude. . . . A clear distinction exists between peonage and the voluntary performance of labor or rendering of services in payment of a debt. In the latter case the debtor, though contracting to pay his indebtedness by labor or service, and subject like any other contractor to an action for damages for the breach of contract, can elect at any time to break it, and no law or force compels performance or a continuance of the service.[39]

Although it implicitly rejected the view of the *Robertson* majority, the *Clyatt* court did not explicitly overrule *Robertson*. Rather, it limited the earlier case to its facts, characterizing the second ground for the decision as the rule of the case, and then it simply brushed the case aside. "We need not stop to consider," Brewer wrote, "any possible limits or exceptional cases, such as the service of a sailor [citing *Robertson v. Baldwin*]."[40] In *Bailey v. Alabama*, decided in 1911, the Supreme Court struck down Alabama's

37 Ibid., 43. 38 Ibid., 120–1, 134.
39 *Clyatt v. United States*, 197 U.S. 207 (1905), 215.
40 Ibid., 216.

false pretenses statute as a violation of the Anti-Peonage Act and the Thirteenth Amendment. Justice Charles E. Hughes, building on the *Clyatt* opinion, declared that the Anti-Peonage Act "necessarily embraces all legislation which seeks to compel the service or labor by making it a crime to refuse or fail to perform it."[41]

Evidently, Northern elites were of two minds on the question of penal sanctions for breaches of labor contracts. When it came to their use against helpless black people in the South, with its history of slavery but also with its distance from Northern labor relations, Northern elites felt inclined to invoke the Indiana tradition that had, after all, first been developed in a similar context. The peonage cases that found their way before the Supreme Court had been initiated by federal authorities and did not grow out of an indigenous movement of black workers. The people responsible for the attack on Southern peonage were Progressives, committed to protecting the weak by reforming government and the legal system.

However, when the question of penal sanctions was posed outside the context of Southern labor relations as an abstract matter of contract law, or in the Northern context where many white workers were organized, possessed suffrage, and where what penal sanctions there were applied only to a tiny portion of the working population, the question seems to have presented greater difficulties for the elites. Not only do we have the decision in *Robertson* to point to, but during the first decade of the twentieth century the legislatures of three Northern states made their sympathy with *Robertson* clear when they enacted false pretenses labor contract statutes of their own. These statutes aimed at enforcing the labor agreements of white workers who had received transportation advances to remote lumbering, mining, or railroad construction sites. Minnesota enacted such a statute in 1901,[42] followed by Michigan in 1903,[43] and Maine in 1907.[44] We do know that the Maine statute was enforced. Fifty or sixty cases were brought before one rural justice of the peace after 1907.[45]

In his dissent in *Bailey*, Oliver Wendell Holmes suggested that the majority's opinion had been improperly swayed by the particular social context in which the case had arisen. "We all agree that this case is to be considered and decided in the same way as if it arose in Idaho or New York. Neither public document nor evidence discloses a law which by its

---

41 *Bailey v. Alabama*, 219 U.S. 219 (1911), 243.
42 *General Laws of Minnesota for 1901*, chap. 165, pp. 212–13.
43 *Michigan Compiled Laws*, §§ 408.582–408.583.
44 *The Revised Statutes of Maine* (1917), chap. 128, § 12.
45 John Clifton Elder, "Peonage in Maine," A Manuscript Report sent to the Attorney General of U.S., National Archives, Record Group #60 Dept. of Justice file #50-34-0, p. 13.

administration is made something different from what it appears on its face, and therefore the fact that in Alabama it mainly concerns the blacks does not matter."[46] He went on to explain how deeply problematic the majority's opinion was. "The Thirteenth Amendment," Holmes wrote,

does not outlaw contracts for labor. That would be at least as great a misfortune for the laborer as for the man that employed him. For it certainly would affect the terms of the bargain unfavorably for the laboring man if it were understood that the employer could do nothing in case the laborer saw fit to break his word. But any legal liability for breach of contract is a disagreeable consequence which tends to make the contractor do as he said he would. Liability to an action for damages has that tendency as well as a fine. If the mere imposition of such consequences as tend to make a man keep to his promise is the creation of peonage when the contract happens to be for labor, I do not see why the allowance of a civil action is not, as well as an indictment ending in a fine. . . . I do not blink the fact that the liability to imprisonment may work as a motive when a fine without it would not, and that it may induce the laborer to keep on when he would like to leave. But it does not strike me as an objection to a law that it is effective. If the contract is one that ought not to be made, prohibit it. But if it is a perfectly fair and proper contract, I can see no reason why the State should not throw its weight on the side of performance.[47]

Holmes was right, of course, that all contract remedies operate to enforce agreements by presenting the breaching party with a choice between performing and a disagreeable alternative. To the extent that a party decides to perform labor in order to avoid the unpleasant alternative, that party may be said to have chosen the lesser evil voluntarily, or to have chosen it under coercion. Either characterization is available, but once we decide to characterize such a choice as coerced, as the majority in *Bailey* did with respect to criminal penalties, then there is no logical ground for saying that any similar choice is "voluntary." We must conclude that labor contracts cannot be enforced through any legal remedy at all consistent with the prohibition against involuntary servitude.

Although Holmes was correct about all this, it did not seem to have bothered the majority in either *Clyatt* or *Bailey*, both of whom blithely ignored the coercive effects of money damages for contract breaches, presenting them, in fact, as the opposite of "compelled" performance. "A clear distinction exists," Justice Brewer wrote in *Clyatt*, "between peonage and the voluntary performance of labor or rendering of services in payment of a debt. In the latter case the debtor, though contracting to pay his indebtedness by labor or service, *and subject like any other contractor to an action for damages*

46 *Bailey v. Alabama*, 219 U.S. 219 (1910), 245–6.
47 Ibid., 246–7.

for breach of that contract, can elect at any time to break it, and no law or force compels performance or a continuance of the service."[48]

It is also true, as Holmes recognized, that certain alternatives to performance are less unpleasant than others, and fewer people will tend to choose performance when confronted with them. But the performance of those who choose to avoid these unpleasant alternatives by rendering the labor service is no more voluntary than the labor service of those who choose to perform to avoid the unpleasant alternative of prison. The decision of the majority is, from a logical standpoint, arbitrary, a decision to draw a line through a continuum and to call certain decisions to perform labor under certain kinds of threats "voluntary" and other decisions to perform labor under other kinds of threats "involuntary." In fact, the decision as to where to draw such a line is not a decision about where coercion begins or ends in labor relations, but rather a normative and political decision about what kinds of hard choices we should continue to allow certain people to force others to make and what kinds we should not permit.

There is no natural or logical point in this process. The peonage cases place criminal penalties for breaches of labor contracts on one side of the line and ordinary money damages on the other, without any explanation or justification for this particular position.

In the peonage cases, the Supreme Court created the modern constitutional standard for free labor by rejecting an earlier constitutional tradition that had defined free labor differently. This decision was forced on the court by the perceived need to combat Southern efforts to reimpose a form of servitude on black people. And it is to this moral and political decision that we must trace the constitutional origins of modern free labor in this country, just as we must trace the origins of modern free labor in England to a political and moral victory of the laboring classes.

Modern free labor did not arise as the result of the spread of liberal ideas or the diffusion of free markets based on free contract. It was the result of a difficult political and moral resolution of fundamental dilemmas within liberalism itself. Liberalism demanded that market transactions be voluntary, not coerced. But liberal ideas provided no objective, value-neutral means for distinguishing coerced from voluntary decisions. Only changing political, constitutional, and moral circumstances in the last quarter of the nineteenth century produced the modern definition of coerced labor that included within that definition voluntary contractual labor enforced through specific performance or penal sanctions. Once an arbitrary line

---

48 Emphasis added. *Clyatt v. United States*, 197 U.S. 207 (1905), 215–16.

had been drawn through a continuum of contract remedies, it became possible to identify coerced contractual labor with contractual slavery. This expansion of the definition of contract of slavery made more justifiable a restriction on the freedom to contract into such relationships.

Most nineteenth-century liberals had long since resolved the conflict between freedom of contract and freedom of person in favor of freedom of person when it came to contracts of slavery. Most took the position that individuals should not be free to alienate their freedom. Once contractual labor enforced through penal sanctions came to be redefined as a form of slavery, the same resolution of this basic liberal dilemma could be adopted in the case of such contracts. Modern free labor is not the result of a regime of perfect freedom of contract, but is the product of restraints placed on freedom of contract in the interest of preserving liberty of person.[49] It represents a particular resolution of fundamental dilemmas within liberalism itself. Other resolutions of these basic problems were possible, leading to regimes of free contract like those in place in England, Prussia, and Illinois during the first two-thirds of the nineteenth century. It was only a set of contingent political events and changing moral standards that produced the modern version of free labor during the late nineteenth and early twentieth centuries.[50]

49 See Binder, "Substantive Liberty," and Knight, *Freedom & Reform.*
50 Ibid.

Index